FREE SPEECH YEARBOOK

Volume 41
2004

Editor
Susan J. Drucker
Hofstra University

Published by
National Communication Association

FREE SPEECH YEARBOOK

The Free Speech Yearbook publishes essays in doctrinal analysis of free speech law, the rhetorical analysis of landmark cases and judges, and theoretical discussions of the freedom to communicate. Approaches that explore interdisciplinary and international issues of free and responsible speech, press, media law, regulation and policy, press freedoms and governance of new media are also welcome. I also am interested in having round-table discussions of 2 important new works on free speech: John Durham Peters' Courting the Abyss: Free Speech and the Liberal Tradition, and Catharine MacKinnon's Women's Lives, Men's Laws.

Submissions should follow MLA style (5th edition). All submissions to FSY undergo blind review by at least two editorial board members. Final manuscripts must be submitted in MS Word format. Digital submissions are now accepted. Please feel free to contact me with any inquiries concerning the Yearbook. Send four high quality copies to:

James Arnt Aune
Editor, *Free Speech Yearbook*
102 Bolton Hall
Texas A&M University
College Station, TX 77843-4234
email: jaune@tamu.edu
telephone: 979.862.7797

Contents

Editor's Introduction

The theme of the articles in this issue ''Free Expression in the New Millennium'' reflects the continuance and change we see as technological developments and political extremes challenge free expression. The technology of communication challenges developments in applicable laws governing expression. Technological convergence challenges the traditional regulatory rationale and vertical industry models while simultaneously testing the traditional approach to regulation by nation-states. Articles in this issue explore, how historically and currently, the changing communication landscape confronts the viability of free speech and press.

As a regular contributor to this publication I found the editorial policy accepting of new ideas and articles sometimes ''on the edge.'' But as an editor I have found the perception of what was appropriate for submission to be relatively narrow. I have become increasingly concerned that we are preventing new ideas from being disseminated because they do not ''fit'' within the walls we've built. I am pleased that during this last year of my editorship we have critically examined ''what is in a name'' and have begun the official process of changing the title to the *Freedom of Expression Annual.* I strongly support this change as it stems from several observations: a) Freedom of speech, of the press, of association, of assembly and petition are associated with the set of guarantees that comprise what is referred to as freedom of expression—a broader term than ''free speech;'' b) technological and industry convergence and globalization are altering the field of free expression. This communication environment calls for an inclusive approach and publication. We hope the *Annual* will be a publication that crosses divisions within NCA and invites submissions and readership from other professional organizations and venues. I am pleased that this process of self examination and change was launched during my editorship.

The change to ''freedom of expression'' is consistent with the language of the *National Communication Association's Credo for Free and Responsible Communication in a Democratic Society*. This Credo reflects a principle central to the NCA. This Credo along with the NCA Credo for Ethical Communication reflects core principles. This issue begins with a conversation about these Credos among noted organizational leaders and scholars.

I am very pleased that this issue continues to provide a United States Supreme Court review by Paul Siegel and carries on my effort to address regions beyond U.S. borders. In this issue Timothy Walters and Jack A. Barwind provide an introduction to issues of free expression in the Middle East with their article on the United Arab Emirates.Thomas Flynn has compiled an extended book review section addressing a wide array of rich cutting edge and historical cases studies.

A small, dedicated editorial board has always been cooperative, reliable, good humored, understanding and supportive. From reviewers to intrepid copyeditor, it has been a delight to work with them. My editorship has spanned many changes in the law, the world and this publication. It has been an honor to serve.

Susan J. Drucker

Credo for Free and Responsible Communication in a Democratic Society

Recognizing the essential place of free and responsible communication in a democratic society, and recognizing the distinction between the freedoms our legal system should respect and the responsibilities our educational system should cultivate, we members of the Speech Communication Association endorse the following statement of principles:

WE BELIEVE that freedom of speech and assembly must hold a central position among Americans constitutional principles, and we express our determined support for the right of peaceful expression by any communicative means available.

WE SUPPORT the proposition that a free society can absorb with equanimity speech which exceeds the boundaries of generally accepted beliefs and mores; that much good and little harm can ensue if we err on the side of freedom, whereas much harm and little good may follow if we err on the side of suppression.

WE CRITICIZE as misguided those who believe that the justice of their cause confers license to interfere physically and coercively with speech of others, and we condemn intimidation, whether by powerful majorities or strident minorities, which attempts to restrict free expression.

WE ACCEPT the responsibility of cultivating by precepts and example, in our classrooms and in our communities, enlightened uses of communication; of developing in our students a respect for precision and accuracy in communication, and for reasoning based upon evidence and a judicious discrimination among values.

WE ENCOURAGE our students to accept the role of well-informed and articulate citizens, to defend the communication rights of those with whom they may disagree, and to expose abuses of the communication process.

WE DEDICATE ourselves fully to these principles, confident in the belief that reason will ultimately prevail in a free marketplace of ideas.

NCA Credo for Ethical Communication

(approved by the NCA Legislative Council in 1999)

Questions of right and wrong arise whenever people communicate. Ethical communication is fundamental to responsible thinking, decision making, and the development of relationships and communities within and across contexts, cultures, channels, and media. Moreover, ethical communication enhances human worth and dignity by fostering truthfulness, fairness, responsibility, personal integrity, and respect for self and others. We believe that unethical communication threatens the quality of all communication and consequently the well-being of individuals and the society in which we live. Therefore we, the members of the National Communication Association, endorse and are committed to practicing the following principles of ethical communication:

We advocate truthfulness, accuracy, honesty, and reason as essential to the integrity of communication.

We endorse freedom of expression, diversity of perspective, and tolerance of dissent to achieve the informed and responsible decision making fundamental to a civil society.

We strive to understand and respect other communicators before evaluating and responding to their messages.

We promote access to communication resources and opportunities as necessary to fulfill human potential and contribute to the well-being of families, communities, and society.

We promote communication climates of caring and mutual understanding that respect the unique needs and characteristics of individual communicators.

We condemn communication that degrades individuals and humanity through distortion, intimidation, coercion, and violence, and through the expression of intolerance and hatred.

We are committed to the courageous expression of personal convictions in pursuit of fairness and justice.

We advocate sharing information, opinions, and feelings when facing significant choices while also respecting privacy and confidentiality.

We accept responsibility for the short- and long-term consequences for our own communication and expect the same of others.

Editor's Comments:

"The National Communication Association is a non-profit organization of researchers, educators, students, and practitioners, whose academic interests span all forms of human communication. The organization articulates its core principles in a collection known as 'CREDOS'." This is the way Thomas Flynn described two panel discussions held at recent conferences convened to consider the CREDOS of the NCA. The aim was to shed light on the history and process by which these documents came into being and to explore the meaning and implications they hold for communication scholarship and pedagogy. The NCA has passed three credos: 1) the Credo on "Free and Responsible Communication in a Democratic Society," 2) the Credo on "Ethical Communication," and 3) The Credo on "Free and Responsible Use of Electronic Communication Technology."

While known to some members of the association, their existence came as something of a surprise to others when the first two were featured prominently at the 2003 NCA Annual Convention at which time they were distributed to the attendees. Further examination led to the discovery that all three had taken up residence on the NCA website under the heading "Policies: External." In turn this set off a chain reaction of telephone calls and correspondence that began with NCA headquarters and wound its way around the country. There was a great deal of curiosity, cooperation and bemusement surrounding their origin and intent. The seemingly simple questions asked were: "who drafted the credo, how was each approved, and when did this take place and why? "

While the CREDOS represent the National Communication Association's core principles, they also raise fundamental questions for what they say on our behalf as individual members of the association and why and what the association is saying on its behalf.

1) Can an academic association take a position on behalf of its constituents?
2) Can an academic association take a political position on behalf of its constituents?
3) What does each of the Credo say or intend?
4) What does each of the Credo mean?
5) Why are there two Credo?
6) Does the adoption of a Credo propose or deny a political position?
7) And, should an academic association remain politically neutral?
8) To what extent does an academic association represent minority positions?

The underlying question, the elephant in the room, is whether a professional, scholarly organization should take on an advocacy role. Should scholars be activists?

The pages that follow represent the thoughts of those engaged in this most recent examination of the CREDOS. Overlap found in these comments reflect common knowledge and lore. I thank all of those who so openly embraced this inquiry and who graciously share their insights. It is my hope that this special section serves as an invitation to readers to join the conversation in these volatile times for Free and Ethical Communication.

Susan J. Drucker

The Development of the NCA Credo for Ethical Communication

Roger Smitter
Executive Director
National Communication Association
Washington, DC

Andersen's (2002) history of the emergence of the formal study of ethics in the National Communication Association begins in ancient times. The Greeks and Romans taught public speaking as a means of civic engagement. For them, ethics was a matter of virtue. The *rhetor* was the "the good man speaking well." Public speaking served a civic good. Virtue was found in the "golden mean" because deliberation of public policy could not long tolerate extremes of behavior and still meet the needs of citizens.

This ideal carried forward well into the twentieth century (Andersen 2002). Textbooks in the 1950's clearly defined public speaking as preparation for participation in public life. Also, textbooks began to formally recognize the role of the message recipient in the communication process, making the idea of audience far more heterogeneous than the Greeks could have imagined. The 1950's also saw the emergence of textbooks devoted to persuasion. All of these changes highlighted the connection between communication and ethics.

Against the backdrop of dramatic social protests of the late 1960's, a host of textbook authors began to systematize the teaching of communication ethics. The first were Nielsen (1966) and Johannesen (1967).

The National Communication Association (NCA) has been very supportive of the study of communication and ethics. In the early 1970's, the then Speech Communication Association (now NCA) published a bibliography on ethics. In 1972 SCA approved the Credo for Free and Responsible Communication in a Democratic Society. Its attempt to define the limits of what was protected expression was clearly formed in response to the upheaval in society at the time. As such, it included many ethical imperatives. In 1973 SCA President Bob Jefferies appointed a committee to investigate the writing of an SCA document on ethics.

By 1982 the interest in ethics had gained sufficient status that NCA officer Ken Andersen made "Communication Ethics and Values" the theme for the annual convention. Two years later, a group that had been meeting informally under the leadership of Jim Jaksa successfully petitioned SCA to form a Communication Ethics Commission. In 1990 the group began hosting a biennial conference on the study of communication ethics. In 1995 the group played a major role in ensuring that a part of the NCA mission statement included a clear reference to the importance of ethical communication.

The 1980's and 1990's saw significant growth in the number of textbooks available for teaching communication ethics. These included updated versions of Johannesen's text (1996) plus Greenberg (1991), Jaksa and Pritchard (1994), Makau and Arnott (1997), Jensen (1997), and Seeger (1997).

By 1998 the communication ethics group was ready to create a major statement about communication ethics. After extensive discussion about whether the statement should be general in nature or focus on specific practices, the group decided to craft a credo which would be aspirational in nature, apply to all forms and settings of communication and function as a social contract in a democratic society. Twenty-five NCA members came together to draft the credo. The majority were members outside the communication ethics group. The document was approved in 1999 by the NCA governing body.

What lies ahead for the Communication Ethics division? What can it and NCA contribute to the on-going controversies about ethics in the public life that have engulfed American society since 1999? In a lengthy classroom discussion of ethics, one of my graduate school instructors reminded us that when (not if) our discipline develops knowledge that others want and need to know, we will have to answer the questions posed by ethics.

That time has arrived. Today we see the confluence of a growing body of knowledge of how communication can affect human behavior and the emergence of increasingly more powerful means of communication. While politicians, marketers and others are asking ''How can we make it more powerful?'' our response should be: ''What is the ethical way to treat your audience'' and ''What good will your message bring to our communities?'' The Communication Ethics Division provides an excellent ''window'' unit for the discipline, giving the world a view of how ethics scholars in communication address these important questions.

Works Cited

Andersen, K. ''Developments in Communication Ethics: The Ethics Commission, Code of Professional Responsibilities, Credo for Ethical Communication. *Journal of the Association for Communication Administration,* 29 (2000) 131-143.

Greenberg, K.J. (Ed.) *Conversations on communication ethics.* Norwood, NJ Ablex. 1991

Jaksa, J. and Pritchard, M. *Communication ethics: methods of analysis.* Belmont, CA: Wadsworth, 1994.

Johannesen, R.L. (Ed.). *Ethics and persuasion: selected readings.* NY: Random House, 1967.

Johannesen, R.L. *Ethics in human communication* (4/e). Prospect Heights, IL Waveland. 1996.

Makau, J.M. & Arnett, R.C. (Eds.) *Communication ethics in an age of diversity.* Urbana, IL: U of Illinois. 1997.

Nilsen, T.R. *Ethics of speech communication.* Indianapolis: Bobbs-Merrill.

Seeger, M.W. *Ethics and organizational communication.* Cresskill, NJ: Hampton, 1997

Where Have All the Credos Gone?

Isa N. Engleberg
Past President, National Communication Association
Prince George's Community College

Credos—formal statements of belief and principles (from Latin *credo*, meaning "I believe")—are not policies or professional codes. Rather, credos epitomize the core beliefs of an institution, organization, or society, as is the case in religious credos that set forth statements of belief and confessions of faith. Thus far, the National Communication Association has formally adopted three credos:

1. Credo for Free and Responsible Communication in a Democratic Society (Adopted December 1972)
2. Credo for Free and Responsible Use of Electronic Communication Networks (Approved 1994)
3. Credo for Ethical Communication (Adopted November 1999)

All three credos can be found on the NCA Website (www.natcom.org) by searching the term *credo*.

At the 2005 Eastern Communication Association Convention, a program entitled "Considering Meaning and Influence of NCA Credos in Teaching and Scholarship" reviewed and discussed the NCA credos. Several questions emerged:

- Are there criteria for defining the purpose and function of NCA credos?
- What is the practical value of these credos?
- Why does the National Communication Association have three credos?
- Does one of these credos subsume the others?
- Could these credos be combined into *one* comprehensive credo for the National Communication Association and the communication discipline?

The belief statements in these credos express core values about the function of communication in a democracy as well as foundational beliefs about the communication discipline. These interrelated roles have been discussed in books, journals and convention programs for decades. For example, in 1990, *Communication Quarterly* published an essay by Ronald Arnett entitled "The Practical Philosophy of Communication and Free Speech as the Foundation for Speech Communication." Arnett presented the argument "that the study of communication ethics and free speech is the practical heart of the disciplinary field known as speech communication" (208). After offering a definition of practical philosophy and its connection to communication studies, Arnett described the practical value of this connection:

> Communication ethics assists us in combating the demagoguery of simply asking, "Can it be done?" without the accompanying ethical question, "Should it be done?" which is likely to generate debate. In a time of medical questions of life and death from abortion to euthanasia, we must be wary of easy answers. . . . Communication ethics requires asking why, not just how, and free speech necessitates examining multiple perspectives.
>
> Free speech makes it possible for ideas other than our own to gain a hearing. Free speech permits us to question (215).

As a participant in and co-facilitator of the summer conference that developed the NCA Credo for Ethical Communication, and as a former NCA President, I find myself in a unique position to examine the questions discussed at the ECA convention panel on NCA credos. I offer a brief history of how the NCA Ethics Credo was developed—and its relationship to the other two credos. Second, I pose several challenges for instructors and programs desiring to integrate the credos into coursework. Third, I offer "modest proposals" for promulgating the NCA credos as a means of advancing communication studies and the NCA mission.

History of NCA Ethics Credo

The best history of the NCA Ethics Credo was written by Kenneth E. Andersen and published in the *Journal of the Association for Communication Administration* in 2000. Andersen traces the evolution of ethical interests and issues by the National Communication Association and the development of the NCA Credo.

Andersen notes that "various forces [such as the Vietnam War] combined to produce the 1972 policy document on freedom of speech which had a clear ethical import as suggested by the title, 'Credo for Free and Responsible Communication in a Democratic Society'" (135). The Credo for Ethical Communication had a longer genesis with roots in the 1982 SCA Convention and its theme of "Communication Ethics and Values." In 1995, the Association for Communication Administration's Summer Conference Defining the Field of Communication developed the following definition: "The field of communication focuses on how people use messages to generate meanings within and across various context, cultures, channels and media. The field promotes the effective and ethical practice of human communication."

During the 1990s, NCA attempted to create a code or standard of ethical practices. The result was a document

> too specific to the inner workings of the NCA. Additionally, it had too much detail, some sections describing standard operating procedures rather than providing an ethical standard. The (Communication Ethics) Commission felt that a separate statement was needed: An overarching statement of the goal and nature of ethical communication. The exemplar invoked was the 1972 Credo for Free and Responsible Communication (Andersen 139).

As a result, NCA sponsored a summer conference in 1999 to write a credo that was, in turn, presented to the NCA Legislative Council for approval in November of 1999. Subsequently, the phrase *effective and ethical* was adopted by NCA as the focal point of its new mission statement:

> The National Communication promotes effective and ethical communication. The Association supports the communication research, teaching, public service, and practice of a diverse community of scholars, educators, administrators, students, practitioners, and publics.

Interestingly, the ethics conference participants did not review or address the NCA Credo for Free and Responsible Use of Electronic Communication Networks, in part, because they were unaware of its existence and its focus on issues related to both free speech and communication ethics. The motivation for developing and approving this credo were similar to those that moved the association to develop and adopt the freedom of expression credo. In this case, the digital divide and the potential denial of technology-enhanced communication resources prompted NCA members to advocate access to all means of expression.

Credo Challenges

The NCA credos present several challenges that should be addressed if the credos are to serve the communication discipline and communities beyond its narrow confines. Many NCA members do not know that the credos exist. And not surprisingly, very few people beyond the communication discipline are aware of the credos and their value. In recent years the NCA has attempted to make the credos more visible by highlighting them at conventions and making them more conspicuous on the NCA Website. Some basic textbook authors now include the NCA Ethics Credo and use its guiding principles as standards for assessing effective and ethical communication. The number of publications on communication ethics has increased, but they are not recognized or generally appropriate for use in basic courses.

Unfortunately, many communication instructors are not prepared to integrate free speech or communication ethics into their basic courses. Those who teach our basic courses may have limited coursework or critical knowledge in either subject. As a result, they may feel unqualified to tackle these important topics without supplementary textbook support or ancillaries. Teaching free speech and ethics requires more than perfunctory discussions about the perils of plagiarism, where you can shout fire in a movie theatre, or simplistic lists of dos and don'ts.

Advancing the NCA Credos

Even a cursory examination of the three credos uncovers major similarities in purpose and wording. All three expound the virtues of free speech and open access to communication resources. All three condemn attempts to constrain communication, regardless of the media. And all share a reverence for truth and accuracy in communication. In light of these similarities and the fact that a credo should represent an organization's formal statement of belief and principles, our discipline could benefit by consolidating the three credos into an overarching statement that echoes the NCA mission statement of promoting "effective and ethical communication."

The task of consolidating these credos will not be easy. Political interests may be reluctant to give up "their" credo. An open-minded and thoughtful process must be developed to ensure universality as well as precision. Perhaps the time has come for NCA to sponsor a summer conference designed for this purpose. An open invitation to members with expertise and interests in freedom of expression, communication ethics, and technology access could provide the synergy needed to articulate the foundational statements of belief and principles in communication studies.

Are we courageous enough to accept the consequences of a foundational credo? When members and affiliate groups call upon the NCA to take public stands on politically charged issues, can an NCA credo or credos provide the basis for such position statements? Consider these examples:

- Should NCA refuse to share communication resources with the Boy Scouts of America because the organization prohibits the appointment of homosexuals as scout leaders?
- Should NCA exhort the news media to thoroughly research background stories on issues such as embryonic stem cell research or right-to-die decisions?
- As defenders of free speech, should the NCA support a position on the Senate filibuster or open access to the Internet?

An NCA credo could serve the association by providing the basis for public commentary. Conversely, it could also lead the association to involvement in issues that members may not believe are within its purview. The adoption of an NCA credo—or the dissemination of current credos— present ironic dilemmas: Are we courageous and wise enough to stand by the foundational beliefs and principles in our credos? Are we fully committed to free speech, communication ethics, and access to communication resources?

Regardless of whether the NCA develops a single credo or not, the association and its members should make its existing credos more visible and helpful to larger audiences. The following suggestions are offered as examples to demonstrate how the NCA could benefit by making its mission of promoting effective and ethical communication better known:

- Publish a monograph for faculty to help them teach and apply credo principles in their courses;
- Give the credos a more prominent place on the NCA Website instead of placing them deep within a section on policy platforms;
- Sponsor a Communicator of the Year Award that recognizes a public figure or group for exemplifying credo principles;
- Sponsor a Communication Advocacy Award that recognizes a person or group within the discipline who has advanced the scholarship or practical application of credo principles;
- Seek grant or foundation support for advancing the scholarship and practice of credo principles through a Center for the Study of Effective and Ethical Communication.

I hope that these suggestions spark interest in those who value our credos and yearn for their recognition and acceptance. In the conclusion of his essay, Ronald Arnett hopes for a time when we "emphasize the practical need for free speech and communication working hand in hand as freedom and responsibility, and the conviction that the best and brightest ideas can be discovered together in conversation." In his final sentence he entreats us to recognize "communication ethics and free speech as a foundation of our discipline (that) provides a base from which we can practically pursue truth together in the midst of difficult and uneasy answers in a complex and ideologically diverse human community" (216). The critical message in our credos may, in fact, be the core that holds us together as a discipline.

Works Cited

Andersen, K. E. (2000). Development in communication ethics: the Ethics Commission, Code of Professional Responsibilities, Credo for Ethical Communication. *Journal of the Association for Communication Administration*, 29, 131-144.

Arnett, R. C. (1990). The practical philosophy of communication and free speech as the foundation for speech communication. *Communication Quarterly*, 38, 208-217.

Credo, Credo on the Wall
or
Credos and Other Good Words Intended to Guide those Who Believe

Gary Gumpert
Communication Landscapers

This article is written with multiple perspectives: What kind of statement is made by a national communication association with the adoption of a credo? Additionally, what does a credo mean to the membership? The Carroll C. Arnold 2003 lecture delivered by Kenneth E. Andersen at the 2003 National Communication Association convention in Miami Beach was titled: *''Recovering the Civic Culture: The Imperative of Ethical Communication.''* The lecture particularly focused on the NCA *Credo for Ethical Communication* (adopted in 1999). At that convention that credo and a previously extant ''Credo for Free and Responsible Communication in a Democratic Society'' were distributed to the attendees and included in the printed lecture later sent to all law-abiding and ethically oriented NCA members. There seemed to be a heightened sense of importance that the delegates revisit and revitalize themselves regarding the matter of ethics.

This nation is in a period of crises regarding the right to communicate and we think it imperative that we guard against both the legal and ethical violations of communication. The Patriot Act, the process of media consolidation, the exponential growth of the Internet and the escalation of global communication, emphasize the responsibility of communication scholars to guard against the violation of the communication process by forces outside the scholarly domain and perhaps to protect or define those within.

Yet that renaissance of NCA Credos triggered a number of questions. Why was there suddenly a need for a new one? Was this a statement by the NCA leadership to scholars at large or was it intended as a means of ''keeping one's house in order?'' Why ''credo?'' What is a ''credo?''

''Credo'' comes from ''Creed''—''An authoritative formulated statement of the chief articles of Christian belief as the Apostles Creed, the Nicene Creed or the Athanasian Creed.'' (The Random House Dictionary of the English Language YR). It is a system of principles or beliefs framed from a fairly broad, sometimes religious, perspective proclaimed as a guiding set of principles for the constituents of the faith. In that light what do and how do the NCA Credos mean? What is the difference between a ''credo'' and the adoption of a ''policy platform?''

In 1995 the NCA Legislative Council approved a policy on political communication.

Resolved, that the NCA urges the Federal Communications Commission or other appropriate governmental body to require the public media to devote, either at their own or at public expense, significant amounts of air time to local and national political debates, conducted in citizen-sensitive formats, and taking advantage of the latest developments in debate theory

In 1996 the Legislative Council approved a policy opposing campus speech codes.

> **Resolved**, That the National Communication Association (NCA) opposes the creation and imposition of any speech codes, codes of conduct, or other regulatory actions that would place any limits on free expression outside the classroom beyond those recognized by the U.S. Supreme Court as valid exceptions to the protections of the First Amendment.

There are numerous other examples of ''policy platforms,'' and they indicate willingness for an academic communication association to take a position regarding national political issues regarding communication.

How credos relate to policy platforms in terms of importance and impact is not clear. The credos in question are well-intentioned statements, but their meaning and intent is surprisingly murky. Who is the intended audience, the NCA scholar or the NCA citizen? In his lecture Kenneth Andersen speaks to the challenges ahead:

> I believe we must be active participants in rebuilding the civil culture. The communication process as it has and is being utilized has played a significant role in the decline of the civic culture. Altering communication activity can play a significant role in rebuilding the civic culture. We accept a role in building the civic community? This field once accepted that responsibility. Are we willing to do so again? Obviously no one individual can do very much. But if each of us does a little we will have significant impact.
>
> First we need to value the incredible relevance of the two credos to our work and enrich the experience of our students by making the principle enunciated in the credos a significant part of their growth and learning. . . .
>
> Second, we need to assist students in developing strategies for dealing with the mass communication stimuli coming at us. . . .
>
> Third, as individuals we must accept our responsibility to be active in our several communities to an appropriate degree and participate with others in maintaining and enhancing those communities (Andersen 2005 21).

But the relationship of the ''ethical Communication'' credo and the ''free and Responsible Communication in a Democratic Society'' is not clear. Further inquiry results in the following insights. Isa Engelberg, past president of NCA (president in 2003) indicated that

> The Ethics Credo was drafted at the 1999 NCA Summer Conference on Communication Ethics. At the core of the conferences were several NCA members with very strong communication ethics credentials. The big ''three'' were Ken Andersen, Matt Seeger, and Paula Tomkins. The Credo was adopted and endorsed by the NCA Legislative Council in November 1999. . . . One reason why we called for such a credo is that the association had one on freedom of speech, but not one on ethics. Our textbooks rarely covered this area in detail, in part, because authors didn't know what to include. Moreover, many other associations had similar credos (Engelberg 2004).

Sherry Morreale reported that ''the NCA Ethics commission saw a need to produce another credo that more specifically speaks to current issues regarding communicating ethically in contemporary society.'' What else could the Ethics Commission work on, other than an Ethic's Credo? Why did we need a second Credo and what precipitated the need at this time?

What is interesting was there was very little recollection of the earlier credo and the circumstances for its adoption. We were able to trace its beginnings to longtime civil libertarian Franklyn Haiman.

> I'm the one who drafted the Credo for Free and Responsible Communication. It wasn't Thomas Jefferson, but it has to be nearly that many years ago. It was so long that I don't remember when. . . . About the only thing I'm absolutely sure about is that I wrote it, because I do remember clearly doing so (Haiman 2004).

Commenting on his reactions to the later credo, Professor Haiman said:

> I have no idea why or when the second credo got written and adopted. As for your question about attempts to get the NCA/SCA/SAA politically active, there was indeed quite an experience back in 1960 when a group of us decided the organization should have a free-speech committee and programs on the subject. The leadership at the time thought it was some kind of subversive/commie plot and would have none of it. They finally relented and let us have a single program at the next convention, and that created quite a to-do. One of the panelists . . . was a disgruntled ex-graduate student from Wayne State, who claimed in his presentation that he been denied his PhD for political reasons. The leadership tried to get their hands on the tape of the program, but Al Goldberg [Denver University], one of us subversives, was chasing around the hotel to get it and keep it. Which he finally succeeded in doing—secretly! Nobody was ever the wiser (Haiman 2004).

Ken Anderson thought that the first credo might have been in response to McCarthyism and other current issues at that time. In response to our questions about the second credo and its intent, he said,

> Obviously I thought it was addressing all in our discipline as people that needed to help translate the credo into their teaching. Through them I hoped it would become both a stimulus to greater concern about communication ethics in their classroom and ultimately greater ethical awareness and ethical communication behavior by their students and ultimately the larger society. Clearly it assumed a relatively democratic society in which individuals are both allowed to and are responsible for their decisions and actions (Andersen 2004).

Asked about the specific circumstances, Andersen stated,

> the impetus in one sense grew out of an effort by the NCA to establish a code of ethics to guide its activities. This was worked on by several folk and reviewed by Richard Johannesen. But it was not really a code of ethics—or at least not just that—but also prescriptions about submitting manuscripts, etc. which are procedures that had no real ethical component. They were just rules of the game. The Communication Ethics Commission said first we needed a statement of values, a kind of credo before we moved on to form a code of ethics. This resulted after some discussion with Bill Eadie on the summer conference proposal. Some of us contributed to that financially as well as formed a steering committee composed of members of the Communication Ethics Commission. The need from my point of view is eternal because there is always an ethical dimension to everything in the communication process. Communication is done by humans to/with/for other humans. Whenever we have more than one person linked we have an ethical dimension or at least the potential of one. In communication I would argue there is always one even if we are not fully or even partially conscious of it (Andersen 2004).

During this period of correspondence we asked "Would it be fair to say that the Credo for Ethical Communication is mildly antithetical to activism? It seems to really emphasize the respect and freedom of expression that should characterize the classroom." Ken Andersen responded,

> I would say no, that the credo is not anti-activism. In fact, if practiced it would encourage it because it encourages others to state their position and for understanding it as a basis for response. It does discourage the kind of shouting match we now get in too many TV programs of shouting partisans. Indeed, I would argue it promotes dialogue and thus activism (Andersen).

The overlapping nature of the two credos was discussed by Kenneth Anderson in a talk delivered at an ethics conference held at Duquesne University in 2004. Admitting some degree of potential confusion, Anderson said the "Free and Responsible Communication Credo largely takes a societal view and focuses upon response to communication of others much more than the initiation of communication.'' He continues . . . ''One focuses upon the importance of the quality of the content and a commitment to the integrity of the ideas and to maintenance—preferably enhancement-of the communication process.''

''The Credo for Free and Responsible Communication in a Democratic Society'' was drafted in the 1960s. It was drafted during a tumultuous period in which protest and concern regarding the Vietnam War was the concern for many, where activism and social conscience was being considered as an NCA option. While Kenneth Andersen acknowledges the ''Credo for Free and Responsible Communication in a Democratic Society'' in his lecture, it is not mentioned within the preamble or text of the ''Credo for Ethical Communication.'' So we have two separate, but equal credos. . . .but another credo is hidden in NCA Credo-land.—The *Credo for Free and Responsible Use of Electronic Communication Networks* drafted and approved by the NCA Legislative council in 1994.

Credo for Free and Responsible Use of Electronic Communication Networks (approved by the NCA Legislative Council in 1994)

The principles of free and responsible communication have long been a hallmark of communication study. Since 1963, the National Communication Association has included among its core documents a Credo for Free and Responsible Communication in a Democratic Society. Recognizing the advent of electronic means of global communication that are accessible to the general public, we members of the National Communication Association endorse the following statement of principles relating to electronic communication:

We take the concept of ''free speech'' literally: there is limited freedom of expression if access to the means of expression is limited by financial ability. We, therefore, urge the development of free and low-cost means of accessing the means for processing and distributing information in electronic forms.

We realize that access is limited if specialized expertise is required to take advantage of the necessary technology. We, therefore, urge the development of hardware and software that requires minimal training but that still allows wide use of worldwide electronic resources.

We support freedom of expression and condemn attempts to constrain information processing or electronic communication, especially expressions that are offensive to some or even most of the populace. Likewise, we support a right to privacy, both in the ability to maintain the integrity of individual message exchanges and in the ability to shield oneself from unwanted messages.

While supporting free expression, we nevertheless consider the maintenance of intellectual property rights to be crucial to the encouragement of creativity and originality. We, therefore, urge the designers and regulators of electronic forms of communication to use special vigilance to insure that the works of individuals or groups are protected from unfair use by others. We encourage communication researchers to produce findings that will guide policy decisions concerning the social impact of electronic communication and to make those findings available widely. Likewise, we encourage the designers and regulators of electronic forms of communication to take credible findings about the social impact of their work into account as they implement new products and services.

We accept the need to teach students not only how to use electronic forms of communication but how to use them both wisely and well.

Finally, we call upon users of information processing and distribution networks to do so responsibly, with respect for language, culture, gender, sexuality, ethnicity, and generational and economic differences they may encounter in others.

This 1994 credo acknowledges the existence of the first credo and recognizes ''the advent of electronic means of global communication.'' The text is, however, curious and limited in scope. The credo urges ''the development of hardware and software that requires minimal training but that still allows wide use of worldwide electronic resources.'' In addition, it expresses a veiled concern regarding offensive communication, supports the right of privacy, and is concerned about intellectual property.

So the NCA has blessed us with three credos. The last of the credos—the ''NCA Credo for Ethical Communication''—does not mention the other two. Even though the period in which the ''Credo for Ethical Communication'' percolated (1994 to 1999) coincides with a period of accelerated electronic communication and the convergence of electronic media, no mention is made of the ''Credo for Free and Responsible Use of Electronic Communication.'' It seems to have been forgotten and admittedly is not a particularly well-articulated credo.

So, three separate discrete credos are there to guide the NCA membership. There apparent separateness is strange. Why the distinction between ''ethics'' and ''free and responsible communication?'' Why were they not merged? Why so little attention paid to electronic communication? At a time when privacy, surveillance, security, mediated communication in all shapes and forms, potential violations of Freedom of Assembly and Freedom of Speech permeate everyday life, ethics, free and responsible communication, and communication technology should have been addressed as one—not as discrete disconnected communication parts. We are left with several additional and gnawing questions linked to the nature of a credo and its relationship to activism. Why a credo? Does such a statement directly affect or guide the personal of the ''Communication Professor?'' Can a credo be the basis of action? Do these particular credos represent the individual member of the National Communication Association? The only recent evidence of political activism among communication associations is the case of the Amicus Brief filed on behalf of NCA in 1996 with regard to the constitutionality of the Communication Decency Act. Seen as the first effort to regulate the Internet, a friend-of-the-Court brief from NCA was part of the proceedings. NCA members who worked on the brief included Dale Herbeck Bruce Gronbeck, and, the principal author, Joseph Tuman. The argument made was that the CDA was inappropriately based on broadcast law, while the Internet is not a broadcast medium. The brief also argued that the Internet provides for the kind of give-and-take that the country's founders envisioned when they included the First Amendment in the Constitution. Bill Eadie, former Associate NCA Director, in writing about the brief at the time noted ''This argument in particular is consistent with NCA's Credo on Free and Responsible Use of Electronic Communication Networks, which the Legislative Council adopted in 1994'' (Tuman 2004). Are there other examples in which the three credos have guided association action?

Was a credo guiding the National Communication Association when it deliberated over whether or not to hold its annual convention in a state that had not ratified the Equal Rights Amendment?

Was it a credo or a set of unspoken principles that steered the National Communication Association when it debated and chose not to take a position regarding the Vietnam War?

Is there ever a time for the National Communication Association to take a position regarding the violation of civil liberties during a period shaped by the fear of terrorism and the search for security?

Do the credos guide us? If not, what are the credos for?

Works Cited

Andersen, K.E. (2005). ''Recovering the civic culture: The imperative of ethical communication.'' *Carroll C. Arnold Distinguished Lecture, National Communication Association.* Boston: MA: Pearson Education, Inc.

Andersen, K.E. (2004). Personal communication, 8 October.

Credo for Free and Responsible Use of Electronic Communication Networks (1994). http://www.natcom.org/nca/Template.2asp?bid=512, Site visited Oct. 1, 2004.

Engelberg, I. (2004). Personal communication, 4 October.
Haiman, F. (2004). Personal communication, 4 October.
Morreale, S. (2004). Personal communication, 4 October.
Tuman, J. (2004). Personal communication, 5 October.

The Strange Career of Credo Talk in NCA

Donald Fishman
Boston College

The word ''credo'' refers to a fundamental set of beliefs. It implies a commitment to a basic set of values from which all other beliefs and actions arise. Credos were popular in America during the nineteenth century, but they have declined in popularity, usage, and influence during the second half of the twentieth century. Using David Reisman's (2001) line of inquiry, there is an ''inner-directed quality'' to a credo, whether that credo is adopted by an individual or company. In the post-modern world where truth is often regarded as contingent and contextual, there is something atavistic about the reliance upon a credo. At the same time, to have a credo means that an individual or organization retains an active ownership over a set of bedrock and authoritative beliefs. Thus, while ''credo talk'' may be atavistic, one also can admire, even envy, the owner of such a credo. Like the inner-directed individual, a credo owner has an identity, stands for something positive, and the very existence of such a credo dispels doubt and uncertainty about an individual's or organization's commitments.

But the National Communication Association now possesses three credos. Credo Number One is the venerable 1960s statement dealing with ''Free and Responsible Communication in a Democratic Society.'' Credo Number Two was approved in 1994, and its subject matter is the ''Free and Responsible Use of Electronic Communication Networks.'' This credo was written to acknowledge the growing influence of electronic communication, especially the advent of the Internet. Credo Number Three, the ''Credo for Ethical Communication,'' was drafted and approved by the Legislative Council in 1999.

During the 2003 Carroll Arnold lecture on civic culture, Kenneth E. Andersen (2003) called attention to Credo Number One and Number Three. He referred to them as ''bookends'' serving to meld together a democratic process for decision-making (p. 19). In the aftermath of Andersen's lecture, Susan J. Drucker and Gary Gumpert began to inquire about the proliferation of credos within NCA. In October of 2004, a convention program on credos was organized at the New York State Communication Association (NYSCA) convention. In April of 2005, another program on credos was held at the Eastern Communication Association (ECA) convention in Pittsburgh. Former NCA president Isa Engleberg, former ECA president Sandra Herndon, and current NCA Executive Director Roger Smitter participated on the ECA program.

As one of the participants on both the NYSCA and ECA panels, I would like to weigh in on the surge of ''credo talk.'' I want to concentrate on two points. First, what explains the proliferation of credos within NCA? Second, what are the contours of activism within a professional association?

The Proliferation of Credos

Gumpert and Drucker seemed puzzled by the proliferation of credos within NCA. They were unable to obtain detailed information on the origins of Credo Number One, or why we needed the subsequent credos. Moreover, they were unsuccessful in obtaining an explanation for how the credos related to each other. In fact, the best available evidence indicates that there was no attempt to provide an overarching explanation for the multiple credos.

How then does one explain the proliferation of credos? One possible answer comes from public choice law. Public choice law postulates that ''lobbies'' that are organized, focused, and resourceful-rich will be able to get legislation enacted because the public at-large tends to be unorganized, unfocused, and lacks the resources to devote sustained attention to a legislative campaign. In the field of copyright law, for instance, a coalition of organized groups was able to extend the duration of copyright law from life of the author plus fifty years, to life of the author plus seventy years (See, *Eldred v. Ashcroft* 2003). This extension came about largely because the public was unfocused and disorganized while advocates of the legislation were not only organized and single-minded, but they had the resources to wage a sustained campaign. Moreover, they had a strong financial incentive to seek new legislation. For the supporters of the extension, the added twenty years substantially increased their revenues. For the public, the technical aspects of copyright were an issue that remained below the radar screen, seemingly without a major impact on everyday life.

Within NCA, a variation on this ''public choice hypothesis'' operates. Not only are some groups organized and focused, but they may have a compelling issue, and they may have leaders with a great deal of ''reputational'' capital to steer the group's interests through the inertia of organizational indifference. Apart from organizational inertia, there typically is no active opposition to the creation of a new credo.

Let me attempt to apply this revised public choice hypothesis to the proliferation of credos within NCA during the past forty-five years. Credo Number One was spearheaded by Franklyn S. Haiman, Alvin Goldberg and a group of activists who organized the Freedom of Speech Commission in the early 1960s. The most likely adoption date is 1963. The drafters of this document were reacting not only to the McCarthyism of the 1950s, but to the conservatism and parochialism rampant in society. Leaders of the Speech Association of America (SAA) were understandably reluctant to support a proposal that might leave the impression of fostering left-wing activities. Indeed, strong proclamations of freedom of speech had been a prominent left-wing strategy during the 1930s and 1940s, and there was a resistance among the leadership of the SAA to adopting the new document.

Haiman wrote the credo. Its principles reflect his basic belief in public deliberations, the open and honest airing of divergent opinions, and the enriching influence of more—not less—speech. Just as President Kennedy and the New Frontier were able to open up society to new ideas, Haiman and his colleagues were able to win widespread support for the credo. The principles enunciated in the credo seemed like bedrock values for an organization dedicated to the improvement of society through speech activities. Incidentally, the credo was adopted before the beginning of the Vietnam War but during the era of the sit-ins and freedom rides. Like Haiman's career, the credo seems to envision an activist-like stance for the owner of the document, and its universal language makes it an ideal document for a statement of principles for a communication-oriented professional association (For a re-publication of this credo, see Andersen 2005, 7-8).

Credo Number Two, the Free and Responsible Use of Electronic Communication Networks, was adopted in 1994. It was a very forward-looking document. Its principal authors were Thomas W. Benson and William F. Eadie. Eadie produced the first draft copy of the proposed document, although he credits Benson as the primary source of the idea. The document was revised editorially by the original group of discussants of the proposal and then submitted to the Legislative Council. With one minor revision, the Electronic Communication Credo was passed overwhelmingly. Substantively, the credo emphasizes the need for a low-cost means of access to the Internet, the development of hardware and software that provides minimal barriers for the average computer user, the protection of privacy, and a respect for intellectual property. At a time when Congress was considering enacting legislation to restrict cyberspace, the authors of the credo issued a forceful statement: ''We support freedom of expression and condemn attempts to constrain information processing or electronic communication, especially expressions that are offensive to some or even most of the populace.'' Three years later in *Reno v. ACLU* (1997), the Supreme Court struck down the Communication Decency Act (CDA) as being overbroad and vague, a position anticipated by the 1994 credo's language criticizing the regulation of offensive speech.

Interestingly, Credo Number Two is the least credo-like statement among the three NCA credos. Instead, it reads like a plank in a political party's platform or a short White Paper. It is sufficiently abstract so that it will outlive the issues of the day, but it lacks the timeless and universal quality of a credo. Instead, this statement is a product of the mid-1990s, influenced by a set of policy issues that dominated society, e.g., obscenity, privacy, the digital divide, and shielding ''oneself from unwanted messages.''

The third credo was adopted in 1999. By contrast with Credo Number Two, its language and structure is very credo-like. Its opening paragraph announces: ''We advocate truthfulness, accuracy, honesty, and reason as essential to the integrity of communication.'' Its last paragraph acknowledges ''We accept responsibility for the short-and long-term consequences for our own communication and expect the same of others.'' The adoption of the credo was spearheaded by Kenneth Andersen, Matthew Seeger, and Paula Tompkins. The sponsors of the credo were able to use the growing interest in ethics to organize a special NCA Summer Conference, and they were able to distinguish the earlier statement on freedom of speech from one devoted to ethical communication. Because of the reputational capital and leadership of Andersen and his colleagues, the Legislative Council approved the credo. Of course, it is hard to imagine that the membership at large would have objected to having a statement on ethical communication. In the face of multiple and continuing examples of misconduct in business, politics, and academic life, such a statement puts the organization on the ''side of the angels.'' But there is a bigger problem with the document—not just with literal meaning of the principles of the credo.

The proliferation of credos can grow into a cottage industry. A group with a specialized interest and several highly credible leaders within the association creates a weekend retreat around an interesting topic. Not only do you get to discuss an issue of importance with your colleagues, you also get the opportunity to draft a credo that later might be enacted by the association. An interesting package: A retreat plus a credo as spin-off benefit. Such a trend may leave us credo-rich, but it will dilute the impact of any given credo. It also creates an oxymoron: the *credo de jour*, which is a radical departure from the timeless language and transcendent objectives that a credo typically embodies.

Instead, it might be time to halt the proliferation of credos. Policy statements, position papers, and White Papers reports are not credos. These documents reflect the thinking of the association at a particular time and place. But they do not pretend to be statements of universal, eternal, and authoritative beliefs. It may be time to cease ''credo talk'' and turn our attention to policy statements and position papers. Adopting multiple credos—even adopting a credo that does not have a transcending purpose—primarily will leave members of the association shaking their heads ten years later wondering what was the rationale underlying the adoption of a well-intentioned but vague set of beliefs. The adoption of each additional credo, moreover, dilutes the impact of the already existing statements of core beliefs.

Let me turn to the other part of Drucker and Gumpert's inquiry: The role of activism in a professional association. There is a problem with adopting a position paper—although it is a lesser one than the promulgation of credos. Nevertheless, it is still one fraught with perils: It is a problem involving the complexities of academic freedom and the unique role that academics and intellectuals play in society.

Academic Association and Activism

Drucker and Gumpert raise a number of questions about associational activism. At the ECA panel session, they ask: ''Can an academic association take a position on behalf of its constituents? Should an academic association remain politically neutral? Should scholars be activists?'' They wonder whether or not the adoption of a credo affirms or denies the stance of taking a political position. In addition, they cite several political positions that NCA has adopted, e.g., a resolution in 1995 against California's Proposition 187, a 1996 resolution against speech codes, a sweeping 1995 resolution on political communication, and the association's role in drafting an Amicus brief in *Reno v. ACLU* (1997). It is not surprising, therefore that they argue ''a professor is, by definition, an activist.''

I agree with Drucker and Gumpert. Professors should be activists. Academics should participate in those decisions that influence the quality and direction of society. They should create ideas, organize, and agitate for change. But the harder questions are: (1) Should professors be able to use their classrooms as a platform for their political beliefs and (2) Should professors use an academic association as a vehicle to promote political objectives. Here I would argue for the limited use of a professional association to foster political goals while not limiting a professor's right to influence the public events in society as an activist.

Academic Freedom in the Classroom

Professors play a unique role in society. They are creators of ideas, repositories of historical knowledge, and disseminators of information to students and society at large. Some of the ideas that professors create and disseminate may be unpopular. Because of their unique role in creating useful, abstract, or unpopular ideas, professors require special safeguards to espouse their beliefs, especially from outside interference.

The problem of employer and public interference with a professor's freedom to propound ideas has a long history. The American Association of University Professors (AAUP) has been the most important vehicle to promote the protection of the rights of professors. In 1915, the AAUP produced its first comprehensive statement on academic freedom. It identified three aspects of academic freedom: (1) freedom of inquiry and research (2) freedom of teaching within the university or college and (3) freedom of extramural utterance and action (Hamilton 1995 164). Prior to the AAUP's 1915 statement, employment law and common practice allowed universities to treat professors as employees ''at will,'' and to fire them without cause for uttering unpopular beliefs or participating in political movements. Written in the midst of World War I, the 1915 Statement of Principles was an attempt to safeguard professors against discipline and dismissal for performing their legitimate activities. If professors could be fired for statements that disturbed trustees, politicians, and the public at large, this would cause a chilling effect creating a restrictive environment in which faculty members could not properly perform their duties. Thus, the 1915 Statement of Principles stated that dismissing professors for advocating a point of view represented ''a radical failure to the social function discharged by the professional scholar,'' and it stressed providing protection for speech activities inside and outside the ''walls of the university'' (Hamilton 360). The 1915 Statement of Principles also created standards and expectations for a faculty member in his or her role as an advocate. As Hamilton (1995) explains, ''The tradition of professional academic freedom grants rights to individual professors conditioned on the performance of correlative duties of competence and ethical conduct'' (5).

In 1940, a broader statement of the basic principles of academic freedom was adopted by the AAUP, and it gained widespread acceptance by most colleges and universities. It has been commonly referred to in academic employment contracts, and most universities and colleges now pride themselves on adhering to the 1940 AAUP statement, and they have incorporated portions of the AAUP statement in their tenure codes.

While the 1915 and 1940 Declaration of Principles frequently were violated by the McCarthyism of the early 1950s, in 1957 the Supreme Court provided special protection for academic freedom under the First Amendment in *Sweezy v. New Hampshire* (1957). In that decision, Justice Frankfurter spoke eloquently about the need to protect the ''spirit of inquiry'' and provided a warning against ''the grave harm resulting from government intrusion into the intellectual life of a university'' (234).

A decade later, the Supreme Court further expanded the protection of academic freedom. In *Keyishian v. Board of Regents*, (1967) the Court struck down the use of loyalty oaths that restricted the academic freedom and the expression of opinion by faculty members. In *Keyishian*, Justice Brennan wrote: [A]cademic freedom is of transcendent value to all of us and not merely to the teachers concerned . . . that freedom is therefore a special concern of the First Amendment, which does not tolerate laws that cast a pall of orthodoxy over the classroom'' (603).

Beginning in the late 1960s, colleges and universities became wide-open forums for the expression and the exploration of new ideas. Between the Vietnam War and the start of the Second Iraqi War in 2001, few professors at research or state universities lost their jobs because of advocacy of unpopular opinion. Academic freedom has survived, even prospered, in times of political stress and disharmony. The outspoken professor has become a commonplace. Even the development of the fervent and often unthinking patriotism following the September 11th crisis was unable to re-create a restrictive climate on college campuses. There were, and are, legitimate anxieties over the use of the 2001 Patriot Act. Under the Patriot Act, the new powers of Federal government include the ability to obtain the business records of library patrons, records of Internet users, bookstore sales, and wide-ranging powers to prevent the disclosure of sensitive research, even though it is unclassified under Federal standards.

The Patriot Act has been the biggest threat to freedom of expression on college campuses during the past twenty-five years. Indeed, after September 11th, concern with national security has been more intense than at any time since the McCarthy era. At the same time, a university professor's right to speak out against the war on terrorism or ill-advised government policies has not generated open reprisals by employers. Sanctions by employers against controversial professors have been rare, and the constitutional protection of academic freedom in the classroom has continued. I do not mean to adopt a starry-eyed view of freedom of speech. There undoubtedly has been censorship and self-censorship of professors. Invitations to speak by certain professors have been withdrawn, new restrictions exist on access to foreign students and visitors, and attacks on academic freedom have persisted. By and large, however, academic freedom in the classroom has been safeguarded, and a professor's right to speak out has been largely unrestricted.

There also is a new twist to the concept of academic freedom. The 1970 AAUP's statement on Freedom and Responsibility emphasizes creating ''an atmosphere conducive to learning'' and the ''even-handed treatment of all aspects of the teacher-student relationship'' (Hamilton 376-379). A professor has a right to speak out on issues of public interest, but he or she has a duty to promote an atmosphere of learning that is fair to the interests of the students. A chemistry professor who devotes a large portion of his or her class to discussing Social Security reforms is abusing that important privilege. Similarly, a professor who imposes an orthodoxy on the views expressed in the classroom is unfairly limiting the academic freedom of students.

Menard (1996) intelligently views academic freedom as a universal principle governed by "a historically circumscribed relationship" (166). From decade to decade, the problems of academic freedom have shifted—from fear of leftists and subversives in one era to speech codes, gender orthodoxies, and students harassing professors in another era. But it is fair to say that the "outspoken professor" has been protected in the classroom, safeguarded in "extramural" activities, and supported in his or her independence from administrative interference and coercion. Few professors who have adopted unpopular and unorthodox stances have faced disciplinary reprisal or dismissal from university administrators.

Associational Activism

Drucker and Gumpert raise an important question about associational activism. As scholars and concerned citizens, they ask, should we be compelled to be politically neutral? Why should an academic association not enter the political arena? Drucker and Gumpert provide evidence of several instances where NCA has taken a political position, many of which seem to be consistent with the dictates of its several credos.

My position is slightly different than the one that Drucker and Gumpert articulated at the ECA convention. Let me develop the position in three points, the third of which represents an interesting qualification to the previous two.

First, I grant that the issue of associational activism is a highly complex one, and when an association like NCA prides itself on being an "engaged discipline," that engagement should involve speaking truth to power and criticizing governmental policies that are adverse to the welfare of society. The tendency to accept government grants, to sit in the chambers of government and discuss issues of health policy, for instance, also must be accompanied by a willingness to criticize foolish decisions and wasteful expenditures of money if the concept of an engaged "academic" discipline is to carry any meaning.

Second, I am reluctant to transform a professional association into a political vehicle. Professional associations in academia exist to promote scholarship, foster good teaching, and provide acts of service based upon the professional competence of its membership. To use the membership of a professional association to engage in political activities and to lobby for a political objective represents an unhealthy departure from our current mode of operations.

I am not opposing activism. But I am encouraging activism on the part of an individual, not a professional association. For instance, I have been a life-long member and activist in a political party. I have attended the last twelve state political conventions of my party in Massachusetts. I have served as the campaign manager for my State House of Representatives member. I have worked to elect candidates at all levels of politics, and I have had coffee and soda with political colleagues in the Massachusetts State House as we have conducted strategy sessions. In the course of these activities, I have discovered how hard it is to rally supporters, form coalitions, and raise money. In fact, it is very hard to round-up and create a constituency to support any political issue. While the ability to solicit funds and to organize people is a difficult task, it is the function of political parties and special interest groups. Academic associations should not be regarded as just another special interest group on the political landscape—this would tend to diminish their credibility and objectivity.

I think it is unfair to attempt to require individuals who join a professional association with vocational goals to begin to support political positions. It is unfair to use the funds of the organization for mailings and meetings. It is unfair to devote hours of the association's time to sifting through the myriad of political issues that confront society as opposed to conducting the business of the association.

My third point represents an interesting qualification. Occasionally, an overriding issue confronts society, such as the war in Vietnam. Allegedly, an academic association had a special mandate to offer an opinion on the war because students were being taken out of the classroom and drafted into a war whose objectives were unclear and ill-advised. When such a compelling issue does arise, and when there is a "direct and tangible relationship" between the goals of the association and the taking of a political position, then it is possible to depart from a position of political neutrality and take a stand. But such as stance should be regarded as the exception, not the rule. There should be a presumption against taking a political position, and it is the burden of those advocating a resolution or a particular course of activities to overcome this presumption.

This talk of political neutrality should not be confused with political inertia or anti-activism. Professors are free to take a position as individuals, to sign petitions, to campaign actively for a particular course of action, and to lend their intelligence and expertise to a cause. But they should have to work to create a constituency and raise funds, and not "capture" an existing professional association as the base of their operations.

Conclusion

The opening pages of the booklet of Kenneth Andersen's Carroll Arnold lecture at the 2003 NCA convention contain a reprint of Credos Number One and Number Three. The language of these two credos is striking and forceful. From the Preamble of Credo Three, for instance, the text states "We believe that unethical communication threatens the quality of communication and consequently the well-being of individuals and the society in which we live" (5). Similarly, from principle six of Credo One, the text indicates that "We encourage our students to accept the role of well-informed and articulate citizens, to defend the communication rights of those with whom they may disagree, and to expose abuses of the communication process" (8).

While examining the credos side-by-side, it is natural to ask how the credos relate to each other, and why the professional association decided to privilege these two statements above all other possibilities. A discerning reading of the credos also raises important questions about whether the credos implicitly endorse professional activism in order to reach the objective embraced by the principles in the various declarations.

The Andersen booklet should be a beginning, rather than the end, of longer discussion on the role of credos and associational activism. The reliance on a credo strikes me as an interesting anomaly: Part public relations ploy, part statement of identity, and part philosophical outlook. But it is worth considering at length whether a pre-modern credo can serve a useful role in guiding an individual's thought and behavior in a post-modern world. In addition, the analysis of associational activism deserves more attention. Activism is a complicated topic. It embraces academic freedom, First Amendment jurisprudence, legal protection against an employer's interference with a professor's right to advocacy, as well as a series of philosophical assumptions about the role of academics and intellectuals in society.

I have argued that "credo talk" and the role of associational activism have undesirable consequences. But this is a topic in which more speech—not less-should be brought to bear on the issues under discussion. There is now a long-standing legal tradition that insulates professors from an employer's interference, especially the intrusion of the state into a faculty member's right to conduct research, engage in teaching, and to espouse, in the words of the 1915 AAUP Declaration of Principles, "intramural as well as extramural utterances." Unfortunately, less attention has been paid to the academic freedom of students in the classroom, a topic that has become prominent in the face of accusations of widespread political correctness on campus and the lack of respect for "conservative ideas" in academia. In light of recent developments with the rights of students and heightened concerns with national security, a re-examination of academic freedom within public and private colleges and universities is warranted.

Almost twenty-five years ago, Professional William Van Alstyne contended that "The price of an exceptional vocational freedom to speak the truth as one sees it . . . is the cost of exceptional care in the representation of that truth and a professional standard of care" (Hamilton 1995 344). What constitutes "exceptional care in the representation of truth" and an acceptance of "professional standards of care" deserves an extended and wide-ranging discussion. We have not heard the last words on "Credos" or "academic activism" by a professional association. The further probing of these concepts is a very desirable and important project to undertake. It is an especially fitting project for legal scholars of communication as well as those concerned with ethics. To date, there has been too little discussion of academic freedom, not too much.

Works Cited

Andersen, K.E. (2005). *Recovering the civic culture: The imperative of ethical communication.* Boston, MA: Pearson Education Inc.

Eldred v. Ashcroft, 123 S. Ct. 769 (2003).

Hamilton, N.W. (1995). *Zealotry and academic freedom: A legal and historical perspective.* New Brunswick, NJ: Transaction Publishers.

Keyishian v. Board of Regents, 385 U.S. 589 (1967).

Menand, L. (1996). Academic freedom as an ethical practice. In L. Menand (Ed.) *The future of academic freedom.* Chicago: The University of Chicago Press, 163-180.

Reno v. ACLU, 521 U.S. 844 (1997).

Riesman, D., Glazer, N. & Denney (2001). *The lonely crowd: A study of the changing American character (Rev. ed).* New Haven, CT: Yale University Press.

Sweezy v. New Hampshire, 354 U.S. 234 (1957).

American Pirate Radio—The New Local Radio?

Harvey C. Jassem

We protect communication and freedom of expression for a multitude of reasons. Free speech as a core value has been linked to our notion of individual growth; a robust marketplace of ideas rewards society with good and better ideas; and the value we call free speech is inherently tied to our belief that in a democratic society it is antithetical to have those who govern limit our ability to know and express.

Measures of freedom of expression vary. Absence of government prohibitions on speech is the pivotal measure for some. Others look for an absence of economic barriers to entry or, better yet, the ability to *effectively* enter and reach the marketplace of ideas, and still others look for the range of diverse ideas/voices/content that is readily available to the audience. However one measures it, there is generally consensus that more freedom of expression is positively associated with more voices in the marketplace, more access to the outlets for effective expression, and more diverse options for the audience. And for most free speech proponents, more is better. In some cases, government intervention in speech related matters serves as a barrier to such freedoms. In others, society is reliant on government intervention to maximize these freedoms. The proper role of government regulation of radio is not entirely settled.

Of the mass media, radio has been one of the more democratic forms of public expression. It began in private hands, unregulated by government, and proved so popular and "easy" to broadcast, that government intervention in the name of freedom became necessary. Today there are a multitude of local stations, approximately 13,600, licensed by the federal government (FCC Broadcast Station Totals 2006). On its face, this might indeed suggest that radio is presenting a robust marketplace of ideas. Certainly, there are more radio stations available to most Americans than there are local television stations, newspapers, or even local magazines. There are a large number of radio formats available on those radio stations as well, also suggesting a robust marketplace. Interestingly, however, throughout the history of radio in America there have been a robust band of "pirates" who have taken it upon themselves to violate federal law and taken to the radio airwaves illegally. They tend to rationalize their actions on the premise that radio fails the democratic test without them. Some point to the shrinking number of conglomerate owners. Others note that regardless of who owns the stations, most stations are commercial in nature and hence are programmed in ways that are geared to maximize financial return. Some say that leads to conformity and a diminution of consumer choice. Others point to the paucity of news and public affairs programming on most commercial stations in their indictment of radio as being less than a bastion of free speech values.

This paper will discuss American pirate radio as a response to government regulation and the resultant radio system.

Values of Radio Regulation

When the Federal Radio Commission (FRC) was established in 1927, its primary function was to bring order to the emerging radio spectrum. The United States government had declared sovereignty over the "radio" spectrum and created the FRC to assign frequencies (and power/location configurations) to a limited number of users in order to further the effective and efficient use of spectrum and to ensure conditions that would permit the growth of commercial radio. Though initially conceived of as a temporary commission the necessity for which would end shortly after radio frequency (license) assignments were made, the FRC continued in operation, replaced in 1934 by the Federal Communications Commission (FCC) which continues to operate today.

Early on it became clear that assigning spectrum allocations was not a value-free function. Theoretically, it could have been. The FRC could have divided up the spectrum into a number of channels and randomly given them to the first lucky applicants, but the Radio Act of 1927 required that radio operate in the public interest, and largely gave the FRC the task of determining what that meant. The FRC, supported by a lengthy record of court decisions, decided it had to be more than a traffic cop of electromagnetic signal interference. In granting and denying licenses, in determining how strong stations' signals could be, in deciding where stations could be based, the Commission developed a hierarchy of values with which to make its decisions.

The 1927 Act gave the FRC the responsibility of regulating in such a way as to encourage "fair, efficient, and equitable radio service." To that end, the Commission decided that some radio service was better than none[1], so it created a class of high power stations ("clear channel") whose signals would travel widely, especially at night, thereby giving even rural Americans, whose small communities did not or could not yet support a radio station of their own, access to radio. It also decided that some local service was better than more total radio service. Thus, lower power (and more local) licenses were carved out. Implicit in this arrangement was the recognition that radio was going to be largely commercially supported, and that its economic viability was linked to the size of the audience reached. There was also the political necessity to assign radio frequencies equitably around the nation.[2] While early proposals that the country be divided into several regions, with each getting the same number of radio channel assignments, were replaced with more flexible notions of equitable assignments, localism was an early goal of FRC/FCC policy.

Localism as a principle is important because it provides opportunities for diverse voices, outlets for local concerns, programming, news, and talents, as well as an opportunity for local businesses to market their wares. But localism, as operationalized by lower-power signals, does not guarantee these uses in and of itself. Theoretically, one could own "all" the local radio stations in town, or even across the country. So ownership restrictions were established to reinforce the values of localism *and* diversity of ownership. Duopoly rules limited owners to one station per market, and nationwide caps limited the number of stations one party could own to seven per service (AM, FM, TV). Owners were required to be American citizens, have access to technical expertise, have the financial resources with which to operate a station, and to have reasonably criminal-free backgrounds.

It is important to note that even if fully enforced, these ownership and signal configuration requirements would not guarantee any particular type of programming. Despite the protests that content-related concerns impinged on broadcasters' First Amendment freedoms, regulators made clear their programming preferences. This came into play primarily when the Commission faced the decision of giving a license to one of several applicants. It would turn to programming-related issues to help it make license award decisions. While it rarely imposed specific programming-related rules, its guidelines (such as the 1946 "Blue Book") encouraged local live programming, sustaining programming (programming that might not be commercially viable), news and public affairs programs, kids' shows, educational programming, farm shows, etc. It encouraged/required stations to discuss local needs with local leaders of civic, political, religious, charity, business, youth, elderly, and other groups. These discussions were to be summarized along with the stations' programming responses to these needs. Again, the regulatory goal here was to encourage stations to program for the local community, and to demonstrate that a variety of sub-communities were being served.

What resulted was a stable system of primarily commercial radio stations. Few radio stations lost their licenses. Some might suggest that that was a result of the FCC's lack of interest in applying its public interest requirements. Others point to the good job performed by broadcasters, thereby obviating much need for government oversight or interference.

The system of American radio that emerged was one in which the high costs of local live programming were generally curbed by the adoption of networked and syndicated programs[3], as well as by reliance on recordings supplied gratis by the major record companies. Though radio networks moved much of their programming from radio to television in the 1950s, radio stations did not use the opportunity to greatly increase their local programming. Instead, they generally increased their reliance on records and the emerging rock and roll. Such programming provided an interesting mix of local/unique and national/standardized content. Local DJs could spin a mix of records that seemed to target local sensibilities, but because the product was generally coming from national recording firms, and because of national exposure and marketing efforts, regional differences have shrunk over the years. Local ads formed the economic bedrock of radio, and the revenue generated by those ads was tied to the size of the audience listening to a given station. Stations had strong economic incentives to increase their audience size while continuing to minimize their programming costs.

Incumbent stations would have preferred a system whereby radio competition was completely stifled, but they didn't get that level of protection. Over the years, the FCC has permitted more AM stations on that band, by marginally diminishing the protection it gave some stations and by increasing the size of the band. More significantly, in the 1940s, the FCC opened the FM band promising higher quality fidelity and local service (since FM signals would be limited by various factors to a range of generally less than 50 miles). In the 1960s, the FCC recognized that FM had gone largely underutilized because many of its licensees were AM stations that were simply simulcasting on both their AM and FM frequencies. The Commission determined that this was not an effective use of the spectrum, and required that these stations stop simulcasting most of the time. FM radio grew impressively after that, thus increasing the radio options available across the country.

Explicit in the creation of an FM radio band was the value of protecting a place for non-commercial radio. The FCC reserved part of the FM band (88-92 MHz) exclusively for non commercial stations, recognizing that even the addition of the many more radio stations that the FM band afforded would not adequately serve the needs of all audiences or "speakers." There were simply some voices that could only be heard if commercial support was not required, or even an option. (Interestingly, commercial broadcasters did not strongly object to the "set-aside" for non-commercial radio or TV frequencies, perhaps believing that noncommercial stations offered less competition than commercial ones might.)

Aside from the 20% of the FM band that was reserved for noncommercial broadcasting, the overall American radio system that was nurtured and shaped by the FRC/FCC is notable for its reliance on commercially supported privately owned stations, with limited concentration of ownership and limited entry by newcomers, little programming interference or direct input from the federal government, and lip service to local programming. While the FCC stubbornly upheld its right to regulate in and for the public interest, it generally spoke to the wisdom of not substituting its own programming judgment for that of the so-called "marketplace." This system dominated by privately owned and operated radio stations has come to be the operational definition of the "public interest."

New Market Entrants

Since 1927, those wanting to broadcast AM or FM radio in the United States had a few options. They could petition the FCC for a license to an unused and available radio frequency in a given location, they could purchase an existing station (or construction permit) from a private broadcaster (pending FCC approval of the transfer of the license from the former holder to the station purchaser), they could operate a carrier-current or closed circuit station (which really isn't broadcasting at all), or they could attempt to subvert the FRC/FCC and operate their station without a license. That last option is known as "pirate" radio.

Whether on AM or FM, when more than one applicant desires an unused frequency, the Commission has had to determine which one should get it. Until recently, that meant a series of comparative hearings and often appeals. Those hearings would attempt to determine which potential broadcaster would best serve the public interest. Preference would be given to minority group members, local owners, owners who did not own any/many other outlets (thereby increasing diversity of ownership), and applicants who proposed more substantial local programming. The applicability of each of these qualities changed at different times in the regulatory history. More recently, the comparative process has given way to auctions.

Purchasing an existing AM or FM station has not necessitated engineering studies or even competing applicants (generally). If a buyer met the FCC's minimal qualifications and if the proposed sale would not violate ownership regulations, buyers who reached agreement with sellers on the terms of a sale could count on receiving the license. Though there have been some small incentives for some sellers to sell to minority group owners (there have been occasional tax incentives, for example), these private sales are made without regard to public policy issues. It is a money-driven marketplace transaction. As is the case with such transactions, those with access to more funding have better likelihood of succeeding and getting on the air.

Assuming an aspiring broadcaster could not get a license by any of these means, they could opt for carrier current status, enabling them to send their signal on the electrical circuitry of a building or a small series of buildings. This, and similarly other restrictive very low power options limit the effective range of such "broadcasts" to approximately 200 feet and do not constitute what anyone means by broadcasting.

The unlicensed aspiring broadcaster could always try to ignore the law and operate without a license. One can certainly build a radio station and transmitter from very legal parts, and the technical expertise necessary for sending out a signal is not particularly hard to come by. Operating a radio station (on frequencies used for AM and FM radio) without a license is a violation of Section 301 of the Communications Act of 1934, subjecting the violator to seizure of his/her equipment and/or financial forfeiture. While some have objected to the licensing requirement, suggesting that it is a violation of their First Amendment right to speak, more than seventy years of judicial review consistently finds that licensing is a reasonable government function/requirement that is not violative of the First Amendment. Unlicensed broadcasters have been thought to pose a threat to the stability of an interference-free and hence functioning broadcast system. Licensed broadcasters are the primary watchdogs who report unlicensed users to the FCC. Such complaints often trigger FCC investigations of the unlicensed broadcasters.

Though it is not easy to get a radio license, the number of licensed broadcast radio stations has increased steadily, from 618 in 1930 to approximately 13,600 today. The FCC constantly gets requests for new radio station licenses. This does not include the interest of those who wish to broadcast *without* a license.

Unlicensed Pirate Radio—The Calling

Precisely because unlicensed radio stations are not registered, and because they are often short lived and somewhat moving targets, it is not possible to know how many such stations have existed or even why. In some cases, unlicensed, or pirate, stations began because champions of particular music or entertainment felt unserved by existing stations and were determined to air what they loved. A chat-room comment by a pirate radio supporter in Great Britain put it like this:

[I]f it were not for pirate radio, there would be no Rock N' Roll. It was Radio Caroline off the coast of the UK in the sixties that broke the Beatles, Stones, The Who and many other British RNR bands. That's because the Beeb refused to play this type of music (Durr).

Others have gotten into pirate radio for more political reasons (some would say that control of entertainment dissemination is political too). In its comments submitted to the FCC in 1999, the National Lawyers Guild Committee on Democratic Communications asks:

When is the last time you heard a city council meeting on a radio station? A high school football game: A play? poetry? The candidate of the Green party? Or the Libertarian party? When is the last time you heard a serious discussion of a local school tax issue? A local labor action? Parents discussing the need for local day care? Or more parks? When is the last time you heard the voice of a homeless person on the radio? An unemployed person? Or someone dying of AIDS or breast cancer? Or a recent immigrant? Or a migrant laborer? (National Lawyers Guild 1999).

These comments were made available on the Internet and received comments of support by self-proclaimed community activists, college professors, folks active in free speech movements, students, pirate broadcasters, former commercial broadcasters, as well as from many who did not identify any "affiliation." There are communities of people who believe that they are not satisfactorily served by either the commercial radio stations or the noncommercial ones. Some because they don't hear the content or the speakers they'd like, others because they simply want the ability to "speak" via radio. They invoke principles of free, robust, and decentralized communication. They also speak of pirate radio as their hobby.

One former pirate spoke fondly of his days setting up a pirate radio station in his college dorm. "It was really wild 'n crazy. . . We got this really funny guy down the hall to be a DJ. . . . And, for some reason, the pretty coeds started hanging around 'station headquarters'. . ." He went on to gush about technical improvements he made to the transmitter as a result of new equipment and advice he read in a magazine. He continued to support other pirate stations, got his B.S. in electrical engineering, and left his pirate radio hobby behind him (McFadden).

Another anonymous commenter wrote "The airwaves are property only a few are licensed to use, but with technology that's within everybody's reach, you can trespass onto these spaces. It is not as though there is no room for it. Every empty channel on your TV set, and every empty frequency on your radio dial could be filled with programming, if more people knew how to hot wire the airwaves."

A representative of Heartland Free Radio noted that their station offered programs that deal with UFOs, ACLU, lewd and obscene programming, and shows from Jim Hightower, Counter-spin, Alternative Radio, and "other voices that don't get heard from around here."

Another pirate broadcaster went from paper pamphleteering to "electronic pamphleteering" by starting a pirate radio station. "It is speech about matters of highest public concern—political and economic reform and the local and international environment." While they've been contacted by the FCC, they claim to still be on the air, two years after they began (Freeradio 1999).

One of the more well known recent pirate radio stations is Free Radio Berkeley, overseen by Stephen Dunifer. It was started in 1993, and operated as a 50 watt 24/7 station on 104.1 FM in the Berkeley/Oakland area. It described itself as "providing community news, discussions and interviews, information, a wide range of music, and more. [I]t is part of an ever growing micropower broadcasting movement to liberate the airwaves and break the corporate broadcast media's stranglehold on the free flow of news, information, ideas, cultural and artistic creativity"

(Free Radio Berkeley 1999). The FCC ordered closure of this station and the US District Court upheld that order in 1998 (*US v. Dunifer*). Dunifer argued that the FCC's refusal to permit low powered FM micro radio stations amounted to unconstitutional content regulation, since such stations would carry programming that would be different than that carried by larger licensed stations. He objected to the FCC's policy of not issuing Class D, low powered FM licenses. Interestingly, the court rejected Dunifer's appeal of the FCC's injunction against his broadcasting by noting that because he hadn't applied for a Class D license, he did not have standing to challenge the FCC's policy of not granting those licenses. His argument that applying for such a license would have been futile, did not persuade the court. Today, according to Free Radio Berkeley's web site, ''Free Radio Berkeley has two somewhat distinct entities—Free Radio Berkeley 104.1 FM, a silenced broadcast station that was operating with 100 volunteer programmers, and—Free Radio Berkeley IRATE (International Radio Action Training, Education), which provides transmitter kits, technical support and training and is involved in national and international outreach and organizing efforts'' (Freeradio).

In another case, pirate broadcaster Rick Strawcutter, whose station he described as primarily Christian and politically oriented, claimed that the FCC's policy of prohibiting unlicensed micro radio is invalid because it violates (1) the First Amendment, (2) the Equal Protection principles of the Fifth Amendment, (3) the Due Process Clause, (4) the FCC's statutory mandate ''to encourage the larger and more effective use of radio in the public interest,'' 47 U.S.C. § 303(g), and (5) Article XIX of the United Nations Declaration of Human Rights and Article XIX of the International Covenant on Civil and Political Rights (*U.S.A. v. Any* 1998).

While this case against Strawcutter was dismissed on procedural grounds, the philosophical arguments he made have not withstood judicial review.

1996 And The Big Change

Complex change is rarely the result of a single influence. Nevertheless, the Telecommunications Act of 1996 has had a tremendous impact on the structure and balance of the American radio system. Significantly, the Act so diluted the radio ownership and operation limitations/requirements, that while private ownership remains the bedrock, diversity in ownership and localism in ownership are no longer on the value radar screen. This was not the first time radio ownership regulations had been loosened. In 1985, the number of stations one owner could own in any one service (AM, FM, TV) was increased from 7 to 12. In 1992, the national radio station ownership caps were raised to 18 in each service, and duopoly rules were relaxed to permit an owner to own two AM and two FM stations in the same market in markets with more than 15 local radio stations. In 1994 the national radio ownership cap was again increased to 20 in each service. But in 1996, Congress removed those numerical limitations entirely, and replaced them with the rule that permitted one company to own all the radio stations it wanted until its stations reached 35% of the national audience, and permitted companies to own as many as eight radio stations in a market.

Radio consolidation followed quickly. In 1997 and 1998 there were approximately 1,800 deals worth a total of more than 24 billion dollars involving the changing ownership of radio stations (Rathbun 1999). When the Act was passed, the two largest group owners accounted for 13% of radio's total revenues. By the end of 1997, the top two accounted for 27% of radio's total revenues (Tristani 1998), and by the end of 1999, the top two groups accounted for 33% of revenues (''Clearly,'' 50). At the end of 2002 the top five owners accounted for 55% of local radio revenues (Safire 2003 A19), and the largest group owner, Clear Channel, owned more than 1,200 radio stations in the United States. The rush to consolidate was a rush to take advantage of the economies and power consolidation afford. A single company owning hundreds of radio stations could consolidate management, sales and programming functions, and they did just that. The heightened efficiency and market power resulted in skyrocketing radio station prices after the 1996 Telecommunications Act. That provided more incentive for stations to sell out to the large group owners, and made it more difficult for new entrants to buy individual stations. Not only would an independent station face leaner, meaner, and more powerful competition from the group owners, but the price of market entry had gone up substantially. And, as group ownership increases, local and diverse ownership declines.

During this period, pirate radio was active, as was the FCC in trying to shut it down. Between September 1997 and October 1998, the FCC closed down 320 pirate radio stations (Monaghan).

Low Power Rule Making

Coincidental to the apparent robust presence of pirate radio and the FCC's attempts to shut it down, was the issuance of its Notice of Proposed Rulemaking re. the creation of new low power FM (LPFM) radio service (FCC Notice, Docket 99-25). Noting that the 1996 Telecommunications Act has resulted in major consolidation of ownership and heightened barriers for new entrants, the proposal called for three classes of low power community FM radio, one class operating at a maximum of 1,000 watts with a service area of approximately 8.8 miles, another operating at a maximum of 100 watts with a service area of 3.5 miles, and possibly a third with a maximum power of 10 watts serving 1 or 2 miles. The Notice said:

> These proposals are in response to two petitions for rule making and related comments indicating substantial interest in, and public support for, increased citizens' access to the airwaves. We believe that these new LPFM stations would provide a low-cost means of serving urban communities and neighborhoods, as well as populations living in smaller rural towns and communities. In creating these new classes of stations, our goals are to address unmet needs for community-oriented radio broadcasting, foster opportunities for new radio broadcast ownership, and promote additional diversity in radio voices and program services. We are proposing that LPFM stations not be subject to certain technical rules currently applied to other classes of radio service. (FCC, Notice Docket 99-25, ¶ 1.).

In 2000, the FCC issued new low power FM rules calling for two classes of LPFM, 10 watts and 100 watts, rather than the three classes (and the 1,000 watts) suggested in its original Notice of Proposed Rulemaking. Permitted stations would be noncommercial, have no ownership interests in other broadcast stations or other media (cable or newspapers), and be reserved for local owners (for a period of two years). LPFM owners could own only one station per market and up to ten nationwide (FCC Creation 2000). Individuals or those entities wishing to support local radio operations with advertising were out of luck.

Reactions to the LPFM rulemaking shed some light on the threats, opportunities and values associated with various local radio options. The established mainstream broadcasters, as represented by the NAB, largely balked at the notion of LPFM, noting that the increased competition it promised would hurt a system that already did an enormous amount of local public service programming. In the spring of 2000, NAB President Eddie Fritts said that "local, over-the-air broadcasting is going to continue to be the key to success" for stations. "If we do not remain local, we're going to lose our franchise to competitors" ("What's"). These comments were made in conjunction with an NAB report that claimed local radio and television stations provided $8.1 billion in annual public service. That figure was extrapolated by the NAB from a survey of commercial broadcasters which asked them to quantify the amount and commercial worth of public service announcements and other public service programming stations carried from August 1998 through July 1999.

The NAB report was issued in April 2000, just as the FCC was making policy regarding new public service obligations on digital broadcast licensees. It is likely that the report was designed to help fend off additional public service obligations. Though the methodology used in the report is somewhat questionable—it presumed that the responding stations' self reports were accurate and that they represented the amount of public service programming being done by stations choosing not to respond to the survey, and it further presumed that the economic value of PSAs could be accurately measured by relying on stations' rate cards—this lengthy report failed to clearly distinguish between *local* public service and *national* public service. In its 70 + pages of anecdotal evidence, it repeatedly pointed to examples of specific PSA campaigns stations did in response to one issue or another, and claimed that "nearly two-thirds . . of the PSAs aired by the average radio station during the year were about local issues" (National Association of Broadcasters 2000). Stations claimed that they assisted fundraising and awareness campaigns and helped organize community events. They did so through PSAs, public affairs programming, and in news segments. In addition, many stations contributed production assistance and money directly to the groups. The line between local and national is not entirely clear, since many of the groups identified as being "local" were local chapters of national organizations (such as the American Red Cross, American Cancer Society, United Way, etc.). The NAB report, while limited in how much reliable information it actually provided, did suggest that many commercial broadcasters played important roles in getting out the word about some public interest concerns. The extent of that help is not clear, however.

The Benton Foundation sponsored two reports examining public affairs programming over a two-year period, and arrived at very different conclusions. Their sample was considerably smaller than the NAB's, but the sampled markets were selected randomly and programming was examined for a specified two-week period. Both of these studies found that stations in the sampled markets provided approximately .3% to .35% of their airtime to local public affairs programming. Benton did not include news segments or PSAs in these totals. The Benton Foundation used its studies to justify its calls for enhanced public service responsibilities for digital broadcasters ("What's" 2000).

Regardless of just how much local public affairs/community service the established broadcasters are doing, it is clear that some folks see the need for more. Indeed, a basic premise of many community non-commercial stations which were excluded from these surveys, is to serve alternative interest "communities." To the extent that this philosophy describes them, the very existence of non-commercial stations, and the people who support those stations through financial and volunteering contributions as well as through their listening, testifies that there are additional needs to be met. So too can this argument be extended to the rationale behind many "pirate" stations.

The FCC responded to appeals that it reconsider its LPFM rulemaking by reaffirming and clarifying those roles (FCC, memo on Reconsideration, Docket 99-25 2000). It noted that

> Our decision to begin licensing low power FM radio stations at this time is . . . in response to the dramatic changes in the radio industry during the last four years since our radio multiple ownership limits were relaxed pursuant to the 1996 Act. Given the substantial consolidation of radio station ownership in recent years, the need for adding diverse voices to the airwaves has grown.

The rules were slightly modified from the earlier 2000 version, but for the most part, the Commission dismissed objections raised (primarily by National Public Radio and other existing radio interests) to LPFM. While reaffirming the need for LPFMs to protect full powered FM signals and not vice versa, it repeatedly pointed to the need for local community based broadcasting. That need would not be compelling enough to permit "pirates" to be eligible for LPFM licenses, since in the FCC's view, they had proven to be unreliable by being pirates.

By 2005 LPFM had grown to approximately 600 stations, primarily in small and mid sized markets, and the FCC opened another inquiry into possible rule changes intended to strengthen LPFM (FCC Second Order on Reconsideration 2005).

Pirates response to LPFM

As noted earlier, due to the somewhat clandestine nature of pirate radio, it isn't easy to get a representative sample of pirates. A check of the "Free Radio Network" web site offers some insights. Fourteen hundred responses to the posted survey question "How do you think the legalization of LPFM will effect [sic] pirate broadcasting activity?" yielded the following results:

no effect	36%
it will decrease	27%
it will increase	20%
not sure	17%

Though this is not a reliable sample either, it suggests that many folks who were interested in pirate radio seemed to think that LPFM would not change pirate radio much. On the pirate chat lines, the "talk" was primarily anti LPFM. Typical comments included:

"Screw the NAB Pirates, long live unlicensed microradio!!!!"

"Let's hope he [President Clinton] veto [sic] the bill [limiting LPFM outlets], but let's remember we can still setup those pirate radio and take back the airwaves ourselves."

"They had their chance, they blew it. [T]hey could have brought us into their tent, and they didn't. Screw the NAB. Screw NPR. Screw CEMA. Screw the fatcat bought and paid for politicians who only represent the corporate interests who've paid them off."

"Screw them all. We're going back on the air, en masse, let them come after us. I have more dirt on the legal licensed broadcasters in my town to write a book."

On the other hand, another chatter wrote in response to this sort of anti-establishment anti-LPFM talk, "This is EXACTLY what broadcasters are using as ammunition as to why lpfm must not be permitted, on ANY basis. If any lpfm is to succeed, this kind of rhetoric has to be minimized, or you just prove Oxley, Gregg, and Co. is correct" (Free Radio Berkeley 1999).

Those commenting "in" the pirate "chat rooms" seem at once angry that the Congress might succeed in limiting LPFM outlets, because doing so limits the number of potential LPFM stations, angry that LPFM is scheduled to take years to roll out across America, and even angry about LPFM in general. There is more advice on line about how to set up pirate stations, and how to build transmitters that will fit into and work from cars (so that they are more difficult to track down), than there is on how to apply for an LPFM license.

Pirate radio enthusiasts also discuss where/when to best hear/broadcast pirate radio internationally on short-wave. Commenters' tag lines such as "Voodoo Radio," "11 meter mayhem," and "what would you like to jam to today?" were not uncommon. These chat lines and help lines seem more focused on encouraging international listening and broadcasting than on anything local.

"Free Radio: A Documentary," is a sympathetic documentary on pirate radio produced by Kevin Keyser. A review of the "director's cut" of the video notes that some currently active pirates are quick to admit that they will continue on without a license [even if LPFM is approved]. Part of the reason is ideological: "a lot of people don't like the idea of being 'licensed' at all by the FCC, because if they can give you a license, they can also take it away.'' Explains Keyser, ''Some people, like Mbanna & . . . Dunifer, don't want the government regulating them or what they can say on the airwaves in any way'' (Free Radio: A Documentary 2000).

A content analysis of broadcast pirate radio in the United States would be a helpful tool in an effort to determine just how pirate stations are serving their local communities. Unfortunately, such a content analysis is infeasible. Given the size of the country and the clandestine ways in which pirate stations operate, it is essentially impossible to know when and where a pirate will broadcast, and impossible to get representative samples from around the country. A search of the literature and Internet finds the Free Radio Network (FRN) Internet site as one of the best portals to this underground world. FRN offered a lengthy sample of pirate radio on its CD ''Pirate Radio, Volume One, 1999, A collection of pirate radio studio recordings in MP3 audio format.'' Most of the samples on this CD are from the mid-1990s, and are not necessarily a representative sample of pirate radio in the US.

The samples of pirate radio on the CD point to a world in which disregard for the conventions of mainstream radio is flaunted. There is a mix of obscure new and older broadly defined ''rock'' music, often with announcers talking over that music. There is parody of some music and established stars (such as the amateur-sounding Bob Dylan sound-alike parodying him on his self-proclaimed ''Bob Dylan Radio''), crude sex/bathroom talk, and rants about how this is radio the government doesn't want you to hear. The premise of such anti-government rants was essentially that big government serves as a censor.

Interestingly, on this particular sample of pirate radio, there appeared to be nothing that the FCC would actually have prohibited had it been broadcast on licensed radio stations. Also, in this particular sample, there was more interest in whether distant listeners could hear the station than there was in anything local. That some of these samples came from short-wave pirates would explain some of that interest in distant listeners, but none of the FM pirate radio sampled mentioned anything local. There was an almost eerie sense of deja-vu conjuring up visions of the very earliest broadcasters in the United States. The low quality audio, accompanied by oft-repeated ''if you can hear us, please send us a postcard to post office box blah-blah-blah'' brought up visions of radio's earliest days.

Characterizing pirate radio in a monolithic fashion is as inaccurate as painting a monolithic picture of licensed radio. Pirates appear to be local religious groups attempting to spread the word over the air to their local communities by the only broadcast facility they can afford, to anarchists for whom part of their mission is to disobey federal laws they don't respect, to hobbyists who use short-wave to send their signals as far as possible and have no particular local focus. Some are commercially supported, others are not.

Pirate radio was and is an outlet for alternative voices. The mainstream commercial AM and FM broadcasters operate in a regulatory and financial structure that rewards a smaller range of options than does the nearly structure-less ''pirate'' radio world. But ''alternative'' does not translate to ''local,'' if by local we mean something more than idiosyncratic to the individual speaker. Excerpts available from the Free Radio documentary portray a range of uses for unlicensed stations. At least one station points to its role as a local community clearing house for information. Another has an open-mic policy, where anybody can come in and have their say for a couple of hours at a time. Such programming has at least minimal and potentially significant local perspective. That is not to say it is well done, but it does suggest that some of these stations are and can be important local outlets. Clearly, there is some programming dealing with local people/tastes/interests *both* on licensed and unlicensed radio.

Localism-Community

One of the ironies of the modern age of media is that we are at once faced with mega-conglomerates controlling more overlapping media interests than has ever been the case in history, and at the same time, we are faced with a bewildering array of media choices, only some of which are controlled by those mega-conglomerates. There is a disorienting chaos in these choices and voices. The technology we are using further complicates the "sense of place." As we become increasingly wired through cable television and various Internet options, as we increasingly become unwired through satellite and wi-fi delivered options, we are tuning to radio and television outlets without being able to distinguish whether the outlet is a local station, a distant station, or some amorphous world-wide locationless entity. To some degree, we may be redefining our own communities as those we share interests with rather than by those with whom we share physical proximity.

Nevertheless, localism in radio, based on community of place, continues to be lauded. It goes beyond the romanticism of championing the local small underdog. For most commercial radio broadcasters, the *business* of radio has primarily been local. Local advertising traditionally represented the largest source of revenue for radio stations. So, regardless of where ownership might be located, commercial radio has always touted its localism. Recently, as the LPFM issue has been in the fore, the National Association of Broadcasters tag line in their promotional material stresses this more than ever. It reads: "Local Broadcasters: Bringing Community Service Home."[4] The NAB's promotions have called attention to the support local stations (radio and television) give to non-profit organizations through coverage, PSAs, donations, etc. The NAB has raised this flag in its fight against LPFM.

Localism was also the rallying cry of those supporting the creation of LPFM. In their cry supporting the FCC's LPFM proposal, the Public Media Center and Media Access Project headlined a full page newspaper ad with "Act now to save America's last chance for local radio" ("Act now," A17). "Low cost, low-power FM is the last chance for radio to return to its truly local, community-service roots," and "Don't let them silence America's real Voice—Yours!" the ad continued.

Localism, then, has served as a rallying cry of the incumbent established radio broadcasters, the emerging LPFM broadcasters, and the pirate broadcasters. Ironically, each entity claims to have a hold on the best of localism and suggests that it can represent that value most effectively, perhaps even more so if some of the local competition would just go away.

To those interested in more radio options—both more listening choices and more opportunities for "speakers" to get their word out—it seems likely that the number of outlets will grow significantly. That *can* mean a growth in the amount of local programming, though it is clear that while content and structure are related, one does not guarantee the other. In other words, "more" radio outlets, even low powered ones, may or may not yield programming that would be considered "local."

If LPFM quickly develops into a robust system, as the FCC plans, and if the number of full powered multi-streaming digital stations explodes, as may well be the case, opportunities for local licensed broadcasting will grow considerably. The interest is there. Indeed, FCC Chairman Kennard reported that there were nearly 12000 applications for LPFM licenses in the first twenty states for which the FCC started taking LPFM license applications (Kennard 2000). The significance of LPFM and multi-streaming stations is unclear, since they will be part of an ever growing number of "radio" options (including direct broadcast satellite, cable, and Internet "radio") and will be taking place at a time when information flow and the resultant sense of community is increasingly insensitive to location. Even in a world filled with "licensed" or "legal" "broadcasters," many of whom will be local and attempting to serve local needs, there will likely continue to be pirates who simply prefer to operate outside the conventional norms. Some of these pirates will likely do their own and local programming. But their reason for being will not be that there are no other local alternatives, for LPFM and the other options make possible many more local outlets.

LPFM has increased the number of voices on radio, but it has not fully opened entry to the marketplace for all those wishing to use radio as a form of expression, as it excludes individuals, other media owners, and those who would rely on commercials to support the station. For the individual or small organization without deep pockets, neither full powered nor low powered licensed radio outlets provide much of an option.

If LPFM is not enacted in a more robust fashion, or if the restrictions put on it are so limiting as to permit only a small number of new stations, and if multi-streaming digital radio and wireless Internet "radio" fail to develop, then pirate radio may well be an important seat of local broadcast radio. It is reasonable to assume that as the walls protecting professional broadcasters break down with technological advances, more and more people will want to try their hand at public communication. Radio is a terrific way to communicate.

If markets work, they reach a point of equilibrium. Supply meets demand. That has not happened in radio, and in the name of localism and free speech many continue to break into the market as suppliers. Their contributions may or may not be of much value. And given the recent opportunities to webcast and podcast legally, it may be possible to reach potentially larger audiences by legal means than it is by illegally broadcasting as a pirate. Still, the pirates continue. One who believes in marketplace forces must take seriously the notion that they are filling unmet needs. Perhaps those needs originate more on the supplier side than on the demand side, and in the marketplace of ideas, that is often the case.

Because the present system of allocating licenses and using the spectrum relies on the exclusion of some who would be broadcasters, because it favors those with deep pockets and complex organizational structures, individuals and small organizations wanting to broadcast continue to violate the law and resort to pirate broadcasting. The Internet is not a perfect substitute. Until such time as the technology and regulatory structure of radio is radically revamped to allow virtually anyone to broadcast, or until such time as people stop wishing to add their voices to the broadcast marketplace, there will be pirates lurking. To the extent that they do not diminish radio service, perhaps to the good.

Endnotes

1. In 1928, the FRC noted that serving the public interest meant bringing about "the best possible broadcasting reception conditions throughout the United States." FRC "Statement on Public Interest, Convenience, or Necessity," 2FRC Ann.Rept.166 (1928), as cited in (Kahn 52).
2. The 1928 "Davis Amendment" directed the FRC to provide "equality of radio broadcasting service . . . to each of . . . five [geographic] zones [of the US]." Davis Amendment, Public Law 195, 70th Congress (Kahn 49).
3. The FCC's 1941 Annual Report noted that over 97% of the nation's total nighttime broadcasting power was utilized by network owned or affiliated stations (Mosco 1979).
4. See www.nab.org, or NAB ads such as the one on the inside back of cover of *Broadcasting and Cable*, 1 May 2000.

Works Cited

"Act now to save America's last chance for local radio." Advertisement, *New York Times* 2 May 2000: A17.

Carroll Broadcasting Co. V. FCC, 258 F.2d 440 (D.C. Cir. 1958).

"Clearly, it's Clear Channel." *Broadcasting and Cable* 18 September 2000: 50-62.

Durr, B. *The Free Radio Network Grapevines.* 1 May, 1999 http://www.frn.net/vines/forum 2/html/000533.html.

FCC, *Broadcast Station Totals as of September 30, 2005.* 14 January, 2006 http://www.fcc.gov/mb/audio/totals/bt050930.html#START.

FCC, *Creation of Low Power Radio Service, MM Docket No. 99-25, RM-9208, RM-9242, Report and Order.* 20 January 2000.

FCC, *Memorandum Opinion and Order on Reconsideration, Creation of Low Power Radio Service, MM Docket 99-25, RM-9208, RM-9242,* 20 September 2000.

FCC, *Notice of Proposed Rule Making, MM Docket No. 99-25, 64 Fed Reg 7577.* 16 Feb. 1999).

FCC, *Second Order on Reconsideration and Further Notice of Proposed Rulemaking, MM Docket 99-25, FCC 05-75.* 16 March 2005.

47 *C.F.R.* §§ 73.211 (a), .511(a), .512 (c).

''Free Radio: A Documentary,'' Anonymous review, 19 March 2000 http://www.freeradio.org

''Free Radio Berkeley'' Press release, AMPB Report #29. 8 April 1999 http://www.freeradio.org.

Freeradio bulletin board. http://www.freeradio.org/amp.

Kahn, F. J. *(Ed.). Documents* of American Broadcasting. Englewood Cliffs, NJ: Prentice Hall, 1978.

Kennard, W. E. (2000). *Statement by FCC Chairman William E. Kennard On Adoption of Order on Reconsideration of Low Power FM Radio Service.* 22 Sept. 2000 http://www.fcc.gov/Speeches/Kennard/Statements/2000/stwek-076.html site visited January 2006.

McFadden, B. *A Brief history of KHOG,* (Nd). http://www.rdrop.com/users/billmc/khog/khog.html.

Monaghan, Peter. ''Exploring Radio's Sociocultural Legacy.'' (Feb. 19, 1999). *The Chronicle of Higher Education* 19 Feb. 1999: A17.

Mosco, V. *Broadcasting in the United States.* Norwood, NJ: Ablex, 1979.

National Association of Broadcasters. ''A National Report on Local Broadcasters' Community Service,'' April 2000: 7.

National Lawyers Guild Committee on Democratic Communications. *Comment of National Lawyers Guild Committee on Democratic Communications, In the matter of Microstation Radio Broadcast Service, Petition for Rulemaking, FCC RM No. 9208.* http://www.hallikainen.com/lpfm/comments/NLG.html 1999.

Rathbun, E. A. ''Going, going, gone ... Slowdown in Radio Consolidation Offset by Broadcasting Megadeals.'' *Broadcasting and Cable* 15 Feb. 1999: 33.

Safire, W. ''On Media Giantism'' *New York Times* 20 January 2003: A19.

Tristani, G. (1998). *Remarks of FCC Commissioner Gloria Tristani before the Texas Broadcasters Association.* http://www.fcc.gov/Speeches/Tristani/spgt811.html 3 Sept. 1998.

U.S.A. v. Any and All Radio Station Transmission Equipment, et al., located at 2903 Bent Oak Highway, Adrian, Michigan, Defendant, Rick Strawcutter, Claimant, 19 F. Supp. 2S 738, 741; 1998 U.S. Dist. Lexis 19488 (U.S. Dist. Court for the Eastern District of Michigan, Southern Division, 1998).

US v. Stephen Paul Dunifer, 997 F. Supp. 1235; (U.S. District Court, Northern District of California, 1998).

''What's Local About Local Broadcasting?—Still Not Much.'' B*roadcasting Extra*, Benton Foundation email, 4 April 2000.

Reading John Locke in Cyberspace: Natural Rights and "The Commons" in a Digital Age

Donald Fishman
Boston College

The metaphors to describe the communication revolution have a conspicuously spatial dimension to them. The "Information Superhighway" is the most prominent of these metaphors. It conjures up miles and miles of smooth pavement or roadway, creating a multi-faceted electronic highway that allows an individual to obtain unlimited information. But terms such as "Celestial Jukebox," "Electronic Bulletin Board," "Electronic Soap Box," "Electronic Frontier," and a globally-connected "Virtual Shopping Mall" continue the tradition of viewing uncharted and evolving developments on the Internet through the prism of conventional spatial metaphors. Similarly, the regulation of cyberspace is perceived spatially as "enclosing" or imposing barriers upon "the modern equivalent of the Western Frontier" (Hunter 2003 442).

Many of the articles and books analyzing the development of the Internet embrace one or more spatial metaphors. These terms are employed to describe the indescribable, i.e., that which we do not know but want some reassuring vision to guide us in forging ahead comfortably. Drucker and Gumpert (1995) contend that "The adoption of spatial terminology may appear a ready and useful mechanism for making the revolutionary changes of the information age less strange, intimidating, and boundless" (p. 50). Johnson and Marks (1993) argue that while cyberspace is "unstable" and "changeable," it exists as an unexplored "territory" that researchers currently are attempting "to map" in order "to determine the rights and duties of participants" in a variety of evolving electronic communities (488). For Kerr (2003), the process of "mapping" includes judiciously selecting the correct metaphors and nomenclature in order to serve the goals of fairness and justice.

Metaphor has long been at the center of conceptions of intellectual property. John Locke's early interpretation of "the commons" provides an enduring justification for a natural rights philosophy in the sphere of intellectual property. However, during the past forty years, the natural rights approach to intellectual property has been overshadowed by an economic interpretation. Economics provides a useful mode of reasoning necessary to make trade-offs between providing incentives to authors and inventors and allowing the public reasonable access to artistic, creative, or utilitarian works. Recently, however, there has been a recognition that the economic interpretation of intellectual property is incomplete, leaving room for a revitalized natural rights philosophy (Wolf 1995; Moore 1997). In fact, still operating under the influence of the old economics paradigm, I envision a rehabilitated natural rights approach serving as a "complementary good," i.e., like tea and sugar, or pizza and soda, most people will want to use both in examining intellectual property in a digital age.

This article follows an emerging pattern of applying tradition-bound concepts to cyberspace (Boyle 1997; Froomkin 2003; Lessig 2001; Litman 2001; Smith 1997; Thierer & Crews 2002). This activity is slowly becoming a cottage industry within communication law. Instead of the more widely followed path of reading the Constitution in cyberspace, I focus upon John Locke and the natural rights theory to achieve the objective of producing a ''complementary good'' to the dominant economics approach to intellectual property. This article is sub-divided into three parts. Part I discusses the strengths and drawbacks of an economics approach to intellectual property. Part II analyzes Locke's philosophy and the much overlooked Lockean Proviso that provides a springboard to balance the rights of owners and information-developers with those of end-users of intellectual property. Part III examines the decision-making in NBA v. Sports Team Analysis and Tracking System, Inc. (1996) and NBA v. Motorola (1997). Part III also discusses how the decisions in these and other cases can be better understood through the perspective offered by the Lockean Proviso.

The Economic Approach to Intellectual Property

The economic approach to intellectual property is part of a larger movement entitled ''Law and Economics.'' This movement began with the appearance of Ronald Coase's pioneering articles relating law to economic analysis (Coase 1937; Coase,1960). However, the Law and Economics movement owes its prominence to the prolific efforts of Richard Posner and his colleagues at the University of Chicago who have popularized a rigorous mathematical approach to controversial legal problems.

The Law and Economics movement begins with the assumption that the principles of microeconomics and welfare economics can be applied to traditional areas of law, such as contracts, torts, and property. The economic principles found most applicable to the law include price elasticity, that all firms are profit maximizers, that substitutes exist for virtually all products, and that costs can be subdivided into sunk, fixed, variable, and transactional factors. Law and Economics also considers spillover effects that may affect a decision, such as externalities (Landes & Posner 200311-36). At bottom, the movement attempts to measure the costs and benefits of an issue, and prescribes to whom the benefits or costs should be allocated in order to construct a rational method of decision-making. As Bunker (1998) observes, Law and Economics proponents ''urge that economic rigor and quantitative analysis, based upon the consequences of legal outcomes, should replace normative legal theory that draws upon controversial and sometimes ill-defined notions of individual rights, morality, and justice'' (p. 517). British economist Dnes (1996) contends that ''Fairness criteria are notoriously difficult to define . . . It is a sad fact that many people see what is in reality only an expression of their own preference in favouring the welfare of some individual or group relative to another as an expression of justice. The advantage of an economic approach is that it avoids interpersonal assessments and is more neutral in its efforts'' (p. 7).

From its inception, there was a harmonious and common-sensical orientation in the Law and Economics approach to intellectual property. The task of adapting economic theory to doctrines in intellectual property, therefore, occurred with relative speed and ease. Landes and Posner (1989) observed, ''Intellectual property is a natural field for economic analysis of the law'' (p. 325). Gordon (1989) similarly wrote, ''That economics should be a focus of attention is unsurprising, since both copyright and patent law are seen as serving primarily economic incentive functions'' (p. 1348). Moreover, the rationale for copyright law seems aptly suited for an explanation based upon economic theory. For instance, Rowley (1998) contends that ''Copyright law endeavors to promote the production of creative works by balancing between two competing policy interests: (1) ensuring that authors have an adequate economic incentive to produce those works; and (2) preserving the public domain by ensuring that the author's monopoly is not so broad that it prevents others from developing competing works'' (p. 481).

The main objective of the Law and Economics approach has been to create a legal regime that neither underprotects nor overprotects innovators and creators; that aims to provide attractive incentives to the next generation of innovators and reasonable access at a fair price to end-users. Given the cross-pressures of these goals, fairness is understandably a difficult objective to achieve. There is a high social cost to a policy of overprotection, which gives a producer the right to prevent the use of a desired work. Underprotection also has serious long-term implications for the aggregate production of artistic, intellectual, and utilitarian works. In addition, there typically is a great deal of anxiety about overprotecting or underprotecting innovative works, such as computer software programs or videotapes, because each product may mature to represent a unique category of works, and each product may eventually develop a separate and distinct market scheme (Gordon 1994).

The Law and Economics movement's interpretation of intellectual property relies heavily upon an array of seemingly uncontested economic truisms. Chief among these are: (1) People respond favorably to incentives; (2) As costs increase, individuals will consume less of a given product; (3) Monopolistic prices tend to be higher than prices in a competitive environment; (4) As prices increase, individuals will search for substitutes; and (5) Free riders are individuals who take advantage of the benefits of an activity without paying for the services or goods. Probably the most controversial element in this outlook is the strong reliance on what has been labeled as Coase's Theorem: That resources tend to gravitate to their most valuable uses if and when voluntary exchanges are encouraged; and, if the parties in a dispute are allowed to bargain freely, any argued-over property will end up in the possession of the individual who values it the most, regardless of the initial assignment of legal rights (Coase 1996). In effect, the profit motive—coupled with efficiency—is the self-executing engine that dominates this perspective. Posner and the supporters of the dominant Chicago School of Law and Economics movement insist that wealth maximization, a comparison of net monetary gains and losses derived in the most efficient manner, should be the overriding objective that the legal system should foster.

From a Law and Economics perspective, the regulation of intellectual property ultimately is anchored in the "intangible nature" of its products. A tangible good, like an egg sandwich, can be consumed only once and by only one person unless that person divides the sandwich into portions. Thus, in dealing with a tangible good, one encounters a zero-sum situation, i.e., whatever portion one person gets automatically will be taken away from the amount available to others. However, an intangible good, like a movie, may be watched by many people without taking away the pleasure from any one of them. As Harrison (1995) observes, the ability of more than one person to consume and appreciate a work warrants the creation of special legal schemes: "Positive externalities and free-riding explain the existence of copyright, trademark, and patent law" (p. 46). Litman (1990) also believes that intangible property creates a unique opportunity-cost problem, especially for authors: "The costs of creating the works is often high, the cost of reproducing them is low, and once created, the work may be reproduced rapaciously without depleting the original. In a world in which such reproduction is not restrained, an author will be unable to recover the costs of creating a work and will therefore forgo the creative endeavor in favor of something more remunerative" (p. 970).

Among the perspective's benefits, the Law and Economics movement provides a vocabulary and a degree of rigor to discuss a wide range of legal issues, and it is especially useful in analyzing intellectual property issues. For instance, the existence of transaction costs raises the question of spending dollars to collect nickels and dimes by users who photocopy materials from copyrighted books and journals. But the introduction of cyberspace also reduces transaction costs to nearly zero for owners and users of intellectual property. In this respect, the Internet has become the world's largest copying machine, and the resulting copies are always nearly perfect and verbatim reproductions. Transaction costs, or a lack of them, become a useful way to analyze the changes created by the Internet.

Most importantly, the Law and Economics movement provides genuine insight into the regulatory process. The issue of intangible property existing within a market structure is a prime example of where Law and Economics theorists have been especially astute. For instance, viewing innovations such as the photocopier and videocassette recorders as operating within a market structure or *waiting for that market to mature in order to segment different types of users becomes a persuasive way to understand the problems of regulating the emerging technologies* (Gordon1982). The Law and Economics approach distinguishes among different types of goods—public and private, or tangible and intangible—and it demonstrates the difficulties that have occurred with public goods and intangible products of the mind and imagination as these products encounter a market structure (Posner 1988, 338-352;). Nobel laureate Gary Becker (1976) argues that a "market structure" exists in many areas of social and political life not traditionally viewed as the subject matter of economic analysis, and that "price," "equilibrium," and "marginal utility" are concepts that serve to coordinate and regulate the complex interactions among an individual's preferences, behaviors, and deeply-held values.

Interestingly, the economic interpretation of intellectual property quickly emerged to become the dominant perspective within this multi-faceted area of copyrights, patents, trademarks, and trade secrets. Earlier intellectual property writers had relied heavily upon a doctrinal approach, stringing together several key concepts to foster an aura of coherence within the varied sub-fields of intellectual property (e.g., Landes & Posner 2003 420-424; Fisher 2001). But these sub-fields were relatively autonomous and unique, apart from the common agreement that producing more works of intellectual property was regarded as a highly desirable goal. Economics provided a useful mechanism to connect these disparate sub-fields. The Constitution had left it open to Congress to determine the optimal level of protection needed to maximize the production of intellectual, artistic, and utilitarian works. The economic analysis was extremely useful in pinpointing the desired degree of legal protection necessary to stimulate innovations, induce creativity, and encourage the production of intangible goods by producers while still allowing reasonable access to these works by the public at large.

Moreover, the Law and Economics approach filled a vacuum in intellectual property: it did not struggle and triumph over an active opposition. The doctrinal orientation was a piecemeal and often idiosyncratic approach. The older tradition of natural rights had decayed long before the beginning of World War II when intellectual property became viewed as a source of instrumental rather than natural rights (Moore 1997. 66). In addition, the instrumentally derived economic interpretation of intellectual property allows authors, trademark owners, and inventors to receive "only those rights which promoted economic efficiency" (Yen 1990 518). An efficiency-based standard was especially suited to the changes occurring within intellectual property law. As American society changed from a manufacturing to an information-oriented economy, the exponential expansion of the number of information producers, developers, and distributors placed a new premium upon an efficient use of resources by each party involved in the production of intangible goods.

However, the economic paradigm of intellectual property law has led to several important criticisms. Yen (1990) contends that the dominant economic paradigm distorts intellectual property decisions in two major respects. First, judges frequently ignore economic considerations in controversial intellectual property cases. Instead, the judges employ non-economic criteria, such as fundamental fairness, equity, or a pre-existing conception of justice (p. 521). In these situations, the economic paradigm provides us with little, if any, information about how a court reaches a decision. The economic model, powerful as it is in providing a coherent interpretation, thus has the potential to become irrelevant in any given case.

A second flaw that Yen (1990) identifies is the widely disparate conclusions yielded by economic models (p. 521). Theorists differ about the consequences of particular actions. Even under the best of economic scenarios, such as utilizing a Pareto adjustment (Pareto superior situations and Pareto optimal situations), the possible policy recommendations from the models lead in vastly different directions. Consequently, economic analysis, while providing an aura of rigor, fails to deliver conclusions that are uniform and consistent. In fact, because of the very flexibility of the Law and Economics model, judges often can find an economic warrant for the predisposition that they initially bring to the case itself.

There is a third major criticism of the economics paradigm that stems from the very ease in the use of the model and its underlying assumptions: that the approach tends toward oversimplification and even crude reductionism. Economics interacts with the law in a myriad of ways, and it does not require a major leap of imagination to envision that economic issues underlie many social problems. But the terms of the economic model can be utilized in a very simple, reductionist way. The use of the model can be analogized to giving a little boy or girl a hammer; all of sudden, he or she discovers that the whole world needs pounding. The economic model creates distortions because judges frequently make decisions on non-consequentialist grounds, and they inconsistently follow the cost-benefit formula provided by the Law and Economics movement. Intangible property diverges from a perfectly competitive model, where price is equal to "marginal" or "average" costs and where the "private costs of creating" and "deadweight losses" (or producer and consumer surpluses) are easy to determine. Judges instead frequently rely upon one economic factor or another, and they may exercise discretion to highlight that factor over other economic considerations. In particular, the concept of providing "more incentives to innovators" frequently has been reduced to a one-way approach expanding the protection for copyright owners at the expense of the general public (Solomon 1999 E2). Overall, the incentives argument has become one of the most oversimplified principles in the analysis of the production of intellectual property (Moore 1997 76-77; McLeod 2001).

These flaws, however, do not argue for abandoning the economic paradigm. Rather, the key terms in the economic paradigm should be treated as stock issues. As such, they provide an initial template for a critic to examine a problem. If the terms do not fit a particular problem, or if market failure provides an incomplete explanation, then non-economic considerations should be included in the discussion. Weinbreb (1987), Yen (1990), and Moore (1997) believe that a revitalized natural rights theory provides a conceptual structure to complement legal positivism and, by implication, to augment the reigning economic paradigm in several spheres of the law. Lessig's (2001) use of Locke's "commons" metaphor, and Litman's (2001) praise for the vitality of the public domain indicate growing modern-day support for a revitalized "commons" and a renewed emphasis on the role of labor in the creative process.

However, a natural rights theory does not begin with a favorable presumption in the field of intellectual property. Instead, there is a widespread and historically based fear against relying upon a natural rights theory to analyze intellectual property theory. Natural rights and labor theory have been associated with "an unprincipled expansion of author's rights which will run amok over the public interest in free access to work" (Yen 546). As a result, natural rights theory has been stigmatized as being too closely associated with expanding the rights of authors and inventors, and it is viewed as failing to offer a mechanism capable of handling situations where a conflict arises between the author-creator and the public at large. In contrast to economic analysis, natural rights theory is viewed as lacking a mode of reasoning for making trade-offs between the rights of a creator-inventor and the rights of the public. However, this conclusion is based upon a very narrow interpretation of natural rights and of Locke's natural rights approach. A broader interpretation of the Lockean Proviso provides a more nuanced concept for judging the public interest.

The Lockean Philosophy and the Lockean Proviso

John Locke (1632-1704) is the leading proponent of the labor theory of property. A physician by training, a literary critic, and a political philosopher, Locke's doctrines became embedded in an influential interpretation of philosophical liberalism. His T*wo Treatises on Government,* completed in 1689 and 1690 respectively, set forth his major political ideas. Locke's first treatise was devoted to attacking Sir Robert Filmer's theoretical support of the doctrine of divine rights for kings. Locke assailed the injustice of monarchy, and he attacked the notion of heredity rights as the best means of transmitting political power and property (Russell1945 619-621). In his second treatise, Locke attempted to explain a theory of natural law, and how labor served as the underlying basis for the creation of property as well as for the development of individual rights and human dignity (Hughes 1988 pp. 296-298). Locke's theory of property starts with the premise that in a state of nature there is no positive law to enforce ownership of private property or to legitimize institutions. Individuals have moral obligations that they extend to each other, but there are no judges to provide a binding interpretation of natural law or to settle disputes. People, therefore, create a "civil society" largely because doing so removes the uncertainties inherent in the state of nature, and because it provides them with an enhanced degree of security.

Locke also begins his labor theory with the pivotal assumption that people own their own bodies and the labor produced by their own efforts. Locke (1960) wrote:

[E]very Man has a *Property* in his own *Person.* This no body has any Right to but himself. The *Labour* of Body and the *Work* of his Hand, we may say, are properly his. Whatsoever then he removes out of the State that Nature hath provided, and left it in, he hath mixed his *Labour* with, and joyned to it something that is his own, and thereby makes it his *Property* (pp. 328-329). The key terms in this passage are "labour" and "joyned" because the resulting mixture leads to the creation of property.

When an individual's labor is mixed with other elements of nature, the resulting creation is owned by the inventor, especially in the realm of intellectual property. Thus, the person who labors industriously is capable of owning more goods than the less productive individual. Locke's labor theory, therefore, is initially designed to explain and justify the private appropriation of goods from the commonwealth of nature (Peters1989. 395; Kramer1997). One of the most controversial aspects of Locke's conception surrounds whether he would allow an unfettered and unrestrained (read: selfish) individualism. For instance, does his labor theory allow for the unlimited expansion of ownership rights by individuals against all claims by the public at large? The threshold question within an intellectual property context is: Does Locke's labor theory provide a warrant for the unlimited expansion of the rights of authors or inventors?

The answer is a resounding "no." Although less emphasized in the interpretation of his theory, Locke's natural rights theory provides for the rights of the public while protecting the rights of authors and creators. In fact, there is an explicit source of affirmative protection within Locke's scheme that protects the public from being harmed by the detrimental acquisitions of any one person (Hailwood 1996 40-43).

At the heart of Locke's labor theory lies the seventeenth-century metaphor of the "commons." The commons is depicted in spatial terms as a large field (Locke1960 329-330), but Locke defines the "commons" as all the fruits, animals, and natural elements, which are owned by humans jointly as tenants in common. Gordon (1993) has labeled the "Lockean Proviso" as the statement within Locke's theory that allows for trade-offs to promote the public welfare (p. 1538). Locke (1960) wrote that "For this Labour being the unquestionable Property of the Labourer, no Man but he can have a right to what is once joyned to, at least where there is enough, and as good left in common for others" (p. 329). This conception of "enough and as good'' remaining in the commons is the *Lockean Proviso*, and it serves as the basis for the protection of the rights of the public at large.

Locke provides a helpful example to illustrate his reasoning on how ''the commons'' operates during its everyday activities. He imagines a commons with acorns or apples that fall from a tree. An individual devotes his or her energies to gathering a pile of the apples or acorns. The pile becomes part of an individual's possession once the labor has been expended to create it. ''That Labour,'' argued Locke, ''put a distinction between them [the gathered commodities] and [the] common. That added something to them more than Nature, the common Mother of all had done; and so they became his private right'' (p. 330). The laborer did not need the consent or approval of anyone to remove the objects from the commons. For Locke, this type of appropriation is the first principle of survival among humans, and it is an assumption that does not even need to be articulated.

Locke intelligently anticipated possible objections to his labor theory of property. He raised the critical issue of the individual who attempts to monopolize the goods in the commons. He then set forth three lines of argument to rebut detractors of his theory.

Locke's first argument is that the commons is rich and abundant, and the supply of goods is inexhaustible. Locke treated land as subjected to his litmus test of labor-providing an-ironclad-title because the ''vast wilderness of the Earth'' offers an abundant supply of land for those who are willing to apply their labor (pp. 334-335). The uninhabited places on the earth would allow an individual to ''sow and reap'' a piece of land that he or she could legally appropriate through the legitimizing effects of their labor. But Locke extended the scope of this argument by including a unique value-added dimension provided by labor to society. Locke asserted that the person ''who appropriates land to himself by his labour, does not lessen but increase[s] the common stock of mankind'' (p. 336). The warrant for this statement was the premise that a cultivated acre of land provides ten times the benefits than does a piece of property that goes unused (p. 336). Intuitively, Locke argued that there is a producer's surplus, or social welfare benefit to society, that arose from mixing labor with the elements of nature.

Locke's second argument postulates that labor is the essential ingredient for the improvement of society. Locke attributed at least ninety percent of societal advancements to labor-based activities (p. 338). Thus, he contends that the protection and promotion of ''honest industry'' by government is the best course of action to achieve long-term benefits (p. 340). He concluded that labor ''put the greatest part of value on land, without which it would scarcely be worth anything'' (p. 340). The individual, therefore, is the source of all value in society to the extent that he or she employs their labor productively. Locke's commitment to a theory that ''labor-creates-wealth'' is unequivocal. He concludes this argument without acknowledging any reservations or even qualifications to his overall thesis that people ''were the great foundation of property'' (p. 341).

Locke's third argument is that people are inherently equal. There may be inequality in the collection of possessions, such as gold and silver, but as long as people had an equal opportunity to cultivate land, they accordingly had an equal opportunity to better themselves. The opportunity to apply one's labor provides a guarantee that the prospects for society to improve would remain intact. In effect, equal opportunity is left for everyone to exploit. For Locke (1960), the image of the ''commons'' provides the basis for a ''common-wealth'' or civilization to evolve (p. 400). Locke explicitly rejects monarchy and oligarchy as the best governing apparatus of the common-wealth, but he does not stipulate or openly endorse the use of ''democracy.'' Instead, he uses the terminology of an ''independent community,'' which he envisioned as having the power to choose its own preferred form of government (pp. 399-400).

All in all, the ''commons'' remains the guiding spatial image in Locke's vision of society. Applying natural rights theory, an individual has the ''right'' to use, transfer, or exclude others from his/her property. Locke provides an account of property as a staple of society, and he posits equality of opportunity among individuals who exist in a world characterized by seemingly inexhaustible resources. The Lockean Proviso requires that an individual take as much as he/she needs as long as what is left in the commons is "enough and as good" as what the individual originally acquired. Gordon (1993) contends that "What Locke posits is a sort of compromise, an entitlement midway between nonownership and tenancy-in-common: freedom to keep one's gains, subject to a duty not to impair others' abilities to draw their own gains from the resource" (p. 1560). Wolfe (1991) explains the Lockean position on freedom and duty in more straightforward terms: "No one has a right to interfere with your person or your possessions unless either you have consented, or you have forfeited your rights by violating the rights of others" (p. 4). Thus, there is a calculus within the Lockean scheme, a series of trade-offs that the proviso permits, and these trade-offs demonstrate that Locke's conception of labor theory was a more richly textured formulation than has been commonly understood.

Locke's interpretation of the "commons" and his mode of reasoning still have applications today, especially in the midst of the unfolding revolution in communications. In a very real sense, Locke's bucolic depiction of the "commons" as the dominant image of the seventeenth-century world has now been replaced by a different spatial metaphor for the twenty-first century: Cyberspace.

There are several conceptual similarities between the "commons" and "cyberspace." For one thing, cyberspace has no limits; it is infinitely malleable, and it has no geographical boundaries or political borders. Like the commons, cyberspace is a source of seemingly inexhaustible resources. To use Locke's terminology, cyberspace is a "vast wilderness" in which individuals can employ their labor to create new products and services. The horizons seem endless. For another thing, value in this new digital environment will lie not only in "owning and possessing" information, but rather in the opportunities presented to use and exploit digitized information as data, voice, and visual images continue to converge (Katsch 1995 224). In the digital world, labor once again plays an all-important role.

Labor becomes the key element in the creation of property because of the very nature of digital products. There will be secondary and tertiary users of information who will take the original or enhanced data and alter it even further as it is transferred from the first producer to the second user-producer and so on down the line. In this digital environment, a collaborative process of authorship is likely to emerge that does not exist in an analog world. Several individuals may add their labor to the information—which, in turn, raises new questions about the scope of ownership rights. *But cyberspace restores the role of labor to a central position in the production process.*

In addition, the rapidly evolving conception of "cyberspace" generates a series of important questions. How much ownership of digitized materials should society allow in this new environment? What kind of economic incentives, and at what level, should society provide for people to encourage new works? Should we limit these incentives by regulatory criteria such as time, money, level of creativity, or "sweat expended" on producing the material? On an even more mundane level, should we allow one company to create a web browser that will dominate the exploration of cyberspace? Or, will the process of innovation and economic development automatically provide a set of changing circumstances that will work against any one individual or firm dominating "cyberspace"? There is even an overriding question about the role of regulations in cyberspace: Will the velocity of change serve as a compelling argument for allowing the marketplace—not the law—to make decisions about the unfolding digital economy?

The economic paradigm is likely to persist as the dominant approach in intellectual property. Its vocabulary, rigor, and common sense orientation will not be easily supplanted. Even in cyberspace, markets will develop for services; firms will attempt to maximize profits; and individuals will seek to optimize their resources. In addition, free riders and externalities will continue to create problems for owners of intellectual property. Meanwhile, cyberspace promises to reduce transaction costs, and it will make a home office with its computer and modem an unprecedented window to a world of commerce and education. For intellectual property, many changes are likely to occur. Copying will be easier; distribution will be faster; and the ability to re-format and create derivative works will be limited only by the prevailing technology. As new markets and innovations develop, the economic paradigm will continue to offer useful insights into the creation, distribution, and protection of intellectual property. The Law and Economics paradigm contains a built-in calculus for weighing benefits and harms, and it allows the trade-offs to be measured with an enviable degree of rigor.

However, the Lockean philosophy of natural rights and the Lockean Proviso also may serve a useful purpose, especially since the velocity of change will undoubtedly outpace revisions in statutory law. Lockean theory provides a means for judges to make common law decisions drawing loosely upon the same criteria of fairness and justice that the image of the "commons" originally sought to promote. Like "the commons" of the seventeenth and eighteenth centuries, cyberspace is boundless and boundary-less. Legislators correctly fear making decisions about cyber-property, cyber-torts, or even cyber-crimes because the technology of the digital world is changing even as they deliberate these issues. Economic transformations and the development of markets and sub-markets increasingly will continue to play a vital role in cyberspace. But, if the history of the photocopier and VCR offer any lessons about technological and economic development, it may take twenty years or more for a particular market structure to emerge. In the meantime, concrete issues will emerge requiring immediate adjudication.

There are several non-economic issues that will need to be addressed in cyberspace, independent of the emergence of any market and sub-market schemes. For instance, as our understanding of cyberspace increases, how big should the public domain be in a digital world? Do we want to provide special a priori protection either by contract or property rights for fact-oriented databases that take years of labor to create and from which commercially valuable information can be transmitted easily over the Internet? And, if inventors and creators are given rights to reap the benefits of their creations, should we also require that "enough and as good" be left in the public domain?

It is very likely to assume that as cyberspace unfolds absent any statutory guidelines, judges may be compelled to rely upon abstract notions of "fairness" and "justice" and not simply utilize the yardstick of "wealth maximization" to address the problems that have come to the legal forefront.

This point is especially true if Litman's (1996) analysis of the digital age is correct, and if copyright stakeholders attempt to impose new "duties" upon private non-commercial users of copyrighted works. Responding to a report from the Clinton Administration's Information Infrastructure Task Force, Litman contended that an economic approach that emphasizes providing incentives to creators should be counter-balanced by a more equitable model to adjust the relationship between the "haves" and "have-nots" in the world of intellectual property. It is equity, not economics, that triggers Litman's pathbreaking proposal to redesign copyright law so that it focuses upon an "exclusive right to commercial exploitation" with her distinction being on "commercial" rather than "private" or "non-commercial" (p. 41). Litman's proposal would allow for reading and making copies of a work in one's home office, but it would prohibit downloading articles and selling an anthology of works to readers. Litman's proposal immunizes the general public from duties that currently would fall only to commercial and institutional users of copyrighted materials.

A few words of explanation may make Litman's thesis less abstract. According to Litman, what is radically new is that the process of digitization coupled with electronic transmission to private, non-commercial home users has created a new category of ''at-home users'' of copyrighted works. This is a category of users who previously were never major players in the reproduction, distribution, display, or creation of derivative works, or in the extensive policy-making efforts to regulate copyright. Indeed, the development of widespread copying and distribution activities that once required sophisticated equipment and considerable expense may now be accomplished with little skill or out-of-pocket costs to a would-be ''copyist'' working at home. Litman insists that extending copyright law to cover the everyday activities of individuals in a non-commercial, non-institutional capacity would amount to a fundamental step backward in copyright law. One of the implications of Litman's analysis is that all copying in a digital world *would not necessarily be an infringement.* In fact, Litman argues ''temporary copies are an unavoidable incident of reading on the Internet'' (p. 46). A second implication of Litman's analysis is that the continued expansion of copyright protection for producers cannot be justified from an economic perspective. Litman's proposal draws upon a sense of equity and justice, not efficiency or transaction costs, to restructure the world of copyright.

Litman's thesis on the perils of expanding the rights of authors in cyberspace is echoed by Netanel (1996). Netanel focuses directly upon the emerging issue of online browsing, but he identifies two separate strands to the question. On the one hand, Netanel argues that extending ''copyright's limited monopoly blithely over all new uses may unduly burden the public domain'' (p. 290). Netanel hypothesizes that the owner of a copyrighted work ''might not only require a payment each time a work is accessed online, but might also charge different users different amounts for the same use, relying on consumer profiles to exact a greater amount for those uses and types of works that an individual consumer values the most'' (p. 316). Netanel views the prospect of charging consumers for each new digital use, or any and all future developments on the Internet, as a logical but unwelcome outcome of the value placed upon giving incentives to producers in the economic interpretation of intellectual property.

On the other hand, Netanel speculates that the changing market structure created by cyberspace and the ''dawn of digitization'' may actually hurt the ability of copyright owners to re-capture the economic value of their work. Even if authors were willing to disseminate their work freely in a digital environment, publishers should be given the ''possibility of recovering their costs in selecting, editing, marketing, and distributing creative works'' (p. 340). In addition, Netanel suggests that it is foolhardy to believe that the digital environment will completely ignore economic considerations and market analysis when determining the scope of copyright protection. Market realities and institutional-risk averseness will continue to play a key role in the decisions on what and when to publish. The resulting content on the Internet also may be influenced heavily by ''vendors'' who provide advertising and on-going services to both content providers and content receivers. Netanel contends that ''with the advent of digital communications, copyright's role in a democratic civil society has become at once more prominent and more problematic'' (p. 364).

Nevertheless, there is a major conclusion that can be broadly inferred from Netanel analysis: As a larger percentage of ''works'' become available on the Internet, and with the breakdown of the pivotal distinction between mass marketing and personal use, it is likely that new political and judicial decisions will be necessary to re-configure the proper role of intellectual property in the rapidly changing digital environment. However, these decisions will not emerge solely from the flawed economic interpretation of the reigning intellectual property paradigm. A sense of fairness and equity for copyright owners, distributors, and users will be needed to guide the evolving system.

Overall, the Lockean Proviso may still yield insights about policy decisions, but this time it will be operating in an electronic environment and not the bucolic surroundings of the ''commons.'' Like the commons of John Locke, once again this will be an environment where labor—

variously characterized as intellectual, creative, utilitarian, and digitally-derived—will be valued greatly. Once again, judges without statutory law or direct legal precedent to guide them will turn to the common law tradition in their quest to translate geographically-bound doctrines into cyberlaw. The lack of statutes, legal precedents, and clear-cut powers of jurisdiction also will place a renewed premium on the role of a judge and may revitalize the long dormant discussion of the role of common law in intellectual property—issues that for the past twenty-seven years in the United States were believed to be settled by federal preemption of all copyright and patent issues. In fact, during the past two decades, any common law issue thought to offer equivalent intellectual property rights to copyright was automatically preempted by Section 301 of the 1976 Copyright Act. Yet, in an age where judges may need some flexibility, an abstract but pragmatically based notion of fairness and equity may be desirable. Accordingly, the Lockean Proviso may be especially employed for decisions related to the use of materials from the "digital commons."

NBA v. Motorola and the Lockean Proviso

The third section of this article attempts to apply the Lockean Proviso to generate insight into the decision-making of courts in intellectual property cases. This section is limited in scope. It is centered upon two decisions where the new technologies have posed a serious problem and where the current statutory copyright scheme does not provide helpful or persuasive answers. The core of the analysis focuses upon the *National Basketball Association v. Sports Team Analysis and Tracking System, Inc.* (1996) and *NBA v. Motorola* (1997). Brief references also are made to *Pro-CD v. Zeidenberg* (1996), *The Washington Post v. Total News* (1997), *Kelley v. Arriba* (1999), and *Los Angles Times v. Free Republic* (2000) insofar as they illustrate technologically novel ways to distribute information.

The two basketball cases focus upon a new technology for relaying basketball-related game information via hand-held pagers. While both cases are rich in economic analysis, the holdings also bring new vitality to the long dormant discussion of the doctrine of misappropriation. Moreover, the cases demonstrate the utility of the Lockean Proviso as a means to explaining the confusing central ruling of the Second Circuit Court in *NBA v. Motorola*. That decision held that a limited misappropriation doctrine survives the preemption standard set forth in Section 301 of the 1976 Copyright Act. However, the Second Circuit Court ruled that the doctrine of misappropriation could not be applied to real-time information about basketball games that were relayed via a pager in the National Basketball Association's (NBA) case.

The District Court Opinion in NBA v. Motorola

The NBA v. Motorola has received widespread attention in the popular and academic press because the case contains an attractive mixture of sports, new technology, and the highly visible failure of statutory law to anticipate the versatility of a hand-held pager. The case itself is a by-product of the ever-changing evolution in communication technology. But the legal importance of the case comes directly from the re-emergence of the common law doctrine of misappropriation within a cyber-age context.

The facts of the case center upon the introduction and diffusion of a new application for digital technology. Motorola manufactured and sold a hand-held paging device that allowed the public to keep track of scores and game information of basketball contests played by the twenty-nine teams in the NBA while the games were still in progress. The SportsTrax pager could be used to follow the score of basketball games on a basket-by-basket basis—thus allowing the recipient of the service to have exciting NBA basketball "in the palm of your hand" (*NBA v. STATS* 1133). The "SportsTrax Pager" came onto the retail market in January, 1996, selling for approximately two hundred dollars. The pager has an inch-and-a half by inch-and-a-half screen that operates in four modes: (a) Current (b) Statistics (c) Final Scores and (d) Demonstration. The contested use focuses upon the information emitted by the pager in the "current mode."

In the current mode, the pager displays six items of information: the teams playing, changes in score, the team in possession of the ball, whether the team is in a free-throw bonus, the quarter of the game, and the time remaining in the quarter. The information is updated every two to three minutes, with more frequent updates occurring at the end of the first half and near the end of the game. There is a two to three minute lag between the game itself and the information displayed on the pager screen.

A company called Sports Team Analysis and Tracking Systems (STATS) supplies the data for the SportsTrax Pagers. STATS relied upon reporters who watched the game on television or listened to the game on radio. These reporters then would type into a personal computer information such as changes in the score, completed and missed free throws, and clock updates. The information was then sent by a modem to a common carrier, and subsequently further transmitted via satellite to various local FM radio networks that, in turn, sent the signals to owners of the SportsTrax pagers.

The information sent by the reporters also was used by America On-Line (AOL), and a home computer attached to a modem for a fee could access STAT's AOL site, where the recipient would receive "slightly" more comprehensive information in "slightly" less lag time than the SportsTrax pagers. But the focus of the NBA's complaint and the court's response was on the SportsTrax pager, not the nascent AOL site. In advertising the pager, Motorola did not claim sponsorship or approval by the NBA, but the company did use the NBA acronym as part of its marketing and promotional activities to sell the pager.

The NBA was victorious in the district court's decision. At the district court level, the NBA's complaint raised five claims for relief: (1) State law related to unfair competition by misappropriation; (2) False advertising and false representation under Section 43A of the Lanham Act; (3) State and common law related to unfair competition; (4) Federal copyright infringement; and (5) Unlawful interception of communication under the Communication Act of 1934. The district court dismissed all of the NBA's allegations except the first one—state law related to unfair competition by misappropriation. The district court held that Motorola and STATS were liable for misappropriation under New York state law, and the court permanently enjoined the parties from distributing data about ongoing NBA games via a pager, the AOL site, or equivalent mechanisms.

The district court was persuaded favorably by the NBA's multi-faceted efforts to regulate real-time transactions of game information. "Real-time" was defined by the court as "information about an ongoing NBA game, such as changing scores, disseminated while the game is in progress" (*NBA v. STATS* 1128). Four mechanisms were highlighted in the district court's opinion of the NBA's resourceful efforts to limit real-time transactions. First, the NBA carefully screened the credentials of the media, and promulgated a list of explicit restrictions prior to allowing any print and broadcast journalists to cover a game. Second, the NBA had given permission to Sportsticker—which is owned by ESPN—to distribute electronically factual information about the games. In turn, Sportsticker created "a data feed with this information" and sold the information to clients for a fee (*NBA v. STATS*, p. 1131). Third, the NBA had created its own system for disseminating statistical information about its games called "Gamestats." This system, while in its initial stage of development, would be directly harmed by the continued existence of STATS, and it limits the ability of the NBA to engage in other licensing efforts to sell "real-time" game information. Fourth, the court was visibly impressed by the NBA's ability to walk a tightrope with respect to transmitting game-type information: The league attempted to provide the public with concrete information to stimulate interest in future NBA games while it attempted to preserve its right to derive revenue from real-time sales (*NBA v. STATS* 1130). ''The activities by [the] NBA,'' declared the district court, ''demonstrate its unequivocal intention not to abandon its proprietary interests in real-time NBA game information'' (*NBA v. STATS* 1157).

At the same time, the district court held that STATS indisputably had engaged in commercial misappropriation. The court found ''without hesitation that their product crosses the boundary from mere media coverage of NBA games into competing commercial appropriation of these games'' (*NBA v. STATS* 1158). SportsTrax offers ''consumers real time NBA data with portable, nationwide, contemporaneous, and core information about NBA games'' (*NBA v. STATS* 1158). The court strongly rejected the argument that SportsTrax could be analogized to ''another version of the evening news'' (*NBA v. STATS* 1158). Drawing upon the most famous aphorism from International News Service v. Associated Press (1918), the district court concluded that the SportsTrax pager ''competes with the NBA's wholly legitimate efforts to reap where it has sown'' (*NBA v. STATS* 1158). Justice Pitney's biblical invocation in *INS v. AP* (1918) expressed concern about a defendant who appropriates and sells news originating from the labor of others and thus who is ''endeavoring to reap where it has not sown.'' This phrase—''reaps where it has not sown''—subsequently has become the signature line on behalf of plaintiffs in misappropriation cases who want to receive quasi-property protection for their data.

INS (1918) is still regarded as the paradigm case in the common law to trigger a restrictive quasi-property approach towards information. Youn (1998) points out that Pitney's use of a commanding agricultural metaphor in *INS* ''has caught the fancy of numerous courts and commentators,'' although *INS* ''ceased to be binding when the Supreme Court decision in *Erie Railroad Co. v. Tompkins* (1938) abolished the general common law upon which *INS* was based'' (p. 269). Despite the abolition of federal common law, New York has retained a state-based common law tort of misappropriation based upon an INS-type harm. In addition, Pitney's less quoted passage of the landmark *INS* decision still provides a succinct and compelling statement of the economic harm caused by misappropriation of information. Pitney insisted that misappropriation occurs when a defendant:

> [A]ppropriates to itself the harvest of those who have sown. Stripped of all disguises, the process amounts to an unauthorized interference with the normal operation . . . precisely at the point where the profit is to be reaped, in order to divert a material portion of the profit from those who have earned it to those who have not (*INS. v. AP*. 239-240).

At bottom, the key question for the district court revolved around whether SportsTrax had affected adversely the NBA's ability to profit from ''real-time game information.'' The court found that SportsTrax had ''misappropriated the essence of the NBA's most valuable property—the excitement of an NBA game in progress'' *(NBA v. STATS* 1128). The court also found that SportsTrax's activities prevented the NBA from negotiating with other information distributors. In issuing a permanent injunction to stop SportsTrax, the district court noted that SportsTrax initially had negotiated with the NBA for rights to distribute the game-information, but then Motorola rushed its product to the marketplace without obtaining approval from the NBA. To the court, this looked liked ''a negotiate-first-but-go-ahead-anyway'' type case of infringement.

The Second Circuit Court Opinion in the NBA Case

The Second Circuit Court reversed the decision of the district court. The Second Circuit examined the case as a misappropriation case arising under the state law of New York, and as to whether the Federal Copyright Act of 1976 preempts the claim of such a violation under state law. The Circuit Court succinctly identified the key issue in the case: "The crux of the dispute concerns the extent to which a state law 'hot news' misappropriation claim based on *International News Service v. Associated Press* . . . survives preemption by the federal Copyright Act and whether the NBA's claim fits within the surviving INS-type claims" (*NBA v. Motorola* 1997 843). The Circuit Court then invoked the "extra-element" test to determine whether the contested issue could survive independent from a claim of copyright and federal preemption. The court concluded that game-type information did not qualify as a "hot-news" exception and thus the 1976 Copyright Act preempts the use of New York State law.

From a Law and Economics perspective, this conclusion is disastrous because both Motorola and STATS represent quintessential examples of free riders (e.g., Landes and Posner, 2003). The Law and Economics perspective provides two major arguments why the NBA should win this case.

First, the NBA is a business entity that generates images and information at considerable cost and expense; the value of the information is highly time-sensitive; and the members of the NBA who pay the salaries of the players recoup a large share of their expenses by selling the rights to broadcast (or in copyright language, to "perform publicly") these games to various distributors, e.g., radio and television stations and networks. Therefore, the control of real-time transmission and real-time game information is crucial to the NBA's ability to earn a profit from its activities.

This argument is bolstered further by the key role of real-time information in providing revenue to the NBA. According to testimony presented before the district court, eighty percent of the revenue that the NBA generates comes from real-time transmissions from broadcast rights or fees collected from admissions prior to or while the game is "in progress." (*NBA v. STATS* 1130). The NBA emphasized the importance of controlling "real-time information" as a distinct and autonomous category because it includes the core element of its business: the audience's attention is focused upon the excitement and entertainment value of a game "in progress."

In turn, the ability of parties such as STATS and Motorola to free-ride on the NBA's efforts eventually would reduce the incentive of the league to produce its product and chief service, or, alternately, the free riders would make the endeavor so lacking in profit that the NBA would find it prohibitive to render this service in comparison with the return on its investment. A second major argument from a Law and Economics perspective is that the existence of SportsTrax hurts the NBA's ability to license its own pager service. In its pleadings before the district court, the NBA indicated that it had introduced stage one of its own pager service called "Gamestats," and that STATS would be in direct competition with "Gamestats." The NBA contended that there is a "separate market for real-time transmission of factual information to pagers" as a derivative work, and that STATS and Motorola were free-riding on the property of the league and its component members. The NBA's licensing argument also relies heavily upon a theory of free-riding—although the elements involving the licensing issue are somewhat different than the NBA's earlier version of the free-rider argument. If STATS and Motorola were able to compete with future NBA endeavors, they could offer their services at a cheaper rate because STATS and Motorola could expend minimal resources to produce and market the basketball games.

It is clear from the Second Circuit Court's reasoning that the novelty of the hand-held pager was an influential factor in its decision. The pager adds a completely new device to transmitting information about the game, and it compelled the court to re-consider two issues: (1) Are basketball games covered under the scope of activities envisioned by the Copyright Act of

1976?, and (2) Is the dissemination of factual information, and facts themselves by STATS and SportsTrax, prohibited by the Copyright Act of 1976?

The Second Circuit Court answered both questions in the negative. Neither the underlying games nor facts about the games warrant protection under the scope of the 1976 Copyright Act. The Second Circuit Court ruled that, while broadcasts of basketball games fall into the scope of copyrightable materials, the underlying work—the actual games themselves—do not. Furthermore, the fact-idea dichotomy precludes an organization from controlling factual materials that should be in the public domain and open for anyone to use. In the aftermath of *Feist Publications Inc. v. Rural Telephone Service Company* (1991), there was unequivocal support for the notion that facts gathered solely by the ''sweat-of-brow'' should not receive special protection as ''works of authorship'' (*NBA v. Motorola* p. 847).

However, there was a third issue that troubled the Second Circuit Court: Does Section 301 of the 1976 Copyright Act preempt the use of New York State unfair competition law? The decision of the Second Circuit Court rejected using the Copyright Act to bolster a credibility-stretching claim by the NBA of ''authorship'' in the basketball games themselves. The court agreed that the underlying basketball games were not covered by Section 101 of the 1976 Copyright Act, and the court emphasized that actual games were not one of the categories of works covered under Section 102. Therefore, on the preemption issue the Second Circuit Court was unwilling to follow the reasoning of the district court in allowing a claim of misappropriation based upon the protectible status of the game under the New York state law of misappropriation. The court also held that Section 301 of the 1976 Copyright Act provided that all rights equivalent to copyright are preempted in the 1976 Copyright Act through the Supremacy Clause of the Constitution (*NBA v. Motorola* 848).

In its decision, the Second Circuit Court closely followed the precedent established in *Baltimore Orioles v. Major League Baseball Players Association* (1986). That court ruled that once a performance is reduced to a tangible medium of expression, there is no remaining distinction between the underlying game and the broadcast. The Second Circuit Court concluded that having a doctrine of ''partial preemption'' would have expanded the reach of state law far beyond what Congress had intended in enacting the 1976 Copyright Act. The court held that (1) the owner of the rights of the game can protect the actual broadcast of a game but not the facts from that game; (2) But that the owner cannot protect the underlying game as ''an original work of authorship'' independent from the broadcast itself. The court's ruling curtailed the doctrine of ''partial preemption'' from emerging as a touchstone for modern copyright cases.

However, the Second Circuit Court did acknowledge one category where the state law of misappropriation could survive the federal preemption standard: hot news (the original subject of controversy in the *INS v. AP* case in 1918). The Court utilized the ''extra element'' test to show how ''hot news'' could survive preemption. The Court held that misappropriation would occur (1) if the information is time-sensitive; (2) if the defendant has had a free ride rather than expended its own resources; and (3) if the defendant's actions will constitute a threat to the existence of the plaintiff's product. Considering that Motorola and STATS were not dealing with time-sensitive or public affairs information, and because they had expended resources to gather the information, the court found that misappropriation law was inapplicable in this case. Moreover, the court found that no harm had occurred to the NBA's core products and thus reversed the injunction.

The Implications of the Second Circuit Court's Decision

In the aftermath of the Second Circuit's NBA decision, there has been considerable controversy about the meaning of this case. Youn, Khadder, and Keller have set forth radically different interpretations of the decision. Youn (1998) praises Justice Winter's opinion as a ground-breaking decision because it separates ''incentives'' from ''remuneration,'' and adds incentives to the list of factors that might be considered an extra-element to permit a state-derived misappropriation claim to survive preemption. Khadder (1998) concludes that Winter's designation of ''incentives'' as an extra-element was unnecessary to a valid misappropriation claim. For Khadder, it is the subject matter of the copying, not the extra-element, that determines either misappropriation or copyright infringement. At the same time, Khadder implies that ''free riding'' is just a vogue-ish term for ''unlawful copying'' (p. 15). Meanwhile, Keller (1997) insists that the decision by the Second Circuit Court ''articulated a multi-factored test capable of providing significant protection to content owners in future cases'' (p. 403).

These various commentaries are strikingly at odds with each other. However, there are some common conclusions that can be inferred from the commentaries. While it is clear that the court's opinion resuscitates the common law tort of misappropriation, the court also narrows the decision of the case to include only those instances where ''hot news'' is an issue. The court's newly formulated test places a heavy emphasis on two factors acting in tandem with each other: (1) The time sensitivity of the information and (2) The direct competition between a plaintiff and defendant. The emphasis placed upon these two factors constitutes a shift from the open-endedness and broad contours of the *Board of Trade v. Dow Jones & Co.* (1983), the most widely cited misappropriation case from the 1980s. In all likelihood, both the ''time axis'' and the ''direct competition axis'' will now be prominently featured analytical elements in a determination of misappropriation.

From a Law and Economics perspective, however, the Second Circuit's decision gives unequivocal legitimacy to Motorola and STATS's activities as free riders. The decision hurts the incentives for the NBA to open new markets. The decision also harms the NBA's ability to develop license agreements for its products and properties; it encourages Motorola and STATS to exploit the work of others at minimal costs; and it allows STATS to directly compete with the NBA's fledgling data service—Gamestats.

The Circuit Court knowingly set aside these economic considerations. The court instead would allow a claim of ''pirated information'' only if there was an issue of hot-news, and then only for a brief period while the news remained ''commercially hot'' and in situations where no resources had been expended by a second party to obtain the information. Curiously, the ''direct competition axis'' was simply ignored in the court's calibrations.

Yet, the reasoning in the Second Circuit decision seems to bolster a Lockean rather than a Law and Economics approach to intellectual property. Motorola and STATS were free to join their labor with the information that was out in ''the commons.'' These companies had expended labor, and they had mixed their labor with factual data. The NBA also had mixed its labor with the data to create a product and the subsequent game-type information that emerged. But the court's decision rejected giving a monopoly to the NBA which would have violated the core element of the Lockean Proviso: *''Enough and as good'' in terms of available factual materials would not have still remained for others to use.*

Some Paretian calculations (Pareto superior and Pareto optimal situations) come into play in analyzing the NBA case from a Lockean viewpoint. These Paretian calculations are the same type of considerations that philosopher Robert Nozick (1974) utilized in his widely discussed theory of justice, where he directly incorporated the Lockean Proviso into his explanation of justice, liberty, and property (pp. 174-182). In Lockean terms, STATS and Motorola are made better off by the existence of the pager; the NBA is made worse-off. But, since Congress and the courts have ruled that factual materials cannot be considered original works of authorship, the use of the hand-held pager does not take anything away from the NBA that the league has a legitimate right to possess. In addition, Motorola and STATS have devoted time, money, and labor to creating a new technique for transmitting information to the public, while not preventing the NBA from using a similar innovation to transmit factual materials. In fact, because of its pre-existing communication connections (which represent a "positive externality"), the NBA will probably have a competitive advantage in developing its own product (Gamestats) into the dominant distributor of pager-type information. But Motorola and STATS are living off "the commons," and they should be free to transmit factual materials without any interference by the NBA.

Of course, it would not be far-fetched to suggest that the NBA is likely to respond to this decision by engaging in "rent-seeking" activities. Law and Economics proponents refer to "rent-seeking" as the use of lobbying and political pressure activities to obtain a statutory exemption from legislators. Under this scenario, the NBA may attempt to secure an amendment to the 1976 Copyright Act designed to protect data-originating organizations from any type of economic competition by outside companies who are able to capitalize on pager-like technology to relay information cheaply and quickly. There is a history of successful rent-seeking in the world of mass communications, and the NBA may attempt to re-assert its controls as it endeavors to reap where it believes that it has "exclusively" sown. Interestingly, the NBA cannot rely heavily upon "incentive theory" in this instance because the pager and its developing market for game-type information are essentially irrelevant to the NBA's incentive to produce and broadcast its core product—basketball games. And the NBA was slow—very slow—to realize the commercial value of this new pager technology.

The Lockean Perspective Extended

Of more enduring importance, *NBA v. Motorola* (1997) is not an anomalous case. Rather, it may be a harbinger of issues that are likely to emerge as the digital revolution unfolds. There are several instances where new technologies are forcing courts to confront issues where rights similar, or equivalent, to copyright are at stake. Two other cases will be mentioned briefly, and a Lockean perspective will be suggested as an alternative way to look at the cases that depart from the dominant economics paradigm.

Pro-CD v. Zeidenberg (1996) is a case in which the Seventh Circuit Court reversed a district court decision and ruled that buyers of computer software must obey the terms of a shrinkwrap license because of the contract-like qualities of the license. As Convotta and Sergeeff (1998) wrote: "Shrinkwrap licenses impose specific restrictions on use, reproduction, transfer, and modification of the software program by consumers in an attempt to prevent unauthorized duplication, and to give the software owner a breach of contract action should the restrictions be violated" (p. 35). In brief, mass-market shrinkwrap and clickwrap licenses have become an ever-present part of purchasing software, although the exact terms of the contract cannot be reviewed until the consumer actually has opened the package—which raises the germane question of whether a consumer has received something that was not bargained for or negotiated.

Zeidenberg purchased from Pro-CD a database containing ninety-five million telephone numbers assembled from over 3,000 directories. Subsequently, Zeidenberg ignored the shrinkwrap license and later re-sold the information that was stored on the purchased CD-ROM disk to people on the Internet. Despite the fact that the materials being protected were completely factual, the Seventh Circuit Court held that the contract terms were not equivalent to copyright, and that the terms had to be obeyed. Thus, Zeidenberg was found to have breached the terms of the shrinkwrap contract.

But there is an important slippery slope argument that the Seventh Circuit Court overlooked in this case: If all telephone books were now to come packaged in a shrinkwrap cellophane cover, the information in a telephone book, when opened, would then be protected under contract law. This conclusion directly contradicts Congressional intention regarding factual materials, and it opens a wide door for abuse. This conclusion also is at odds with the Supreme Court's holding in *Feist Publications v. Rural Telephone Service Company* (1991), where the Court refused to extend recognition to factual materials as qualifying for being a work of "original" authorship. Moreover, Aoki (1998) contends that shrinkwrap "agreements make an end run around the Copyright Act's 'first sale' doctrine" (pp. 268-269)

A Lockean approach to the case would have found on behalf of Zeidenberg because "factual" materials were the subject matter in the case, and because "enough and as good" was not left in the commons after Pro-CD had completed its work. Not only does the case seem like a contract of adhesion; but Pro-CD also wants special protection for the misappropriation of facts. Of course, Zeidenberg is not an ideal Lockean candidate because the defendant expended minimal labor and time in gathering the information. This is a major Lockean blemish against his record. Zeidenberg also is competing in the same market that Pro-CD is attempting to establish. At the same time, Pro-CD seems to be benefiting from using contract law to substitute for, or be equivalent to, copyright. The Lockean perspective does not provide an air-tight solution in this case. But the Law and Economics approach that the Seventh Circuit adopted allows contract law to trump copyright in a fashion that the Copyright Act of 1976 explicitly sought to prevent.

The second new technologies case is the *Washington Post v. Total News* (1997). In *Washington Post v. Total News*, an organization called Total News provided a one-click website to the contents of new reports of other widely known news organizations, such as the *Washington Post* and CNN. The website had to be accessed through a Total News computer-window frame, which also carried a separate advertisement banner that financially supported Total News. Total News resourcefully claimed that it did not "cache, or otherwise create any 'copies' of the copyrighted materials posted by the news organizations on their respective sites" (Keller 1997. 401). Thus, their actions did not violate the 1976 Copyright Act. But the publishers of the respective news organizations insisted that Total News infringed upon their exclusive rights under Section 106 of the Copyright Act. The publishers also perceived Total News as a high-tech free rider using materials that they expended no resources to collect.

From a Lockean point of view, the publishers had a right to control the use of the information because they had expended energy, money, and time in collecting the information. Had Total News devoted resources to collecting the news, then the organization could have used the same factual materials on its website. But Total News could not simply utilize materials that others had gathered and published without paying a licensing fee. Total News had independently gathered no news nor sought permission to use information gathered by others. "Hot news" is still the strongest bastion in the Lockean rampart, and this was a case where "enough and as good" still remained in the commons for all genuinely industrious parties to obtain.

It is worth underscoring that both of these cases after NBA v. Motorola (1997) address issues dealing with new technologies, and both incorporate novel ways of transmitting information. A Lockean perspective provides insights that may differ from a Law and Economics approach. For instance, the decision in Zeidenberg written by Judge Frank Easterbrook, a strong proponent of the Law and Economics movement, reverses the Lockean interpretation of allowing "good and enough" to survive. But, most importantly, a Lockean approach in Zeidenberg provides a standard of equity and justice where statutory law is silent and judges are required to made a decision. A Lockean interpretation may be ideally suited as a complement to the dominant economics paradigm during the coming era.

Cases such as *Kelley v. Arriba* (1999) and *Los Angeles Times v. Free Republic* (2000) also represent new use of the Internet to disseminate information. *Kelly* deals with the distribution of thumbnail pictures of the Gold Strike era in California while *Free Republic* deals with a bulletin board that posted complete articles from newspapers for viewers to comment upon. The courts allowed the Internet distribution in *Kelly* while preventing the defendants in *Free Republic* from displaying the full text of news articles. Both cases profit from a Lockean interpretation, and the interpretation is strongest precisely because statutory authority is absent or vague.

Keller (1997) astutely has pointed out that the ''common law has emerged as a source of protection for intellectual property rights throughout this century whenever statutory protection for new forms of media were still evolving'' (p. 402). This is because of the flexibility that the common law provides to reconcile new innovations to traditional legal principles. But common law is limited to a specific jurisdiction and to a particular set of facts. Nevertheless, it also is worth emphasizing that the common law is most effective during periods of change when new technologies are still evolving and when the rules of a nascent industry are unclear. Judges thus are allowed to bring a discerning flexibility to an issue before the bigger picture crystallizes. The Lockean approach provides an orientation to assist judges who may be compelled to draw upon common law doctrines to adjust new technologies to emerging economic realities.

Overall, the significance of NBA v. Motorola is its role as an exemplar of the early digital cases to emerge in a legal environment where statutory controls are silent as to what is protected or prohibited, and where the common law of misappropriation once again manifests itself after a long period of dormancy. Of course, the Law and Economics perspective will continue to frame the major issues and provide the key concepts when examining controversial cases in intellectual property. But the Lockean approach and its accompanying Proviso also provide a set of useful parameters to trigger a ''just'' and ''equitable'' decision in lieu of either statutory or Congressional guidance.

Conclusion

This article has examined John Locke's theory of labor and applied the Lockean Proviso to a digitally based technology. It continues the growing tradition of reading land-based documents and doctrines in cyberspace. Many legal commentators believed that as the twenty-first century progressed, we would abandon black-letter law as well as doctrinal analysis and move into an era of sophisticated legal interpretation and post-modernist approaches in legal analysis. But this has not been the most prominent legal trend of our era. Instead, we are confronting a major *translation problem:* How to translate doctrines that first were applied to libel, privacy, obscenity, and intellectual property within a fixed geographic area to the *tabula rasa* of cyberspace, where there are no borders, no spheres of jurisdiction, and where older doctrines can only approximate the activities now occurring in a digital environment.

Metaphoric images will continue to serve as a rich and fertile basis for framing the evolving issues in cyberspace. As Lemley (2003) suggests, ''Metaphors exist to help us think through new problems by analogizing them to old ones'' (p. 542). Ultimately a metaphor is a cognitive scheme designed to assist us in organizing our thinking. Spatial metaphors from the ''Great Chain of Being'' to the ''public sphere'' have been useful vehicles to identify the contours of a given debate. The term ''space'' conveys not only a boundlessness, but it embodies an entity with boundaries and parameters that have been charted and mapped—a territory with dimensions that are both ''known'' and ''unknown.''

Space is thus a comforting metaphor precisely because it embraces the ''known'' and ''unknown,'' and researchers can focus on either dimension. There is the mystery and disquietude in confronting the ''unknown'' domain. But there also is a ''known'' component that can be built upon and extended, and there is a subsidiary and commonplace vocabulary of "milestones," "landmarks," "turning points," and "benchmarks" that can be employed to measure our progress in obtaining this hard-earned knowledge. All of these metaphors share a common desire: to make sense out of a rapidly changing world and to apply a "concept" that we know—space—to something that may become known only after a long period of investigation. In the final analysis, the metaphoric vocabulary that has evolved is designed to reduce our anxieties and fears about the "unknown" dimension.

Steen (1994) depicts "metaphor" as an instrument to conceptualize reality—not as a "figure of language" to avoid reality (pp. 3-26). As the digital environment continues to expand, we will continue to require new concepts to comprehend the developments that are at sharp variance with our past history. We are unquestionably in the midst of a revolution in communication technology where each day the public witnesses the emergence of a new development or application.

We also are in the midst of an "Age of Translation" where applying land-based doctrines in cyberspace will continue to be a major activity for communication law scholars. Cyberspace which began as a "poetic" metaphor will continue to be extended and developed until it acquires a literal and very pragmatic set of meanings. Cyberspace has become the all-purpose metaphor that serves as a prism for moving from an analog to a digital environment. In a time of uncertainty, cyberspace depicts an environment with physical dimensions, and it gives us a touchstone to discuss the profound and massive changes that are occurring in the dissemination of information. Cyberspace has become John Locke's "commons" for a digital age.

Works Cited

Aoki, Keith. (1998). The stakes of intellectual property law. In D. Kairys (Ed.), The Politics of the Law, 3rd ed. (pp. 259-278). New York: Basic Books.

Baltimore Orioles v. Major League Baseball Players Association 805 F. 2d. 663 (7th Cir., 1986).

Becker, Gary.S. (1976). The economic approach to human behavior. Chicago: University of Chicago Press.

Board of Trade v. Dow Jones & Co. 98 Ill. 2d 109 (1983).

Bunker, Matthew D. (1998). Imperial paradigms: First Amendment theory, legal interdisciplinarity and reductionism. Communication Law and Policy, 3, 551-562.

Coase, Ronald. H. (1937). The nature of the firm. Ecomomica, 4, 368-405.

Coase, Ronald. H. (1960). The problem of social cost. Journal of Law and Economics, 3, 1-44.

Coase, Ronald. H. (1996). Law and economics and A.W. Brian Simpson. Journal of Legal Studies, 25, 103-119.

Covotta, Brian. & Sergeeff, Pamela. (1998). ProCD, Inc. v. Zeidenberg. Berkeley Technology Law Journal, 13, 34-54.

Dnes, A.W. (1996). The economics of law (London: International Thomson Business Press).

Drucker, Susan. & Gumpert, Gary. (1995). Freedom and liability in cyberspace: Media, metaphors and paths of regulation. Free Speech Yearbook, 33, 49-64.

Feist Publications Inc. v. Rural Telephone Service Company, 499 U.S. 340 (1991).

Fisher, William W. (2001). Theories of intellectual property. Retrieved on November 6, 2001 from the World Wide Web: http:// www.law.harvard.edu/academic affairs/coursepages/tfisher/iphistory.html

Froomkin, A. Michael. (2003). Habermas@discourse.net: Toward a critical theory of cyberspace. Harvard Law Review, 116, 749-873.

Gordon, Wendy. J. (1982). Fair use as market failure: A structural and economic analysis of the Betamax case and it predecessors. Columbia Law Review, 82, 1600-1657.

Gordon, Wendy. J. (1989). An inquiry into the merits of copyright: The challenges of consistency, consent, and encouragement theory. Stanford Law Review 41, 1343-1469.

Gordon, Wendy. J. (1993). A property right in self-expression: Equality and individualism in the natural law of intellectual property. Yale Law Journal, 102, 1533-1609.

Gordon, Wendy. J. (1994). Assertive modesty: An economics of intangibles. Columbia Law Review, 94, 2579-2591.

Hailwood, Simon. A. (1996). Exploring Nozick: Beyond anarchy, state and utopia. Brookfield, VT: Ashgate Publishing Company.

Hughes, Justin. (1988). The philosophy of intellectual property. The Georgetown Law Journal, 77, 287-366.

Hunter, Dan. (2003). Cyberspace as place and the tragedy of the digital anticommons. California Law Review, 91, 441-519.

International New Service v. Associated Press 248 U.S. 215 (1918).

Johnson, David. R. & Marks, Kevin. A. (1993). Mapping electronic data communications onto existing legal metaphors: Should we let our conscience (and our contracts) be our guide? Villanova Law Review, 38, 487-516.

Katsh, M.Ethan. (1995). Law in a digital world. New York: Oxford University Press.

Keller, Bruce .P. (1998). Condemned to repeat the past: The reemergence of misappropriation and other common law theories of protection for intellectual property. Harvard Journal of Law & Technology, 11, 401-427.

Kelly v. Arriba Soft Corp. 77 F. Supp. 2d 1116 (Central District of CA, 1999).

Kerr, Orin S. (2003). The problem of perspective in Internet law. The Georgetown Law Journal, 91, 357-405.

Khadder, Nick. (1998). National Basketball Association v. Motorola, Inc. Berkeley Technology Law Journal, 13, 3-19.

Kramer, Matthew. (1997). John Locke and the origins of private property. New York: Cambridge University Press.

Landes, William. M. & Posner, Richard. (1989). An economic analysis of copyright law. Journal of Legal Studies, 18, 325-363.

Landes, William .M. & Posner, Richard. (2003). The economic structure of intellectual property law. Cambridge, MA: Harvard University Press.

Lemley, Mark .A. (2003). Place and space. California Law Review, 91, 521-542.

Lessig, Lawrence. (1996a). Reading the constitution in cyberspace. Emory Law Journal, 45, 869-910.

Lessig, Lawrence. (1996b). The zones of cyberspace. Stanford Law Review, 48, 1403-1411.

Lessig, Lawrence (2001). The future of ideas: The fate of the commons in a connected world. New York: Random House.

Litman, Jessica. (1990). The public domain. Emory Law Journal, 39, 965-1023.

Litman, Jessica. (1996). Revising copyright law for the information age. Oregon Law Review, 75, 19-48.

Litman, Jessica. (2001). Digital copyright. Amherst, NY: Prometheus Books.

Locke, John. (1960). Two treatises of government. In P. Laslett, ed., Critical and Rev. Ed. (New York: Mentor Books).

Los Angeles Times v. Free Republic, 54 U.S.P. Q. 2d 1453 (C.D. Cal. 2000).

McLeod, Kembrew. (2001). Owning culture: authorship, ownership, & intellectual property law. New York: Peter Lang.

Miller, Arthur. R. & Davis, Michale. H. (1983). Intellectual property. (St. Paul: West Publishing Co.).

Moore, Adam. (1997). A Lockean theory of intellectual property. Hamline Law Review, 21, 65-108.

National Basketball Association v. Sports Team Analysis and Tracking System, Inc., 931 F. Supp. 1124 (S.D. N.Y., 1996).

National Basketball Association v. Motorola, 105 F. 3d 841 (1997).

Netanel, Neil .W. (1996). Copyright and a democratic civil society. Yale Law Journal, 106, 283-387.

Nozick, Robert. (1974). Anarchy, state, and utopia. New York: Basic Books, Inc.

Peters, John. Durham. (1989). John Locke, the individual, and the origin of communication. The Quarterly Journal of Speech, 75, 387-399.

Posner, Richard. (1988). Law and literature. Cambridge, MA: Harvard University Press.

ProCD, Inc. v. Zeidenberg, 86 F. 3d 1447 (1997).

Rowley, Fred .A. (1998). Dynamic copyright law: Its problems and a possible solution. Harvard Journal of Law & Technology, 11, 481-528.

Russell, Bertrand. (1945). A history of western philosophy. New York: Simon & Schuster.

Smith, Stephen (1994). Communication and the Constitution in cyberspace. Communication Education, 43, 87-101.

Solomon, John (1999, January 3). Rhapsody in green. Boston Globe, p. E2.

Steen, Gerard. (1994). Understanding metaphor in literature. New York: Longman.

Thierer, Adam , & Crew, Clyde.W., Jr. (2002). Copyfights: The future of intellectual property in the information age. Washington, D.C.: Cato Institute.

Weinreb, Lloyd (1987). Natural law and justice. Cambridge, MA: Harvard University Press.

Wolf, Clark. (1995). Contemporary property rights, Lockean provisos, and the interests of future generations. Ethics, 105, 791-818.

Wolfe, Jonathan. (1991). Robert Nozick: Property, justice and the minimal state. Stanford, CA: Stanford University Press.

Yen, Alfred. C. (1990). Restoring the natural law: Copyright as labor and possession. Ohio State Law Journal, 51, 517-559.

Youn, Monica.Y. (1997) Neither intellectual nor property. The Yale Law Journal, 107, 267-272.

Democratic Space: Mass Media Connections to Public Forum Law

Peggy J. Bowers
Clemson University

"In a free society protest serves to produce stability, not to undermine it."

—Justice Anthony Kennedy, *Hill v. Colorado* (2000)

In the months before the 2004 Democratic National Convention in Boston, city officials unveiled a plan to deal with the anticipated thousands of protesters who would descend on the city to make their views known to the candidates, delegates and citizens. The "free-speech zone" was a small triangle of land bounded by train tracks, service roads and a parking lot for buses and media trucks, mostly out of sight of the Fleet Center where the delegates would gather. The zone would hold only about 400 people at a time. "What's the point to just have a rally, when you don't have an audience for whom the rally is organized?" said Urszula Masney-Latos, executive director of the National Lawyers Guild's Massachusetts chapter (Klein 2004). Carl Rose, Massachusetts ACLU executive director, put it more succinctly: "We don't want it to be a free-speech pen."

Such a dilemma has become all too commonplace across the country as government officials, claiming a host of competing concerns such as public safety, relegate meaningful public speech to the hinterlands of democracy, physically and figuratively. The use of public space for free speech is hardly ever questioned in principle but finds itself increasingly threatened in practice, and for the reason Masney-Latos and Rose have noted, namely, a disconnection exists in contemporary society between the idea of free speech as a constitutional right and the practice of free speech in a meaningful way. The disjuncture is embodied in our attitudes toward physical space and its relationship to free expression. The physical expression of free speech, speakers' ability to move fluidly among those with whom they wish to communicate, is symbolic of its robustness to significantly reach the public for whom and by whom free speech is intended. Take the protests against the World Trade Organization and the Free Trade Areas of the Americas summit, staged in Seattle and in Miami, respectively, as examples. While Seattle was subject to the passion that free speech often breeds (Thomas 2000), the city of Miami had learned Seattle's lesson well. Protesters were restrained from staging their protests within eyesight or earshot of delegates who cut their private deliberations short by a day and took ocean excursions to keep protesters from airing their views (Pain 2003; Nielsen 2003). Indeed, consider the differences in number and practice of public protests in the Vietnam era and those of the war in Iraq. Thus, even as public officials make the exchange of ideas increasingly difficult in physical space, citizens have gradually acculturated to the notion that their voices are no longer necessary or possible.

Protest has been physically removed from the sites of commerce and pleasure, and symbolically removed as well in its evisceration, slowly and deliberately by the Supreme Court aided by the conventions and professional values of the mass media. Public protest is a vital context in which citizens are exposed to alternative points of view. The elimination of public discussion from our midst as normal, holds serious consequences for the nature and robustness of free speech and consequently to the meaning of a free press as well. Free speech requires more than tolerance; it must be nurtured.

The definition of free speech is dependent on an understanding of its relationship to culture. Publics take their form from what the culture can imagine, as John Lennon urged during the Vietnam War. In fact, the very existence of the public depends on whether the culture can envision and embrace such a concept. Without cultural sanction the people who comprise the public cannot conceive of themselves configured that way. As cultural historians of the French Revolution have observed (Hunt 1992; Baker1990), only the cultural changes slowly brought about through years of regal abuse, the influence of the American Revolution and even the Terror allowed the French people to perceive of themselves as a public. Even then, the character of a public depends on how the culture permits that public to take shape.

Some would claim that in America today the public is an amorphous term, meaning too many things to too many people, and in a multicultural society best left in the plural or eliminated altogether (Dean 2002)[1]. True, the face of the public is no longer uniform, if it ever was, and so scholars such as Jurgen Habermas and his notion of the public sphere come under a great deal of criticism as being unrealistic and elitist.[1] Nancy Fraser (1992), most prominently, and others have criticized Habermas for being particularly male in his conception of a public as well as for failing to recognize the plurality of publics. But as difficult as it may seem to define a public, we in society live according to some conception of a public, realistic or not, organize our social values and ideals around it, and indeed distinguish it from the private realm which is the purview of the interpersonal.[2] Realistically, then, various notions of the public compete for dominance to organize our conventions and rules for how people may address one another.

As John Dewey (1922) noted almost a century ago, in order to function as active participants in a democracy, publics must be given meaningful work to do. Citizens have to believe in their ability to effect change, he argued. The sharp increase in voter interest for the 2004 presidential election (McInturff 2004) seems to testify to this principle, as public service campaigns urging, "my vote counts" and a mounting sense of importance for the outcome sparked a record turnout at the polls. Publics must also feel actively engaged, spoken to as conversational partners rather than passive recipients, servants or even judges (Hallin 1994). Iris Marion Young (2000,168) has characterized public communication as "messy, many-leveled, playful, emotional." Most fundamentally, the character of the speech flows from the character of the public from whom it originates.

Conceiving of a public sphere as an active entity has consequences for the shape of our free speech. Young (2000) suggests that a spatial metaphor is most apt to describe a public sphere, for it advances the notion that public discussion is an ongoing, dynamic process that individuals enter and exit, providing unity of experience while acknowledging situated difference. Viewing public citizens as active—engaged in a meaningful way in guiding the form of our institutions and our national priorities, contrasts with a passive notion of the public which chooses from among options presented, but rarely creates a vision to implement.[3] While an active public sphere as the means by which citizens can exert influence over policy decisions is a commonly viewed function of that entity, often overlooked are the abilities for citizens to engage (and expose) power for purposes of opposition and accountability. Even more profoundly, Young (2000) notes that moral appeals by the powerless in an active public sphere shame the powerful out of their selfish, dishonest and bullying ways. For instance, she recounts the story of a group of nuns marching through the streets of Manila who forced soldiers to shoot or give up. For these things to occur, publics must see themselves as communities, as active, as decision makers. Cultural conceptions in place, the speech reinforces the culture that gave it life.

Two models of free speech mirroring that of our understanding of the public become crucial to our discussion. First, conceiving of speech as competitive holds particular consequences for the public forum and our political system. Competitions require winners and losers, with individual competitors seeking ideological hegemony. Consensus is not a possibility. At the social level, such a model takes the form of aggregates of individuals taking sides, as societies view speech as a form of non-violent struggle. This is essentially the political model that prevails today in the United States. Jodi Dean (2002) contends that this makes some ways of living unequal to others, and hence contrary to the core values of democracy that society imagines. She writes (173), "fundamental antagonism involves a political claim on behalf of some modes of living and against others. These other views, then, are in no way equal: calling them that . . . misses the point of contestation, namely, winning." When speech is seen as conversational, though, the implications are far different. Speech becomes not a performance of ideas, but the creation and refinement of them (Sunstein 1993). Once speech is not a competition of agendas, but rather a means to set agendas and a way to connect to others, speech becomes the act of creating community. Following this model it is inherently relational rather than confrontational. Nurturing free speech requires an understanding of its nature in order to know how to cultivate it.

It makes sense, then, that these cultural predispositions would also define, if not, indeed, make media possible. In other words, media are relevant only to the extent that culture views them as such. A public can certainly exist apart from media, and have, both in the past and even more recently, as the example of Eastern Europe, the fall of the Soviet Union or occurrences in Latin America or South Africa can illustrate (Young 2000). When the media were not considered trustworthy, the public formed without their involvement. As much as media representatives wish to think otherwise, they are not a requirement for participatory democracy to work. Rather, they make themselves relevant or irrelevant to democracy by their conduct and content. Should they fail at providing the information and context citizens need to participate in the affairs of state, citizens so inclined will take the initiative to function without them. The Hutchins Commission issued such a warning almost 60 years ago in their now famous report on the freedom of the press. When the founders of the United States deemed the press relevant to democracy, and ensured its freedom as a mouthpiece of the people through the First Amendment to the Constitution, they bestowed on it a cultural legitimacy it could not have asserted for itself. More importantly, however, media are relevant only in the context of a culturally legitimated and formulated public sphere. Plainly stated, the public is the reason for the media's existence, and not the other way around. Indeed, James Carey (1987) has called the public the "god term" for American journalism. And, though the media have much to say about the health, sustenance and tenor of the public sphere, as this paper will argue, they cannot single-handedly bring a public sphere into being ex nihilo. A public sphere must obtain already for the press to have a reason to exist. If citizens conceive of themselves as such and are participating in an open and public discussion with one another, engaged in a shared life together about which they must make decisions, then the purpose of the press is one of facilitating meaningful public discussion and information sharing, a vital cog in the wheel of participatory democracy.

Free speech is therefore culturally conceived, culturally malleable, and thus vulnerable and fragile. Although the Hutchins Commission linked free expression to our very humanness, a fundamental moral right, indeed a duty, in order to be fully human, it is no less true that such a right must be recognized, acknowledged and fostered by societies in order to exist. The Commission wrote (8-9), "The indispensable function of expressing ideas is one of obligation—to the community and also to something beyond the community . . . we see that public discussion is a necessary condition of a free society and that freedom of expression is a necessary condition of adequate public discussion.'' Certainly the Commission saw the press as vulnerable to lose that freedom, and thus by extension, the public itself is made vulnerable. The waning passion for public ideological exchange is a cultural phenomenon precipitated by conceiving of speech as competitive and conflict-oriented. Under this cultural weight, the fragility of free speech makes it vulnerable. This paper will illustrate that the public space on which a free exchange of ideas is so dependent is transformed to consumer space, designed to serve the ends of commerce and the ideological goals of the merchant, and that the Supreme Court has aided this transformation. Yet media make meaning only in the context of the physical realm. Not even the Web can support the cultural practices that enable democracy; it is not a simple translation from space to cyberspace. In this way, the Court has unwittingly aided the decay of free speech in part by socializing citizens to embrace the cultural values that undermine a vibrant democracy. As the bonds of a community life weaken, the work of a democratic polity is hampered. The press, whose own function depends on a vigorous cultural conception of free speech, becomes all the more vulnerable in terms of its freedom to present political ideas. The most basic rights are thus always precarious.

The Courts and the Commercialization of Public Space

In a case that has served as precedent for 40 years, the Supreme Court extended a broad privilege to the people, and to the press by extension, to voice opinion, especially in public affairs. *New York Times Co. v. Sullivan* (1964) was more than the inclusion of libel as a First Amendment issue, or the birth of actual malice as its standard against public officials. The Court used this opportunity to remind the American public about the importance of free expression as a mainstay of democracy, and to mandate citizens' constitutional right and responsibility to criticize the government (see also Lewis 1991).[4] The Court's position on the role of speech at this time is revealing. Speaking out against the government, interacting as citizens with one another and with government, is not merely available should one choose to take the opportunity. In a decision that echoed the Hutchins Commission almost two decades earlier and was in keeping with early models of civic republicanism, the Court made it clear that citizens have a duty to speak against public policy, and to hold their government accountable for the decisions it makes. Justice Black, in his concurrence, wrote,

> ... Freedom to discuss public affairs and public officials is unquestionably, as the Court today holds, the kind of speech the First Amendment was primarily designed to keep within the area of free discussion. ... I doubt that a country can live in freedom where its people can be made to suffer physically or financially for criticizing their government, its actions or its officials ... An unconditional right to say what one pleases about public affairs is what I consider to be the minimum guarantee of the First Amendment.

This rather strong notion of the purpose of free speech is weakened in the Court's case law of the past several decades. In effect, as robustly as the Court maintains the right to speak, it undermines the opportunity to speak by shrinking the amount and relevance of public spaces where the protection and privilege to speak is the most obvious, appropriate and protected.

It is legitimate then to examine briefly a portion of the case law and jurisprudence that has tended toward a narrowing public forum. The Court has historically negotiated the philosophical and practical tensions generated between ''guaranteed access'' and ''equal access'' approaches that guide free speech. The first presumes a constitutional guarantee of access to some public places, stemming from the philosophy that assembly in public places serves an invaluable function to democracy as the ''poor man's printing press'' and as such must be protected, even at the expense of non-speech interests. In an early forum case, Justice Roberts (*Hague v. CIO* 1939) laid out the rationale for this approach:

> Wherever the title of streets and parks may rest they have immemorially been held in trust for the use of the public and, time out of mind, have been used for purposes of assembly, communicating thoughts between citizens, and discussing public questions.... The privilege to use the streets and parks for communication of views on national questions may be regulated in the interest of all; [but] it must not, in the guise of regulation, be abridged or denied (Gunther, 1250).

On the other hand, the equal access approach draws from the dicta of Justice Oliver Wendell Holmes who wrote, "for the legislature absolutely or conditionally to forbid public speaking in a highway or public park is no more an infringement of the rights of a member of the public than for the owner of a private house to forbid it in his house" (Gunther 1250). Under this approach the government is obligated only to provide access nondiscriminatory to places it chooses to provide, with no obligations to provide anything. The distinctions in these two philosophies illustrate perfectly what is at stake for public places. The former is active, the latter passive to the political role of public places. As this paper argues, for free speech to be nurtured and allowed to play a role in sustaining a rich understanding of democracy, so must public space.

Oscillation, if not competition, between the two approaches has unfortunately produced what constitutional scholars have lamented as "an elaborate, even Byzantine scheme of constitutional rules designed to ascertain when members of the general public can use government property for communicative purposes" (Post 1715). As focus shifts from streets and parks to nontraditional forums, the Court has found it difficult to adapt its jurisprudence to the increasingly complex competing claims to freedom of expression in a changing society. Although the Court seemed ambivalent in its early cases[5], by the mid-1960s the tide turned with a pair of decisions that proved disastrous for freedom of expression and the guaranteed access position (*Cox v. Louisiana*, 1965; known as Cox I and II).[6] Although the decisions were not made on First Amendment grounds, the Court reaffirmed the notion that "the right of peaceful protest does not mean that everyone with opinions or beliefs to express may do so at any time and at any place." Decisions in the following years relied on Cox (see for example, *Adderley v. Florida* 1966 and *Lehman v. Shaker Heights* 1974), rejecting the guaranteed access position, and viewing the issue as one of commerce, an important turn in the Court's jurisprudence. In short, the sphere for legitimate public debate was gradually shrinking, effectively limiting public expression and the public's ability to use this means to offer meaningful input in the democratic process.

The modern court, beginning in the 1980s, was only more elusive in dealing with First Amendment issues in the public forum and more obscure and complex in outlining an approach to public forum cases. The Court held, for example, that demonstrators could not sleep in Washington, D.C.'s Lafayette Park to protest the plight of the homeless (*Clark v. Community for Creative Non-Violence* 1984), and citizens could not use First Amendment privilege on a sidewalk running in front of a post office (*U.S. v. Kokinda* 1990). Justice O'Connor's plurality opinion concluded that this was not the kind of sidewalk the Court meant when it designated sidewalks as a traditional public forum.[7] More than traditional public forums were under scrutiny, however. The Court also has a pattern of limiting spaces that now function as public places, such as malls and airports, even though they are under private ownership (see for example *ISKON v. Lee* 1992). Interestingly, in objectifying democratic processes courts have reduced discussions of public deliberation to a management of space. This allows the courts to maintain the veneer of objectivity, while simultaneously limiting public debate by denying access to particular forums. In other words, democratic processes are nothing more than a set of boundaries and authorized spaces. Equal access may be the easiest way to solve such dilemmas, but it is also the one that has the most severe consequences for creating a cultural climate for speech.

More specifically, one of the means by which the Court has seemingly objectively controlled democratic expression is content neutrality, the idea that flat bans on speech are permissible if the ban is not content-based. Given its roots in Enlightenment rationality, legal debate often promotes proceduralist practices that help maintain the Court's authority by embedding sometimes anti-democratic principles through the dictates of objectivity. Mary Ryan (1992), for example, argues that while the tenets that have typically guided public debate attempt to speak from a neutral position, there is often a set of implied interests that this neutrality in fact masks. This problem clearly persists into contemporary legal debates surrounding democratic expression where "neutral" standards become a means for regulating discourse. Legal scholars and even Supreme Court justices have noted that public forum doctrine sometimes obfuscates the very First Amendment values it is supposed to protect. It can do this by reducing the size of the available public space in which debate can occur since there is a direct correlation between the two (Goodman 1998). Moreover, content neutrality actually suppresses views outside the mainstream of opinion, as Justice Thurgood Marshall noted in his dissent to Clark v. Community for Creative Non-Violence (1984): "A content-neutral regulation that restricts an inexpensive mode of communication will fall most heavily upon relatively poor speakers and the points of view that such speakers typically espouse."[8] This makes easy access to public property all the more important. Often the Court has been reluctant to classify areas as traditional public forums, thus restricting their freedoms, but most places that commonly come before the Court have no history of expression, or no history at all. With a static idea of what constitutes "public," the Court cannot accommodate the intentions or spirit of public forum law—to provide speech opportunities for citizens to discuss ideas and thereby strengthen the democratic process—in a changing societal structure. For the past decade or so, however, Justice Anthony Kennedy has urged that the Court look at a forum's suitability for speech rather than its classification or history. He has often argued that a public place is wherever people gather, and the right to speak there ought to be as unfettered as possible. He wrote, "[In] a country where most citizens travel by automobile, and parks all too often become locales for crime rather than social intercourse, our failure to recognize that new types of government property may be appropriate forums for speech will lead to a serious curtailment of our expressive activity." (*ISKON v. Lee* 1992).

In spite of these efforts, the most recent cases have extended the Court's propensity toward content neutrality and narrowly defined public places to further limit expression. In Hill v. Colorado (2000), the Court affirmed a Colorado statute against approaching without consent within 8 feet of another person who is nearer than 100 feet to an entrance to any health care facility in order to pass a leaflet, display a sign, or engage in oral protest, education or counseling, what some might view as a very reactive piece of legislation. In the majority decision Justice Stevens asserted that the Court was regulating the "approaching," not speech, that the regulation was content neutral, and was weighed against the right to be left alone, even in confrontational public settings. Justice Kennedy, in his dissent, characterized the decision as "a most troubling abdication of our responsibility to enforce the First Amendment." In effect, he argued, "the Court tears away from the protesters the guarantees of the First Amendment when they most need it." Claiming this case was a troubling precedent to bar citizens from communicating a message to one another in a public place, "which ought to be the heart of civilized discourse," he warned, "If . . . the Court repeats its grave errors of analysis, we shall have no longer the proud tradition of free and open discourse in a public forum."[9] The pattern has continued on the Court, although no case as major as *Hill v. Colorado* has been decided.[10] In essence, the

Court has been remarkably inclined to narrow public spaces, and to protect private spaces *from* speech—to insulate spaces of commerce and pleasure from the unpopular and sobering prospect of confronting controversial ideas.

Increasingly, and perhaps even more profoundly, public spaces have become intertwined with the practices of consumer society. Justice Kennedy's argument that protecting free speech must adapt to the shifting notions of public places, even if those public places are now privately owned, has had a reluctant and resistant hearing on the Court. Even though malls are now arguably the "new town square" they are also places of commerce,[11] privately owned. And just as merchants historically have shied away from advertising on the news pages of a newspaper because the seriousness and negativity of war, crime and pain that often comprise the news put consumers in an unhappy mood, those same merchants have expended considerable effort to create a consumptive ambience that they wish to preserve, even at the expense of free speech. That is, owners of private property do not always see free speech as being in their best interests, and certainly the designated use for their property is often at odds with the purposes of free speech. When we view the physical space so necessary for speech in economic terms, speech in turn becomes a product, subject to the laws of the market rather than those of civil discourse.

Changing social patterns, an extension of this phenomenon, have contributed to the decay of meaningful public spaces as well. Malls and movie theaters have so much significance as public spaces because people have shifted their social activities to revolve around consumption, often on private property. Public life centers around pursuit of private leisure and organizational employment, as people socialize commonly at the mall or the movie theater, or even at work or company-organized activities. Possibly as a result, people don't see themselves as seeking civic activity. Very few people socialize at the city council meeting, school board meeting or political rally, for example (Bradley 1995).

Shifting patterns in physical space have contributed to this lack of civic life. Since the 1950s suburban housing developments have changed the American landscape and with it social routines of life. The average American worker commutes some distance to the workplace, then spends much leisure time devoted to children's organized social, athletic or educational activities, creating "bedroom communities" where little time or emotional investment can be designated for civic affairs. Consumptive patterns usually dictate that people retreat into ever larger suburban homes, and what time is not devoted to family life is devoted to maintenance of homes and lawns, as evidenced by the plethora of home improvement stores springing up in the suburbs. Leisure activity followed. Movie theaters and malls located themselves in remote areas with copious, relatively cheap land, usually at the intersections of major highways close to suburban neighborhoods. Yet these places have no place for people to congregate other than inside the buildings and grounds of these commercial establishments—private property. Moreover, most American cities are also laid out in patterns unfriendly to pedestrian traffic. The result of this reorganization (or privatization) of public interaction, and the uses to which people put public spaces (see for example Drucker and Gumpert 1997), is a reorganization and reconceptualization of how people use the right to speak.

The consequences for free speech and democracy and the institutions that thrive on, or support the same, are profound. Given the fact that public spaces are usually the only sites that allow everyone to have equal access, expunging these spaces of all political debate completely silences large portions of society. That seems a price far too high to pay, one that destroys any real notion of a public and subsequently of democracy itself, and one that runs the risk of rendering other public forums, such as those inhabited by journalists and other social commentators, inconsequential.

Understanding how the public addresses one another is a crucial element in illuminating the dynamics of our social life and its consequences. Two predominant models of speech shape the public and dictate the nature of competition. Under a marketplace model of speech, communication involves citizens as consumers buying speech as a product for profit and consumption. The economic metaphor is not a convenience of clarity. Rather, it suggests that speech as a product must compete for allegiance by being popular, an idea that holds a profound consequence for democracy. Consumers must be pleased, appealed to with the comfortable and familiar. While the occasional novelty slips through, manufacturers are safer to produce according to the formula that has already proven itself to be saleable, resulting in commercialized speech as homogeneous. Minority voices become lost. Examples from the film and music industry, or even journalism, illustrate this process. Media products are remarkably similar because they sell. Even ''alternative'' voices become mainstreamed, losing their creative control and their distinction.[12] The civic republican model of speech, on the other hand, which some find overly romantic, is advanced by scholars such as Cass Sunstein and Michael Sandel. Here speech is idea-driven and the public autonomous authors of their own government. Speech is not competitive, or economically driven, but rather a relational process in which consensus, not mere compromise, is the goal. Thus communication that creates something different than any one person could achieve alone, is not about promoting some pre-determined agenda others must follow. Instead, citizens discuss their public life together, and generate a suitable outcome to some social problem. Citizens shape the quality of their public life, rather than choosing someone to formulate a plan that best represents their individual interests. Under this model, the minority voice is valuable as a viable force in influencing public life, and community holds intrinsic value. The outcome is driven by the process. The tension between these two models in the public consciousness is evidenced, for example, in the Iowa caucuses of the 2004 presidential primary season. The press reported that some of the caucuses were hosted in people's homes—creating the expectation of real conversation to generate consensus on a political candidate, but then ''the arm twisting begins,'' as if to say that the natural law of speech, if you will, is competitive in nature. These two views of speech are key to framing people's expectations of the quality and character of public life, or even what sort of role public life should play in individual lives, but they require a certain view of public space to support them, as do the media. Yet public space is a matter for the Supreme Court to decide, as well as how citizens may use that space. How the Court has privileged private over public holds profound implications for our democracy and our press.

Media and Public Spaces

Media are inextricably linked to public spaces. In turn, they are linked to the quality of free speech, a cornerstone of a vibrant democracy. To see this crucial relationship between media and physical space, consider this: media must function in the realm of the tangible because of the unique constraints and limitations of the media themselves. Modern news has certain characteristics. These qualities function better, or sometimes at all, only in physical, tangible terms. Similarly, it is easier to describe a real-life event according to the conventions of journalistic objectivity than it is to explain an issue or explain causality (Carey 1986; Romano 1986; cf. Kovach and Rosenstiel 2001). In effect, journalists have created this dependence on physical space by their reliance on objectivity as the hallowed value and practice of the profession, above all others. In her seminal early work on journalistic objectivity, Gaye Tuchman (1972) reveals why journalists have clung to this standard so tenaciously. Pragmatically, it functions as a shield from blame or criticism. The practice of it, routinized and ritualized, offers a procedure that removes the journalist from any attachment or involvement in the story. Without engagement or participation, the outcome is entirely outside the control of the journalist. This is why journalists can vehemently deny responsibility for the content of the story, but answer only for the method used to gather it, similar to the American jury system in which a set of procedures, followed by any set of rational persons, is assumed to wield justice. Objectivity is, Tuchman writes, "the talisman to ward off evil spirits." Any number of studies have affirmed her work (see for example Reese 1990; Soloski 1989; Eliasoph 1988). In his book, *Discovering the News*, Michael Schudson (1978) traces the historical origins of this standard, pointing out that although it is now virtually a moral principle in the practice of journalism, it began as an economic decision enabling a newspaper such as the *New York Times* to garner more readership by eschewing political partisanship so as not to offend readers, and to compete with popular and powerful newspapers such as William Randolph Hearst's *New York Journal* and Joseph Pulitzer's *New York World* by offering an alternative to the lurid, sensational "yellow journalism" of its day. In fact, *Times* owner Adolph Ochs elevated objectivity to a sacred rite, the standard by which all journalism should be judged, and the benchmark of journalistic ethics. The reliance on this objective style of journalism and its consequent moral high ground, set the stage for a marriage between physical space and journalism. As professional schools adopted the *Times* style of journalism, and advanced that newspaper to the paragon of journalistic practice, they simultaneously embraced the scientific epistemology from which it was drawn. This functioned both to automatically legitimize them as well as to commit them to science's basic tenets. Thus, journalists were wed forever after to impartial observation of objects to discover truth, which was then their mission to convey as accurately and pristinely as possible. Observation, the scientists' tool to report on the world around them, was now the journalists' tool, linking them to a tangible world as their only legitimate purview.

Visuality, too, serves to reinforce the media's relationship to physical space. Visuality is an essential component of the media, whether literal, as is increasingly the case even in print or certainly the Internet, or merely vicariously through verbal descriptions, as on radio, for example. The most basic principle of television journalism, for instance, is to have a relevant image for everything said in the script (Tuggle et al. 2004). Such images are easier to obtain while covering an event or talking about an issue by using an event staged in physical space. Even the reporter's stand-up, a standard part of any video package, is best photographed by having the reporter interact with some element of the physical environment. Similarly, personalities are easier to cover than abstract issues, and one of the journalistic conventions of dramatic narrative is to feature a person to represent an issue. For example, news stories are often event-driven and conflict-oriented[13], requiring physical space, if not for their existence, then certainly for their drama. Who can argue against the idea that the best conflict is person-centered, preferably in a face-to-face confrontation? That is why demonstrations are a sure way to draw public attention to one's cause or ideas, and so events are often staged for this very purpose. In short, because audiences historically more readily respond to the concrete and perceptible, media rely on this as an essential element of journalism. Without the physical world, the present media cannot tell their stories with relevancy.

More profoundly, perhaps, the set of visual conventions inherent to the press organize free speech, holding sobering and immeasurable implications for that speech. Media dependent on visuality report only that speech which is visible, and only in the way that this speech visually makes sense. Limiting public spaces in effect makes speech invisible. The intent of public spaces is, the Court has argued, to function as a sort of town hall, a place for speech relevant to civic life. When there are fewer places for criticism, and no people to perform that criticism, it lends the impression that there is less dissension. Indeed, it stands to reason that limiting public spaces limits dissension, but equally important, it limits the general perception of dissension. When criticism is removed from the public eye, people become passive and complacent. Corporate media, economically driven to reflect majority sentiment and thus the status quo, have even less motivation to express the minority view. Visuality in media mandates that creating a story about dissent contain a spatial requirement. Though this entails that many stories will vanish in a shrinking public forum, the stories that do see publication irrevocably change the face of free speech, and this is perhaps an even more insidious consequence. The visual component coupled with media conventions of conflict means that those who do what is necessary to gain media attention are seen as radical and inflammatory, thus marginalizing and unfairly and narrowly characterizing the nature of true dissent. Those unwilling to be arrested have nowhere to dissent. The alternative to conflict in dissent is to stage the banal spectacle, which the media will settle for almost as well. For example, while protests against the invasion of Iraq might have been limited in 2003, those who saw the protesters as (ironically) unpatriotic staged events such as the ''Dixie Chicks Drop-off'' in Wichita, Kansas, so that country music fans could register their disgust with the political views of the band by discarding their music. More specifically, the media capitalized on perceived public sentiment to enable and to cover this event. It would seem that criticism of the government, what the Court most wanted to protect in cases like *Times v. Sullivan*, is precisely the kind of dissent that is limited. Public space preserves dissent. By limiting it, the Court has unwittingly created a culture in which dissent is not popular, and in so doing, and with the media's willing participation, has changed the character of free speech. Thus the Court, as Lee Bollinger (1991 61) writes, ''is continually creating images of what American journalism is and of what it should be.'' The media, in turn, through their visual conventions, aid the Court also to create a picture of what the public are and can be by creating the boundaries (physical and philosophical) of free speech. According to Bollinger, ''it is important to understand that the Court is addressing a larger reality than the technical legal issues placed before it, year after year, for decision.'' A lack of public space militates against *Times v. Sullivan*, essentially contradicting some of the most influencial and longstanding dictum in free speech jurisprudence.

Ideas, too, require physical space. Without it they lose their power, even in a mass-mediated world (or especially so). Paradoxically, mass mediated ideas do not have as much power, though the opposite would seem to be true. Yes, ideas receive more circulation and a wider spread in distance, perhaps, in the mass media, but merely reaching more people does not mean those people are equipped to receive the ideas. That is, mass mediating a message by itself does not produce power. Spreading ideas widely must be coupled with a culture that is ready to respond to those ideas. Physical space is the tangible expression of those ideas.

An apathetic polity undermines the media's ability to function in a robust, participatory democracy. Media's public function depends on people who seek political information. Media entertain, and certainly a good deal of political material comes to the passive eyes and ears of citizens whose interests are directed elsewhere, but more information, particularly stripped of context or meaning or rigorous debate regarding interpretation, does not comprise an active polity. If people don't desire and search for the information that helps them make reasoned judgments about public affairs, media are talking to themselves, at least as it pertains to issues affecting our social lives. People must engage the ideas, or the information is meaningless. Yet the public is increasingly apathetic, and with severe social consequences, as Robert Putnam's (2000) work has so astutely documented. He contends that our increasing disconnection from community and democratic structures has caused a decline in social capital, or the benefits obtained from trust and reciprocity associated with social networks. These social networks are the lifeblood of collective action, itself the genesis of social change. Public space is an essential element in enabling those relationships.

The Ambitions and the Limits of the World Wide Web

Many people have argued that the World Wide Web can be the new public space (see for example Trippi 2004). As with any new media technology, great hope surrounded the advent of the World Wide Web, that it would be the elixir for the related areas of community and democracy. Its accessibility, interactivity, and ability to create communities were thought to hold the key to reinvigorate the polity. But as Dean (2002 3) writes cynically, "In technoculture we can have the privilege and convenience of democracy without the unsightly mess, as millions and millions of people participate in a great big public sphere. Or at least that's the fantasy." Though the Web has provided a valuable forum for speechand chat rooms, list servers and e-mail are available for political, ideological and public discussion; overall the Internet cannot support the kind of cultural practices that will enable a robust, participatory democracy.

Most media scholars are by now quite familiar with the cultural assets proved by Internet technology. Many proponents of the Web see it as a way to encourage younger people to be interested in and participate in the political process. For example, in the 2004 democratic presidential primary, Gov. Howard Dean was able to raise more than $50 million, much of that online in increments of $100 or less (Trippi 2004). His success was due in part to an array of online tools, including blogs, a device that many young people use already to post their thoughts and hold Internet conversations (Faler 2004). As a result, many younger voters were Dean supporters, and now most presidential candidates are using this technology to reach previously inaccessible audiences. John Kerry also used technology to his advantage in both the primaries and in his quest for the presidency. For example, as the election neared, he used pop-up ads in places such as Yahoo!, with videostream playing silently and hotlinks to pages regarding his policies and platform. At the listener's discretion, sound was available, but the main ideas also appeared graphically on the video itself. Such techniques not only reach voters who are inaccessible to print and television, but potentially provide a more efficient way to reach the minority of voters in states already viewed as partisan for the opponent. It is true that political candidates now are almost obliged to post Web pages, and representatives of legislative and executive branches have e-mail addresses so constituents can contact them electronically, which is surely a more instantaneous means of making a voter's will known. Most importantly, they note, the Web has the potential to enable connections among people that transcend geographic space, thus creating new communities. Of course, some communities have been created around political interests, ideological beliefs or other types of social interests or functions.

Whether these are the sort of communities that one can point to as creating radical change in political interest, however, is questionable. Furthermore, some of the most prolific and ubiquitous political activity on the Web is actually political satire, such as the jibjab.com animation of John Kerry and George W. Bush singing insults to one another, which registered more than 65 million hits during the campaign (CBS Early Show Nov. 3, 2004). What may trouble some political analysts and campaign managers is the fact that at least some voters use this form of information to decide for whom they will vote (NBC Nightly News Nov. 2, 2004). The digital divide aside[14], the World Wide Web cannot foster all the particular qualities necessary for participatory democracy to flourish. At least some shared values are also prerequisite to a society in which persons not only want to participate in decision-making, but are empowered to do so (Sandel 1996; Barber, 2004; Young 2000).

Many political scholars have long argued that citizens must possess a sense of sacrifice in order for such a political system to be able to function optimally in the inevitable adversities of social existence. Another important quality for a robust democracy is a sense of commonality. Richard Sennett (1974 16) says the lack of public space is the result of a "change that began with the fall of the ancient regime and the formation of a new capitalist, secular, urban culture." According to this thesis, the business of public culture is no longer authentic and the people are now fragmented to the point where they cannot experience any community. These cultural values have a profound impact on how Web users view the very purpose of Internet use. If communities are already fragmented and little cohesion exists to engender self-sacrifice, the

Web must overcome these cultural handicaps in order to provide the cure for our social ills. The World Wide Web as a medium has qualities that reinforce the cultural values that can hurt free speech. For example, it is a highly individualistic medium. Although it is highly interactive with at least the content, users have a high degree of autonomy as to what they will view and when. As such, it depends on selective exposure to controversial content. If someone doesn't particularly want to interact with opinions or ideas he or she may not agree with, or simply differ from, then that person may choose to ignore all such content, whether it be about world events, political ideas or community affairs. The Web also reinforces the construction of narrowly focused communities. Of course, communities form on the Web. Most of the time these ''specialty'' communities, however, center on one or two dimensions, such as an avocation or common medical condition. These can be very beneficial to their members, certainly, often providing important information or social support to the otherwise isolated, however, these communities cannot be broad based enough to resurrect an active polis.

Because of the highly individualistic and sometimes idiosyncratic nature of Web use and interaction, people are mostly left to their own knowledge to interpret information. That is, the Web is useful to uncover a wealth of information on a given topic, but in the absence of meaningful debate and discussion, its utility for societal affairs and social life is limited. And though it may be easier to e-mail a congressional representative than to write a letter or attend a town hall meeting, access to public officials electronically still depends on their willingness to interact. To be sure, the Internet has fostered some types of communities and provided a valuable tool for information to countless millions. The question remains whether this type of information exchange or specialty community support can sustain participatory democracy.

Another feature of the Internet that is often touted for its potential to revitalize public life is its global nature, but there are social dangers here as well as cyberculture challenges to our conceptions of time, space, and place (Huyssen 2000). Although real-time conversations do exist on the Internet, most people still seek messages individually on their own time. Thus, most conversation is still out of synchronization with the conversational partner or partners. News, political information, and other types of messages as well as e-mail and blogs are retrieved and responded to in various intervals to their actual happening or communication. As we mold the rhythms of the daily newspaper to the Web, however, fundamental shifts expand and contract our notions of time. We may still have our morning ''paper'' but news is posted continually throughout the day, and we have the option of never encountering the paper in its entirety, or even glancing at articles we haven't self-selected as of interest. Moreover, globalization and cybercapitalization erode our concept of space. The result here is a blurring of public and private. Where space used to be definitively demarcated as public or private, now the lack of tangible boundaries and the almost limitless access to personal web pages undermine the concept of space. Finally, globalization and cybercapitalism erode our concept of place. As a result, government experiences disconnect even more with the physical community. Democracies depend on citizens retaining a sense of the physical because social and individual problems involving the spatial characterize many of those that government must solve. Thus, despite its global nature, the Web cannot entirely surmount the challenges posed to it in creating viable community.

The Future of the Public in Public Spaces

Thus far the paper has argued that the public forum, a cherished element of civic life underlying the fundamental freedoms of the First Amendment, is vanishing under the very auspices of the Supreme Court, which is unwittingly aiding its disappearance and socializing the public not to notice or regret its departure. Because notions of free speech, the public, and indeed the media are cultural and relational, they require a vibrant public forum to sustain and enrich them. The physical public spaces on which the media are so dependent for their foundational purpose and activities are dangerously close to extinction or worse, triviality. The Internet, fraught with cultural impediments, will not be enough to overcome society's dependence on the concrete for its core freedoms.

As we have seen, more than media presence alone is necessary to give speech meaning. It requires physical space, not for its own sake, but because of what a certain sort of physical space enables, and the cultural qualities that represents. Cultural practices enable both free speech and media. Physical space understood as public space, supported by a culture that nurtures ideas and discussion, is the bedrock of democracy. As Justice Kennedy has written, "The liberties protected by our doctrine derive from the Assembly, as well as the Speech and Press Clauses of the First Amendment, and are essential to a functioning democracy. Public places are of necessity the locus for discussion of public issues, as well as protest against arbitrary government action. [In] a free nation citizens must have the right to gather and speak with other persons in public places."(*ISKON* v. Lee 1992) The great irony is that while the Court strives to preserve and protect free speech, it really undermines it in this regard. The Court stresses to the American Public not just the value of free expression as a marker of individual identity, but as a sacred right and duty to engage oneself in public affairs. In a recent decision, Justice Kennedy speaking on behalf of the Court, wrote, "First Amendment freedoms are most in danger when the government seeks to control thought or to justify its laws for that impermissible end. The right to think is the beginning of freedom, and speech must be protected from the government because speech is the beginning of thought." (*Ashcroft v. Free Speech Coalition* 2002). Yet, by limiting the public forum as it has done, especially in favor of private enterprise, it unwittingly undermines free speech by thwarting or precluding the diversity of ideas to interact with the mainstream.

Physical space is in danger of losing its cultural meaning at a great cost to media and to ideologically driven free speech. Cultural changes in notions of community, self-expression and hypercommercialism, reinforced by a Court steeped in individualism and privileging private enterprise, has slowly transformed physical space from the bedrock of cultural exchange and social metamorphosis to an atomistic bastion of personal pursuits. Without public space, and an engaged public, media have no political import. Only an active *polis*, of which public space is an indispensable component, can make the provision of public affairs information meaningful. Without public space, ideologically driven free speech is impotent to reach "the other." Natural affinities and relationships find expression beyond physicality, though successful ones must, in its absence, find other means to compensate for its lack. Relationships to those who differ culturally, ideologically or politically are not so seamlessly formed; creating space for the encounter is deliberate and sometimes arduous (Buber 2002). Physical space is therefore crucial to facilitate the opportunity. As Young (168) has written, "If public communication aims at inclusion, debate, and promoting justice . . . it must include multiple forms of protest action—rallies, marches, strikes, boycotts, commemorations and ceremonies, non-violent illegal blockades, and so on." In the absence of public space and the culture to encourage such encounters, space becomes commodified. If it is not a tool for social discussion, it is reduced to commerce and pleasure.[15]

Current jurisprudence in public forum law is socializing citizens to be more individualistic. In the precedents it sets, in the practices it protects, and in the dicta with which it preaches core American values, the Court influences the boundaries of the good in free expression and its concomitant elements. Recall the Court's long held position that citizens' autonomy permits them to avert their eyes from speech they wish to ignore. It is a dark observation that for the social good, there is no such thing as a message one has to hear. Although justices have occasionally raised an objection to the notion that the First Amendment protects one from unpleasant ideas (see *Colorado v. Hill*), clearly the Court believes that free speech is individualistic in the speaker and the listener. In effect, the Court undermines free speech by supporting values that undermine it, such as failing to recognize or protect the social aspect to free speech. Thus, the Court advances the notion that difficult or controversial ideas must be sought out. This inevitably puts the burden (and the disadvantage) precisely on the very speakers whose ideas hold the most potential for social change or who offer an important source of social reflection. Therefore, the Court seems to suggest that different or controversial ideas are an ideological battle and the public becomes a battleground. Nobody wins when speech is a tool of division rather than community.

Civic republicanism is precluded and a robust democracy loses strength as any meaningful expression of the public forum vanishes. Democracy as representative (weak democracy) gains momentum as the political is viewed as an ideological struggle, with individual interests reflected in the aggregate rather than consensus and mutual decision making. Under this model, the political candidate as official takes the burden and responsibility for fighting for the individual by proxy. Many political campaigns successfully exploit the theme that government is the enemy, a separate entity intent on thwarting individual goods if not for the "outsider" who struggles against it, not on behalf of the community, but for the individual citizen. A strong sense of democracy as public participation loses momentum in this environment. As Sen. Bill Bradley (1995) reminds us, "the government and the market are not enough to make a civilization. There must also be a healthy, robust civic sector—a space in which the bonds of community can flourish." Remember that Dewey links the fall of public space to the degradation of rational, open debate. The cornerstone of liberal democracy is therefore the ability to come together and communicate freely in a common area. When a meaningful public forum vanishes physically and in spirit, the public loses its forum for significant public participation. If, in other words, there is nothing substantive for citizens to do, and nowhere to do it, relegating the business of government to representative agents seems that much more inevitable and nonproblematic.

In the wake of a Court that in effect privileges individuality, autonomy and private enterprise over the social and shared, media degenerate into purveyors of private pleasures rather than the linchpins of democracy. Autonomy is not bad; individuality is not bad. But these offer an incomplete picture of speech, lacking an understanding of the inherently social nature of language and its constitutive powers. Viewing speech this way holds profound consequences for our social life together, the nature and quality of our democracy, and our own abilities to change, to hear and be heard. When media are reduced to peddlers of commercial interests, they lose what they view as their most fundamental purpose, betray their self-avowed core values and trivialize the political process. As many scholars have noted, private enterprise is at odds with the diversity of ideas (see, for example, McChesney 1999; 2004). To the extent that democracy decays for lack of the physical space, media's public function declines. The chautauquas exemplify this claim. A grassroots political movement to activate the citizenry on a host of political and ideological causes, the chautauquas serve no particular political interest, but are concerned with revitalizing the polity. They hold meetings around the nation, believing that democracy functions better in person. While they use the Web for follow up to face-to-face contact, participants feel there is no substitute for the spatial (CBS News, February 2004). This principle is further illustrated in the movement to crack down on drug trafficking in Ireland after the murder of journalist Veronica Guerin. Groups of citizens, marching nightly in the streets, not only forced drug dealers out of local neighborhoods, but pressured Ireland's government to create laws enabling officials to seize assets of suspected criminals. Journalism cannot afford to be self-interested when it concerns the public forum. Speech and assembly share the burden of sustaining a thriving democracy as much as the press does. When one is threatened, all are in peril. Journalists cannot blindly claim their own autonomy, then assume that their own privileges may not one day be equally eroded. Aside from the interweaving concerns and relationship these elements share, if the press' self-proclaimed goal is to foster democracy, it should give more than a passing glance to whatever endangers democracy. Journalists' apathy toward the decline of a viable public forum mirrors the political indifference frequently lamented in the body politic. Stanley Aronowitz writes that "the public sphere is always a restricted space" and individuals must present cases to allow themselves entry into it. What is unfortunate now is that these battles are frequently understated within the mass media. Such lack of interest on the press' part can only hasten its own uselessness and further alienate the citizenry from a political system in which it feels isolated if not impotent. The ties between the press and the public forum cannot remain unacknowledged much longer without substantial cost. If they do, we risk erosion of free speech and press and a reduction of our government to that of a democracy in name only.[16]

Endnotes

1. In fact, she has quite startlingly written (p. 175), "For the sake of democracy, it is time to abandon the public."
2. Habermas himself has noted that his model of a public sphere was meant to be an ideal for interaction, not a historical claim, or a realistic portrait of public life.
3. Many scholars have discussed the blurring lines between public and private and mass media's contribution to this redefinition of boundary, but this is beyond the scope of this paper. Here the notion of public is in the sense of public affairs, or our social life together, and not how widely the details of our personal relationships are known.
4. Interestingly, the mass media under control of transnational conglomerates has provoked criticism for giving "consumer choice" but not "consumer control." That the institution of the mass media itself operates on just such a passive and economic assumption about the public, only lends support to the argument here.
5. Justice Anthony Kennedy has indicated that the Court, in fact, writes decisions hoping the American people will read them, not just law students and constitutional attorneys.
6. Several cases in the late 1930s that involved permit schemes and other time, place and manner restrictions seemed to the Court to be thinly veiled attempts from public officials to suppress unpopular ideas [see *Lovell v. Griffin* 1938; *Schneider v. State* 1939; *Cantwell v. Connecticut* 1940] but the Court seemed to contradict itself in *Cox v. New Hampshire* 1941 when it upheld a state law prohibiting Jehovah's Witnesses from holding a parade without a permit.
7. The Court has often contradicted itself in alternating between the two approaches. Usually when the guaranteed access position wins it is subsequently read very narrowly and consequently it is of little use in setting precedent [compare, for example, *Flower v. U.S.* 1972 and *Greer v. Spock* 1976].
8. Justice Brennan's dissent made the point that the Court's distinction had no basis in prior law.
9. This line of argument would be repeated by Justice Kennedy in *Hill v. Colorado* 2000.
10. Kennedy also argued that people do not have the right to avoid unpopular speech in a public place, and that this statute in spirit, and in practice, was aimed at limiting a particular kind of controversial speech. Hiding behind content neutrality produces a false sense of fairness, he said. In essence, the Court had twisted legal logic to its own ends, he charged. "To say that one citizen can approach another to ask the time or the weather forecast or the directions to Main Street but not to initiate discussion on one of the most basic moral and political issues in all of contemporary discourse, a question touching profound ideas in philosophy and theology, is an astonishing view of the First Amendment."
11. In 2002, the Court once again relied on content neutrality to affirm the Chicago Park District's regulation via permit of a traditional public forum. This case also involved controversial speech regarding legalization of marijuana. [Thomas v. Chicago Park District] While the Court did affirm a right to door-to-door speech without a permit in Watchtower v. Village of Stratton (2002), significantly, Rehnquist, [Scalia and Thomas in part] dissented, using content neutrality and the countervailing interests of privacy and crime prevention. *Virginia v. Hicks* (2003) involved an ordinance changing some streets within a public housing development to private rather than public streets, but the Court narrowly considered a trespassing charge against Hicks, which it found not to violate his First Amendment rights.
12. As are airports, no less commercial, designed for speed and efficiency, even though public discourse (and for that matter, democracy) are distinctly inefficient processes.

13. Recently a 60 million dollar loss from Madonna's recording label prompted the parent company to assume creative control until the debt is paid, for example.
14. Journalist Steve Smith has called conflict the ''mother's milk'' of news reporting.
15. This is not an inconsequential question. Millions of people have limited or even no access to Internet providers or the World Wide Web. For example, only forty-two percent of American households had Internet access in August 2000. Black and Hispanic Americans' rates of household access was 23.5% and 23.6%, respectively. As important, many nations originate almost no Web pages, even if they can read pages posted in the West. As the Court has pointed out, moreover, usually the indigent are the ones without technological access or training. It is they whose ideas become even more marginalized through the reliance on the Internet to express ideas and create communities. A thorough discussion of the digital divide is beyond the scope of this paper, however. For a more detailed treatment of this topic, see National Telecomm. and Info Administration, U.S. Dept. of Commerce, Falling through the net: Toward digital inclusion, Exec. Summary (2000), http://www.ntia.doc.gov/ntiahome/fttn0/contents00.html.
16. The Web is a primary example, if one views it as a figurative space. Two primary activities of Internet users are e-mail (mostly for personal messages) and shopping. (Campbell 2005)

Works Cited

Aronowitz, S. (1993). Is a democracy possible? The decline of the public in American debate. In B. Robbins (Ed.), *The phantom public sphere*). Minneapolis: U of Minnesota Press, 75-92

Baker, K.M. (1990). *Inventing the French Revolution: Essays on French political culture in the 18th century*. Cambridge, England: Cambridge University Press.

Barber, B. (2004). *Strong democracy: Participatory politics for a new age, twentieth anniversary*. Berkeley: University of California Press.

Bradley, B. (1995, Feb. 9). *America's challenge: Revitalizing our national community*. Speech to the National Press Club, Washington, D.C.

Buber, M. (2002). *Between man and man*. Tr. R. Gregor-Smith. London: Routledge.

Carey, J. (1987, March). The press and public discourse. *The Center Magazine*, 4-16.

Carey, J. (1986). The dark continent of American journalism. In Robert Manoff and Michael Schudson, eds. *Reading the news*. NY: Pantheon, 46-196.

Chafee, Z. (1948). *Free speech in the United States*. Cambridge, MA: Harvard University Press.

Chalaby, J. (1998). The media transformation of the public sphere in the new independent states. *Innovation*, 11, 73-85.

Cohen, J. (1990). Discourse ethics and civil society. In D.M. Rasmussen (Ed.), *Universalism v. communitarianism*. Cambridge, MA: MIT Press, 83-105.

Dean, J. (2002). *Publicity's secret: How technoculture capitalizes on democracy*. Ithaca, NY: Cornell University Press.

Dewey, J. (1927). *The public and its problems*. Chicago: Swallow.

Drucker, S. and G. Gumpert, Eds. (1997). *Voices in the street: Explorations in gender, media and public space*. Cresskill, NJ: Hampton Press.

Eliasoph, N. (1988). Routines and the making of oppositional news. *Critical Studies in Mass Communication*, 5, 313-334.

Faler, B. (2004, Feb. 20). Dean leaves legacy of online campaign. *Washington Post*, p. A12.

Farber, D. and Nowak, J. (1984). The misleading nature of public forum analysis: Content and context in the First Amendment adjudication. *Virginia Law Review*, 70, 1219-1265.

Fraser, N. (1992). Rethinking the public sphere: A contribution to the critique of actually existing democracy. In C. Calhoun (Ed.) *Habermas and the public sphere*. Cambridge: MIT Press, 121-140.

Goldberger, D. (1983). Judicial scrutiny in public forum cases: Misplaced trust in the judgment of public officials. *Buffalo Law Review*, 32, 175-220.

Goodman, A. (1998). A shrinkage of public space. *Studies in political planning*, 57, 149-162.

Goodnight, T. (1982). The personal, technical and public spheres of argument. *Journal of the American Forensic Association*, 18, 212-219.

Gouldner, A. (1976). Toward a media-critical politics. In *The dialectic of ideology and technology*. New York: Seasbury Press, 138-166.

Gunther, G. (1991). *Constitutional law*. New York: The Foundation Press.

Habermas, J. (1989). *The structural transformation of the public sphere*. Cambridge: MIT Press.

Hallin, D.C. (1994). *We keep America on top of the world: Television journalism and the public sphere*. NY: Routledge.

Hunt, L.A. (1992). *The family romance of the French Revolution*. Berkeley: University of California Press.

Huyssen, A. (2000). Present pasts: Media, politics, amnesia. *Public Culture*, 12, 21-38.

Lewis, A. (1991). *Make no law: The Sullivan case and the First Amendment*. NY: Random House.

McChesney, R. (1999). *Rich media, poor democracy*. Champaign: University of Illinois Press.

McChesney, R. (2004). *The problem of the media: U.S. communication politics in the twenty-first century*. Monthly Review Press.

McInturff, B. (2004, Oct. 31). Interview on NBC News' *Meet the Press*. NBC News.

Nielsen, K. (2003, Dec. 11). Headbangers ball: Claims that police didn't aim at FTAA protesters' upper bodies get a black eye. *Miami New Times*.

Pain, J. (2003, Nov. 14). Miami braces for protesters, trade disputes at globalization talks. *The Associated Press Worldstream*.

Putnam, R. (2000). *Bowling alone: The collapse and revival of American community*. NY: Simon & Schuster.

Raskin, J.B. and C.L. LeBlanc. (2001). Disfavored speech about favored rights: *Hill v. Colorado*, the vanishing public forum and the need for an objective speech discrimination test. *American University Law Review*, 51: 179-228.

Reese, S. (1990). The news paradigm and the ideology of objectivity: A socialist at the *Wall Street Journal*. *Critical Studies in Mass Communication*, 7, 390-409.

Romano, C. (1986). The grisly truth about the bare facts. In *Reading the news*. Robert Manoff and Michael Schudson, eds. (pp. 38-78). NY: Pantheon.

Rosen, J. (1991). Making journalism more public. *Communication*, 12, 267-284.

Ryan, M. (1992). Gender and public access: Women's politics in nineteenth century America. In C. Calhoun (Ed.) *Habermas and the public sphere* Cambridge, MA: MIT Press, 271-289.

Saco, D. (2002). *Cybering democracy: Public space and the Internet*. Minneapolis: University of Minnesota Press.

Sandel, M.J. (1996). *Democracy's discontent: America in search of a public philosophy*. Cambridge, MA: Belknap Press of Harvard University Press.

Schauer, F. (1992). *Constitutional law*. New York: The Foundation Press.

Schudson, M. (1978). *Discovering the news: A social history of American newspapers*. NY: Basic Books.

Sennett, R. (1974). *The fall of public man*. New York: Norton.

Soloski, J. (1989). News reporting and professionalism: Some constraints on the reporting of the news. *Media, Culture & Society*, 11, 207-228.

Sunstein, C. (1993). *The partial Constitution*. Cambridge, MA: Harvard University Press.

Thomas, J. (2000). *The battle in Seattle: The story behind and beyond the WTO demonstrations*. Golden, CO: Fulcrum Publishing.

Trippi, J. (2004). *The revolution will not be televised: Democracy, the Internet, and the overthrow of everything*. NY: HarperCollins.

Tuchman, G. (1972). Objectivity as strategic ritual: An examination of newsmen's notions of objectivity. *American Journal of Sociology*, 77, 660-679.

Tuggle, C.A., F. Carr and S. Huffman (2004). *Broadcast news handbook: Writing, reporting and producing in a converging media world*. NY: McGraw-Hill.

Young, I.M. (2000). *Inclusion and democracy*. NY: Oxford University Press.

I Got You Babe: The Dysfunctional Relationship Among the Copyright Clause, the First Amendment, and the Internet as an Engine of Innovation in the Aftermath of *Eldred v. Ashcroft*

Christina M. Bates
Arizona State University

In the spring of 1995, Eric Eldred, a technical analyst for a computer magazine, began thinking about a way to inspire his triplet teenage daughters to read more (Fonda 1999). The three sophomores at Pinkerton Academy in Derry, New Hampshire were complaining about reading Nathaniel Hawthorne's *The Scarlet Letter* (Fonda). Eldred began to brainstorm about how to spark his daughters' interest in Hawthorne's classic.

Eldred turned to the Internet for possible resources, and having found only inferior electronic versions of Hawthorne's classic work, he decided to create his own on-line edition that he then supplemented with a glossary, timeline, illustrations, and a biography of Hawthorne (Fonda). Eldred then began to envision his own global e-library that would make unusual and out-of-print books available to the public (Fonda) He dismissed the issue of copyright permission, as he would only publish those books with an expired copyright that were a part of the public domain (Fonda).

Eldred's website hit count rapidly grew to 20,000 people and, in 1997, the National Endowment for the Humanities recognized his Eldritch Press as one of the 20 best humanities sites on the Web (Fonda). Furthermore, the Nathaniel Hawthorne Society and the William Dean Howells Society endorsed Internet links to Eldred's web site (Fonda).

However, Eldred's Eldritch Press would prove to be short-lived. On October 27, 1998, President Clinton signed into law the Copyright Term Extension Act (also commonly referred to as the ''Sonny Bono Copyright Term Extension Act'')(hereinafter the ''CTEA'') (17 U.S.C. § 302 (a)). While the CTEA significantly extended the copyright terms of cultural icons such as Mickey Mouse and books such as *The Great Gatsby*, it also affected non-commercial interests (17 U.S.C. § 302 (a)). Following the enactment of the CTEA, several of Eldred's favorite works fell out of the public domain and were no longer available for publication on the Eldritch Press.

In protest of the CTEA, Eldred shut down his web site for a few days and began publicizing his cause. Harvard Law School professor Lawrence Lessig read about Eldred's situation in a news article and inquired as to whether Eldred wanted to challenge the constitutionality of the CTEA. Eldred agreed and a series of lawsuits ensued culminating with the United States Supreme Court decision, *Eldred v. Ashcroft*, decided on January 15, 2003 (*Eldred et al v. Ashcroft* 2003).

In *Eldred v. Ashcroft* the United States Supreme Court decided that the CTEA did not violate either the First Amendment or the Copyright Clause of the United States Constitution (*Eldred et al v. Ashcroft*). While those in Hollywood breathed a sigh of relief following the decision, those in favor of free speech, innovation and creativity were dealt a resounding blow as they witnessed the whittling away of the First Amendment and the Copyright Clause.

While the *Eldred* decision closed the door on the Court's further inquiry, at this time, regarding the relationship between the First Amendment and the Copyright Clause, it failed to examine the potentially devastating effects of such a decision. Finding that the Fair Use provision of Copyright Law sufficiently balances First Amendment rights with the language and intent of the Copyright Clause, the Court dismissed any concern regarding the stifling effect that the decision would likely have on creativity, innovation, progress and free speech.

With *Eldred* now "on the books," what does the future of innovation hold? What is left of the First Amendment after it has been "gutted" by the Copyright Clause under the guise of Fair Use? Where can we, as a society, expect to go from here?

This article explores the aftermath of *Eldred* in terms of the chilling effects it will likely have on innovation, creativity, progress and free speech. Part I provides an overview of the historical relationship between the First Amendment and the Copyright Clause. Part II examines the *Eldred* decision in relation to the newly defined relationship between the First Amendment and the Copyright Clause. Finally, Part III explores some of the effects of the *Eldred* decision particularly in relation to the original intent of the Internet.

The Copyright Clause and the First Amendment

Article 1, section 8, clause 8 of the United States Constitution states that "The Congress shall have the power to promote the Progress of Science and useful Arts, by securing for limited Times to Authors and Inventors the exclusive Right to their respective Writings and Discoveries" (U.S. Constitution. Art. I., § 8, cl. 8). This power was granted to Congress to provide an economic incentive for authors and inventors in order to stimulate creativity, innovation, and progress (Bowker 1912). However, the earliest version of what came to be our modern-day Copyright Clause was known as the Statute of Anne (Gorman and Ginsburg 1993).

In 1710, the Statute of Anne (hereinafter "the Statute") established the protection of books from being copied by unauthorized publishers and thus ended the monopoly on book publishing in England (Gorman and Ginsburg). [1]The Statute's objective was to dissolve the publisher's monopoly by replacing it with an author's monopoly of limited duration (Gorman and Ginsburg). The Statute provided authors with copyrights on new works for a term of 14 years, renewable for an additional 14 years. However, it also replaced booksellers' perpetual rights in existing works with a single 21-year term. Thus, the Statute granted government the power to limit the price at which protected books could be sold and to fine publishers and booksellers for overcharging and excessive fees (Gorman and Ginsburg). Therefore, under "An Act for the Encouragement of Learning, by Vesting the Copies of Printed Books in the Authors of Purchasers of such Copies, during the Times therein mentioned," unauthorized publishers were prohibited from copying original, protected works (Gorman and Ginsburg).

Displeased with the changes brought about by the Statute, the booksellers, in 1735 proposed an amendment that sought to extend the terms of existing copyrights until 1756 (Gorman and Ginsburg). Opponents of the proposed amendment argued that it would "be establishing a perpetual Monopoly . . . only to increase the private Gain of the Booksellers . . ." (Gorman and Ginsburg). The amendment was ultimately defeated and the booksellers lost their opportunity to have, in effect, a perpetual monopoly (Gorman and Ginsburg).

The first opportunity the English courts had to interpret the meaning of the Statute came in 1774 with the case of Donaldson v. Becket (4 Burr. 2408; 98 Eng. Rep. 257 (H.L. 1774). In *Donaldson*, the English court decided, *inter alia*, that the Statute, in effect, trounced the common law right of an author to have perpetual rights to the publishing of his work. It has been argued that the holding in *Donaldson* became the basis for the Copyright Clause of the U.S. Constitution in that the Copyright Clause appears to mirror the Donaldson holding to the extent that it contains the words ''for limited times'' thereby eradicating the perpetual rights that *Donaldson* addressed in 1774 (Bowker).

Upon gaining their independence from Great Britain, the American colonies, through the new Continental Congress, passed a resolution urging the States to ''secure to the authors or publishers of any new books not hitherto printed . . . the copy right of such books for a certain time not less than fourteen years from the first publication; and to secure to the said authors, if they shall survive the first term mentioned . . . the copy right of such books for another term of time not less than fourteen years'' (Resolution of May 2, 1783 1906 11).

It was not until the Constitutional Convention in 1787 that proposals were submitted by Charles Pinckney of South Carolina and James Madison of Virginia to empower Congress to grant copyrights and patents (Fenning, 1925). In each of the proposals Madison and Pinckney suggested that copyrights and patents should be granted only for a ''limited time'' or a ''certain time'' (Fenning 112-113).

The Madison and Pinckney proposals served as the basis for the Patent and Copyright Clause as it currently exists (Donner 1992 370-1). The congressional delegates unanimously approved the Clause with no debat (Donner 371) and, in 1790, Congress passed ''An Act for the Encouragement of Learning'' that essentially restricted the domain of copyright law to federal law solely (Act for the Encouragement of Learning 1790).

However, the Clause was later mentioned in the ratification debates following the initial Constitutional Convention. In the *Federalist No. 43*, James Madison noted: ''. . . The copy right of authors has been solemnly adjudged in Great Britain to be a right at Common Law. The right to useful inventions seems with equal reason to belong to the inventors. The public good coincides in both cases with the claims of individuals . . .'' (Madison 1941 279). As this record is admittedly sparse, scholars tend to look to the first copyright statute, the Copyright Act of 1790, to determine the meaning of ''for limited Times'' (Cargill and Moran 1971 927).

Known as the Nation's first copyright statute, the Copyright Act of 1790 (hereinafter the ''1790 Act''), provided for a federal copyright term of 14 years from the date of publication, renewable for an additional 14 years should the author survive the first term (1790 Act §1, 1 Stat.124). This renewable 14-year term applied to existing works (works already published and/ or works created but not published) as well as future works (1790 Act §1, 1 Stat. 124). Thus, assuming an author survived the first term, she could conceivably have a copyright term of 28 years total, after which point the work(s) at issue would fall into the public domain.

Approximately 41 years later, in 1831, Congress expanded the copyright term from a total possible term of 28 years to 42 years (essentially 28 years from publication, renewable for an additional 14 years should the author survive the first term) (Act of Feb. 3, 1831). Again, the Copyright Act of 1831 (hereinafter the ''1831 Act''), just as the 1790 Act, applied to existing, as well as future, works (Act of Feb. 3, 1831). However, to qualify for the extension, an existing work had to be in its initial copyright term at the time that the 1831 Act became effective (Act of Feb. 3, 1831). In this manner, the 1831 Act was more stringent than the 1790 Act in that the eligibility for the additional 28-year extension was qualified in terms of whether the work at issue was in its initial term under the 1790 Act upon the 1831 Act becoming effective (Act of Feb. 3, 1831). Perhaps, the inclusion of this additional criterion is evidence of the balancing that Congress felt was necessary to ensure that the author would have sufficient incentive to create, while recognizing the importance of having works fall into the public domain within a reasonable period of time.

However, in 1909, Congress extended the copyright term from a possible total of 42 years to a possible total of 56 years (28 years from publication, renewable for an additional 28 years) (Act of March 4, 1909). Just as the 1790 and 1831 Acts, the Copyright Act of 1909 (hereinafter the "1909 Act") applied to existing, as well as future, works (Act of March 4, 1909). Thus, over a period of 119 years Congress extended the copyright term of existing and future works twice. It was not until 67 years later that Congress revisited the issue of copyright terms. However, this revamping would prove to be significantly different than its predecessors.

The language and intent of the Acts of 1790, 1831, and 1909 sought to encourage the expansion of the amount of works within the public domain. However, the Copyright Act of 1976 demonstrated a dramatic change in the balance between protected works and the desire to expand the wealth of information that comprises the public domain. This change served to be the starting point of a shift from a desire to balance authors' rights against the idea that a robust public domain is a societal necessity. In terms of progress and innovation a desire not to reward authors for excessive periods of time and, in doing so, sacrifice the needs of society as concerns a plentiful public domain of works.

In 1976 Congress significantly changed the manner in which copyright terms would be calculated. The difference hinged upon "creation" vs. "publication." Now, unlike the Acts of 1790, 1831, and 1909, federal copyright protection would be afforded a work upon its creation, as opposed to its publication (1976 Act §§ 302-304). This protection would run for fifty years after the author's death (1976 Act §§ 302-304).[2] Furthermore, the Copyright Act of 1976 (hereinafter the "1976 Act") governed all works not published by its effective date of January 1, 1978, regardless of when the works were actually created (1976 Act §§ 302-304). For those works published with existing copyrights as of January 1, 1978, the copyright term was 75 years from the date of publication (1976 Act §§ 302-304).

Thus, the 1976 Act significantly altered the copyright term landscape in that it eliminated the requirement of author survival in order for extension to apply—the term automatically extended for fifty years after the author's death. Thus, assuming an author lived to be 90 years old and received copyright protection for her work at the age of 30, the copyright term on that particular work would last for 110 years. This example demonstrates just one of the dramatic changes that was brought about by the 1976 Act.

Furthermore, the 1976 Act introduced the concept of copyright terms that run from the "creation" of a work rather than from the "publication" of a work (1976 Act §§ 302-304). This change afforded an author copyright protection upon creation of his work—thus, an author need not publish work to benefit from copyright protection (1976 Act §§ 302-304).

The final blow to the public domain theory came in the form of the 1998 CTEA (Copyright Term Extension Act). The CTEA, while retaining the general structure of the 1976 Act, extends the terms of all existing and future copyrights by 20 years (Copyright Term Extension Act). Thus, the copyright term now lasts for the author's life plus an additional 70 years. Under the CTEA, any work that would have otherwise fallen into the public domain as of December 21, 1998 would now continue to enjoy copyright protection for an additional 20 years (Copyright Term Extension Act). Furthermore, for works published before 1978 with existing copyrights as of the CTEA's effective date, the CTEA extends the term to 95 years from publication (Copyright Term Extension Act). So, assuming that a work received copyright protection in 1977, and thus had an existing copyright before 1978, that work would have protection until the year 2072 under the CTEA (Copyright Term Extension Act). Many would seriously question whether this example falls under the "for limited times" language contained in the Copyright Clause. However, in *Eldred* the United States Supreme Court recently decided that it does, so the author will not belabor this point.

While many would argue that the CTEA has stretched the Copyright Clause far beyond its language and intent, others are even more ill-at-ease regarding the dysfunctional relationship that has formed between the Copyright Clause and the First Amendment (Nimmer 1970 1180). Justice Breyer characterized the CTEA as "a statute that exceeds proper Copyright Clause bounds . . . [and] . . . may set Clause and Amendment at cross-purposes, thereby depriving the public of the speech-related benefits that the Founders, through both, have promised'' *(Eldred et al. v Ashcroft)*. Justice Breyer's statement invites a further exploration of what that relationship now looks like in the aftermath of *Eldred.*

The First Amendment states that ''Congress shall make no law . . . abridging the freedom of speech, or of the press . . . '' (US Constitution Amendment 1). Constitutional history tells us that the Copyright Clause and the First Amendment were adopted very close in time. Therefore, one may theorize that the Founders intended for the ''limited monopoly'' aspect of the Copyright Clause to be balanced with free speech principles. Thus, the Founders likely intended for each to be read and interpreted in light of the other. In fact, the US Supreme Court has stated that ''the Framers intended copyright itself to be the engine of free expression'' (558) and the First Amendment to be the means by which that expression is protected in terms of access by the public. As Justice Breyer stated in his dissenting opinion in *Eldred*, '' The Copyright Clause and the First Amendment seek related objectives—the creation and dissemination of information. When working in tandem, these provisions mutually reinforce each other, the first serving as an 'engine of free expression', the second assuring that government throws up no obstacle to its dissemination'' *(Eldred, Justice Breyer dissenting)*

Justice Breyer's statement accurately describes the relationship between the Copyright Clause and the First Amendment *before* the *Eldred* decision. Many have argued that the *Eldred* decision stretched the appropriate bounds of the Copyright Clause and, in doing so, created a dysfunctional relationship between it and the First Amendment. The balance that once existed between the two no longer exists (Tushnet 2000 35). The *Eldred* Court appears to have favored the ''limited monopoly'' aspects of the Copyright Clause over the free expression rights guaranteed by the First Amendment.

Two Worlds Collide: the Eldred Decision v. the Original Intent of the Internet

In his book, ''The Future of Ideas: The Fate of the Commons in a Connected World,'' Professor Lawrence Lessig states ''the Single most striking feature of copyright law is its ability to give owners the power to control innovation in the context of the Net'' (Lessig 2002 253).[3] Lessig made this statement prior to the *Eldred* decision. What does his statement now mean in light of *Eldred?* Did the Court simply increase ''the power to control innovation'' that Lessig foresaw? The remainder of this article explores how the *Eldred* decision flies in the face of one of the original purposes of the Internet—innovation—and what this now means for societal progress.

The architecture of the original internet network, commonly referred to as ''end-to-end,'' was built upon the premise that the network itself would *not* control how it (the network) would grow and change—the applications would control such growth and change. Tim Berners-Lee, the inventor of the World Wide Web, captured this idea very succinctly when describing the foundations of the Web: ''. . . if the Web was to be a universal resource, it had to be able to grow in an unlimited way. Technically, if there was any centralized point of control, it would rapidly become a bottleneck that restricted the Web's growth, and the Web would never scale ''(37).[4] Here, Berners-Lee touched on a number of issues that, when examined closely, pinpoint the potentially devastating effects that the *Eldred* decision will likely have on the Internet as a universal resource and engine of innovation.

First, Berners-Lee spoke of the Web as ''a universal resource.'' Implicit in this statement is the idea that the Web was designed to be, and should be treated as, a universal resource available to, and for the benefit of, the public good (as any other universal resource is typically described and treated) (Lessig). Thus, as a universal resource, the Web must be able to grow ''in an unlimited way.'' Therefore, anything, whether based in technology or law, that would limit the growth of the Web as a universal resource would eventually deplete, and ultimately destroy, the Web in its capacity as a universal resource and engine of innovation.

Next, Berners-Lee noted that if there were any type of centralized control over the Web, that control would rapidly become a bottleneck restricting the Web's growth and ultimately destroying the Web's value as a universal resource and engine of innovation (Lessig). Berners-Lee did not expound on what is meant by ''centralized point of control'' or whether a number of items, grouped together and acting as one, would be the equivalent of a centralized point of control. For purposes of this article, the author argues that ''centralized point of control'' could be, for example, a history of case law that slowly, yet consistently, erodes the freedom of the Internet and its value as a universal resource and an engine of innovation.

Finally, Berners-Lee stated that, if the aforementioned bottleneck were to occur, and consequently the Web's growth were to be restricted, then the ''Web would never scale up.'' Thus, the Web would ultimately become a stagnant source of information (which would be relatively useless in terms of a universal resource) and cease to be an engine of innovation and progress.

So, how does Berners-Lee's description of the Web as a ''universal resource'' relate to the *Eldred* decision? The author believes that the *Eldred* decision is simply another contributor to the ''bottleneck'' that restricts the Internet's growth and will ultimately lead to its demise as a universal resource and engine of innovation. This, the author knows, is a bold leap requiring further explanation.

As stated earlier in this article, the *Eldred* court held that the CTEA did not exceed Congress' power under the Copyright Clause of the U.S. Constitution, nor did it violate the First Amendment (*Eldred* 3). While one may debate whether this decision is a correct interpretation of Congress' power under the Copyright Clause, as well as the relationship between the Copyright Clause and the First Amendment, one would be hard pressed to argue that this decision does not, in some fashion, restrict the growth of the Internet as a universal resource and an engine of innovation.

Again, recall that Eric Eldred brought suit because, in his maintenance of the Eldritch Press, he was asked to cease publishing on the Internet the complete text of books that, prior to the CTEA, were within the public domain. Here, Eldred seized the power of the Internet to reach an infinite number of people around the globe and created an online library where anyone could access the text of classic literature to do with it as they saw fit. Are Eldred's actions not the epitome of innovation and progress? He used works that were within the public domain and transcribed those works into a format that would make them more easily accessible to anyone, anywhere. Is this not the ''beauty'' of the Internet? Would this not be a perfect example of Berners-Lee's ''universal resource'' description of the Internet?

Apparently, the *Eldred* Court did not agree and the *Eldred* decision is now part of Berners-Lee's bottleneck that stunts the growth of the Internet.

Future Implications of Eldred

Since *Eldred*, further and increasingly aggressive attacks on the public domain and free speech have occurred. In mid-2003 the music industry sued four college students who, it claimed, were operating ''little Napsters'' at their universities (Heins 2003). Within a week, the students settled the lawsuits and agreed to pay the music industry \$12,000-\$15,000 each and to shut down the software programs that had been used to operate the Napster-like web sites.

Furthermore, the music industry recently continued its fight against file-sharing by demanding, in what have come to be referred to as ''take-down'' letters, that academic and non-academic

Internet service providers (ISPs) remove web sites, search engines, or other online material that the music industry believes to contain copyright-protected works (Heins). Under a section of the current Digital Millennium Copyright Act (hereinafter the ''DMCA''), these ISPs may be liable for copyright infringement by users unless compliance with ''take-down'' notices is expeditious.

Verizon Internet Services (an ISP) recently challenged the DMCA's subpoena provision which permits copyright owners to obtain subpoenas from a federal court that require ISPs to identify users who are allegedly engaged in infringement (*In re Verizon Internet Services* 2003). Verizon argued that the DMCA provides no built-in protection of the type that the United States Supreme Court specifically noted in *Eldred* was an essential element of copyright. However, Verizon's arguments were rejected and it was ordered to comply with the subpoena and identify the relevant users (*In re Verizon Internet Services).* Verizon's case is currently on appeal.

With the current *Verizon* decision on record, the music industry then delivered in excess of 1,000 subpoenas to various ISPs that demanded the identities of users alleged to be engaging in the illegal sharing of copyrighted music. Most ISPs have complied with the subpoenas and have supplied, and continue to supply, the music industry with the identities of users. By September of 2003, the music industry had filed in excess of 250 lawsuits against alleged ''file-sharers.''

Perhaps the most outrageous actions thus far have come in the form of the music industry's reported actions to sabotage file-swapping and sharing networks by contaminating them with corrupt versions of songs and videos in the hopes of frustrating users to the point where they no longer utilize that particular web site (Borland 2002; Straus 2002). The music industry has also quietly begun embarking on the development of software that would sabotage the computers and/or Internet connections of users suspected of downloading ''pirated'' music (Sorkin 2003). The sabotage may consist of either a redirection of users to web sites where they may legally purchase songs and videos, the scanning of the user's personal computer files for music files that are thought to be illegally copied and the subsequent deletion of those suspected files, and the freezing of a user's computer system in its entirety (Sorkin).

Conclusion

In the preface to his book ''The Future of Ideas: The Fate of the Commons in a Connected World'', Professor Lawrence Lessig observed the following:

> This *is* a war about basic American values. It is about the values of balance and measure that should limit the government's role in choosing the future of creativity. It is about the opportunity for creators to build on the past. It is about limiting the control that legal structures such as copyright give to the industries of yesterday to ensure that they can't use law to constrain creators of tomorrow . . . you can believe in copyright without believing copyright should be perpetual . . . You can believe in these tools to inspire innovation without believing these tools should become so bloated as to destroy the opportunity for innovation'' (Lessig xvi-xvii).

Does the *Eldred* decision further the opportunity for creators to build on the past? Does it exemplify the values of balance and measure in terms of Congress' role, via the CTEA, in choosing the future of creativity? Does it limit the control that copyright gives to industries of yesterday to ensure that they cannot use copyright law to constrain the creators of tomorrow? It is doubtful that one would respond in agreement.

Endnotes

1. For further historical information regarding the Stature of Anne, see Benjamin Kaplan, AN Unhurried View of Copyright 2-7 (1967) and Paul Goldstein, *Copyright's Highway: From Gutenberg to the Celestial Jukebox* 39-43 (1994).
2. This clause became known as "life plus fifty:"
3. In this statement, the "owners" that Lessig refers to are owners of copyright protections.
4. Lessig quotes Berners-Lee to support the proposition that the Net was founded on principles of innovation and that its very survival depends upon unlimited growth in order to achieve this purpose.

Works Cited

Act of Feb. 3, 1831, ch. 16, §§ 1, 16, 4 Stat. 436,.

Act of March 4, 1909,ch. 320, §§ 23-24, 35 Stat. 1080-1081 (1909 Act).

Act for the Encouragement of Learning. (1790, May 31). Chapter 15, 1 Stat. (repealed and replaced 1831).

Borland, J. (2002, September 22). "New Kazaa Likely to raise labels' ire"." *CNET News.com.*

Bowker, R.R. (1912). *Copyright, Its History and its Law REST OF CITE*

Copyright Term Extension Act, note 1

Cargill & Moran (1971). Copyright Duration v. The Constitution, 17 *Wayne Law Review* 917-.

Donner, I. (1992). *The Copyright Clause of the U.S. Constitution: Why Did the Framers Include it Unanimous Approval?* 36 Journal of American Legal History, 361, 370-71.

Eldred et al. v. Ashcroft, 537 U.S. ____186______ (2003).

Fenning, K. (1925). *The Origin of the Patent and Copyright Clause of the Constitution,* 17 GEO.L. 109-113.

Fonda, Daren, *Copyright's Crusader,* THE BOSTON GLOBE MAGAZINE, August 29, 1999.

Gorman, R. and Ginsburg, J. (1993).*Copyright for the Nineties (4th ed.).* reprinted from An Act for the Encouragement of Learning, 1710, 8 Anne, ch. 19: England.

Heins, M. (2003). "The Progress of Science and Useful Arts: Why Copyright Today Threatens Intellectual Freedom. 37

In re Verizon Internet Services, 240 F. Supp. 2d 24 (D.D.C. 2003).

Lessig, L. (2002). *The Future of ideas: The fate of the commons in a connected world."* Vintage Books.

Madison, J. (1941). *The Federalist* No. 43. Modern Library Edition.

Resolution of May 2, 1783 Copyright Office Bulletin No. 3, Copyright Enactments of the United States, 1783-1906 (2d ed. 1906).

Nimmer, M.B. (1970). "Does Copyright abridge the First Amendment guarantees of free speech and press?" 17 *UCLA Law Review* 1180.

Sorkin, A. (2003, May 4). "Software Bullet is Sought to Kill Musical Piracy." *New York Times,* 1, 36.

Straus, N. (2002, September 25). "Online Fans Start to Pay the Piper." *New York Times,* E 1, E 7.

Tushnet, R. (2000). *Copyright as a model for free speech law.* 42 B.C.L. Review 1.

1790 Act §1, 1 Stat. 124).

1976 Act §§ 302-304

98 Eng. Rep. 257 (H.L. 1774).

"Mere conduits" Or Editors?
ISPs, Web Masters, Immunity and Safe Harbor in Online Defamation versus Online Intellectual Property Cases

*Juliet Dee**
University of Delaware

With the "information superhighway" approaching adolescence, certain glaring discrepancies in Internet law are becoming harder and harder to ignore. For example, the Digital Millennium Copyright Act (DMCA) of 1998 does *not* provide immunity for Internet Service Providers (ISPs) who facilitate copyright infringement. In contrast, Section 230 of the Communications Decency Act (CDA) of 1996 *does* provide total immunity to Internet Service Providers (ISPs) who facilitate defamation and even distribution of advertising for child pornography online.

It is the thesis of this paper that Congress needs to amend Section 230 of the CDA so that it follows the DMCA model for redress of grievances caused by copyright infringement. The DMCA at least provides for "notice-and-take-down" of material that infringes on a copyright, rather than the blanket immunity that the CDA provides to ISPs and "users" of "interactive computer services" in defamation cases. This discussion will focus on the discrepancies between the CDA and the DMCA, past consequences of these discrepancies in terms of economic harm to individuals, harm to victims of defamation or to copyright holders, and an analysis of the implications of these statutory inconsistencies.

Statutes

Let us begin with a close look at the language of both the Communications Decency Act (CDA) and the DMCA. Congress passed the CDA as part of the Telecommunications Act of 1996. Section 230 states that

> (1) No provider or user of an interactive computer service shall be treated as the publisher or speaker of any information provided by another information content provider (47 USCS S 230(c)(1)).

That is it. The statute never explicitly states that "providers" (meaning Internet service providers or ISPs) are granted *immunity* from liability, but courts have granted ISPs immunity from liability based on content originating with third parties based on this one statement in Section 230(c)(1). The next statement provides the infamous "Good Samaritan" protection for ISPs:

> (2) No provider or user of an interactive computer service shall be held liable on account of . . .

---

* The author wishes to thank Professor Paul Siegel, Director of the School of Communication of the University of Hartford, for his constructive comments and suggestions on an earlier version of this paper.

1) any action voluntarily taken in good faith to restrict access to or availability of material that the provider or user considers to be obscene, lewd, lascivious, filthy, excessively violent, harassing, or otherwise objectionable, whether or not such material is constitutionally protected . . . (S 230)(c)(2)(A).

This ''Good Samaritan'' provision means that ISPs will not be held liable if they take any ''good faith'' actions to shut down obscene web sites, for example. At the same time, the clause above it means that ISPs will be immune from liability if even if they do nothing; in other words, they are not liable if they take down an offensive web site, and they are likewise not liable if they leave it up. It is a win-win situation for ISPs, and a great incentive for them to remain unresponsive should they receive complaints about offensive material on web sites or bulletin boards created by their subscribers.

Section 230 also provides a definition for an ''interactive computer service:''

The term ''interactive computer service'' means any information service, system or access software provider that provides or enables computer access by multiple users to a computer server, including specifically a service or system that provides access to the Internet . . . (S 230)(f)(2).

Section 230 never uses the term ''Internet service provider,'' although it seems clear that a ''provider . . . of an interactive computer service'' would be an ISP. It is more problematic, however, when Section 230 refers to the ''user of an interactive computer service'' (S 230)(1) because the term ''user'' is never clearly defined. Would a ''user'' be a web master? Would a ''user'' be an individual sending an e-mail message to one other person? If so, would such a ''user'' likewise be immune from liability if he or she defames someone on a web site or in an e-mail message? This vagueness in the terms of Section 230 has opened the floodgates of litigation, as is discussed below.

Another clause in the CDA cautions that Section 230 will have ''no effect on intellectual property law.'' Nothing in this section shall be construed to limit or expand any law pertaining to ''intellectual property'' (Section 230)(e)(2).

Two years after Congress passed the CDA it passed the Digital Millennium Copyright Act (DMCA) (17 USCS S 512), which was Congress' first attempt to devise a legal framework for dealing with copyright infringement online. SS 512(b)(c)(d) contains the so-called ''notice-and-take-down'' provision. It provides that the ISP must respond ''expeditiously to remove, or disable access to, the material that is claimed to be infringing'' (17 U.S.C. SS 512(b)(2)(E). If the ISP does not remove the infringing material it may be held liable for copyright infringement itself.

The DMCA gives a more detailed definition of a ''service provider'' than does the CDA; the DMCA defines a ''service provider'' as follows:

An entity offering the transmission, routing, or providing of connections for digital online communications, between or among points specified by a user, of material of the user's choosing, without modification to the content of the material as sent or received (S 512)(k)(1).

Although the definition of ''service provider'' in the DMCA might suggest that an ISP is identical to a common carrier such as a telephone company, this is not the case. The U.S. Supreme Court has defined a common carrier as one that ''makes a public offering to provide [communications facilities] whereby all members of the public who choose to employ such facilities may communicate or transmit intelligence of their own design and choosing'' (*FCC v. Midwest Video Corp.* 701). The FCC has concluded that common carriers offer ''basic'' information transport rather than "enhanced" services which implicate the transfer and storage of information that subscribers can access. In the Telecommunications Act of 1996 Congress provided that "nothing in this section shall be construed to treat interactive computer services as common carriers" (47 U.S.C. S 223(e)(6). The FCC has stated that hybrid services like those offered by America Online [AOL] are "enhanced services, and are not telecommunication services . . ." [meaning common carriers]. "AOL does not act as a mere conduit for information. Even chat rooms, where subscribers can exchange messages in 'real time' are under AOL's control and may be reformatted or edited" (*In re Federal-State Joint Board on Universal Service* 13 *FCC Record* 11537-11539). Courts have also upheld the FCC's rule that ISPs such as AOL are not common carriers (*Howard v. America Online, Inc.* 753).

Of course, in terms of avoiding litigation, it would be to an ISP's advantage to enjoy the same legal status as a common carrier. It has been well established for more than a decade that common carriers such as the Baby Bells or AT&T cannot be held liable for indecent material such as "dial-a-porn" audio services that utilize telephone lines (*Sable v. FCC*; *Dial Information Services v. Thornburgh*). The CDA (Section 230) provides a "negative" definition of an interactive computer service in the sense that we know that it does *not* have the legal status of a publisher or speaker, but there is no "positive" definition. In interpreting the CDA, courts have generally granted an "interactive computer service" the legal status of a "distributor" such as a magazine store or a newspaper stand. For example, just as a magazine store can cover its "indecent" magazines with brown wrappers or refuse to carry such magazines altogether, the larger ISPs such as AOL and Cox Cable have editorial policies that forbid subscribers to post obscene material on web sites that the ISPs themselves provide.

Another glaring discrepancy between the DMCA and the CDA is that the former provides for a specific "notice-and-take-down" procedure whereas the latter has nothing resembling the "notice-and-take-down" provisions of the DMCA. For example, if a plaintiff succeeds in determining the identity of his/her defamer, there is still no incentive whatsoever for the ISP to shut down a defamatory web site. It is difficult to persuade a judge that the elements necessary to bring a libel suit to trial are present (identification, publication, defamation, and fault). It is also difficult for the plaintiff because a great deal of speech that appears at first glance to be defamatory can constitute one's personal opinion and will receive a great deal of First Amendment protection.

Even if the plaintiff can persuade a judge as a matter of law that the elements of libel are present, an ISP would have no incentive to remove a defamatory posting because the CDA provides for no sanctions against an ISP for leaving a defamatory posting up indefinitely. Whereas the plaintiff in a traditional libel suit can recover damages against a newspaper, the plaintiff in an online defamation suit can recover damages *only* from the individual who defames him or her; thus, an online defamation suit is more akin to *Dun & Bradstreet, Inc. v. Greenmoss Builders, Inc.* This 1985 case involved a non-media defendant (a credit reporting agency that falsely reported that Greenmoss Builders, Inc. was bankrupt). The U.S. Supreme Court held that plaintiffs suing non-media defendants did *not* have to establish actual malice or negligence in cases involving purely private matters. This created a new "private matters" test in libel law; courts must now make a public-versus-private-matter determination in defamation cases. This further complicates online defamation cases. If an anonymous poster charges that a company's accounting practices are fraudulent and the company's stock prices fall as a result, is this a "private matter" or a "matter of public concern?" If a court treats such a case as a private matter but a widespread pattern of anonymous defamatory postings begins to take a palpable toll on the stock prices of small companies, does this become a "matter of public concern?"

Legal Precedents in Online Defamation Cases

In response to conflicting court decisions in *Cubby v. CompuServe* and *Stratton Oakmont, Inc. v. Prodigy Services Company,* Congress passed the CDA as part of the Telecommunications Act of 1996, as is mentioned above. In *Blumenthal v. Drudge*, the first legal test of the CDA, a court upheld AOL's immunity from suit despite the fact that AOL was paying Matt Drudge for his "Drudge Report" in which he falsely stated that White House aide Sidney Blumenthal had a history of spousal abuse.

Whereas in *Blumenthal v. Drudge* it was clear that Matt Drudge himself was the defamer, there followed numerous cases in which those committing defamation were anonymous. In some of these cases the anonymous defamers even assumed the identities of innocent parties to make it appear as if the unsuspecting innocent party was the source of the defamatory statements. The most egregious of these cases was *Zeran v. America Online, Inc.* In this 1997 case a vicious prankster made it appear as if the unsuspecting Ken Zeran was trying to sell T-shirts glorifying Timothy McVeigh's massacre of 168 people in the Oklahoma City bombing in 1995. When AOL flatly refused to assist Zeran in learning the identity of the prankster, however, the U.S. Court of Appeals for the Fourth Circuit held AOL to be immune from liability under Section 230 of the CDA. Thus, Ken Zeran was unable to recover damages despite serious threats to his own safety and that of his parents, due to hate mail and community outrage from those who mistakenly believed that Zeran was trying to sell the T-shirts.

The Fourth Circuit's ruling set a precedent for *Lunney v. Prodigy Services Company* in which Alex Lunney, like Ken Zeran, was the victim of a vicious prank whereby someone usurped his identity and sent e-mail messages threatening to harm the sons of Lunney's Boy Scout leader. Like AOL, Prodigy refused to assist Lunney in learning the identity of the prankster; thus Lunney was unable to recover damages.

Following *Zeran* and *Lunney*, there are a number of cases in which anonymous pranksters defame unsuspecting parties. But the outcomes of these cases appear in sharp contrast to *Zeran* and *Lunney* because the ISPs did in fact assist the victims of online defamation in learning the identities of the pranksters who were defaming them (*HealthSouth Corporation v. Krum, Attkisson v. Doe, Attkisson v. Gerstein, Graham v. Oppenheimer, Sabbato v. Hardy*).

In the cases above the plaintiffs were individuals who sued "John Doe" in order to obtain subpoenas to learn the identities of those who were defaming them. In contrast to these cases involving individual plaintiffs, there have been a number of cases in which the plaintiffs are corporations issuing subpoenas in order to learn the identities of anonymous posters criticizing corporate policies. These cases are sometimes barred by anti-SLAPP laws (Strategic Lawsuits Against Public Participation). But even when courts dismiss the cases as a matter of law, if the corporations learn that those criticizing them are current employees, the employees are usually fired or referred for "corporate counseling" (*Raytheon v. Does 1-21*, Aquacool *2000 v. Yahoo! Inc., Dendrite International, Inc. v. Doe No. 3*).

Dendrite International, Inc. v. Doe No. 3 is significant. When the company issued subpoenas to learn the identities of those alleging changes in its accounting practices, the New Jersey appellate court established a three-part test designed to balance "the well-established First Amendment right to speak anonymously, and the right of the plaintiff to protect its proprietary interest and reputation through the assertion of recognizable claims based on the actionable conduct of the anonymous . . . defendants" (*Dendrite International, Inc. v. Doe No. 3,* 760-761). The New Jersey appellate court found that despite Dendrite International's claim that the anonymous postings had hurt its stock prices, this was not reflected in trading records; thus the court required Dendrite International to notify anonymous posters that they were subjects of a subpoena.

Republication of (Reposting) Defamatory Material Online

When Congress used the term ''interactive computer service'' in Section 230, it made no attempt to distinguish between web masters and ISPs. Whereas web masters might be in a position to exercise editorial control over the information on their web sites, ISPs have thousands of subscribers, making it extremely difficult or impossible to monitor the enormous volume of information being exchanged. Courts have been inconsistent in decisions involving the question of whether web masters should be granted immunity based on Section 230. For example, in *Curzon-Brown and Wall v. San Francisco Community College District, Ryan Lathouwers, Associated Students and Doe's 1-25*, the Superior Court of the City and County of San Francisco held that Section 230 of the CDA granted immunity to the web master (Professors who charged that web master was fabricating defamatory ''student evaluations'' dropped their suit after court held that web master had immunity). But in *Sabbato v. Hardy* the Ohio Court of Appeals held that Section 230 of the CDA did *not* guarantee immunity to the web master (web master held to act as a ''referee'' because he participated in the ''conversations'' on his web site).

In addition to the question of whether a web master should receive immunity, there is the question of whether someone who re-posts a defamatory statement should receive immunity under Section 230. In traditional libel law, the republication rule holds that if a newspaper, for example, repeats a defamatory allegation by a third party, even if the newspaper attributes the allegation to the third party, the victim of defamation can still successfully sue the newspaper for *republication* of the defamation. But in the online defamation case *Barrett v. Rosenthal* the court granted Section 230's immunity to the defendant who had republished a defamatory statement. Does this mean that the republication rule that has governed libel law for centuries has been thrown out with regard to online defamation? If so, there would clearly be one set of rules for hard copy print media and another set of rules for information posted on the Internet.

The next two cases involve online defamation in cases that raise questions such as 1) whether the operator of a newsgroup should be liable for re-posting (republishing) defamatory material, and 2) whether the person committing defamation can be held liable if he or she did not *intend* for his/her defamatory comments to be distributed on a listserve.

Barrett v. Clark (2001), sub nom Barrett v. Rosenthal (2003)

The case of *Barrett v. Clark* began when physicians Stephen Barrett and Terry Polevoy operated ''Quackwatch,'' a 32 year-old nonprofit organization ''to combat health-related frauds, myths, fads and fallacies.'' Barrett and Polevoy launched Quackwatch's web site in 1996. It includes information about fraudulent health care practices and contains criticisms of alternative medicine. Barrett and Polevoy became victims of online defamation; for example, one Timothy Bolen accused Dr. Polevoy of stalking Christine McPhee, who hosted a radio talk-show about alternative medicine in Canada.

Ilena Rosenthal, Director of the Humantics Foundation for Women in San Diego (a center for alternative health care), and operator of a Usenet newsgroup for women who have had problems with breast implants, then reposted Tim Bolen's defamatory message to one or more news groups. Barrett contacted Rosenthal and informed her that Timothy Bolen's original message contained false and defamatory information about Polevoy; he also threatened to sue Rosenthal. Instead of withdrawing the message accusing Polevoy of stalking, however, Rosenthal posted messages about Barrett's threat to sue and claimed that Barrett was an arrogant bully who tried to ''extort'' her; she then attached a re-posting of Bolen's defamatory statement.

Rosenthal and Bolen prevailed on the grounds that Section 230(c)(1) of the CDA immunized Rosenthal from liability because the message was created by a third party (Timothy Bolen). Judge James A. Richman of the Superior Court of Alameda County, California, explained: ''As the user of an interactive computer service, that is, a news group, Rosenthal is not the publisher or speaker of the piece. Thus, she cannot be civilly liable for posting it on the Internet. She is immune'' (*Barrett v. Clark* 9).

Judge Richman held that Timothy Bolen was the guilty party and could face legal action and damages. But the cyber-talebearer who re-posts the defamatory statement is completely shielded from liability, Judge Richman explained.

Barrett v. Clark was thus a case of first impression in which Judge Richman ruled that an individual who re-posts defamatory information originally authored by another person on the Internet is granted immunity from suit by Section 230(C)(1) of the CDA. Legal scholar Stephanie Blumstein argued that this was unfair—that an individual Internet moderator ''does not deserve the protection reserved for ISPs'' (Blumstein 408). Like Blumstein, legal commentator Carl S. Kaplan observed that ''courts are expanding Section 230's scope beyond what Congress intended, thereby creating a gaping hole in ISP accountability'' (Kaplan, 2001). Blumstein added: ''Further complicating this mounting problem of accountability, the *Barrett* court extended CDA immunity to protect not only the ISP, but also the user of an ISP when the user fails to monitor and remove defamatory statements under [her] control'' (Blumstein 418). Blumstein continued:

> . . . the re-poster of prior published material is far from ignorant of the message's content, and allowing people to re-post potentially libelous material on the Internet with impunity will spur reckless behavior. . . . If a defamatory message makes it into a moderated newsgroup, it should not be because the moderator is starting [her] own private ''flame wars'' and using [her] immunity privilege to defame with impunity (Blumstein 422).

In contrast to Judge Richman's decision in *Barrett,* Blumstein pointed approvingly to *Sabbato v. Hardy* in which the court held that ''if a webmaster requires an access password . . . and the webmaster may use his discretion to refuse access to anyone, then Section 230 will not necessarily protect him with an 'automatic cloak of immunity''' (*Sabbato v. Hardy*, cited in Blumstein 422).

When Barrett and Polevoy appealed, the Court of Appeals of California affirmed Judge Richman's order in most respects. But the Court of Appeals reversed the order as it applied to Dr. Terry Polevoy, whom Timothy Bolen had accused of stalking the Canadian talk-show host Christine McPhee, because Bolen was falsely accusing Polevoy of criminal activity *(Barrett v. Rosenthal* 757-758).

In its decision the court explained that ''the central question in this case is the extent to which [Section 230 of the CDA] abrogated the common law of defamation'' (*Barrett v. Rosenthal* 761). The court continued, observing that under the common law, those who re-publish another's defamatory comments may be treated as

> 1) primary publishers (such as book or newspaper publishers); 2) as conduits (such as a telephone company); or 3) as distributors (such as a book store, library or news dealer) . . . .Distributors . . . are subject to an intermediate standard of responsibility and may only be held liable as publishers if they know . . . of the defamatory nature of matter they disseminate (*Barrett v. Rosenthal* 761).

The court then considered whether Section 230 barred treating Rosenthal as a ''distributor'' and subjecting her to notice-based liability. Barrett and Polevoy argued that if Judge Richman's interpretation of Section 230 were upheld, then ''a clever libeler could easily escape liability by having some other Internet user . . . publish libelous statements which another 'Internet user' is free to re-publish'' *(Barrett v. Rosenthal* 763). The court continued:

We agree [with Barrett and Polevoy] that [Section 230] cannot be deemed to abrogate the common law principle that one who re-publishes defamatory matter originated by a third person is subject to liability *if he or she knows . . . of its defamatory character*. . . . By construing Section 230 as conferring an absolute immunity, the trial court erred (*Barrett v. Rosenthal* 763).

The Court of Appeals of California thus remanded the case to the trial court for further proceedings. The case is pending.

Batzel v. Cremers (2003)

At the same time *Barrett v. Rosenthal* was wending its way through California's state courts, *Batzel v. Cremers* was being considered in California's federal courts. The facts of *Batzel* parallel those of *Barrett. Batzel v. Cremers* involves online defamation in which a listserve operator forwarded a defamatory message to his list. He also posted the defamatory message in the form of a ''blog.'' Before *Batzel*, no court had really addressed bloggers or list serve operators. Blogs (short for web logs) are online diaries updated frequently by writers who use the medium to comment on current events and everyday life.

This case began when North Carolina handyman Robert Smith did some painting for Ellen Batzel and there was a dispute over his fee. He later claimed that he had overheard attorney Ellen Batzel say that she was descended from top Nazi politican Heinrich Himmler. Smith also claimed that Batzel had European paintings in her house. Smith e-mailed Ton Cremers, former Director of Security at Amsterdam's famous Rijksmuseum and sole operator of the Museum Security Network, suggesting that Batzel might possess paintings the Nazis had stolen from the Jewish people. Cremers' web site attempts to locate stolen works of art by disseminating information to museums and law enforcement personnel. Cremers posted Smith's e-mail message to his listserve. Cremers later contacted Smith to ask for additional information, at which point Smith told Cremers that if he [Smith] had thought his e-mail ''message would be posted on an international message board, he never would have sent it in the first place'' (*Batzel v. Cremers* 1022). Cremers apologized for the confusion and told Smith in an e-mail message that ''You were not a subscriber to the list and I believe that you did not realize your message would be forwarded to the mailing list'' (*Batzel v. Cremers* 1022).

But Ellen Batzel had already seen the e-mail message about her. She sued Smith, Cremers, and the Museum Security Network for defamation. She denied ever saying that she was a descendant of a Nazi official, denied inheriting any art, and charged that Smith had maliciously defamed her out of pique because Batzel had refused to show her Hollywood contacts a screenplay that Smith had written. The district court ''declined to extend the legislative grant of immunity pursuant to S 230(c) to Cremers and his Museum Security Network, holding that the Network is not ''an Internet service provider'' (ISP) and therefore is not covered by the statute'' (*Batzel v. Cremers* 1026). Thus Batzel won her case in the district court.

Cremers appealed, and the U.S. Court of Appeals for the Ninth Circuit disagreed with the district court's reading of S 230. The Ninth Circuit ruled that Cremers, as a provider of ''an interactive computer service'' should be immune from liability under S 230. The Ninth Circuit thus extended immunity to listserve operators as well as ISP's. This would normally end matters, the Ninth Circuit observed,

. . . but this case presents one twist on the usual S 230 analysis: Smith maintains that he never ''imagined [his] message would be posted on an international message board or [he] never would have sent it in the first place.''

. . . Smith's confusion, even if legitimate, does not matter, Cremers maintains, because the S 230(c)(1) immunity should be available simply because Smith was the author of the e-mail, without more.

> We disagree. Under Cremers' broad interpretation of S 230(c), . . . providers of interactive computer services could with impunity intentionally post material they knew was never meant to be put on the Internet. . . . The result would be nearly limitless immunity for speech never meant to be [disseminated] over the Internet (*Batzel v. Cremers* 1033).

The Ninth Circuit thus explained that noncommercial web site hosts are liable only when they post information that a reasonable person would have known was not meant for publication.

Because Cremers' prior knowledge was not entirely clear from the record, the Ninth Circuit then remanded the case to the district court to determine whether Cremers knew or should have known that Smith *did not intend* to publish any information about Ellen Batzel (*Batzel v. Cremers* 1035).

Judge Ronald Gould dissented in part, arguing that Ton Cremers should not be granted immunity for re-publishing Robert Smith's defamatory comments under any circumstances.

> The majority's rule will be incomprehensible to most citizens, who will be unable to plan their own conduct mindful of the law's requirements. . . . By shifting its inquiry away from the defendant's conduct, the majority has crafted a rule that encourages the casual spread of harmful lies. . . . The majority's rule licenses professional rumor-mongers and gossip-hounds to spread false and hurtful information with impunity. . . . Nothing in the CDA's text or legislative history suggests that Congress intended CDA immunity to extend so far (*Batzel v. Cremers* 1038).

Ellen Batzel appealed, requesting a rehearing *en banc*, but Judges William Canby and Marsha Berzon of the Ninth Circuit denied her petition for a rehearing. Again, Judge Gould dissented, arguing that Batzel should be granted a rehearing *en banc:*

> Make no mistake: the panel majority coldly goes where no circuit court has gone before, . . . providing broader automatic immunity of the most callous and damaging defamation that anyone might maliciously post on the Internet. . . . No federal Court of Appeals, save the panel majority in *Batzel,* has ever held that statutory immunity should be given for the pre-publication selection and posting of harshly defamatory material (*Batzel v. Cremers, petition for rehearing* 908).

Judge Gould explained that Congress recognized a difference between "selection" and "screening:"

> Screeners of matters posted by others get immunity; those who select what is posted do not. Section 230 demonstrates a clear Congressional intent to immunize screening and post-publication removal, but shows no corresponding Congressional intent to immunize pre-publication selection and editing. . . . Congress provided immunity for web site operators who edit or remove what another has placed on the Internet. But Congress did not provide for immunity for web site operators who place, for the first time, defamatory information on the Internet (*Batzel v. Cremers, petition for rehearing* 909-910).

Judge Gould stresses that the panel majority has stretched the meaning of Section 230 far beyond what Congress had originally intended:

> Human reputations, built on good conduct over decades, should be not so easily tarnished and lost in a second of global Internet defamation. Under the panel majority's rule, . . . there is no remedy against the person who willingly chooses, with no exercise of care, to amplify a malicious defamation by lodging it on the Internet. . . . Unless the result were commanded by Congress, we should not create such a system (*Batzel v. Cremers, petition for rehearing* 910).

After her petition for rehearing *en banc* was denied, Batzel's case was remanded to the federal district court, where it is pending.

Immunity for AOL in a Case Involving Child Pornography

In *Doe v. America Online, Inc.* (2001), the mother of an 11 year-old plaintiff who was lured into making child pornography sued AOL after Richard Lee Russell used AOL's ''chat rooms'' to market this pornography; AOL refused to suspend Russell's Internet service, and Supreme Court of Florida held that AOL was immune from liability under Section 230 of CDA.

Invasion of Privacy: Is Linking to a Web Site Like Trespassing?

In addition to the problem of granting immunity to ISPs even when child pornography is advertised in their chat rooms, another recent case involves public disclosure of private facts. This case raises the question of whether a defendant may include a link on his/her web site that links others to the web site of the person whose privacy is invaded.

Johnson v. Max (2003)

The case *Johnson v. Max* involves invasion of privacy and raises the former question above regarding linking one's web site to another's when the defendant is disclosing private facts about the plaintiff. This case is popularly known as that of ''the beauty queen versus the cad'' (*Johnson v. Max* 1). It began with 27 year-old Tucker Max, a man so enamoured of his own sexual prowess that he posted an application form on his web site so that women could apply for the privilege of dating him, along with ''an amalgamation of debauchery, sexual exploits and self-promotion'' (*Johnson v. Max* 1).

Without benefit of the purported date application, however, Max, author of *The Definitive Book of Pick-Up Lines,* initiated a relationship with Katy Johnson, (Miss Vermont 1999 and Miss Vermont USA 2001, and author of *True Beauty: A Sunny Face Means a Happy Heart*). Although their personal relationship was short-lived, upon seeing Katy Johnson's web site which generally urges abstinence from sex and alcohol, Max apparently felt compelled to post an essay called ''The Miss Vermont Story'' on his web site. In this essay Max described a personal relationship he had had with Katy Johnson in graphic detail (Max, ''The Miss Vermont Story''). Indeed, Max dragged the ''kiss-and-tell'' genre to astonishing new depths, ''casting serious aspersions on [Katy Johnson's] adherence to the ideals promoted by her web site'' (*Johnson v. Max* 2). In addition to posting ''The Miss Vermont Story'' on his web site, Max included a link to Katy Johnson's web site (Johnson).

Katy Johnson filed suit, charging public disclosure of private facts. She obtained a temporary injunction from Judge Diana Lewis of the Fifteenth Judicial Circuit Court in Palm Beach County, Florida, enjoining Max from

1) using, including or even making reference to ''the name 'Katy Johnson,' 'Katy,' 'Johnson' or title 'Miss Vermont' in any periodical or books, and on his website located at www.tuckermax.com''
2) ''Disclosing any stories or information, notwithstanding its truth, about any intimate or sexual act engaged in by'' Katy Johnson; and
3) linking [Johnson's] web site (www.katyjohnson.com) to [Max's] web site (*Johnson v. Max,* Temporary Injunction).

Max's attorney John C. Carey filed a motion to dismiss (*Johnson v. Max*, Defendant's Motion to Dismiss). The American Civil Liberties Union (ACLU) of Florida also filed an amicus brief on Max's behalf. The ACLU of Florida argued that the temporary injunction was an illegal prior restraint, adding:

> Particularly disturbing . . . is the prohibition against Max using any hyperlink on his web site to link to Johnson's web site. The notion that one World Wide Web user can prohibit another World Wide Web user from utilizing what is

essentially a public address is very disturbing. The utility of the Internet would collapse if the use of web site addresses were dependent upon permission of the ''owner'' of the web site (*Johnson v. Max*, Memorandum of *Amicus Curiae* American Civil Liberties Union of Florida 4).

Law professor Susan P. Crawford agreed with the ACLU that ''to block the ability to link is in effect to say that [Katy Johnson's] web site is her own private property'' (Liptak A13).

The ACLU also noted certain discrepancies in Katy Johnson's arguments; for example, in her complaint her attorney Michael Santucci argued that Max ''continues to publicly disseminate private facts of and concerning Plaintiff,'' whereas Santucci had also issued a press release stating that ''Katy Johnson emphatically denies the story contained on Tucker Max's web site'' (*Johnson v. Max,* Memorandum of *Amicus Curiae* American Civil Liberties Union of Florida in Support of Defendant's Emergency Motion to Dissolve Temporary Injunction, 6). The obvious implication is that if Max's story were false, Katy Johnson could have sued for defamation, but she sued only for public disclosure of private facts, thus tacitly admitting that the story is factual.

U.S. District Judge Daniel Hurley dismissed Johnson's suit and dissolved the temporary injunction. Thus Katy Johnson's suit did not set any legal precedent, although during May and June 2003 when the circuit court's injunction was in effect, her case received national attention.

Digital Millennium Copyright Act (DMCA)

Congress implemented the Digital Millennium Copyright Act (DMCA) in part so that U.S. law would comply with ratified treaties. In other words, Congress passed the DMCA in furtherance of the World Intellectual Property Organization Copyright Treaties Implementation Act (Nimmer & Nimmer 9). In 1996 there was a conference in Geneva, Switzerland in which nations negotiated treaties on a global scale designed to protect copyrighted material such as records, audiotapes and compact discs (Nimmer & Nimmer 9). Section 512 of the DMCA, referred to as the Online Copyright Infringement Liability Limitation Act (OCILLA), provides ISPs with more specific guidance regarding circumstances in which the ISPs will be liable for copyright infringement (Limitations on Liability Relating to Material Online).

Although traditionally copyright infringement is a strict liability standard, the DMCA provides a safe harbor for ISPs under certain circumstances. Specifically, an ISP could be liable for contributory infringement if the ISP had actual knowledge of the infringing activity (*Religious Technical Center v. Netcom On-Line Communication Services, Inc.* 1383). The reason for creating a ''safe harbor'' from direct liability for an ISP is that the ISP would be unaware of the content of thousands of messages unless it were to censor every single message (Nimmer & Nimmer 11).

Thus, the DMCA protects ISPs from liability only if they expend their resources to evaluate copyright infringement complaints; then they must immediately remove or block access to the posting and notify the offending poster that he or she has infringed on copyrighted material.

Discussion

Notice-based liability or government subsidy?

Comparing the notice-based liability upheld in European courts with the total immunity granted in Section 230 of the CDA, legal scholar Matthew Schruers applies an economic analysis and concludes that it would be economically inefficient for U.S. ISPs to return to a notice-based liability regime. Instead, he argues that the government should subsidize efforts to monitor the Internet (Schruers 264).

More Speech

Free speech advocate Mike Godwin appears to argue for ''more speech'' rather than for mounting litigation:

> . . . the preferred response . . . to a defamation problem is to fix it yourself, and a major goal of libel law has been leveling the playing field for private individuals who have been libeled by the media and do not have access to an outlet powerful enough to counteract the resultant reputational damage. This theory breaks down within the context of the Internet, however, as the ''low barrier'' to speaking online allows those who . . . have been defamed the ability to respond to the statements within the same medium and, in the case of many bulletin boards and chat rooms, the exact same context in which the original messages were posted. Often this provides plaintiffs with a means of redressing reputation damage that is ''a lot more satisfying'' than seeking legal redress, and provides a remedy in ''only minutes'' (Godwin 81-82).

Indeed, some companies have already implemented systems that strive to correct defamatory statements with the truth. For example, someone placed a message on an AOL bulletin board alleging that Boston Market's ''homemade'' potatoes were actually instant potatoes from Sysco. Instead of filing a lawsuit, Boston Market posted a reply to the same bulletin board explaining that ''Sysco trucks the potatoes in, but they are not Sysco brand potatoes. They are whole potatoes. And they really do have big mashers in the back of every [Boston Market] restaurant'' (Lorek 1996). Thus, some corporations such as Boston Market have avoided litigation simply by turning to ''more speech'' as an alternative.

The broad immunity created by Section 230 of the Communication Decency Act (CDA) has sometimes led to troubling results, however. For example, a service provider that cannot be held liable for posting a defamatory message may have little or no incentive to take such material down even if informed that the material is defamatory.

One solution to this problem created by statute is Congress' approach in the Digital Millennium Copyright Act (DMCA). The DMCA includes immunity provisions, similar to those of the Communications Decency Act, that protect Internet service providers from liability for content provided by third parties. The DMCA, however, unlike the CDA, provides specific notice, take-down and put-back procedures that carefully balance the First Amendment rights of users with the rights of a potentially injured copyright holder (17 U.S.C. SS 512(c) and (g) (describing the DMCA's take-down and put-back procedures). But Congress has not amended S 230 to provide for similar take-down and put-back procedures.

Thus, the most important difference between the CDA and the DMCA is that the DMCA requires the ISP to take action immediately upon receiving notification of copyright-infringing material, whereas the CDA requires no such action. Indeed, the CDA does not require the ISP to do anything—even after receiving notification. Under the CDA, the ISP may either remove the defamatory material or may ignore all requests to do so; in either case the ISP does not face liability. Comparing the two laws, legal scholar David Hallett comments: ''Congress already addressed the answer [to online copyright infringement] in the DMCA; now all that needs to be done is simply to apply these same principles to afford protection for a defamed individual'' (Hallett 259).

Legal scholar Susan Freiwald strongly agrees with David Hallett:

> Congress erred when it granted immunity from defamation liability to cyberspace intermediaries in [Section 230 of the CDA]. [Section 230 of the CDA] . . . ignored the needs of potential victims of online defamation. In effect, Congress wrote half a statute, one that granted intermediaries some vague rights, but failed to clearly impose any countervailing responsibilities on them. . . . Moreover, total immunity grants intermediaries excessive freedom; they face no liability

for failing to stem online defamation, even if they knew about the defamatory postings and could easily remove them. Furthermore, total immunity denies legal remedy to those victims who cannot identify their defamers (Freiwald 572-573).

Freiwald argues that ''the courts, not Congress'' would have been the least imperfect institution to determine intermediary liability for defamation (Freiwald 574). She observes that ''not only may Congress be ill-suited to make a change, but once it does, that decision may compromise the ability of other institutions to solve the problem'' (Freiwald 582).

Like Hallett, Freiwald points to the discrepancy between the DMCA and Section 230 of the CDA:

New digital copyright laws require all intermediaries to publicize their agent for service of process on the World Wide Web. By contrast, in several of the cases so far brought against intermediaries for online defamation of others, the plaintiff could not identify the original author. Even the intermediaries who host them may not know their posters' true identities. No current legal rule prevents an individual from operating under an untraceable pseudonym, nor can one necessarily force disclosure of a defamation perpetrator's identity by an intermediary who knows it. Thus, if a victim of online defamation cannot recover from the intermediary who carried the posting, she may well not be able to recover at all (Freiwald 586-587).

Freiwald argues that ISPs should have the same legal status as ''distributors'' such as booksellers, libraries and news vendors who do not review the actual content of their publications in the normal course of their business. Freiwald then focuses on the question of whether ISPs should face ''distributor liability, a standard that does not require them to review materials prior to disseminating them, but that does require them to take action once they know . . . that they are disseminating defamatory material'' (Freiwald 590-591).

Even worse, ''given the prevalent use of aliases such as screen names, [ISPs' refusal to act] increases the likelihood that a defamation victim may never learn the identity of the author [of defamatory material]. Finally the agreements [between ISPs and users] generally require that users indemnify [ISPs] against any third-party claims arising out of the user's actions'' (Freiwald 635).

Freiwald observes that there is a potential for Congress to be biased in any legal question involving ''a skewed distribution, where a group with diffuse interests [victims of online defamation] battles a group with concentrated interests'' [ISPs that want to avoid liability for online defamation] (Freiwald 652).

In litigation, ISPs have claimed that they cannot take steps to reduce problems such as online defamation, but this is disingenuous. In fact, they can take such steps, but at a cost (*United States v. Thomas* 711) (finding that defendant ISPs in an obscenity case could determine the jurisdiction of their users with some effort at some cost).

Like David Hallett and Susan Freiwald, legal scholar Stephanie Blumstein argues that Congress should amend Section 230 of the CDA in order to hold ISPs to a notice-based liability scheme; in other words, ''Congress should provide a standard for a notification process similar to that used in the DMCA'' (Blumstein 431-432).

The recent case of *Universal City Studios et al. V. Eric Corley and 2600 Enterprises, Inc.* (2001) indicates that copyright holders will play hardball with those who infringe on copyrights. In this case the Second Circuit held that Eric Corley could not post on his web site a computer program that decrypts the encryption code for DVD movies. Furthermore, Corley could not provide links to other web sites containing the same decryption program.

More recently, the Recording Industry Association of America (RIAA) has put increasing pressure on file swappers, and during the past few years this pressure has pushed file swappers to adopt more and more drastic means of evasion. First there was Napster, a system of centralized servers, but American courts quickly identified Napster as an enabler of copyright infringement due to the manner in which Napster's servers facilitated illegal music file trading.

The next generation of file-swapping configurations eliminated central servers and built peer-to-peer (P2P) networks that directly connected file sharers to each other. These P2P networks have proven to be more impervious to lawsuits. The companies that make the P2P software needed to create these networks have argued that P2P could just as easily be used for legitimate purposes such as sharing personal photographs or other forms of non-copyrighted content (Salkever 2004).

The current generation of decentralized file-swapping networks makes little or no effort to mask the digital fingerprints of individual users. Thus, researchers working for the RIAA can easily log onto the networks, download pirated songs, and note the IP addresses of particularly egregious file sharers. The RIAA identifies egregious file sharers as those who are offering 800 or more songs for download (Salkever 2004).

Despite the RIAA's attempt to play hardball, they have encountered a dramatic setback in *Recording Industry Association of America, Inc. v. Verizon*. In December 2003 the U.S. Court of Appeals for the District of Columbia Circuit threw a spanner in the works when it decided *Recording Industry Association of America (RIAA) v. Verizon* (2003) in Verizon's favor. The court upheld Verizon's refusal to cooperate with the RIAA's request for subpoenas in order to determine the identities of Verizon subscribers who were sharing large music files. In doing so, the court, although not completely de-fanging the DMCA, perhaps filed down its teeth, setting a precedent whereby copyright holders will find it more difficult to identify those who are illegally downloading copyrighted material.

In this case a federal district court had ruled that the RIAA could use subpoenas under the DMCA to ascertain the identities of peer-to-peer music file sharers from ISPs that act as ''mere conduits'' in providing the file sharers with Internet access accounts. But the U.S. Court of Appeals for the District of Columbia Circuit reversed. It relied on the plain language of Section 512(h) requiring a subpoena application to identify the specific material ''to be removed or access to which is to be disabled.'' The court then concluded that the subpoena applies only to situations involving the storage of infringing material or links on the ISP's own servers. The court explained that the subpoena can legally extend to activities falling under the caching, hosting or storage, and information-locating-tool ''safe harbors'' of Sections 512(b), (c) and (d). But the subpoena cannot extend to activity such as the routing of e-mail instant messages or P2P file transfers subject only to the ''mere conduit'' safe harbor of Section 512(a). The court thus held that the RIAA's attempt to force ISPs (Verizon and others) to disclose the identities of alleged file swappers is barred because to apply the DMCA to force disclosure in this way is unconstitutional. The court in effect ruled that the provision of the DMCA violated due process (Cox 2004).

Of course the ruling by the D.C. Circuit is not binding on courts in other circuits. But clerks in federal district courts who process DMCA subpoena applications will no doubt take the D.C. Circuit's ruling into account.

The RIAA has not yet decided whether to appeal the *Verizon* decision, but in January 2004 it announced a new round of lawsuits against 532 peer-to-peer users (Cox 2004). Legal commentators predict that peer-to-peer file swappers will resort to encryption, at which point the RIAA ''will have to become a lot more like the code-cracking National Security Agency in an escalating cat-and-mouse game with programmers who write encrypted file-sharing network software'' (Salkever 2004). Alex Salkever explains that most ominous to creators of copyrighted content is the fact that ''the shift to encrypted P2P networks will allow not only continued trading of pirated music but also of pirated software and movies'' (Salkever 2004). After all this, ''the pirates will remain untouchable underground—thanks to the RIAA's misguided legal missiles'' (Salkever 2004).

The Motion Picture Association of America (MPAA) followed the RIAA's lead in November 2004, announcing a campaign to stamp out online movie-swapping before it becomes rampant. Movie sharing ''still represents less than 2% of all online file sharing, compared with 60% for music and other audio files, according to BigChampagne LLC, a company that tracks illegal file sharing'' (McBride B1). There are also legal alternatives for movie fans, such as MovieLink and CinemaNow, which permit viewers to pay for movies that they download (McBride B3).

Conclusion

Of the cases discussed above, perhaps the least problematic is that of *Johnson v. Max.* The outcome of the case would probably have been the same even if Tucker Max had published a hard copy tabloid story about his intimate relationship with Katy Johnson. Those who sue for public disclosure of private facts face a nearly insurmountable hurdle because the defendant can always argue that the story is ''newsworthy.'' What was unusual about the ''Miss Vermont'' case was that a Florida judge was willing to issue a restraining order prohibiting Tucker Max from linking his web site to Katy Johnson's web site in the first place. Of course, this restraining order was soon dissolved on appeal; thus, the case did not set a new precedent in the area of privacy law.

There is also the question of whether web masters and listserve operators should receive the benefits of Section 230's immunity guarantee even when they are active participants in re-posting defamatory statements originating from others. Whereas the courts in *Curzon-Brown* and *Barrett* did indeed grant Section 230's immunity to the webmasters in question, treating them as if they were ''users of an interactive computer service,'' the court in *Sabbato* declined to grant immunity to the webmaster. *Batzel* is pending following the Ninth Circuit's decision to remand *Batzel* to the trial court in order to determine whether Cremers knew that Smith had not intended to post his comments about Ellen Batzel on a listserve or a web site.

Of the cases outlined above in which the identity of the person committing defamation was at first unknown, the victim of defamation was able to use a subpoena to discover the defamer's identity in the majority of cases (*HealthSouth, Raytheon, Attkisson, Aquacool 2000, Graham,* and *Sabbato).* In three cases, however, *(Zeran, Lunney* and *Curzon-Brown*), the victims of defamation were *never* able to learn the identities of those who defamed them because of the refusal of AOL, Prodigy and the web master Ryan Lathouwers, respectively, to cooperate.

Congress no doubt had good intentions when it passed Section 230 of the CDA, effectively granting the legal status of a magazine store to ISPs. But no one in Congress could have anticipated the incredibly shabby treatment Kenneth Zeran received from AOL when Zeran's and his parents' safety were threatened by an anonymous prankster. AOL made no effort whatsoever to learn the identity of the person playing the vicious prank upon Ken Zeran, and there was no legal mechanism giving AOL any incentive to do so.

If we compare AOL's nonchalant responses in *Zeran* and *Doe* (AOL's chat room used to advertise child pornography; even after being notified AOL made no effort to stop the producer of child pornography) with the way in which a telephone company would treat the victim of an obscene phone call, one might wonder whether AOL deserves ''magazine store'' status at all. Telephone companies (common carriers) cooperate with law enforcement personnel in order to identify and detain those who make obscene phone calls. In contrast, AOL and other ISPs immediately realized that Section 230's immunity provision was in fact a convenient guarantee promising that no matter how irresponsible AOL was, even to the point of permitting advertising of child pornography after being notified by the child victim's mother (*Doe v. America Online*), there would be no negative consequences for AOL.

If Congress ever gets around to amending Section 230 to alleviate its cumbersome ambiguity, Congress might look to the laws of various European and Asian countries to inform themselves of other possible solutions to the problem of online defamation. Although the laws and legal precedents of other countries are beyond the scope of this paper, other legal scholars have suggested that there are more workable solutions than that provided by Section 230 (Determann, Amadei, Williams et al., Savage, Sterling).

Sometimes market forces can exert pressure in favor of "the little guy" such as the victim of online defamation despite the fact that Congress has stacked the decks in the ISPs' favor. For example, the cases involving Sidney Blumenthal, Ken Zeran, and the victim of child pornography in *Doe v. America Online* were catastrophic for the plaintiffs when courts interpreted the CDA to grant immunity to America Online. One might ask, however, about the extent to which America Online won or lost in the court of public opinion following these cases. In other words, if potential customers turned away from AOL and selected a different ISP such as Comcast, for example, because AOL was gaining a reputation for being an ISP that did not care how badly "the little guy" suffered as a result of its asserted immunity, then AOL would have to do some damage control from a public relations perspective.

In some of the more recent cases (*HealthSouth Corporation v. Krum, Attkisson v. Gerstein, Graham v. Oppenheimer* and *Sabbato v. Hardy*, for example), the ISPs may have been responding to market forces (or at least the court of public opinion). In these cases the ISPs assisted victims of anonymous defamation in learning their defamers' identities despite the fact that there was no legal incentive to do so.

Of course, the most elegant response to online defamation was that of Boston Market, which exercised the "more speech" option rather than filing a lawsuit when someone charged that it used instant potatoes rather than "home made" mashed potatoes. A well-known corporation such as Boston Market with ready access to the media can indeed jump into the fray and respond to defamatory bulletin board postings, thus defending its reputation.

But for a private person such as Ellen Batzel, the "more speech" option may be ineffective. Batzel lost several clients in California, and she was investigated by the North Carolina Bar Association after Ton Cremers posted Robert Smith's accusation that she possessed paintings stolen from Jewish families by the Nazis.

One cannot help noticing the huge discrepancy between the relative power and influence of copyright owners (such as Disney Corporation or the RIAA) and "the little guy" who may be a victim of online defamation, who is frequently an individual with limited financial resources. Whereas the DMCA includes a "notice-and-take-down" provision, Section 230 of the CDA has no such provision. Of course in the wake of *RIAA v. Verizon* (2003), the DMCA apparently provides less ammunition for copyright holders than they would prefer. The DMCA still authorizes the issuance of a subpoena to an ISP that *stores* infringing material on its servers, but does *not* authorize issuance of a subpoena to an ISP that acts as a "mere conduit" in transmitting infringing material (*Recording Industry Association of America v. Verizon, 2003).* Nonetheless, the DMCA at least contains a mechanism for "notice-and-take-down" provisions whereas Section 230 of the CDA provides no series of steps that might protect victims of online defamation.

Part of the problem, of course, is that it is difficult to determine what "notice-and-take-down" provisions would entail for online defamation. First there is the problem of determining whether a critical comment is merely opinion (protected by the First Amendment), whether it is genuinely defamatory, whether it is false, and whether it was made with negligence or malice. We must concede that the sheer volume of messages and information that ISPs convey each moment would render an attempt to screen out defamatory comments prohibitive. Second, if an ISP *does* receive notification of alleged defamation online, to immediately remove the offending statement without investigation would deny the defendant due process. This is not to excuse AOL for ignoring the pleas of Ken Zeran or the pleas of the mother whose 11 year-old son was lured into child pornography which was advertised on AOL. Rather, this is to say that Congress should fine-tune Section 230 of the CDA. Congress should *require* ISPs to make some effort to immediately rectify situations in which, once they are notified, they are in a position to assist real and potential victims of online defamation, especially when the victim's physical safety is endangered due to usurped identity, as in the case of Ken Zeran.

Just as telephone companies have the financial resources to help identify those who make obscene telephone calls, ISPs have the financial resources to identify those who play vicious but anonymous pranks, re-publish defamatory comments without bothering to check their credibility, or advertise child pornography. It is time to call their bluff.

Works Cited

Amadei, Xavier. "Note: Standards of Liability for Internet Service Providers: A Comparative Study of France and the United States with a Specific Focus on Copyright, Defamation and Illicit Content." *Cornell International Law Journal* 35 (November 2001/February 2002):189-229.

Aquacool 2000 v. Yahoo! Inc. CV 00-04993 (C. D. Cal. 2000). Complaint (filed May 11, 2000). Available at http://epic.org/privacy/anonymity/## (Site visited September 16, 2004).

Attkisson v. Doe, No. 99VS178988A (State Court, FultonCounty, Georgia, filed January 28, 1999).

Attkisson v. Gerstein, No. 1999CV06397 (Superior Court, Fulton County, Georgia, filed March 18, 1999; dismissed June 19, 2000).

Barrett v. Clark, No. 833021-5, 2001 WL 881259 (Cal. Super. Ct. July 25, 2001).

Barrett v. Rosenthal, 112 Cal. App. 4th 749; 5 Cal. Rptr. 3d 416, 2003 Cal. App. LEXIS 1551 (Cal. App. 1st Dist. Div. 2, October 15, 2003).

Batzel v. Cremers, 333 F. 3d 1018, 2003 U.S. App. LEXIS 12736 (Ninth Circuit 2003), petition for rehearing *en banc.,* 351 F. 3d 904, 2003 U.S. App. LEXIS 24304 (Ninth Circuit 2003).

Blumenthal v. Drudge, 992 F. Supp. 44 (D.D.C. 1998).

Blumstein, Stephanie. "The New Immunity in Cyberspace: The Expanded Reach of the Communications Decency Act to the Libelous 'Re-Poster.'" *Boston University Journal of Science and Technology Law* 9 (Summer 2003):407-432.

Common Carrier Regulation. 47 USCS S 223 (2003).

Communications Decency Act. 47 USCS S 230 (2003).

Cox, Evan R. "RIAA Resumes Legal Offensive: Recording Industry Association Uses John Doe Lawsuits Against P2P File-Swapping Post-Verizon." *The Internet Newsletter* (January 28, 2004).

Cubby v. CompuServe, 776 F. Supp. 135 (S.D.N.Y. 1991).

Curzon-Brown and Wall v. San Francisco Community College District, Ryan Lathouwers, Associated Students and Does 1-25, No. 307335 (Cal. Super. Ct., City and County of San Francisco, filed October 20, 2000).

Defamation Act, Chapter 31, 1(1), (1996) (England).

Dendrite International, Inc. v. Doe No. 3, 775 A. 2d 756 (N.J. Super. Ct. App. Div. 2001).

Determann, Lothar. "Case Update: German CompuServe Director Acquitted on Appeal." *Hastings International and Comparative Law Review* 23 (Fall 1999):109-123.

Dial Information Services Corp. v. Thornburgh, 502 U.S. 1072, 117 L. Ed. 2d 132, 112 S.Ct. 966 (1992).

Digital Millenium Copyright Act. 17 USCS S 512 (2003).

Doe v. America Online, Inc. 783 So. 2d 1010 (Supreme Court of Florida, 2001).

Dun & Bradstreet, Inc. V. Greenmoss Builders, Inc. 472 U.S. 749 (1985).

FCC v. Midwest Video Corp. 440 U.S. 689 (1979).

Freiwald, Susan. "Comparative Institutional Analysis in Cyberspace: The Case of Intermediary Liability for Defamation." *Harvard Journal of Law & Technology* 14 (Spring 2001):569-655.

Graham v. Oppenheimer, No. 3:00CV57 (E.D. Va., filed October 23, 2000).

Godwin, Mike (1998). *Cyber Rights: Defending Free Speech in the Digital Age.* New York: Times Books, Random House.

Hallett, David E. "How to Destroy a Reputation and Get Away With It: The Communication Decency Act Examined: Do the Policies and Standards Set Out in the Digital Millenium Copyright Act Provide a Solution for a Person Defamed Online?" *IDEA: The Journal of Law and Technology* 41 (2001): 259-267.

HealthSouth Corp. v. Krum, No. 98-2812 (Pa. C.P. Centre County, filed October 28, 1998) (1998).

Howard v. America Online, Inc. 208 F. 3d 741 (9th Cir. 2000).

In re Federal-State Joint Board on Universal Service, 13 *FCC Record* 11501 at 11537-11539.

Johnson, Katy. www.katyjohnson.com (Site visited September 30, 2004).

Johnson v. Max, No. 03-Civ-80515, Defendant's Motion to Dismiss and for More Definite Statement and Incorporated Memorandum of Law (S.D. Florida, West Palm Beach Division, filed June 13, 2003).

Johnson v. Max, Memorandum of *Amicus Curiae* American Civil Liberties Union of Florida in Support of Defendant's Emergency Motion to Dissolve Temporary Injunction, 1, No. 03-Civ-80515 (S.D. Florida, filed June 17, 2003).

Johnson v. Max, Temporary Injunction, No. 03-Civ-80515 (Palm Beach County Circuit Court, filed May 6, 2003).

Kaplan, Carl S. ''How Is Libel Different in Cyberspace?'' *New York Times on the Web*, August 9, 2001. http://www.nytimes.com/2001/08/09/technology/10CYBERLAW.html

Limitations on liability relating to material online. 17 U.S.C.S. S 512 (2003).

Liptak, Adam. ''Internet Battle Raises Questions About Privacy and the First Amendment.'' *New York Times* June 2, 2003:A13.

Lorek, L.A. ''Companies Entangled by the Web, Internet an Easy Tool for Corporate Critics.'' *Sun-Sentinel* March 3, 1996:WL 2490219.

Lunney v. Prodigy Services Company, 683 N.Y.S.2d 557 (Supreme Court of New York, Appellate Division, Second Department (1998).

Max, Tucker. www.tuckermax.com (Site visited September 16, 2004).

Max, Tucker. ''The Miss Vermont Story.'' http://www-2.cx.cmu.edu/~dst/Katy-Johnson (Site last visited June 13, 2003).

McBride, Sarah. ''Film Industry Vows Crackdown on Online Movie Thieves.'' *Wall Street Journal* November 5, 2004 B1, B3).

Nimmer, Melville & David Nimmer. *Nimmer on Copyright* Vol. 10, App. 5, 9 (Matthew Bender & Co., 2000).

Raytheon v. Does 1-21, Motion to Quash, No. 99-816 (Mass. Super. Ct. Middlesex County, Complaint filed Feb. 1, 1999).

Religious Technical Center v. Netcom On-Line Communication Services, 907 F. Supp. 1361 (N.D. Cal. 1995).

Recording Industry of Association of America, Inc. v. Verizon Internet Services, Inc., No. 03-7015; No. 03-7053, 2004 U.S. App. LEXIS 3563 (U.S. Court of Appeals, D.C. Circuit, filed February 24, 2004).

Salkever, Alex. ''Big Music's Worst Move Yet; The RIAA's Newest Legal Assault on File Swappers is Pushing Them to Encrypted Networks, where the Damage Could Become Catastrophic.'' *Business Week Online* January 27, 2004.

Savage, Ryan. ''E-Commerce: Between a Rock and a Hard Place: Defamation and Internet Service Providers.'' *Aspen Review of International Business and Trade Law* 2 (2002):107-121.

Sabbato v. Hardy and Rudy, 1999 CV 02909; 2000 CA 00136, 2000 Ohio App. LEXIS 6154 (Court of Appeals, Fifth Appellate Division, Stark County, Ohio, 2000).

Sable Communications of California, Inc. v. FCC, 492 U.S. 115, 106 L.Ed. 2d 93, 109 S.Ct. 2829, 16 Media Law Reporter 1951 (1989).

Schruers, Matthew. ''Note: The History and Economics of ISP Liability for Third Party Content.'' *Virginia Law Review* 88 (March 2002): 205-264.

Sterling, Scott. ''International Law of Mystery: Holding Internet Service Providers Liable for Defamation and the Need for a Comprehensive International Solution.'' *Loyola of Los Angeles Entertainment Law Review* 21 (2001): 327-351.

Stratton Oakmont, Inc. v. Prodigy Services Co. 23 Media Law Reporter 1794 (N.Y. Sup. 1995).

United States v. Thomas, 74 F. 3d 701 (6th Cir. 1996).

Universal City Studios et al. V. Eric Corley and 2600 Enterprises, Inc. 273 F.3d 429 (2nd Cir. 2001).

Williams, Alan et al. ''England and Wales.'' In *International Media Liability: Civil Liability in the Information Age,* 107-112. Christian Campbell, editor. (Chichester, New York: Wiley, 1997).

Zeran v. America online, Inc. 129 F. 3d 327 (4th Cir. 1997).

Freedom of Speech in Occupied Nations: What should be the Obligations of an Occupying Power?

Douglas Fraleigh

Freedom of expression issues came to the forefront in Iraq shortly after the collapse of Saddam Hussein's regime. On April 9, 2003, a crowd of Iraqis danced in Baghdad's Firdos Square after U.S. Marines used an armored recovery vehicle to topple a large statue of Saddam Hussein (Cable News Network 2003). This spontaneous celebration did not herald a new era of freedom of speech in Iraq. After seizing control of the only TV station in the city of Mosul, Major General David Petraeus said that "we have every right as an occupying power to stop the broadcast of something that will incite violence." The U.S. civilian administrator in Iraq, Paul Bremer, promulgated a list of prohibited categories of expression (Jayasekera 2003a).

Restrictions on expression imposed by occupying powers are not limited to the United States' policies in Iraq. After a NATO force entered Bosnia to enforce the 1995 Dayton Peace Accords, an Independent Media Commission was established to regulate the Bosnian media. The UN administration in Kosovo promulgated restrictions on the print and broadcast media there after UN troops moved in to enforce the peace settlement between NATO and Yugoslavia in 1999.

The twenty-first century is likely to be characterized by an increase in military occupations led by the United States or international organizations that include the United States. In the aftermath of September 11, 2001, the U.S. has announced a new National Security Strategy that includes preemptive war as a means to prevent terrorist attacks (National Security Strategy 2002 6) and also a determination to promote "free and open societies on every continent" (p. 1).

Furthermore, the historical constraints on military intervention by the UN or NATO have diminished. The international regulation of Iraq after the 1991 Gulf War "was seen as a legal precedent for universal human rights-based intervention," leading to UN-authorized actions in Somalia and Bosnia (Chandler 2002, 8-9). The *Report of the Panel on United Nations Peace Operations* (2000) stated that during the Cold War United Nations peacekeeping operations usually focused on monitoring cease-fires, rather than actively building the peace. However, "since the end of the Cold War, United Nations peacekeeping has often combined with peace-building in complex peace operations . . . " (p. 3). Peace building includes reintegrating former combatants into civilian society, improving respect for human rights, and technical assistance for democratic development, including electoral assistance and support for free media (p. 3).

This propensity for military intervention and subsequent occupation makes increasingly salient the question of whether freedom of expression rights ought to be guaranteed to the citizens of an occupied nation.

This article will defend the position that freedom of expression should be guaranteed by an occupying power, particularly when the motivation for occupation includes the protection of human rights and the establishment of self-government. The first section of this article will summarize the freedom of speech issues raised by three major recent occupations: the U.S.-led occupation of Iraq, the NATO occupation of Bosnia, and the UN occupation of Kosovo. Next, the reasons why occupying powers should provide for freedom of expression will be developed, and finally, typical justifications for occupying power censorship will be analyzed and critiqued.

Occupying Power Restrictions on Expression

Freedom of expression issues have been particularly significant in three recent occupations by the U.S. and its allies in Iraq and by NATO forces (authorized by the United Nations) in Bosnia and Kosovo.

Control of Expression in Iraq

The U.S. and its allies have influenced expression in Iraq through direct controls and also by U.S. control of its own media network in Iraq. Freedom of expression issues are also implicated when coalition forces respond to outbreaks of violence during demonstrations in Iraq. *Controls on the Content of Expression.*

The U.S. Civilian Administrator in Iraq, Paul Bremer, promulgated a nine point list of Prohibited Activities. These include:

> ''Incitement to racial, ethnic, or religious hatred, advocating support for the banned pre-war Ba'ath party, and publishing material that is 'patently false and is calculated to provoke opposition to the Coalition Provisional Authority or undermine legitimate processes towards self-government' '' (Jayasekera 2003a).

Bremer also required all Iraqi media to be registered and noted that media outlets that break the rules will have their licenses revoked and their equipment confiscated. Individual violators may be prosecuted and sentenced to one year in prison and a $1,000 fine. The only appeal is to Bremer, whose decision is final (Jayasekera 2003a).

Iraqi media outlets have been sanctioned when the content of their messages was objectionable to leaders of the occupation. In Mosul, Major General David Petraeus, commanding officer of the 101st Airborne Division, seized editorial control over the city's only TV station, contending the station broadcast ''predominantly non-factual/unbalanced news coverage'' (Zerbisias 2003). The station had aired Al-Jazeera's coverage of a letter allegedly written by Saddam Hussein calling for Iraqis to rise up against the invaders. Another newspaper, Al Mustaqila, was shut down for publishing the statement ''Death to all spies and those who cooperate with the U.S.'' (Oppel 2003). Furthermore, the Iraqi Governing Council acted with the approval of the Bush administration and shut down the Baghdad office of Dubai-based Al-Arabiya (''Losing the Media War'' 2003). On November 16, 2003, Al-Arabiya had broadcast an audio tape purportedly made by Saddam Hussein. The message called on Iraqis to fight foreign soldiers as a patriotic duty (Deans 2003).

United States Controlled Media in Iraq

In addition to regulating the Iraqi media, the U.S. has funded the Iraqi media network (IMN). This network is under the authority of Chief Civilian Administrator Bremer, and it has taken control of the property of the pre-war ministry of information. The IMN is reclaiming old government equipment from local media that sprung up after the fall of Hussein (Jayasekera 2003b). According to Stephen Claypole, a veteran newspaper adviser who had worked for the U.S. and Britain, the IMN ''was the stuff of dreams for the White House and No. 10 [Downing Street]—direct control over the content of the evening news'' (Byrne 2003). Changes have been required by coalition leaders. IMN managers ''were told to drop the readings from the Koran, the 'vox-pop' [person] in the street interviews (usually critical of the US invasion) and even to run the content past the wife of a US-friendly Iraqi Kurdish leader'' (Jayasekera 2003a). Although station managers initially rejected these demands, IMN was transformed. Paul Bremer reserved the right to advise the IMN on any matter of content, and retained the power to hire and fire IMN employees. The end result is that "the man in absolute authority over the country's largest, richest and best equipped media network is also his own regulator and regulator of his rivals" (Jayasekera 2003a).

Outbreaks of Violence During Demonstrations

The shooting deaths of Iraqi citizens during protests have raised other freedom of speech issues. For example, on April 28 in the town of al-Falluja, between 100-250 Iraqis participated in a demonstration, shouting slogans such as "God is great!" and "No to Saddam! No to the U.S." When the demonstration reached a local school, shooting broke out. Exact casualty numbers are in dispute, but according to different sources between ten and seventeen Iraqis were killed and a larger number were wounded (Human Rights Watch 2003 "Violent Response").

The protesters claimed that U.S. soldiers fired on them without provocation, whereas the U.S. military maintained that persons in the crowd were shooting at American soldiers, and that U.S. forces responded to them with precision fire (Human Rights Watch 2003 "Violent Response"). A Human Rights Watch investigation did not find bullet damage to support the claim that U.S. forces had come under fire first, and the impact pattern of U.S. bullets did not seem limited to a precise response. U.S. commanders contended that there were provocateurs in the crowd, perhaps paid by the Ba'ath party to shoot at U.S. troops. Human Rights Watch concluded that this scenario was possible (Human Rights Watch 2003 "Violent Response").

On April 30, a demonstration protesting the U.S. presence in Iraq and the shootings of April 28 took place in front of the U.S. Army's primary base in al-Falluja. During the protest, a U.S. convoy rolled past. Some of the demonstrators threw rocks at the convoy, breaking a window in the lead vehicle and hitting one soldier in the head and knocking another's tooth out. U.S. military leaders argued that persons in the crowd had also fired on the crowd, whereas the participants argued that they had no weapons. The lead vehicle fired a warning shot and then the trail vehicle fired at the crowd with a machinegun. Three Iraqis died and sixteen were wounded (Human Rights Watch 2003).

There have been other incidents of violence during demonstrations in Iraq. For example, nine Iraqis died and twenty-nine were wounded in Mosul while shooting guns into the air to celebrate Saddam Hussein's birthday. A majority died at the hands of the celebrants' gunfire, but some Iraqis were shot by U.S. troops who perceived that the celebratory gunfire was an attack (Fisher 2003).

Control of Expression in Bosnia

In the early 1990s, Bosnia was plagued by intense conflict after a majority voted for Bosnia to become an independent republic. Many Bosnian Serbs opposed independence and their forces seized substantial territory and carried out a campaign of ethnic cleansing against Bosnian Muslims, that nation's largest ethnic group. The Dayton Peace Agreement in 1995 led to a cessation of hostilities between Serb, Croat, and Bosnian factions in Bosnia (Hanson 2001). Under the accords, a NATO force would enforce the peace settlement (Chandler 2002), and the Organisation for Security and Cooperation in Europe (OSCE) would organize elections that would be supervised by the United Nations (Price 2000). Bosnian Serb media sources were highly critical of many developments that occurred in the aftermath of the Dayton Accords, and their partisan rhetoric was answered with restrictions on expression.

Controversial Expression in Bosnia

Bosnian Serbs spoke out against political candidates who were preferred by the West. For example, during a key election in the summer of 1997, Bosnian Serb-controlled SRT (Serb Radio and Television) criticized Biljana Plavsic, a presidential candidate who was favored by the international community. SRT contended that she was a "traitor to the Serb nation" and "a pawn of the international community" (Price 2000).

The Bosnian Serb media also aired critical and potentially incendiary statements about NATO troops in Bosnia. After Serb Radio and Television refused a request to inform its listeners about an international agreement intended to create a more pluralistic media, it went on to compare the NATO force to the Nazis, and alternated images of NATO soldiers and German Storm troopers (Price 2000). During a time when U.S. troops were being harassed by stone-throwing crowds, Serb radio encouraged the populace to "fight against the occupiers" and "kick out the [international supervisor]" (Thompson and De Luce 2002).

Serb criticism of war crime prosecutions was another contentious issue. Serb Radio and Television responded to a press conference by the chief prosecutor of the International Criminal Tribunal for the Former Yugoslavia, Louise Arbour, by claiming that the Tribunal "was a political instrument and prejudiced against the Serbs" (Thompson and De Luce 2002). The broadcast also referred to two indicted war criminals as heroes.

Controls on Expression in Bosnia

After the Bosnian Serb criticism of the war crimes tribunal, the UN and the International Tribunal required SRT to broadcast a public apology along with the full press conference by Louise Arbour. The broadcast was accompanied by an introduction written by the war crimes tribunal (Thompson and De Luce 2002).

NATO troops also took control of four key Bosnian Serb television transmitters on October 1, 1997, because of "broadcasts considered hostile to the 1995 Dayton Peace Accord" (Cable News Network Interactive 1997). NATO Secretary General Javier Solana decided that SRT was obstructing the peace process through its criticism of the War Crimes Tribunal and its support for Radovan Karadzic, a former Bosnian Serb leader who was wanted by the tribunal to stand trial for alleged atrocities committed during the Bosnian war (CNN Interactive 1997).

To provide a more systematic method of regulating expression in Bosnia, an Independent Media Commission was established. The Commission established standards for program content, including a ban on material that incited ethnic or religious hatred and a rule requiring conformity to community standards of decency and civility. The media could not promote the interests of a single political party and there was a right to reply to a broadcast which "unjustly places a person in an unfavourable light" (Price 2000). The Commission's divisions would monitor the media and investigate complaints, license broadcasters, and impose sanctions when appropriate. The sanctioning tribunal could require apologies, prohibit rebroadcasting of an offending program, and impose financial penalties.

Control of Expression in Kosovo

In 1998-99, fighting between the ethnic Albanian majority in Kosovo intensified (a province in the territory of Yugoslavia) and the Yugoslavian government headed by Slobodan Milosevi. Kosovo Albanians strongly supported separation from Yugoslavia and Milosevic's response was an increasingly violent campaign against the Albanians. NATO leaders asked Milosevic to voluntarily accept their terms to settle the conflict. When the Serbian president refused, NATO launched a bombing campaign against Yugoslavia. After seventy-eight days, Milosevic relented and accepted a peace settlement (Mertus and Thompson 2002). The agreement between the United Nations, NATO, and Yugoslavia provided for a UN Interim Administration Mission in Kosovo (UNMIK), and a UN Kosovo Force (KFOR) moved into Kosovo. UNMIK was to provide transitional administration and facilitate the development of democratic self-government (Herring 2001).

Following the settlement, controversial statements were expressed in the ethnic-Albanian media in Kosovo. Some media sources began publishing the names of Serbs who they believed had committed war crimes in Kosovo, along with their home addresses and work places (Sullivan 2000). After an American representative from Human Rights Watch issued a report condemning Albanian revenge attacks against the Serbs, the anti-Serbian newspaper *Bota Sot* printed an article stating that the representative was gay. The newspaper accused another journalist and human rights advocate of being a Russian spy (Sullivan 2000).

In response to what they considered a ''deteriorating situation'' (Mertus and Thompson 2002), UNMIK promulgated several restrictions on expression in Kosovo. Regulation 2000/4 prohibited ''inciting national, racial, religious or ethnic hatred, discord, or intolerance'' (OSCE 2000). This restriction provided for five year prison terms for violations, and terms of up to ten years for persons who took advantage of their position (as politicians, community leaders, journalists, publishers, and teachers) while committing these acts. A Code of Conduct for the broadcast media was also created (Temporary Media Commissioner September 8). This code placed a variety of restrictions on broadcast communication, including:

1. A requirement that all programming meet generally accepted international standards of civility.
2. A ban on broadcasting any material that encourages crime or criminal activities, denigrates an ethnic or religious group, any material that attributes criminal responsibility to any individual prior to a finding of guilt by a lawful tribunal, and any material before undertaking a prudent and reasonable inquiry to ensure the veracity of the material.
3. A requirement that broadcasters will strive to ensure accuracy, fairness, and impartiality in all reporting.
4. A requirement that broadcasters extend a right to reply when they have broadcast material that places a person, group, or institution in an unfavorable light, when fairness and impartiality require it.

A similar Code of Conduct, 2000/37, was promulgated for the print media (Temporary Media Commissioner 2000, June 17). A Media Appeals Board was given the power to modify, uphold, or rescind decisions made by the Temporary Media Commissioner pursuant to the media and broadcast codes of conduct.

The newspaper, *Dita,* was prosecuted for violating the media regulations. An article in Dita had claimed that Petar Topoljski (a Serb who worked for the U.N. in Kosovo) was a paramilitary thug who took part in the beating, robbing, and expulsion of ethnic Albanians the previous year. Eleven days later, Topoljski disappeared. His body was found on a secluded riverbank—he had been stabbed in the chest and his throat had been cut. (Mertens 2000). Another article in *Dita* was titled ''Crimes and Criminals Have Names: They Live Undisturbed.'' The article included photographs, names, and addresses of two persons (described as Orthodox priests), along with the allegation that they had participated in crimes. Two days later, two Orthodox priests (one who worked in a place mentioned in the article) were shot and hospitalized (*Beqaj v. Temporary Media Commissioner* 2000).

The UN Mission in Kosovo shut down *Dita* for eight days (Reeker 2000) and the Temporary Media Commissioner imposed a fine of DEM 25,000 for publishing the ''Crimes and Criminals Have Names'' article. *Dita* appealed the decision to the Media Appeals Board in Kosovo, which held that the article was prohibited (because it published personal details that posed a serious threat to life and safety) and that UNMIK Regulation 2000/37 did not restrict political speech on matters of public interest. The Media Appeals Board did find that the procedures followed created an "appearance of arbitrary decision making" and remanded the case for redetermination (*Beqaj v. Temporary Media Commissioner* 2000).

The actions by the occupying powers in Kosovo, Bosnia, and Iraq illustrate how freedom of speech is restricted through ad hoc decisions and more formal regulations. Although censorship by occupying powers is a typical practice, it is questionable whether these restrictions are always in the best interest of the citizens of the occupied nation or the broader world community.

Freedom of Expression is Important in Occupied Nations

Freedom of expression ought to be guaranteed to persons living in occupied nations and such freedom is particularly important when the intervention is justified on humanitarian grounds. If a goal of an intervention is to liberate the occupied nation from civil war or a repressive regime, and to ease the transition to democratic self-government, freedom of expression is imperative.

Occupying Power Restrictions Will Have a Substantial Chilling Effect

Occupying power restrictions threaten a wide range of expression. The doctrines of vagueness and overbreadth are premised "upon the danger of tolerating, in the area of First Amendment freedoms, the existence of a penal statute susceptible of sweeping and improper application" (*NAACP v. Button* 1963). A law regulating speech will be deemed overbroad "if it sweeps within its ambit a substantial amount of protected speech along with that which it may legitimately regulate" (*Doe v. University of Michigan* 1989). Furthermore, a statute is unconstitutionally vague when persons "of common intelligence must necessarily guess at its meaning" (*Doe v. University of Michigan*).

The broad, imprecise language that has been used to define prohibited speech in occupied nations meets the criteria for vagueness and overbreadth. For example, the Code of Conduct for Broadcast Media in Kosovo requires broadcasters to insure accuracy, fairness, and impartiality, and prohibits denigration of any ethnic group. The Independent Media Commission in Bosnia requires conformity to community standards of decency and civility and expects that the media will not promote the interests of a single political party. In Iraq, broadcasters may not transmit information that is "patently false" or calculated to provoke opposition to the coalition provisional authority. The terms in these regulations are highly subjective and could be used by an occupying power to ban almost any speech that it finds objectionable.

The vague and subjective nature of these restrictions is particularly troubling due to the penalties that may be imposed. The consequences include fines, loss of a broadcasting license, seizure of broadcasting technology, and imprisonment (one year in Iraq and five years or more in Kosovo). Such severe penalties will create a chilling effect. As the U.S. Supreme Court noted in *Reno v. ACLU* (1997), "the severity of criminal penalties may well cause speakers to remain silent rather than communicate even arguably unlawful words, ideas and images."

It is unrealistic to assume that the leadership of an occupying power will err on the side of freedom of speech when implementing these regulations. An occupying power is not a benevolent dictatorship. It will have substantial incentives to manage the information that comes out of an occupied country. First, the leaders of the occupation have their own images to protect. Occupiers will manage the news in a way that makes their occupation look good. Secondly, the leaders of the occupation must answer to political leaders back home. The civilian leadership will want the world to hear that the occupation is going well and most of the local citizens are happy.

Political leaders may need good news on the war front to make up for troubles at home. For example, shortly after the impeachment trial in the Senate, Bill Clinton turned his attention to Kosovo. "Clinton's focus on an international issue was perhaps not surprising, he has had several successes in that arena during the past 13 months while the Lewinsky scandal unfolded" (Lawmakers Pick Up Pieces 1999). George W. Bush began the invasion of Iraq during a time when he was under criticism for a slow economic recovery and a growing budget deficit. Political analyst Bill Schneider (2003) noted "in 2004, the U.S. will still be in Iraq, maybe even running the country. Is that good for Republicans? It is if things are going well. But if Americans find themselves under attack, they might ask 'What are we still doing in Iraq?' " In a high-stakes political environment it will be difficult for any occupying power, no matter how well-intentioned, to be objective.

Broad, general regulations, enforced by criminal sanctions, will discourage citizens of an occupied nation from voicing their viewpoint. These constraints on expression have a variety of undesirable consequences.

Occupying Power Restrictions Have Unfavorable Results

Restrictions on Expression are Dehumanizing

If an intervention is carried out on behalf of the citizens of the occupied nation, respecting the rights of those citizens is necessary. When an occupying power controls expression in the territory that it occupies, it limits the humanity of the persons it controls. The right to self-expression is inherent in any political system which respects individual dignity (*Guglielmi v. Spelling-Goldberg Production* 1979, Bird, C.J., concurring).

The citizens of an occupied nation will have strong feelings about their circumstances. Some persons are likely to have experienced severe injustices and deprivations under the previous regime, particularly a totalitarian one. They will want to share their hopes and aspirations for the future and may have strong feelings about the appropriate future direction of their nation. While they may appreciate the occupier's removal of an unjust regime, they may also feel frustrated by their inability to remove the regime themselves. The residents of an occupied nation may feel shortchanged by the occupying power or wonder when the troops will be going home. Some citizens are likely to have strong reactions to events during the occupation and to want to voice their responses.

It is dehumanizing to deny the citizens of an occupied nation the ability to express such sentiments. This dehumanization has been characterized by a variety of unflattering terms. The International Crisis Group (1999), a non-governmental organization that advocates international conflict resolution, noted that the international powers should "work harder to treat Kosovars less like *errant children* in want of firm parenting and more like the self-respecting, accountable citizens on whose behalf it has been asked to serve." Roberts (1990) argues that by keeping the inhabitants of occupied territory in a separate legal category, denying them normal political activity, they become *second-class citizens*, and the occupation becomes more akin to *colonialism*. Erlanger (1999) also refers to a "colonialist mentality" in which "foreigners impose their standards and codes of conduct on journalists in Kosovo when there was a perfectly adequate independent Albanian-language press before the war."

Restrictions on Expression Inhibit the Consent of the Governed

If the people of a nation are to determine their own future, rather than having it imposed by an occupying power, they need to be able to express their viewpoint on the directions that their country should take.The assurance of free expression rights once an occupier takes power is particularly important when a justification for military action was to liberate an oppressed people. The moral basis for such an intervention is to take power from a totalitarian regime and return that power to the citizens of the occupied nation. Yet ''there is no mechanism to make the actions of the world's most powerful states accountable to the citizens of the states they choose to intervene in'' (Chandler 2002 72). When the establishment of political institutions is delayed, the citizens of an occupied nation are in ''political limbo,'' neither offered citizenship by the occupying state nor entitled to exercise other political rights. This situation can be compared with apartheid (Roberts 1990 52).

The citizens of an occupied nation do not have a right to vote for the political leaders of the nations that occupy their country and dictate the conditions of the occupation. Freedom of expression provides these citizens with a potential remedy to this lack of power. By expressing their attitudes about the occupation to key target audiences (such as the military and political leaders of the occupying nation, the voters of the occupying nation, and citizens and leaders in other nations who may support their cause), the people whose territory is occupied may be able to facilitate desired changes in the policies of the occupier.

Restrictions on Expression Inhibit the Search for Truths

Contemporary First Amendment jurisprudence in the United States is significantly influenced by Justice Holmes' dictum that ''the ultimate good desired is better reached by free trade in ideas,—that the best test of truth is the power of the thought to get itself accepted in competition of the market'' (*Abrams v. U.S.,* 1919, Holmes, J., dissenting). This premise is important to resolving factual and value questions relating to occupied nations.

Occupying powers do not have a monopoly on the truths concerning factual issues that arise during the occupation. When the citizens of an occupied nation are denied free expression, relevant perspectives cannot be voiced. For example, when describing individual incidents (such as the shootings that occurred during the protests at al-Fallujah), different witnesses will have differing perceptions of the events. They may or may not believe that they have been given the opportunity to tell their story. If they believe that injustices were committed and not properly rectified, they may wish to try to take their case to the world community. If these viewpoints can be suppressed, a truthful resolution of the issue is less likely.

Free expression is also required to resolve factual questions concerning the time period prior to the occupation. In places such as Rwanda, East Timor, Bosnia, Kosovo, and Iraq, there were extensive human rights violations prior to any international intervention. Citizens of these societies who experienced these abuses first hand will have information about accused violators that the occupying powers could not know. The occupying power may not aggressively pursue such violations due to political considerations or financial constraints. For example, in Bosnia, a frequently heard charge was that some of the most notorious war criminals remained at large. It was also argued that occupying forces were not actively pursuing indicted war criminals who should be brought to trial at The Hague (Hanson 2001 92-93). To ban or chill allegations of war crimes (or lax prosecution of war crimes) may prevent the truth from coming to light. Unless the accusations constitute an incitement to imminent violence, they should not be prohibited.

Freedom of expression is also imperative when resolving value questions raised by an occupation. An occupying power is hardly a neutral evaluator of its own motives and policies. The citizens of the occupied nation may wish to challenge the occupying power's self-assessment of its policies. If they are denied a voice, alternative perspectives will be excluded from the dialog about the occupation. For example, it has been argued that the Dayton Peacc Accords in Bosnia were motivated more by the U.S. government's desire to strengthen the NATO alliance and American leadership than by "the need to promote unity and democracy within the multiethnic state of Bosnia" (Hanson 2001 95). It is debatable whether the U.S. and its allies have acted as quickly as possible to restore essential services in Iraq and whether the U.S. is motivated primarily by a desire to bring freedom to the Iraqi people or to achieve other objectives (such as preserving access to oil or installing a pro-American government). United Nations policies during the transition to self-government in East Timor are also open to question. There, the leading political group was denied office space in the capital city and there were "daily protests at the UN's high-handed rule over the territory" (Chandler 2002 204).

The people affected by the occupation should be able to speak their mind on the policies that are being implemented in their name, without fear of being sanctioned. As the Supreme Court noted in *New York Times v. Sullivan* (1964), "debate on public issues should be uninhibited, robust, and wide-open" and it may include "vehement, caustic, and sometimes unpleasantly sharp attacks on government." When an Iraqi is highly critical of the occupying forces during a "person on the street" interview or Bosnian Serbs claim that NATO forces are like Nazis, these comments are similar to the strident political rhetoric that one hears during election campaigns in Western democracies.

Another group of stakeholders who need access to all relevant information about an occupation are the voters in the nations that are occupying other countries. These individuals also have a right to know the perspectives of the people in the occupied countries. The governments that are engaged in an occupation have a political incentive to report that the citizens of the occupied nation are very supportive of the occupation. If the people whose countries are occupied do not have the freedom to voice their criticisms of the occupier, the voters back home in occupying nations will lose an important source of information needed to evaluate whether their own government is telling them the truth.

Restrictions on Expression Inhibit the Transition to Self-Government

Freedom of expression is at the core of democratic decision-making whether it is in the United States or abroad. A free, independent media is "a crucial step towards the reconstruction of democratic institutions immediately after the conflict has ended" (UNESCO 2000).

Censorship is said to be necessary in the short-run in order to create more favorable conditions for self-rule in the long-run. Thus, occupying powers have excluded disfavored groups and ideas from the marketplace of ideas. For example, support for the Ba'ath Party was not permitted in post-war Iraq. Defense Secretary Donald Rumsfeld also pointed out that even if a majority of Iraqis voted for an Islamic Republic, the U.S. would not accept an Islamic regime (Ramonet 2003). In Bosnia, after nationalist parties prevailed in the 1996 elections, High Representative Carl Bildt and the Western governments concluded that candidates who supported the Dayton Accords had no chance to prevail in a hostile media environment. Therefore, Bildt sought the authority to reform the indigenous media networks and take action against inflammatory reports (Thompson and De Luce 2002 207-08). The occupying powers later took control of Bosnian Serb radio stations.

Far from creating a stable democracy, censorship inhibits the development of a lasting, peaceful, system of self government in the occupied nation. The risks associated with giving *control* of the post-occupation government to any single faction should not be conflated with the merits of denying any faction the freedom to *participate* in the debate about the nature of the post-occupation government. The disfavored interests in occupied societies are unlikely to respond to censorship by forgetting their grievances and embracing political candidates and perspectives that are acceptable to the occupying power. Shutting the disfavored factions' perspectives out of the marketplace of ideas will not make them go away. They must be expressed and be seriously considered along with other ideas about the occupied society's political future if a viable system of government is to be achieved.

All of the major interests in a society must have the opportunity to debate and negotiate their political future. Chandler (2002) argues that when consensus is imposed, rather than negotiated by the stakeholders, neither the majority nor the minority has an incentive to reach a solution that could be viable in the long run. He argues that in East Timor, Bosnia, and Kosovo, the political sphere has been colonized by external regulation with negative consequences for any self-sustaining solution. In Afghanistan, any successor government to the Taliban must have the support of factions constituting the Northern Alliance and also the Pushtun, constituting about half the population and living to the south (''Afghanistan after the Taliban'' 2001). When expression is limited, it impairs the successful transition to self-government. The long-term success of any system of government implemented by an occupying power depends on the support of the citizens of the occupied nation. If citizens cannot show their support or voice their grievances regarding the direction that democratization of their country is taking, it will not be known whether they have ''bought in'' to the process. If they have not, disfavored factions are likely to work to subvert the system once the occupier has left.

If a new government is established in an environment where the public sphere is regulated by foreign powers, the new government may be perceived as a puppet of the occupiers by those who have been excluded from that public sphere. Such a government would lack the credibility that is necessary to establish a new political system. For example, if a new leader is seen as a ''tool of American interests,'' support for that leader is likely to evaporate (''After the Taliban'' 2001). This consideration would be particularly important in a situation where significant numbers of citizens may not trust the occupying power's motives.

Past U.S. involvement in Iran shows the perils of superpower attempts to force a government on another nation. As then-U.S. Secretary of State Madeline Albright noted, ''in 1953, the U.S. played a significant role in orchestrating the overthrow of Iran's popular prime minister, Mohammad Mossadegh'' (Kinzer 2003 212). This paved the way for dictatorial rule by the Shah of Iran for twenty-six years. Historian James Bill noted that the American policy ''deeply alienated Iranian patriots of all social classes and weakened the moderate, liberal nationalists'' (Kinzer 2003 212). Kinzer notes that ''from the seething streets of Tehran and other Islamic capitals to the scenes of terror attacks around the world, Operation Ajax (the 1953 CIA sponsored coup) has left a haunting and terrible legacy'' (p. 215).

Reservations About Freedom of Expression in Occupied Nations

It has been argued that individual rights such as freedom of expression are uniquely western values and that it would be ethnocentric to impose such a value on the citizens of an occupied nation. It has also been argued that restrictions on expression are necessary in occupied nations as a means to prevent violence. These reservations will be addressed here.

Are Guarantees of Freedom of Expression Ethnocentric?

The primacy of personal freedom has been characterized as a western value (Kausikan 1998 22-23). For example, the Beijing government's 1991 White Paper, 'Human Rights in China' contended that social turmoil might pose a threat to the people's most important right, the right to subsistence. This perspective implies that ''the state has a moral responsibility to curtail individual freedoms and political participation in the name of the higher good of the community'' (Dunne and Wheeler 1999 13).

Galtung (1998) distinguishes between "I-cultures" and "we-cultures." I-cultures emphasize the individual, who should be free to make decisions without submitting to the compulsion of society. On the other hand, in we cultures, individuals are situated in a "web of social relations." Solidarity with the "we" is typical and ego-assertiveness is rare (p. 220). Galtung notes that human rights laws come from western law and I-culture. He notes that to a Muslim true believer, Salman Rushdie's book, *The Satanic Verses*, constitutes a sacrilege against one of the key symbols of a we-culture. Thus, Islamic leaders declared a fatwa, "mobilizing the faithful to come to the rescue of the faith, the cement of that culture" (p. 221). This response is diametrically opposed to the protection afforded to controversial expression that violates majority norms in an I-culture.

The imposition of free expression by an occupying power could be classified as cultural hegemony. Evans (1998) argues that imposing the human rights that are favored by the West is motivated by the "preservation of self interest and the perpetuation of dominance" (citing Muzaffar 1995) "rather than a real concern to create the conditions for human dignity" (p. 18).

Regardless of one's perspective on the issue of whether freedom of expression should be a universal human right, there can be no justification for censorship *by an occupying power*. An occupying power exacerbates the problems of cultural hegemony that are inherent in any occupation when it decrees what expression is permissible. Limits on expression will be imposed based on the occupying power's self-interest, not on an altruistic desire to preserve the cultural norms of the occupied people. The regulations in Iraq, Bosnia, and Kosovo do not include a criterion such as "violation of cultural norms" as a basis for sanctioning expression. At best, the restrictions address speech that might incite violence, at worst, they forbid criticism of the occupying powers and their policies.

Freedom from restrictions on expression by an occupying power is needed if the occupied population is to develop a self-governing society that is consistent with its cultural values. If an occupying power can limit discourse about the appropriate form of government, or censor criticism of the form of government preferred by the occupier, that is cultural hegemony.

The thesis that an occupying power should guarantee freedom of expression during the occupation, is distinct from the issue of whether the occupying power should mandate the type of government that is permissible after the occupation ends. If it is hoped that the occupied nation will embrace the values of a liberal, western-style democracy, censorship during the occupation is an unlikely means of creating an affinity for a human-rights respecting democratic government. The occupying power commits a performative contradiction when it denies free speech rights during the time of its rule, but insists that the newly-formed government must respect individual rights. It is doubtful that the people of an occupied nation will embrace the protection of individual rights because the occupier forces them to accept these values without question. An illusory consensus may be created if a democratic government is mandated and anyone who disagrees is excluded from the public sphere. However, this government will not have the legitimacy to govern once the occupying troops have withdrawn. Conversely, according to Egyptian democracy advocate Saad Eddin Ibrahim, "Islamic militants are tamable through accommodative politics of inclusion. Running for office, or once in it, they recognize the complexities of the real world and the need for gradualism and toleration" (Chua 2003 277).

If the people of the occupied nation are free to discuss and debate the merits of a liberal democracy, and compare it to alternative proposals, then it is possible that the citizens will come to support a human-rights based form of self-government on their own volition. Referring to free local elections in Iraq, Yale Law Professors Amy Chua and Jed Rubenfeld (2004) note:

> "To be sure, some Iraqi towns might elect fundamentalist clerics as their lawmakers. The coalition must not try to suppress such results. Let the Iraqis see their decisions respected. Let them see some towns where fundamentalism reigns and some where it does not. The hopes of a democratic Middle East may depend on it" (p. 23).

Are Restrictions on Expression Necessary to Prevent Violence?

Advocates of restrictions on expression by occupying powers contend that the freedom of expression enjoyed by U.S. citizens is unrealistic in a post-conflict environment. For example, Sullivan (2000) argues that:

''Incitement to racial, ethnic, or religious hatred, advocating support for the banned pre-war Ba'ath party, and publishing material that is 'patently false and is calculated to provoke opposition to the Coalition Provisional Authority or undermine legitimate processes towards self-government' '' (Jayasekera 2003a).

Major General David Petraeus, commanding officer of the 101st Airborne Division, made a similar argument with respect to Iraq: ''we have every right as an occupying power to stop the broadcast of something that will incite violence. Yes, what we are looking at is censorship, but you can censor something that is intended to inflame passions'' (Zerbisias 2003).

Broad, open-ended censorship provisions are not the answer to violence in occupied nations. Nor should assemblies and demonstrations be limited on the grounds that violence might break out. Although the existence of ongoing violence in an occupied nation may be a factor in the *application* of free expression principles, it is not a justification for abandoning those principles.

Restricting Advocacy of Violence

One advocacy of violence issue is whether general calls for resistance should be banned. it may be argued that exhortations such as ''fight against the occupiers,'' or ''death to all spies'' need to be regulated in occupied nations because they may cause acts of violence. However, if such words are prohibited, both critical political rhetoric and true threats or incitement to violence will be sanctioned. These two categories of expression need to be distinguished. In the United States, hostile rhetoric that constitutes political hyperbole (''If they make me carry a rifle, the first man I want to get in my sights is LBJ'') or antagonism toward authority figures (''I will eliminate all pigs from the President on down'') rather than a ''true threat'' is protected by the First Amendment (*Watts v. U.S.* 1969, *U.S. v. Fredrickson 1979*). In *Brandenburg v. Ohio* (1969), the Supreme Court held that ''the mere abstract teaching . . . of the moral propriety or even moral necessity for a resort to force and violence is not the same as preparing a group for violent action and steeling it to such action.'' An occupying power should not be able to punish hyperbolic rhetoric unless there is proof of a true threat or incitement to violence.

A second issue has been raised by allegations against specific individuals. These expressions are exemplified by the publication of war crime accusations in Kosovo that were discussed in part 1 of this article. It would be possible to blame the assaults against alleged war criminals in Kosovo on the allegations that were published in the media. This would rely on an effect-to-cause argument that because accusations in the media preceded the assaults, the media accusations caused the assaults. Under the *Brandenburg* standard (expression must be intended to cause imminent lawless action and likely to produce such action), an occupying power might be able to prove that the publisher of these allegations did intend to cause imminent assaults on the alleged war criminals, and that their reports were the cause of the attacks. However, an occupying power should have to prove its case rather than assuming the media are responsible.

The newspaper war crimes accusations may not have been the cause of the attacks in Kosovo. If the journalists discovered the names and addresses of the alleged war criminals from other sources, then that information was already known to other Albanian Kosovars. Those who knew this information could have had the motive and knowledge needed to commit these attacks regardless of what was reported in the media. It is also unlikely that persons would be persuaded by the media reports unless they were already predisposed to commit such an attack. Bailey (1987) argues that it cannot be proven that advocacy caused violence, unless the audience was predisposed towards committing violence. He notes that if the audience is predisposed, it is not possible to separate the speaker's contribution from the audience. The media publication could only be argued to be a cause of the attacks if there were people in the community who were predisposed to commit these crimes, and would not have discovered the location of the alleged war criminals but for the publication of this information.

Restricting Assemblies

Protests are not inherently violent, and death and injury are not necessary outcomes. For example, in Iraq, deaths and injuries did result during the April 28 and 30, 2003 demonstrations at al-Fallujah. However, other assemblies and demonstrations have taken place without violence and casualties. For example, nearly one-half million mourners came to Najaf for the burial of Shia cleric Ayatollah Muhammad Baqr al-Hakim on September 2, 2003. Although the Ayatollah's brother blamed the U.S. for failing to prevent the bombing and called for occupying forces to leave Iraq during his eulogy, the BBC reported that the crowd was calm and somber (BBC News 2003).

If an occupying power is given carte blanche to restrict assemblies because violence may occur, there is a significant opportunity for content discrimination. Some demonstrations are supported by an occupying power. When a column of U.S. Marines advanced into Firdos Square in Baghdad, on April 9, 2003, Iraqis tore down portraits of Saddam Hussein, began throwing shoes (a serious insult in the Arab world) and chipped away at the base of a statue of Hussein before U.S. Marines toppled the statue (Cable News Network 2003). This incident was cited by coalition leaders as proof that the Iraqis supported the U.S. invasion. If the leaders of the occupation can pick and choose which demonstrations to allow, they would have the ability to manage the world's understanding of Iraqi citizens' perspective.

If the forces of the occupying power are properly trained for a policing role, violence during demonstrations can be minimized. Human Rights Watch noted that the 82nd Airborne Division troops placed in al-Fallujah was a combat unit that came straight from battle. They had not been trained in law enforcement, they lacked tear gas or other forms of non-lethal crowd control, and they did not have enough translators to communicate with the community (Human Rights Watch 2003 ''Violent Response''). Article 2 of the United Nations Code of Conduct for Law Enforcement Officials notes that while performing their duties, law enforcement officials must uphold the human rights of all persons. Article 3 provides that law enforcement officials may use force only when strictly necessary and to the extent required for the performance of their duty (Office of the High Commissioner for Human Rights 1979). Lethal force may only be used when strictly unavoidable to protect life (Human Rights Watch 2003 ''Violent Response''). By properly training its forces who will be involved in police duties, both public safety and freedom of expression can be maintained.

When violence between the occupying power and persons at a demonstration occurs, any claims that the occupying power unjustly caused casualties should be open to resolution through an independent judicial process. Protesters who are injured by the police during demonstrations in the U.S. have the opportunity to file lawsuits claiming that their constitutional rights were violated. Persons in the Israeli occupied territories of the West Bank and Gaza have a right to petition the Israeli Supreme Court against arbitrary or illegal acts by the military commander and other authorities (Roberts 1990 88). When a nation is occupied on humanitarian grounds, the case for allowing citizens of the occupied nation to make claims that their freedom of expression was abridged, to the occupying power's judicial system is particularly strong.

Using More Speech as an Alternative to Censorship

Although violence prevention may be the stated goal of limits on expression, such restrictions may actually exacerbate violence. Groups who are excluded from the public sphere will turn back to the ethnic networks they relied on for survival in the past (Chandler 2002 206). The excluded groups are also more likely to resort to violence when they are denied the right to participate. Referring to Afghanistan, Chandler (2002) notes that ''plans to impose a 'friendly' administration, which vets political parties and those the West disapproves of, seem likely to lead to more civil conflict rather than less.''

''More speech'' provides an alternative to censorship as a means to counter groups that are perceived to be dangerous. Media Freedom NGOs (nongovernmental organizations) have even taken the position that media assistance should be part of the humanitarian aid that is given to conflict-ridden societies. Darbishire (2002) notes that ''even in a developed crisis, NGOs prefer to support alternative voices and greater plurality rather than take restrictive measures'' (p. 338). Timely support of democratic development of the media sphere can help prevent the escalation of conflicts (p. 359). At a UNESCO meeting on 'Propaganda Inciting to Commit Genocide in Rwanda,' it was resolved that ''genocide propaganda be countered by supporting or creating independent media, in particular radio, thus permitting the population to be informed in a non-partisan way and allowing voices of tolerance and reason to be heard'' (p. 338).

Conclusion

In the twenty-first century, the new U.S. National Security Strategy and the post-Cold War international political environment will increase the propensity for military interventions and subsequent occupations. The rationale for these interventions, in whole or in part, will be the establishment of democracy and the protection of human rights in the occupied nations.

When one or more nations occupy another country, the occupying powers ought to guarantee freedom of expression. Restrictions on expression dehumanize the occupied population, inhibit the development of a self-governing society, and prevent the search for truths that need to be brought to light as part of the healing process in an occupied nation. Censorship will not achieve its stated objectives of reducing violence and creating the conditions for self-government in an atmosphere of respect for human rights. The citizens of democratic nations have been the beneficiaries of expanding free expression rights during the past century. When their governments take control of other nations, the citizens of the occupied countries deserve the same liberties.

Works Cited

Abrams v. U.S., 250 U.S. 616 (1919) (Holmes, J., dissenting).

Afghanistan After the Taliban. (2001, October 6). *The Economist.*

Bailey, W. (1987). ''The Supreme Court and Communication Theory: Contrasting Models of Speech Efficacy.'' Perspectives *on Freedom of Speech.* Carbondale, IL: Southern Illinois Press.

BBC News.(2003, September 2). ''Thousands bid Cleric Farewell,'' *BBC News UK Edition.* Retrieved October 6, 2003 from the World Wide Web: http://news.bbc.co.uk/1/hi/world/middle east/3200009.stm.

Beqaj v. Temporary Media Commissioner (Kosovo Media Appeals Board, 2000). Retrieved July 20, 2003 from the World Wide Web: http://www.asil.org/ilib/ilib0327.thm

Brandenburg v. Ohio, 395 U.S. 444 (1969).

Byrne, C. (2003, July 9). '' Iraqi TV was Coalitions 'Stuff of Dreams, *Guardian Unlimited.''* Retrieved August 12, 2003 from the World Wide Web: http://media.guardian.co.uk/broadcast/story/0,7493,994192,00.html.

Cable News Network (2003, April 9). ''Saddam Statue Toppled in Central Baghdad.'' Retrieved April 9, 2003 from the World Wide Web: http://www.cnn.com/2003/WORLD/meast/04/09/sprj.irq.statue/index.html

Cable News Network Interactive (1997, October 1). ''NATO Troops Stop Hard-Line Bosnian Serb Broadcasts,'' *World News Story Page.*

Chandler, D. (2002). *From Kosovo to Kabul: Human Rights and International Intervention.* London: Pluto Press.

Chua, A. (2003). *World on Fire: How Exporting Free Market Democracy Breeds Ethnic Hatred and Global Instability.* New York, N.Y.: Doubleday.

Chua, A. & Rubenfeld, J. (2004, January 12-18). ''A Meltdown, Not a Melting Pot.'' *Washington Post National Weekly Edition*, 23.

Darbishire, H. (2002). ''Non-Governmental Perspectives: Media Freedom versus Information Intervention?'' In *Forging Peace: Intervention, Human Rights, and the Management of Media Space* (M.E. Price and M. Thompson, eds.) Indiana University Press, 329-364

Deans, J. (2003, November 25). ''Iraqi Ousting of Arab TV Channel Sparks Freedom Fears.'' *The Guardian.* Retrieved December 12, 2003 from the World Wide Web: http://media.guardian.co.uk/print/ 0,3838,4804858-111303,00.html

Doe v. University of Michigan, 721 F. Supp. 852 (E.D. Mich. 1989).

Dunne, T. & Wheeler, N. J. (1999). *Human Rights in Global Politics* Cambridge, U.K.: Cambridge University Press.

Erlanger, S. (1999, August 16). ''NATO Peacekeepers Plan a System of Controls for the News Media in Kosovo.'' *The New York Times on the Web.* Retrieved July 20, 2003 from the World Wide Web: http://www.freerepublic.com/forum/a37b8769a24.ee.htm.

Evans, T. (1998). ''Introduction: Power, Hegemony and the Universalization of Human Rights.'' In *Human Rights Fifty Years On: A Reappraisal* (T. Evans, ed). Manchester, U.K.: Manchester University Press, 1-23

Fisher, I. (2003, April 30). ''Americans Kill 13 Iraqis at Rally.'' *The Fresno Bee,* A1.

Galtung, J. (1998). ''The Third World and Human Rights in the post-1989 World Order.'' In *Human Rights Fifty Years On: A Reappraisal* (T. Evans, ed.,) (Manchester, U.K.: Manchester University Press, 211-31.

Guglielmi v. Spelling-Goldberg Productions, 25 Cal. 3d 860 (1979) (Bird, C.J., Concurring).

Hanson, M. (2001). ''Warnings from Bosnia: The Dayton Agreement and the Implementation of Human Rights.'' In *The Kosovo Tragedy: The Human Rights Dimensions* (K. Booth, ed). London: Frank Cass, 87-104.

Herring, E. (2001). ''From Rambouillet to the Kosovo Accords: NATO's War Against Serbia and its Aftermath.'' In *The Kosovo Tragedy: The Human Rights Dimensions* (K. Booth, ed.). London: Frank Cass, 225-45.

Human Rights Watch (2003, June). ''Violent Response: The U.S. Army in al-Fallujah,'' 15 *Human Rights Watch* No. 7.

International Crisis Group (1999, December 13). ''Starting from Scratch in Kosovo: The Honeymoon is Over.'' *ICG Balkans Report,* No. 83: 11.

Jayasekera, R. (2003a). ''Gives With One Hand, Takes Away With the Other.'' *Index on Censorship Webpage.* Retrieved June 21, 2003 from the World Wide Web: http://www.indexonline.org/news/20030611 iraq.shtml.

Jayasekera, R. (2003b). ''A Limit to the Demands of Military Security.'' *Index on Censorship Webpage.* Retrieved August 11, 2003 from the World Wide Web: http://www.indexonline.org/news/20030727 iraq.shtml.

Kausikan, B. (1998). ''A Universal Definition of Human Rights Ignores Cultural Diversity.'' In *Human Rights: Opposing Viewpoints* (M.E. Williams, Ed.,). San Diego, Ca.: Greenhaven Press, 21-24

Kinzer, S. (2003). *All the Shah's Men: An American Coup and the Roots of Middle East Terror.* Hoboken, N. J.: John Wiley & Sons.

''Lawmakers Pick Up Pieces After Impeachment Ordeal'' (1999, February 13). *CNN.com/Allpolitics.* Retrieved January 26, 2004 from the World Wide Web: http://www.cnn.com/ALLPOLITICS/stories/1999/02/13/ impeachment.01/index.html.

''Losing the Media War'' (2003, December 8-14). *Washington Post National Weekly Edition,* 24.

Mertens, R. (2000, August 7). ''UN Muzzles 'Vigilante' Press.'' *St. Petersburg Times Online.* Retrieved July 20, 2003 from the World Wide Web: http://www.sptimes.com/News/080700/news pf/Worldandnation/UN muzzles vigilante.

Mertus, J. & Thompson, M. (2002). ''The Learning Curve: Media Development in Kosovo. *In Forging Peace: Intervention, Human Rights, and the Management of Media Space.* (M.E. Price and M. Thompson, eds.). Indiana University Press, 259-86.

Muzzafar, C. (1995). ''From Human Rights to Human Dignity.'' *Bulletin of Concerned Asian Scholars, 27,* 6-8.

NAACP v. Button, 371 U.S. 415 (1963).

The National Security Strategy of the United States of America (2002, September). *New York Times v. Sullivan*, 376 U.S. 254 (1964).

Noto v. U.S., 367 U.S. 290 (1961).

Office of the High Commissioner for Human Rights (1979, December). *Code of Conduct For Law Enforcement Officials.* General Assembly Resolution 34/169.

OSCE (2000, February 9). ''Press Release: Regulation Against Incitement of Hatred is Key for a Democratic Kosovo.'' *OSCE Online.* Retrieved August 25, 2003 from the World Wide Web: http://www.osce.org/news/Generate.php3?-news id=206.

Oppel, Jr., R. (2003, August 6). ''Citizens, Still Wary, are now Overwhelmed.'' *International Herald Tribune Online.* Retrieved August 13, 2003 from the World Wide Web: *http://www.iht.com/articles/105346.html.*

Price, M.E. (2000 May). ''Restructuring the Media in Post-Conflict Societies: Four Perspectives.'' *(COJCR: Online Journal of Conflict Resolution).* Retrieved July 24, 2003 from the World Wide Web: http://archiv.medienhilfe.ch/Reports/cojcr-bih.htm.

Ramonet, I. (2003, May 1). ''Transition to an Empire.'' Le Monde Diplomatique. Retrieved June 13, 2003 from the World Wide Web: http://www.globalpolicy.org/security/issues/iraq/attack/law/2003/0501empire.htm.

Reeker, P. (2000, June 5). ''UN Shuts Temporarily Kosovo Newspaper 'Dita.''' *U.S. Office Pristina Webpage.* Retrieved July 20, 2003 from the World Wide Web: http://www.usoffice.pristina.rpo.at/dita/htm

Reno v. ACLU, 520 U.S. 1113 (1997).

Report of the Panel on United Nations Peace Operations (2000). Document A/55/035. S/2000/809.

Roberts, A. (1990, January). ''Prolonged Military Occupation: The Israeli-Occupied Territories Since 1967.'' *The American Journal of International Law, 84,* 44-103.

Schneider, B. (2003, April 22). ''Analysis: Comparing Post-War Politics in 1992 with 2004.'' *CNN.com./Inside Politics.* Retrieved January 26, 2004 from the World Wide Web: http://www.cnn.com/2003/ALLPOLITICS/ 04/22/war.lessons/indes.html

Sullivan, S. (2000, May). ''The Case Studies: Kosovo.'' In Restructuring the Media in Post-Conflict Societies: Four Perspectives. *COJCR: Online Journal of Conflict Resolution* (M. Price, Ed.) Retrieved July 24, 2003 from the World Wide Web: http://archiv.medienhilfe.ch/Reports/cojcr-bih.htm.

Temporary Media Commissioner (2000, September 8). ''Code of Conduct for the Broadcast Media in Kosovo.'' *OSCE Homepage.* Retrieved August 25, 2003 from the World Wide Web: http://www.osce.org/kosovo/bodies/tmc/bcoc.php3?lg = e.

Temporary Media Commissioner (2000, June 17). ''Temporary Code of Conduct for the Print Media in Kosovo.'' *OSCE Homepage.* Retrieved August 25, 2003 from the World Wide Web: http://www.osce.org/kosovo/bodies/tmc/pcoc.php3?lg = e.

Thompson, M. & De Luce, D. (2002). ''Escalating to Success? The Media Intervention in Bosnia and Herzegovina.'' In *Forging Peace: Intervention, Human Rights, and the Management of Media Space* (M.E. Price and M. Thompson, eds.). Indiana University Press, 200-35.

UNESCO (2000). ''Media in Conflict and Post-Conflict Areas: What Should the Role of the International Community Be?'' *Communication and Democracy Webpage.* Retrieved July 20, 2003 from the World Wide Web: http://www.unesco.org/webworld/wpfd 00/back conflict.html.

U.S. v. Fredrickson, 601 F.2d 1358 (8th Cir.), *cert. den.,* 444 U.S. 934 (1979).

Watts v. U.S., 394 U.S. 705 (1969).

Zerbisias, A. (2003, May 18). ''Iraqi Democracy Means a Free Press.'' *The Toronto Star.*

Galileo and the Aristotelian Cardinals: A Study of Suppression

Craig R. Smith
California State University, Long Beach

In Rome on a very hot August 13th, 1600, Giordano Bruno, a Dominican Friar, was burned at the stake for endorsing Nicholas Copernicus' heliocentric theory and claiming that Christ was not divine. The smoke from the immolation spread a pall over the scientific community. Prior to Bruno's martyrdom, the philosopher Patrizi had been forced to recant his Platonism. The works of Dante, Telesio, Charron, and Campenella were put on the Catholic Church's *Index* of forbidden books. The deluge of attacks on heresy was a reaction to the Protestant reformation; it would swamp Galileo Galilei, and demonstrate how the pope could retard scientific discovery.

This study will proceed in several stages. First, it will provide the historic context to Galileo's trial by following the incorporation of Aristotelian thought into Catholic orthodoxy. Second, it will examine the relationship between church censorship and science by examining the argumentation of Galileo's famous *Dialogue on the Two Chief Systems*, for which he was brought to trial. Third, it will re-evaluate Galileo's sentencing in light of the contextual and argumentative reading of his work.

By the time of Galileo's birth the papacy had re-established its hold over the church, having weathered Martin Luther's revolt. Cardinal Caraffa, who became Paul IV, put a counter-reformation in place. He created the "Holy Office" which took up investigations of church matters in all of the known Catholic world. Caraffa's attack on immorality is credited with re-establishing moral leadership among Catholics, though by this time England had fallen away due to the defection of Henry VIII.

As the war between Catholics and Protestants raged, the popes became more concerned than ever about heresy. The devout Bernardino Ochino, who founded the Capuchin order, refused a call to Rome, fearing for his life, and retreated to Protestant Geneva for safe haven. Followers of Erasmus were silenced and his books put on the Index. After some turmoil (see below), the Dominicans and Franciscans had adopted Aristotle, particularly his method of argumentation, as their guide, after aligning some of his claims with scripture. The incorporation of Aristotle would be important to the story of Galileo since the Franciscans, the Dominicans, and the Jesuits were for the most part devout Aristotelians. Their initial love for Aristotle's *Organon* carried over to his work in the sciences, some of which was badly flawed. Since Galileo's findings would undercut some of Aristotle's scientific claims, he would come into the sites of the Aristotelians in the Catholic Church.

The Rise of Aristotelianism in the Catholic Church

Since Aristotle was considered a pagan, he was not initially embraced by the church. As late as 1300, one could find strong resistance in the Catholic Church to teachings of Aristotle. However, just as Augustine had incorporated Plato and Cicero into church teachings, thereby overturning Tertullian's injunction against them, so too would later church scholars incorporate Aristotle's works. The Christian Boethius translated the *Organon* while serving Theodoric as Master of Offices. He began the "scholastic" tradition of relying on reason to support Biblical interpretations. The monk Abelard relied on Aristotle's *Categories* to refine his argumentation. He was fascinated with Aristotelian dialectic and incorporated it into the *logica modernorum* of the time.(Colish 1997 275). However, Abelard's controversial life style retarded the spread of Aristotelian teachings within the church. In 1179, another hurdle was placed before Aristotelians when in reaction to the Cathar heresy the Third Lateran Council called on the faithful to take up arms against heretics. The Cathars were experts at using Aristotle to defend their positions (Rubenstein 2003). Some in the church were smart enough to realize that they too could use Aristotle in defense of their positions. Pope Innocent III ordered Domingo de Guzman, the founder of the Dominican order, to do battle with the Cathars, and he proved their equal by using their Aristotelian dialectic. Soon all of Aristotle's works that were extant, including those found in the Muslim strongholds of Spain,[1] were being examined in Rome and at the universities of Paris and Bologna, which enjoyed more academic freedom than their counterparts in Byzantium. The *Physics* proved to be one of the most popular with its definition of an "unmoved mover" and its depiction of the earth as the center of the universe. However, it would be an uphill battle for Aristotelians. In 1210 a council of bishops banned Aristotle's works in Paris on penalty of excommunication (Steenberghen 1970). That allowed the University of Padua, founded in 1222, where Galileo would eventually teach, to advertise that it was a place where Aristotle could be studied.

Perhaps the most important reversal in church thinking on the matter occurred in 1231 when Pope Gregory IX restored the right to explore Aristotle's works in Paris under strict supervision. From Paris, Aristotelianism would spread across Europe under the guise of being corrected commentary on the great philosopher. Thomas Aquinas, a Dominican, played no small part in this conversion, arguing through Aristotelian demonstrations that reason came from God and could lead us back to God as the ultimate cause of all creation. As a student of Albert the Great, Aquinas had become familiar with all of Aristotle's major works and attempted to reconcile them with Christian theology. He returned to Paris in 1252 where he met Bonaventure; the two were able to convince the University of Paris to require Aristotelian studies of all undergraduates. Thus, what Augustine was to Platonic thought, Aquinas was to Aristotelian thought. His commentary on Aristotle's *Politics* had been widely circulated by the end of the 13th Century. For our purposes, it is interesting to note that the commentary endorses public participation in government.

Despite a setback in 1270, when once again the Bishop of Paris forbade the teaching of Aristotle, Aquinas' *Summa Contra Gentiles* set a new standard for the use of Aristotelian demonstration in defense of the faith. He also used his logical machine—Aristotle corrected by scripture—to defend his notion of free will. Again, the church balked at issuing the Condemnations of 1277 which listed over 200 Aristotelian statements that were incorrect. Some of these statements came directly from Aristotle's *Physics*.

Despite these injunctions, the Dominicans continued to use Aristotle as the basis of the teaching in their universities. When they secured the canonization of Aquinas in 1323, Aristotelianism was reinforced. The condemnations and bans were rescinded in Paris. Its university sought to catch up with the University of Padua in terms of scholasticism (Rubenstein 237). In the meantime, the Franciscans, relying in part on Duns Scotus and William of Ockham, found their own way to Aristotle (Rubenstein 253). While Aquinas sought to define the role of reason in nature, Scotus and Ockham opened the door to empirical science with their focus on knowable facts, though Ockham had to battle charges of heresy along the way. Like Luther, Ockham needed the protection of a political prince. Once he found him, Ockham's speculations were safe. His story may have caused Galileo to believe that he was protected while under the Medici roof. What Galileo needed to understand, however, was that for most of the two centuries leading up to his discoveries, Aristotelianism dominated the curricula of Europe despite the incessant infighting between Dominicans and Franciscans. He also needed to understand that the Catholic Church had recently been traumatized by the Avignon captivity of the popes and the great schism in the church of 1378 to 1417. From his protected perch, Ockham claimed these popes were heretics. To end the schism, the College of Cardinals deposed all claimants to the papacy and installed Martin V as the new pope. As a result of this turmoil, when the popes returned to Rome they fortified and isolated themselves at Castel Sant' Agnelo. It was during this time that the Vatican area emerged as their private, secure state.

Galileo's Revolution

Several scholars inspired Galileo's scientific investigations. Aristotle's theory had been refuted by Claudius Ptolemy, and then revised by Copernicus when he published *De revolutionibus* in 1543, which he dedicated to Pope Paul III. Paul had condoned the re-activation of the Inquisition in Italy, half a century after the Inquisition had been re-ignited in Spain by Ferdinand and Isabella. In fact, in Italy prosecutions were carried out with even harsher results.[2] With the exception of martyred Giordano Bruno, the Dominicans joined with Franciscans to enforce orthodoxy and prevent compromise with the Protestants. Ignatius Loyola, who founded the Jesuits in 1540, made loyalty to the "Hierarchical Church" its first rule of obedience. The Jesuits, having studied Aquinas, became superb logicians on the front lines of the Counter Reformation. They knew that Luther had condemned Aristotle: "Aristotle is to divinity, as darkness is to light," he had said (Grimm 1957 12). Nothing strengthened Aristotle's position in the Catholic Church more than Luther's condemnation of him and the scholastics that had advanced his theories.

The pope also contributed men to fight for Holy Roman Emperor Charles V in the Thirty Years War, which would create a context for the trial of Galileo. The Council of Trent, which ended in 1563, also played a role in Galileo's trial because the Council reinforced the influence of Aristotelian scholasticism on Church doctrine, making it more rigid than ever. Luther's teachings were condemned; Jerome's *Vulgate* endorsed as the only true Bible. Paul IV, who endorsed the conservatives in his bull *Benedictus Deus*, lectured on what constituted proper art, and revised the *Index of Prohibited Books.*

Into this context was born Galileo Galilei (1564-1642), a renaissance man, who had memorized epic Italian poems while being educated at the University of Pisa near his home town.[3] He entered that university in 1581 to study medicine, but soon shifted his studies to mathematics. He then taught in Florence before returning to the University of Pisa in 1589 as professor of mathematics, where he learned that Tuscany, because of political past, was enmeshed in vitriolic dialectic that carried over into the academic community (Pesic 2002). Nonetheless, he began to study Copernicus and also undercut Aristotle's theory concerning falling objects. Galileo's contract was terminated when he indicated his support for heliocentrism and argued that the earth rotated on an axis. In 1592, the University of Padua, under the control of Venice, hired Galileo. There, he studied Tycho Brache's theories of astronomy. By 1597 he was an avid empiricist and Copernican, a position reinforced by his study of pendulums in 1602 (Galileo 1994).

Galileo's time in Venice is important because that city was much more tolerant of dissent than other city-states. In fact, Venice considered itself a counter-weight to Rome both politically and in terms of religious toleration. This may be why Galileo would set his controversial dialogues in the city of Venice, which had long been a stellar republic surrounded by monarchies. When Venice led the defeat of the Turks at Leponto, the city became more independent of the papacy than ever. Venice claimed that it was the savior of Christendom. Prior to Galileo's arrival in Venice, popes had been hostile to the city because of its independence. In fact, Julius II won a war against Venice and the city-state regularly allied itself with enemies of the popes. Pius V and Gregory XIII were suspicious that the sea-faring Venetians were regularly exposed to heresy. These popes named no cardinals from the city during their tenures. Like other popes, these two made Florence their political favorite. Thus, Galileo's association with Venice may have hurt his reputation with the papacy while instilling a false sense of security about how his theories would be received.

In 1604, an observation would provide Galileo with evidence for an anti-Aristotelian argument. Galileo saw a supernova and began to doubt Aristotle's theory concerning the permanence of the heavens. Galileo raised eyebrows when he wrote a comic dialogue in the vernacular between two peasants who ridiculed Aristotelian science. This argumentative technique was a favorite of the time, (Rubenstein 161), and Galileo would return to it again. The problem was that it tended to harden the hearts of his opponents.

Galileo was familiar with the works of Ludovico Carbone and Antonio Riccobono (Moss & Wallace 2004). The latter provided a new commentary on Aristotle's *Rhetoric*. Carbone wrote on many subjects, but it may have his *On Oratorical and Dialectical Invention* that caught Galileo's attention. Because of the give and take between Protestants and Counter-Reformation forces within the Catholic Church, argumentation enjoyed a resurgence. Along the canals of Venice, publishing houses turned out many of these books. Galileo adopted the style of argumentation used in many of them.

More importantly, Galileo soon supported Copernicus's theory with empirical evidence observed from his newly invented telescope. As the powers of the telescope were increased, Galileo could see ships at sea hours before harbor masters could, and thus, he became a consultant to the Venetian Navy (Galileo). Smartly, he made a gift of his new invention to the Venetian Senate in 1609, and the sea power rewarded him with tenure at Padua. He was an academic success who felt comfortable advancing his controversial thesis.

A year later, Galileo was called home to Tuscany at the request of his former pupil Cosimo de Medici II, who had become Grand Duke. At the University of Pisa, which reported to the Medici, Galileo discovered the isochronism of the pendulum using his own pulse. In September of 1611, he engaged Aristotelians in a debate that was hosted by the Grand Duke and observed by two visiting Cardinals, one of whom was Moffeo Barberini who eventually became Pope Urban VIII. Barberini believed Galileo had won the debate and came to admire the physicist, yet another factor that created a false sense of security in the scientist.[4] It gave him the courage to display his telescope to the papal court, where he was made a member of the Roman Accademia dei Lincei, one of the first learned societies. He was feted by important Cardinals including Barberini. During this visit, Galileo also met with Pope Paul V, who had resisted reform, had further fortified the Vatican, and had excommunicated the entire Venetian senate because it had imposed taxes on church property. Nonetheless, Paul treated Galileo as royalty. Galileo's success led to jealous backbiting on the part of his academic colleagues in Florence and Pisa.

In 1612, Galileo successfully predicted the eclipses of the moons around Jupiter; he then further verified Copernicus' theory using the phases of Venus, based on a tip from Benedetto Castelli.[5] He went on to write a thesis on the center of gravity in solid bodies and to invent a hydrostatic balance theory that correctly revised Archimedes. Galileo's work *Bodies in Water* was published in the vernacular and again challenged Aristotle's physics. Galileo's book prompted Cardinal Carlo Conti to assure Galileo that the Bible did not support Aristotle's physics and astronomy. The book further roiled Galileo's colleagues. Worse, the Dominicans in Florence condemned Copernicus in the same year.

Galileo soon provided his new Medici patron with a treatise on Jupiter called *The Starry Messenger*. Galileo had discovered four moons circling the huge planet. Galileo's observations allowed him to put natural law into mathematical formulas, a procedure that would greatly advance the scientific method and become the basis of modern mechanics. Since Venice was more tolerant of new ideas than either Florence or Rome, the book was published there and eventually found its way into the hands of Johannes Kepler (1571-1630), who would help in the struggle to get Copernicus' theory accepted.

In 1613, when he wrote his treatise on sunspots, he re-confirmed Copernicus' theory. Galileo challenged Aristotle's theory that bodies can remain in motion only if there is some force acting on them; Galileo argued that no such force was necessary once the body was set in motion. This was the primitive notion of inertia that would inspire Isaac Newton, who was born in the year that Galileo died.

These new theories raised so much suspicion and controversy that Galileo felt obligated to write a letter to a pupil who had offended the Grand Duchess Christina of Lorraine by defending Galileo's teaching. In the letter he explained that nothing he wrote or taught was meant to suggest that the scriptures were in error. However, Galileo allowed that the Bible was metaphorical and often adapted to the common wisdom of its time for rhetorical effect. This letter had been widely circulated by the end of 1614. It provides the first indication that Galileo was aware of the possibility that he might be charged with heresy. In Florence, Galileo might have been alerted to certain danger when he was condemned from the pulpit of Santa Maria Novella as a heretic; but church officials quickly apologized for the rants of the Dominican friar who attacked Galileo (Galileo 171). In the meantime, Galileo's letter made its way to an inquisitor. By 1615, Galileo had written an apologia addressed to the Grand Duchess, in which he stated "... the increase of known truths stimulates investigation, establishment, and growth of the arts." (Sobel 1999 67). Galileo used an array of church saints to defend his investigations, an argumentative strategy he would wish he had retained in later life.

Amidst the growing controversy, Galileo traveled to Rome to try to clear his name. While there, he wrote his theory of tides at the Medici villa in 1616, arguing that the rotation of the earth creates a sloshing in the ocean that causes tidal changes. Newton, among others, would correct this theory explaining the gravitational pull of the moon. But at the time, Galileo received a serious warning from the Aristotelian Cardinals surrounding the papacy. He therefore opened a liaison with Pope Paul V through the Medici Cardinal Orsini. The pope convened his counselors to assess Galileo's new theory. The leader of this group was Cardinal Roberto Bellarmino, a conservative Medici, but an admirer of Galileo nonetheless. He brought Galileo the bad news. Heliocentrism was condemned and Galileo was told to only speak about it as a hypothetical theory. Bellarmino put his understanding of the case into a letter to Galileo. It would play an important role in his trial years later.

Matters seemed to go from bad to worse when, on March 5, 1616, Copernicus' work was put on the *Index*. Six days later the pope met with Galileo to receive his apologia. Luckily, Paul V believed Galileo to be sincere and allowed his return to Florence.

In 1618, Galileo was too ill to view the comets that streaked through the skies over Florence. However, a year later, he published his theory of comets through one of his students. He may have done this because the treatise attacked two Jesuit scientists. Galileo's ruse did not work. The priests immediately determined that Galileo had written the paper; they published rebuttals to it. Galileo then responded in his own name. By 1620, this debate had caught the attention of the pope, who wanted assurance that no mention of Copernicus was made. By this time it was clear that Galileo was fond of three types of argumentation to advance his theories. First was empirical evidence out of which he crafted his strongest arguments; second was demonstration in the fashion of Aquinas; third was refutation, often encased in sarcastic dialogues. It was this latter method of arguing that would cause resentment among Galileo's peers, though such diatribes were not uncommon at the time. Thomas Conley has made clear that vituperation was common by Galileo's time, and this too may have given the scientist a false sense of security (Conley 2004).[6 7]

In 1621 Pope Paul V died and so did Cardinal Bellarmino. Thus, those with a first hand knowledge of the agreement with Galileo on Copernicus' theory were no longer on the scene. In 1622 the short lived Gregory XV was succeeded by Urban VIII, formerly Cardinal Barberini. Delighted, Galileo completed and published his book on comets, *The Assayer*; which he dedicated to the new pope, whom, as we have seen, Galileo had known since 1611 and who, as late as 1620, had addressed Galileo as "your brother" (Sobel 102). The pope had the book read aloud at various gatherings. More good fortune shined on Galileo when a student he had mentored, the pope's nephew, was made a cardinal in his own right. This appointment provided Galileo with another powerful ally in the church, which strengthened his false sense of security.

When Urban intimated in his coronation address that he would intensify the church's role in the Thirty Years War, many in the audience felt the chill of censorship sweep through the room[8]. Urban not only studied under Jesuits but made the canonization of Ignatius Loyola his top priority. Urban knew astronomy and welcomed scholars into his curia on a regular basis; but these seminars gave the scholars an opportunity to denounce their rivals, one of whom was Galileo.

None of this seemed to have an affect on the pope. Galileo came to Rome in the Spring of 1624 and met privately with the pope on at least six occasions. In June, the pope wrote of Galileo, "We embrace with paternal love this great man whose fame shines in the heavens and goes on earth far and wide" (Sobel 138). Galileo felt secure enough to re-open the Copernican debate in writing. He believed he had an agreement with the pope to clarify the Edict of 1616. The Edict, as Galileo understood it, was aimed not at scientific discovery but at protecting scriptural interpretations made by the Catholic Church. Since Thomas Aquinas' famous dicta on the subject, the church held the position that scripture was superior to science. Where science contradicted scripture, science was simply wrong. Humans were too limited intellectually to work out these contradictions, which the church viewed as illusions. Scriptural interpretations were not to be called into question, but hypothetical speculation could advance.

In 1625 Cardinal Zollern reported to Urban that German Protestants embraced the Copernican doctrine. This aroused the zealous pope to extend the Thirty Years War to science. At the same time, Galileo assuming the pope was with him, launched a dismissive and arrogant literary shot at Monsignor Francessa Ingoli, a Jesuit. In the paper, Galileo claimed that the pope was his friend and called for the acceptance of Copernicus on theoretical but non-theological grounds. Galileo's delusion was reinforced when the pope accepted the 50-page polemic, complimenting Galileo on a thoughtful piece. This acceptance of Galileo's sarcastic and cutting refutational dialogic method encouraged further use of the same method in his major work.

The Dialogue on Two Chief Systems

The pope's praise emboldened Galileo to write his fateful *Dialogue on the Two Chief Systems of the World, the Ptolemaic and the Copernican*. It would take six years to complete. While he retained the view that nature is fundamentally based on mathematically determinable shapes, such as triangles, trapezoids, and the like, he demonstrated that Aristotle's theory of mechanics was deeply flawed and that Copernicus was correct in his assessment of the relationship between the sun and the planets.

The work is constructed as a conversation in the vernacular among three learned friends in four settings. Galileo represented Aristotelian thinking in the character Simplicio, an arrogant philosopher who is made to look foolish throughout the *Dialogue*. The character would prove Galileo's undoing when offended Aristotelians around the pope convinced Urban that Simplicio was meant to be the pope himself.

In the beginning of the *Dialogue,* Galileo differentiated between Ptolemy's and Copernicus' theories. He took the Copernican side in the debate "proceeding as with a pure mathematical hypothesis and striving by every artifice to represent it as superior to supposing the earth motionless"(Galileo 5). Note that Galileo tried to abide by the agreement of 1616 by claiming his speculation was hypothetical, but that he intended to use every available means of persuasion to make his point. The former claim as to protect him from prosecution; the latter would get him into trouble because of the abrasive argumentation he used.

For example, he referred to the Aristotelians as "Peripatetics," those who taught in Aristotle's school, and claimed that "These men indeed deserve not even that name, for they do not walk about; they are content to adore the shadows, philosophizing not with due circumspection but merely from having memorized a few ill-understood principles" (Galileo 6). Galileo not only echoed Callicles attack on philosophy from the *Gorgias*, he insulted his rivals for hypocrisy and ignorance.[9] [10]

In the fashion of Plato, Galileo then turned the argument over to his three characters, Simplicio, Sagredo, and Salviati. In the initial passages and throughout, there are moments when the characters live up to the Platonic ideal of questioning, arguing and seeking the truth. Note the argumentative progression in the following passage:

SAGR. Does not this cannon ball, sent perpendicularly upward by the force of the charge, continually decelerate in its motion until finally it reaches its ultimate height, where it comes to rest? And in diminishing its velocity—or I mean in increasing its slowness—is it not reasonable that it makes the change from 10 degrees to 11 sooner than from 10 to 12? And from 1,000 to 1,001 sooner than 1,002? And, in short, from any degree to a closer one rather than to one more remote?

SIMP. That is reasonable.

SAGR. But what degree of slowness is there that is so distant from any degree of motion that the state of rest (which is infinite slowness) is not still farther from it? Whence no doubt can remain that the ball, before reaching the point of rest, passes through all the greater and greater gradations of slowness, and consequently through that one at which it would not traverse the distance of one inch in a thousand years. Such being the case, as it certainly is, it should not seem improbable to you, Simplicio, that the same ball in returning downward, leaving rest, recovers the velocity of its motion by returning through those same degrees of slowness through which it passed going up; nor should it, on leaving the larger degrees of slowness which are closer to the state of rest, pass by a jump to those farther away.

SIMP. This argument convinces me (Galileo 35).[11]

However, the argumentation of ridicule is far more typical of the tone of the work. Simplicio, the Aristotelian, appears thick headed because of his inability to argue well. He says in one passage added after the initial draft, "Please put it down to my lack of practice in the mathematical sciences if I say freely that your arguments are based upon 'greater ratios' and 'lesser proportions' and other terms which I do not sufficiently understand" (Galileo 30). Simplicio tries to defend Aristotle's theory of falling weights, which Galileo had discredited while at Pisa:

SALV. That makes no difference at all, for a ball of one, ten, a hundred, or a thousand pounds will all cover the same hundred yards in the same time.

SIMP. Oh, that I do not believe, nor does Aristotle believe it either; for he writes that the speeds of falling heavy bodies have among themselves the same proportions as their weights.

SALV. Since you do not want to admit this, Simplicio, you must also believe that a hundred-pound ball and a one-pound ball of the same material being dropped at the same moment from a height of one hundred yards, the larger will reach the ground before the smaller has fallen a single yard. Now try, if you can, to picture in your mind the large ball striking the ground while the small one is less than a yard from the top of the tower (Galileo 223).

The others characters patronize Simplicio, further reducing his credibility. Sagredo often has to explain what Salviati is saying to Simplicio because Salviati has a superior intellect (Galileo 30). Simplicio is portrayed as ''confused and perplexed'' (Galileo 56). His thoughts are often reworded for him. In exchange after exchange, he is ridiculed but fails to see what is being done to him. For example, when Simplicio affirms Aristotle's opinion that the heavens have an ''impenetrable hardness,'' Sagredo replies, ''What excellent stuff, the sky, for anyone who could get hold of it for building a palace!'' Salviati chimes in that these are ''castles in the air'' (Galileo 69). At one point, Salviati condescendingly claims that he will help relieve Simplicio's ''incredulity'' (Galileo 30).[12] At another, Salviati says, ''Perhaps you had better tell us about it so that Simplicio will not go on thinking your mirth was directed at him'' (Galileo 108). Simplicio complains on page 158, ''Stop your sneering.'' Salviati accuses Simplicio of being ''one of that herd who . . . retired into their studies and glance through an index and a table of contents to see whether Aristotle has said anything about them'' (Galileo 185). Later Salviati continues this line of attack: ''It is indeed remarkable to me that Simplicio himself, in granting this assumption . . . does not see the enormous absurdity contained in it'' (Galileo 220). Often, when Sagredo has completed his translation of Salviati's thought for Simplicio, Salviati is allowed to continue. Though this device allowed Galileo to make his point twice, once for the learned, and once for the common reader, it was insulting to Aristotelians.

Salviati directly attacks Simplicio at various points when he loses patience with his lack of argumentative ability: ''I am surprised that you should need to have Aristotle's fallacy revealed, it being so obvious, and I wonder at your failure to perceive that Aristotle assumes what is in question'' (Galileo 35). Later Salviati uses hyperbole to claim that Simplicio prefers rhetoric to science when it comes to solving the problems of physics: ''A thousand Demostheneses and a thousand Aristotles would be left in the lurch by every mediocre wit who happened to hit upon truth for himself'' (Galileo 53-54). Salviati claims that in dealing with the Aristotelians he has to repeat his point a thousand times, once again relying on hyperbole to deliver his critique. Later in the dialogue, they are accused of having attacked Copernicus without having read his work. The Aristotelians are also accused of falling victim to their own sophistry. Since they have convinced the ignorant ''silly sheep'' that his theories are true, they turn around and become persuaded by the masses that they must be true because so many people believe them to be true:

SAGR: Such people remind me of that sculptor who, having transformed a huge block of marble into the image of a Hercules or a thundering Jove, I forget which, and having with consummate art made it so lifelike and fierce that it moved everyone with terror who beheld it, he himself began to be afraid, though all its vivacity and power were the work of his own hands; and his terror was such that he no longer dared affront it with his mallet and chisel (Galileo 112).[13]

He then accuses Simplicio of sophistry, ''to that which is false become true in the defiance of nature'' (Galileo 54). This charge was particularly galling to a group of scientific clerics who believed they were following in the steps of Aristotle and Aquinas. At various points fallacies are put into Simplicio's mouth. For example, he argues that because Aristotle is an ancient, his theories should receive more respect: ''His antiquity alone, and the mighty name he has acquired among so many men of distinguished mind, should be enough to earn him respect among all the learned'' (Galileo 110). Throughout the dialogue he consistently commits the fallacy of authority: ''SIMP. Still, I am much more impressed by the authority of so many great authors, and in particular . . . You shake your head, Sagredo, and smile, as if I had uttered some absurdity'' (Galileo 107-108).

This use of authority is condemned in several ways. First, Salviati complains about the use of testimony instead of real, material evidence. Second, he complains about using historians and others, as if they were philosophers (scientists):

> [W]hat is more revolting in a public dispute, when someone is dealing with demonstrable conclusions, than to hear him interrupted by a text (often written to some quite different purpose) thrown into his teeth by an opponent? If, indeed, you wish to continue in this method of studying, then put aside the name of philosophers and call yourselves historians, or memory experts; for it is not proper that those who never philosophize should usurp the honorable title of philosopher (Galileo 113).

The Aristotelians are also accused of throwing good money after bad because they have invested so much in their theory:

> I pity [Simplicio] no less than I should some fine gentleman who, having built a magnificent palace at great trouble and expense, employing hundreds and hundreds of artisans, and then beholding it threatened with ruin because of poor foundations, should attempt, in order to avoid the grief of seeing the walls destroyed, adorned as they are with so many lovely murals, or the columns fall, which sustain the superb galleries, or the gilded beams, or the doors spoiled, or the pediments and the marble cornices, brought in at so much cost—should attempt, I say, to prevent the collapse with chains, props, iron bars, buttresses and shores. (Galileo 56).

This elaborate and windy metaphor is ridicule at its finest, not unlike Edmund Burke's famous attack on Lord North's ''finely tessellated'' cabinet. The metaphor's hundreds of artisans call to mind the army of Aristotelian priests defending the old order. The structure itself reminds one of the pope's palaces; thus, it may have been this passage more than any other that caused Pope Urban VIII to believe he was being ridiculed in the dialogue.

Simplicio and the Aristotelians are also accused of dogmatism. He holds ''inveterate affection'' for ''deeply rooted opinion'' (Galileo 97). Simplicio says at one point: ''I have not observed such things; second, that I do not believe them; and then, in the third place, if you should assure me of them, and show me proofs of them, that you would be a veritable demon'' (Galileo 157).[14] Simplicio is no friend of the scientific method of Aristotle, and is chastised for this bigotry: ''And you are so credulous as to let yourself be persuaded of this nonsense, when you have your own senses to refute it and to learn the truth?'' (Galileo 151). This appeal for empiricism is later followed by the accusation that the Aristotlelians use scripture for their own purposes in ''apish puerilities'' (Galileo 357). There are more calls for empiricism. In a lengthy analogy, Sagredo shows that Aristotelians rejected the anatomical lessons of the Galenists even when shown the physical evidence as proof of their theories.[15] He demonstrates the ''absurdity of this Peripetics reply'' (Galileo 108). Then he asks a rhetorical question to clinch the argument: ''Is it possible for you to doubt, that if Aristotle should see the new discoveries in the sky he would change his opinions and correct his books and embrace the most sensible doctrines, casting away from himself those people so weak-minded as to be induced to go on abjectly maintaining everything he ever said?'' (Galileo 111). This rhetorical flourish is common at the end of the arguments in the dialogue. They are marked with rhetorical questions, periodic style, and such figures as repetition and polysyndeton.

Simplicio's circle is eventually charged with doing more harm to Aristotle's reputation than good. Aristotle, it is argued, was, after all, an empiricist, who was capable of changing his mind. Salviati says, "I often wonder how it can be that these strict supporters of Aristotle's every word fail to perceive how great a hindrance to his credit and reputation they are, and how the more they desire to increase his authority, the more they actually detract from it" (Galileo 111-112). Sagredo attempts to explain this phenomenon by arguing that these Aristotelians are more interested in saving their own reputation than Aristotle's. He concludes with a sarcastic rhetorical question, again demonstrating Galileo's diverse argumentative arsenal: "Now what is this but to make an oracle out of a log of wood, and run to it for answers; to fear it, revere it, and adore it?" (Galileo 113). Various Aristotelian theories are then taken apart, such as the one on air resistance. Salviati concludes the argument: "How many propositions I have noted in Aristotle's science that are not only wrong, but wrong in such a way that their diametrical opposites are true!" (Galileo 153). On the other hand, Aristotle himself is praised for teaching how to undo fallacies (Galileo 131).

The Aristotelians are also attacked with other forms of colorful vitriol: "Such men really deserve to encounter a Medusa's head which would transmute them into statues of jasper or of diamond, and thus make them more perfect than they are" (Galileo 59). The sarcasm combines with the reference to mythology to give the attack an uncanny *ethos*.

At the same time, the Copernican theory is advanced and defended using many of the same rhetorical devices. Sagredo claims that everyone who has been properly exposed to it has been converted. In making this case, he commits a similar fallacy to the one attributed to Simplicio. Just because everyone agrees to a theory does not make it true.

In these constructive sections, the ridicule of Simplicio continues. He is accused of "pretending" to be stupid (Galileo 220). The condescension continues throughout. Phrases such as "Now try, if you can . . . (Galileo 223) and "I am giving you the very best that is in me" (Galileo 258) punctuate the exchanges. Salviati claims that the Aristotelians have made the "Italians" into "laughing stock for foreigners" (Galileo 280). Finally, Sagredo claims that Copernicus is too sophisticated for the prejudiced and ignorant (Galileo 329).

One wonders what would have happened to Galileo had he restrained himself rhetorically and simply written a straightforward paper on the two systems under consideration. The ridicule of the Aristotelians certainly caught their attention, but it would also lead to Galileo's trial and obscure his findings for years to come.

In 1629, Galileo submitted the *Dialogue* to the Inquisition for approval and arrived in Rome in 1630 to obtain a license to print the manuscript. Luckily, the review of the *Dialogue* was undertaken by Father Riccardi, who had approved *The Assayer*. When he approved the *Dialogue*, Galileo was delighted. However, the prince in Rome who was to publish the work suddenly died, and Galileo was forced to find another publisher. Before he could seek one in Florence, he had to submit the manuscript to the Inquisition there. Once the Florentine review was underway, Father Riccardi in Rome decided that more changes were needed in the preface and conclusion. The book was not published until 1632 and then with certain changes. It immediately sold out. Galileo's preface makes much of the fact that the *Dialogue* had been subject to prior restraint and had been approved by church censors in two cities. Galileo must have felt very secure at this moment of publication that he was safe from persecution. Furthermore, since the *Dialogue* was fictional and speculative, he had not violated the Edict of 1616 requiring that all writing about Copernicus be limited to the hypothetical. However, in the same preface, Galileo hinted that the Edict of 1616 was like other injunctions against scientific research that should be discarded:

> Several years ago there was published in Rome a salutary edict which, in order to obviate the dangerous tendencies of our present age, imposed a seasonable silence upon the Pythagorean opinion that the earth moves. There were those who impudently asserted that this decree had its origin not in judicious inquiry, but in passion none too well informed.

Complaints were to be heard that advisors who were totally unskilled at astronomical observations ought not to clip the wings of reflective intellects by means of rash prohibitions. Upon hearing such carping insolence, my zeal could not be contained (Galileo 5).

This argument coming so early in the work must have set censors buzzing.

Galileo on Trial

The pope took the narrow path because the war against the Protestants was going badly, he was losing the allegiance of some nations, and he felt the need to stamp out dissent wherever possible. Convinced and insulted that the Simplicio character represented him, Urban banned Galileo's *Dialogue* and ordered him to Rome for a hearing before the Holy Office of the Church. Cardinal Niccolini and the pope's nephew, the new Cardinal Barberini, immediately tried to intercede on Galileo's behalf, in part, because the scientist was too ill to travel. An indication of the pope's anger can be seen in the fact that he refused to believe the doctors examining Galileo and demanded that he be brought to Rome. Ferdinand Medici II had succeeded to the throne of Tuscany and threw his weight behind Galileo. When the pope was unmoved, the 68 year old Galileo was carried in the Grand Duke's litter to the Tuscan Embassy in Rome.

Galileo referred to Cardinal Bellarmino's letter of 1615 allowing "hypothetical" discussion of Copernicus' theory (Sobel 247).This letter along with Galileo's health delayed the trial into his 69th year.[16] On April 12, 1633, Galileo met with two inquisitors and their secretary. They questioned Galileo on his understanding of the Bellarmino letter. In the next week, the *Dialogue* was examined and found to endorse Copernicus' theory in no uncertain terms. That the book was written in the vernacular, had been revised before publication, and had a change of publishers, aroused the suspicion of the inquisitors. Galileo was portrayed as a duplicitous seducer of the common folk. Thus, the pope summoned ten Cardinals to serve as a jury in the trial of Galileo.

Though distressed at the turn of events, Galileo took some comfort in the fact that his former student, the pope's nephew, was on the panel. On April 30, 1633, Galileo was given a second hearing at which, as suggested by his advisors, he admitted to bad judgment. Galileo said, "I freely confess that in several places it seemed to me set forth in such a form that a reader ignorant of my real purpose might have reason to suppose that the arguments brought on the false side, and which it was my intention to confute, were so expressed as to be calculated rather to compel conviction by their cogency than to be easy of solution" (Sobel 257-58). Specifically, he claimed his theory of tides was presented too much as if it were fact instead of speculation. He then condemned his own "vainglorious ambition." For two weeks, Galileo had been confined at the Holy Office, after which he was permitted to return to the Tuscan Embassy.

On May 10, 1633, Galileo arrived before his questioners with a written statement that re-asserted his misunderstanding of the Bellarmino letter and the Edict of 1616. He pled for forgiveness. Pressured by Urban, Ferdinand II suddenly cut off financial support for Galileo, though the Tuscan ambassador continued to provide food and housing. Urban also encouraged a unanimous verdict from his jury of Cardinals, knowing he already had a majority. On June 16, the pope met with the jury and ordered them to question Galileo with regard to his intentions in publishing the *Dialogue*. He was examined in this regard on June 21, where he said, "I do not hold this opinion of Copernicus. . . . I am here to obey" (Sobel 272). The next day, Galileo was found guilty of heresy; his *Dialogue* was banned. Seven of the ten jurors signed the verdict. Galileo believed all was lost, including his honor.

After some negotiation it was announced that Galileo would be kept under house arrest at the Tuscan Embassy and do penance for three years. Galileo disputed two of the charges: that he was a bad Catholic and that he had gotten his book published by changing venues. He then knelt and recanted his heresy: "I curse and detest said errors and heresies" (Sobel 276). It is most likely a myth that he added, "But it still moves," referring to the earth. Had he done that, he would have been burned at the stake, or at the very least, have badly embarrassed those negotiating for his release.

The activity of Urban VIII behind the scenes indicates not only how affronted he was by Galileo's writing, but how intent he was on stamping out heresy in the church. In the end, however, and perhaps because Galileo recanted, Urban showed mercy and allowed Galileo to leave Rome in the custody of the Duke of Siena.[17]

News of Galileo's sentence had many effects. In July of 1633, Ascanio Piccolomini, the Archbishop of Siena, endorsed the *Dialogue* and took custody of Galileo at his palace. Galileo suffered a nervous breakdown and Piccolomini nursed him back to health. Despite its being banned, the *Dialogue* sold well on the black market. Rene Descartes, however, decided not to publish *Le Monde*, in which he had endorsed Copernicus' theory.

Once recovered, Galileo took up the question of motion; he methodically refuted Aristotle. Eventually these studies resulted in his final book *Discourse and Mathematical Demonstration Concerning Two New Sciences.* He used the dialogue method again with the same three characters from the book that had gotten him into trouble. However, this new dialogue was much more civil and much less arrogant that the previous one. Galileo later said it was his most important work. It proved his most difficult to get published. Inquisitors challenged him in Venice; Jesuits fought him in Germany. Finally, he procured a contract in Holland.

Jealous clerics then sent word to Urban that Piccolomini was indulging Galileo and encouraging more heretical thinking. Urban solved this problem by allowing Galileo to move home to Arcetri under house arrest. He was also not allowed scholarly visitors nor was he allowed to teach pupils. He was allowed to attend mass and to visit his daughter at her nunnery in their home town of Arceti where she died in 1634.[18] Those around Galileo saw that he was crushed and regularly allowed violations of the visitor sanction. Thomas Hobbes and John Milton, for example, came to Arcetri to visit the scientist. By 1638, Galileo was blind. He died in 1642.

While many praised Galileo for his teaching and his tenacity at publishing his theories, Pope Urban refused to eulogize him. Almost a hundred years later, Pope Clement XII, a Florentine, erected a tomb for Galileo in Santa Croce near Michelangelo's burial place. The great artist had died only hours before Galileo was born, and some believe the soul of the sculptor was re-incarnated in Galileo.

Conclusion

Over time, Galileo's trial and treatment have taken on mythic elements. While Galileo was kept under house arrest, he was never in a dungeon, nor anything resembling one. He was housed in embassies, palaces, and eventually his own home during the periods of sentencing and probation. Though the pope's attack on Galileo destroyed the Roman Academia, his followers established the Florentine Accademia del Cimento in 1657 to carry on his work. However, Galileo's *Dialogue* was not removed from the Index until 1835. And only on Halloween of 1992, three and a half centuries after his death, did the Pope John Paul II admit that errors had been made by the Aristotelian advisors to the pope. Thus, while Urban VIII and some of his jurors must take blame for the shameless treatment of Galileo, it should not be shared by the Catholic Church as a whole. Three of Galileo's jury supported him, as did many other Cardinals and church officials.

In fact, there is plenty of blame to go around. The academic community deserves as much blame as the clerical for its stiff-necked defense of Aristotelianism. Then as now, professors were not above insidious attacks on those that differed with them.

Finally, we need to note that Galileo's argumentation is also to blame for his plight. He began his career on the right path. He sought to combine observation with reason and mathematics to produce proofs. Reason needed empirical verification, and observation needed to be guided by reason. Together they could test theory and persuade others to embrace it. He sought a mathematical explanation of nature in general, and the universe in particular. It was not long before Newton and Descartes were building on Galileo's work to advance it into the modern era.

However, as we have seen, Galileo's writing was sarcastic, cutting, dismissive and arrogant. The characters he developed in his dialogues engaged in hurtful satire that enraged his enemies and eventually offended his friend the pope. While those who defend freedom of expression certainly would defend Galileo's right to use these tactics, those who teach the criticism of argumentation might point out that his strategies often made his message unpalatable. In this way, Galileo bears some responsibility for the delays in advancing his theory.

Endnotes

1. There were 70 libraries in Cordoba alone.
2. Catholic officials used the Inquisition as far back as the 1100s.
3. Around 1585, actually mapped Dante's hell from the *Divine Comedy* and then gave lectures on the subject. Later he repudiated this work as inaccurate.
4. The Barberini family symbol was the bee. One can still see them above the altar of Saint Peter in St. Peter's Cathedral in the Vatican.
5. Ptolemy used mathematics to deduce a geocentric theory of the universe. He invented epicyclic theories of motion that allows him to differentiate planets from stars. Copernicus (1473-1543) corrected Ptolemy by developing a heliocentric theory. *De Revolutionibus Orbium Coelestium* was published the year of his death, and somewhat suppressed by those prejudiced in favor of Aristotelian science.
6. Thomas Conley, "Vituperation in Early Seventeenth Century Historical Studies," *Rhetorica*, 22 (2004): 169-182. It is interesting to note that Jesuits were often involved in this type of rhetoric. See pp. 170, 173, 175. Since many of these diatribes concerned science, it is safe to assume that was familiar with them. See p. 177. Conley writes, "The virulence of this scholarly vituperation is not hard to explain if we bear in mind that what sometimes appears to be mere quibbling about manuscript readings or astronomical lore must be read against the background of fierce contestations over such matters as
7. Urban's foreign policy was a disaster. At one point, he allied the papacy with France even while it was using Protestant armies against the Catholic Habsburg rulers of the Germanic provinces.
8. When heard the report of this misrepresentation, he felt like Boethius who was falsely accused of betraying his emperor, Theodoric.
9. Of course, Aristotle's school was called the Lyceum. However, because its faculty tended to pace while teaching, it got dubbed the Peripatetic school.
10. Of course, Aristotle's school was called the Lyceum. However, because its faculty tended to pace while teacing, It got dubbed the Peripatetic school.
11. In the next few lines, the spirit of Plat is extended: "SALV Simplicio, we are engaging in friendly discussion among ourselves in order to investigate certain truths. I shall never take it ill that you exposed my errors; when I have not followed the thought of Aristotle, rebuke me freely, and I shall take it in good part. Only let me expound my doubts and reply somewhat to your last remarks."
12. Later on p. 59, he refers to Simplicio's "stupidity" (Galileo).
13. The masses are regularly referred to as the "herd," "sheep," "ignorant," and so forth.
14. The dogmatism in these remarks may have echoed that of Urban VIII.
15. Since the episode reportedly takes place in Venice, it is very likely that Galileo actually witnessed the event. The rejection of William Gilbert's theory of magnetism is used later in the dialogue to document the dogmatism of the Aristotelians.
16. In the trial transcript, he is mistakenly identified as being 70 years of age.
17. It should be noted that the Doctrine of Papal Infallibility was propounded in 1870 by Vatican I. It applies only to matters of theology.
18. Virginia, who took the name Maria Celeste when she took her holy orders, was one of two illegitimate daughters that put into nunneries. We have her letters to her father, but not his responses. Galileo also had an illegitimate son.

Works Cited

Colish, Marcia L. *Medieval Foundations of the Western intellectual tradition, 400-1400* New Haven. Yale U. Press, 1997.

Galileo, Galilei, *Dialogue concerning the two chief systems*, Tran Drake, Stillman. Berkeley: University of California Press, 1967.

Grimm H. J., ed Martin Luther, ''Against Scholastic Theology,'' in *Luther's Works,* Vol. 31: *Career of the Reformer*, Philadelphia: Muhlenberg Press, 1957.

Moss, J. Dietz & W. A. Wallace, *Rhetoric and Dialectic in the Time of Galileo.* (Baltimore: The Catholic University of America Press, 2004.

Pesic, P. ''Comment on 'Galileo's Discovery of Scaling Laws,' by Mark A. Peterson,'' *American Journal of Physics* 70 (2002): 1160-61.

Rubenstein, R. E. *Aristotle's Children: How Christians, Muslims, and Jews rediscovered ancient wisdom and illuminated the Dark Ages.* New York: Harcourt, 2003.

Steenberghen, F. *Aristotle in the West: The Origins of Latin Aristotelianism*, Leonard Johnson, trans. New York: Humanities Press, 1970.

Sobel, D. *Galileo's Daughter* New York: Walker and Company, 1999.

Benefits and Drawbacks of Anonymous Online Communication: Legal Challenges and Communicative Recommendations

"Bronco" (a.k.a. Craig R. Scott)
The University of Texas at Austin

Anonymous communication has a relatively long and sometimes controversial history in this country. From the anonymous publishing of the *Federalist Papers* under the pseudonym ''Publius'' over two centuries ago to anonymous sources such as ''Deep Throat'' during the Watergate scandal, anonymity has played and continues to perform a unique role in American culture. The ability to communicate anonymously is viewed as part of our basic right to free speech—an interpretation historically upheld in U.S. courts (Bowman 2001) but increasingly problematized by new communication technologies (see Lipinski 2002). Indeed, concerns and debates about anonymous communication may well be at an all time high. Even though we all experience anonymity in a variety of somewhat mundane ways (e.g., anonymous letters to the editor/media, tips to law enforcement, organizational evaluations/appraisals, ''leaks'' and ''whistleblowing,'' church confessionals, suggestion boxes, ''secret'' admirers, letters with no return address, call-in radio show comments, anonymous gift giving, caller-id blocking, some forms of electronic mail, certain online meetings, and a range of support groups; see Anonymous 1998; Marx 1999), recent events have propelled discussions of anonymity to the national stage. The anthrax-laced letters anonymously sent to various influential individuals in our country in late 2001 and the invasive legislation prompted in part by such actions, as well as the growing use (and some would argue, *mis*use) of new communication technologies affording users at least some anonymity,point to two influential explanations for our growing interest and concern about anonymous communication.

First, in the ongoing aftermath from the events of September 11, 2001, there exists a climate of suspicion and heightened security that seems increasingly interested in establishing identity. Terrorists' use of the Internet to communicate with one another covertly has furthered concerns by law enforcement and others (Wieland 2001). Indeed, Marx (2001) confirms that identification technologies have greatly expanded in recent years (e.g., facial/retinal/vocal recognition systems). As will be examined in more detail below, judicial and organizational officials are increasingly likely to take actions limiting one's privacy and to provide identifying information in the name of national security—all of which erodes anonymity. However, this has led, in part, to resistance through anonymity. Samoriski (2002) suggests

> ''the retreat from the prying eyes of surveillance has led to the spread of technologies of anonymity . . . citizens are seeking privacy and anonymity at a time when the government and the business sector are using information technology to compile bigger databases [of information about citizens]'' (161).

Diane Saco (2002), in her book *Cybering Democracy*, advises ''Precisely because we live in a context wherein surveillance has become ubiquitous . . . anonymity can become a viable and even advisable form of resistance'' (119).

Another driving force centers on technology. This issue is most real in the virtual, online environment(s) of the Internet (and other networked communication technologies). In many ways, communication technology makes anonymity more possible—given the obvious challenges of maintaining anonymity in unmediated situations. For example, individuals have the ability to communicate anonymously or pseudonymously using chat rooms, discussion boards, multi-user domains (MUDs), instant messaging (IM), group decision support systems, caller-id blocking as well as anonymous remailers and anonymous web surfing.[1] Of course, some experts (see Turkle 1995) describe the online experience as being largely anonymous in general also. For some, the ease with which people can now communicate anonymously is cause for concern. Not surprisingly then, these same technologies are also used to trace individuals. For example, several of the technologies mentioned here create logs indicating the message and/or computer source. The use of certain screen names or other pseudonyms may also reveal identity. I have playfully penned (keyboarded?) this chapter under the pseudonym ''Bronco''—which I regularly use as an online identity based on my fanaticism about Denver's professional football franchise. Also, system operators and service providers are typically able to ultimately identify the source of an otherwise anonymous message.

As a result of these forces, previously protected rights to free speech via anonymous online communication are now being questioned. As one legal scholar noted: ''The status of anonymous speech as a protected right is contracting, and given technological changes, the anonymous speaker faces unprecedented new challenges. Given the changing nature of anonymous speech from the eighteenth century to the twenty-first, it is likely that the anonymous writer Publius—celebrated by the Founding generation—will soon be dead'' (Wieland 2001 590). Before ''Anonymous'' potentially suffers such a fate, and perhaps to prevent its death completely, we need to better understand the dangers and necessity of anonymous online communication. To that end, this essay begins by more thoroughly defining anonymous online communication and considering its most commonly discussed drawbacks and benefits. Next, court cases regarding anonymous online communication are reviewed to gain a clearer sense of this issue—focusing heavily on what have been termed ''John Doe'' and ''cybersmearing'' cases. Finally, based on that casework and current legal opinions, several critiques and communicative recommendations are offered to more thoroughly address the complex challenges posed by online anonymity. If the *Fast Company* magazine columnist who recently proclaimed, ''we're entering an era of anonymity'' (Godin 2001 86) is correct, then it is imperative that such analysis take place to ultimately preserve anonymous online communication as an increasingly important form of free speech.

Background: Defining Online Anonymity

Williams's (1988) argument, ''anonymity is a notion that ought to be thought, taught and written about much more than it is at present'' (765) is perhaps even more true today with the widespread use of various online communication tools that provide at least some sense of anonymity. In thinking about this construct, it is essential to define it relative to related constructs and talk about various types of anonymity. Most simply, *anonymity*—whether online or not—is the condition in which a message source is absent or largely unknown to a message recipient. Similarly, an anonymous source is one with no known name or acknowledged identity. *Confidentiality* differs in that the source of a comment is known to a few, but the identity of the source is not further revealed to the ultimate message recipients. Thus, the source is absent to all with anonymity; however, confidentiality is a condition in which the source can be connected to his or her comments by some (e.g., researchers, reporters) who agree not to reveal the source to others (see Anonymous 1998). Furthermore, a sense of anonymity may be achieved through a fictitious alternative identity called a *pseudonym* (e.g., ''Bronco''). These fictitious identities take two general forms: sources perceived as fictitious to the message receiver and sources perceived as factual to the message receiver. The former most closely fit ideas related to online anonymity. The latter (taking on another person's actual identity, assuming an invented identity) is substantially different because receivers may have no reason to suspect that the apparent message source is not the actual message source. Although issues related to identity theft and the use of aliases are indeed fascinating and deserving of more attention from communication scholars, they are not immediately relevant to a discussion of free speech and online anonymity.

Elsewhere (Anonymous 1998) I have suggested the following definition of anonymity for communication scholars: the degree to which a communicator perceives the message source is *unknown* and *unspecified.* By *source specification* I mean the extent to which a message source is distinguished from other possible sources. Generally, this dimension ranges from being a general member of some large public grouping to recognition as a specific, singular (though not necessarily known) individual. *Source knowledge* concerns the degree of familiarity between the source and the receiver, and may range from the two being complete strangers to being close friends. In more communicative terms, knowledge level varies between instances where a receiver has had no prior interactions with or information about the source, to situations where the receiver has had numerous prior interactions and may possess a fair amount of information about the source (e.g., knowing one by name).

There are several different types of anonymity. *Physical* (i.e., visual) anonymity is when one cannot sense the physical presence of a message source (e.g., hooding subjects in research studies). *Discursive* anonymity, on the other hand, is the condition in which specific comments cannot be attributed to a specific individual source; thus, it is tied directly to verbal communication. Kling, Lee, Teich, and Frankel (1999) also distinguish between *traceable anonymous communication, untraceable anonymous communication, traceable pseudonymous communication, and untraceable pseudonymity.* Additionally, there are differences between *self-anonymity* (a sender's perceived anonymity to others when he/she is the message source) and *other-anonymity* (the anonymity experienced when a user receives communication from an unidentified source). As Spears and Lea (1994) note, self- and other-anonymity are ''related but conceptually distinct'' (430), leading them to distinguish between what they call ''identifiability'' (self's anonymity to others) and ''anonymity'' (others' anonymity to self).

Perhaps most relevant here is the distinction between what Johnson (1997) labels *offline* anonymity (including face to face, telephone, and traditional media) and *online* anonymity (when using computer-based network systems, primarily the Internet). This author suggests that achieving anonymity in the former requires sender effort but that it is more the natural state of affairs in the latter. Although the types of anonymity outlined in the previous paragraph are all possible online, there are other aspects of online anonymity that make it potentially even more powerful. Most notably, because the Internet is highly accessible and relatively cheap (Crump 2003), it provides a wide range of the population with a channel for voicing dissent. Chiger (2002) adds that ''speaking in an Internet forum is tantamount to making a conference call with half the planet'' (52); thus, with ability to copy, repost, and mass mail, anonymous communicators can reach far greater numbers of recipients. O'Brien (2002) adds that Internet statements may be longer lasting, lacking in editorial oversight, and more capable of finding a receptive audience.

Two other characteristics help to define how online anonymity *should* be viewed. First, anonymity must be considered to exist along a continuum from fully anonymous to fully identified. Thus, a source is not simply anonymous or identified, but may also be partially so. Second, anonymity is usefully viewed as a perception of the communicators involved. Although certain processes and technologies may claim to be anonymous (or not), usage behavior and other effects likely depend far more on the extent to which communicators perceive anonymity. Although such views are consistent with recent theorizing about anonymity (Anonymous, 1998; Marx, 1999), much of the work in legal and other scholarly circles tends to treat online anonymity as an on/off feature of specific technologies. Legal experts often talk about the ''perfect'' anonymity of the Internet (see Crump 2003), though others have reminded their scholars that ''the phrase 'Internet anonymity' is innately an oxymoron'' (Chiger 2002 53). In summary, anonymous online communication may differ in several key ways from other forms of anonymity—most notably in that it can reach more people with less cost, and greater potential power. Furthermore, it has a great deal to do with the level of perceived anonymity in a communicative situation, even though it has historically been considered in more simplistic ways. Given its potential impact and social nature, a closer examination of the pros and cons of anonymous online communication is warranted.

Dangers and Benefits of Anonymous Online Communication

Perhaps any discussion of pros and cons should begin with the disclaimer that ''anonymous communication online is morally neutral'' (Teich et al. 1999 72), meaning any dangers or benefits concern how it is used. Without question, it has and almost certainly will continue to be used for purposes that facilitate both beneficial and detrimental outcomes. I begin with an overview of the major arguments related to the dangers of anonymity, especially online. Next, the beneficial uses of anonymity are reviewed as an important point of comparison.

Dangers

I was recently struck by a response from an organizational employee to an open-ended survey question I had sent about when anonymity might be appropriate, because it captures some of the most extreme concerns about anonymous communication: ''I don't really believe it's appropriate. I want accountability. I answer the telephone with my full name. I put my full name on my answering machine at home and work. I feel that America's obsession with 'anonymity' is a copout; it breeds irresponsibility, non-accountability and shabby work. In the extreme case it breeds a lifestyle of sinfulness and overindulgence.'' Beyond the irony that this comment was made anonymously, it illustrates that accountability for one's actions seems to underlie most concerns about the dangers of anonymity— especially online anonymity given its potential for wider access and impact. Lemley (1999) describes the lack of accountability as ''both the greatest virtue and the greatest problem with anonymity'' (262). Stein (2003 193) suggests that ''with respect to accountability, there are two potential repercussions of anonymity that are cause for concern: first, anonymity will lead to crime; and second, anonymity will undermine free speech rather than advance it.'' A speaker who feels anonymous may choose to libel, slander, and defame (even though such actions are illegal). In fact, perhaps the fastest growing issue related to online anonymity concerns issues of what is sometimes called cybersmearing, where individuals use online anonymity to promote false statements about other people or organizations. Free speech does not extend to defamation, for instance, so anonymity is inappropriate then (see Lipinski 2002); however, because some individuals are able to successfully hide behind the veil of anonymity and disparage others (e.g., current/former employers may be criticized on Internet financial forums which can drive down stock prices), many individuals view this troubling use of anonymity as an especially strong drawback.

Another concern about anonymity directly related to free speech concerns flaming. Defined as the exchange of rude or hostile messages between online participants (Barnes 2003), flaming may be facilitated by the sense of anonymity and the reduced accountability the participants feel online. Although it is probably the most publicized form of online misbehavior (Barnes), recent work has questioned just how widespread this is and has pointed to the need to entirely reconceptualize the construct (O'Sullivan & Flanagin 2003).

Although they are less directly related to free speech concerns, accountability is also at issue regarding the use of the Internet to conduct terrorist activities and other threats to national security. Dystopian rhetoric about the use of anonymity for high tech pedophilia, virtual pornography, destructive computer viruses, and other forms of cybercrime all point to potential negatives associated with the lack of online accountability.

Another set of concerns centers not so much around accountability, but the possibility that anonymity actually ''undermines rather than improves public debate on important issues'' (Stein 2003 193). Audiences have a harder time evaluating credibility, and there is more room for deception and frivolousness. ''Knowing a speaker's identity is necessary to better evaluate the truthfulness of the assertions'' (Barnes 1999 386). People communicating anonymously may believe they have to do so because it would be unsafe to do otherwise—further undermining the value we may perceive as individuals in speaking openly and in an identified fashion. Anonymous speech may seem like less sincere and less involved participation for many. Related to this are concerns about trust. Nissenbaum (2003) contends that online anonymity decreases trust, because we know relatively little about personal character and even the nature of the relationships in which we are involved. To the extent that one lacks a history with a communication partner online (which can be overcome in pseudonymous exchanges), it is difficult to either establish a reputation or to build trust.

Several other more general drawbacks can briefly be mentioned. When interacting anonymously (online or otherwise), individuals may not get credit for their input/ideas, which runs counter to other values in our society. People may also be less influential and less identified with their organizations and work teams when exchanging messages anonymously (see Scott 1999; Scott & Easton 1996), both of which may limit effective decision-making. As another example, scholars have argued about the dangers of anonymous sources and leaks to the media by top government officials (Erickson & Fleuriet 1991).

In a broader sense, some legal experts have suggested that even though anonymity was necessary at earlier times in this country when people might not otherwise have voiced their views, this is no longer true in the information rich society of today (Wieland, 2001). This author further contends that the vast quantities of information online today demand that citizens better know who is speaking. All this represents just one more way in which the possible dangers of anonymous online communication are weighed against the potential benefits. We turn to those next.

Advantages

''The value of anonymous speech in society is regarded as a cornerstone of democratic government'' (Lipinski 2002 95). Indeed, the right to communicate anonymously has generally been considered part of our first amendment right of free speech in the U.S.; i.e., the right to free speech includes the right to speak anonymously. Anonymity encourages free expression and the ability to voice opinions on unpopular ideas. This right is associated with a variety of benefits outlined below.

Marx (2001) offers several reasons as to why we need anonymous communication in general, though they apply to online anonymity as well. These include (a) facilitating the flow of communication on public issues without killing the messenger (e.g., tiplines, whistleblowing, unsigned political communication, etc.); (b) obtaining sensitive information (such as in research); (c) focusing attention on message content rather than status of source; (d) encouraging reporting, sharing, etc. for stigmatized situations; (e) protecting one from subsequent contact (e.g., anonymous donors); (f) avoiding persecution and retaliation for one's beliefs; (g) encouraging risk-taking, innovation, and experimentation; and (h) enhancing play/recreational interaction. I have also argued, anonymously of course (Anonymous 1998), that reasons we anonymize include having less relational status than the message receiver, needing to convey sensitive or suspect information, having low concerns about credibility and low need for credit, and when it is easy to do so (and one believes they will not be detected). Shedletsky and Aitken (2004) note that users may desire online anonymity in situations where they have been harassed/stalked, experienced previous embarrassment, wish to avoid recognition by others on multiple lists, want to voice controversial statements, or need to discuss personal/intimate topics. In all these instances, individuals are able to speak more freely (or even do so at all) because of the anonymity provided. As Barnes (1999) notes, "members of marginalized social groups can use anonymity to express their point of view without fear of social ostracism" (385).

To some extent, even the philosophical writing of Habermas (1989) seems to support the advantages of anonymity. Diane Saco (2002) asserts that "A defense of anonymity can be read out of Habermas's theory of the public sphere, particularly with respect to the construction of a universalized public voice" (206). Additionally, Habermas also expresses a concern as to how anonymity can facilitate individual safety. Even more powerful is the relevance of Habermas when it comes to his writing about the ideal speech situation. For Habermas, truth is rational consensus, which depends on communicative freedom and responsibility being shared and asserted by relevant parties. Anonymous communication would be advantageous in helping to reach this ideal speech situation because anonymity (a) allows all parties must have an equal opportunity to speak, and (b) makes them more free to advance any kind of claim and free to question or challenge claims made by others.

Another set of advantages associated with anonymous speech center on democratic participation. Samoriski (2002) contends that "anonymous speech and free speech have become closely related and continue to play an important part in democratic movements" (p. 161). This happens by providing a means/role in informing and shaping opinion (with many experts agreeing that efforts to identify individuals may serve to chill expression (Samoriski 2002). Additionally, "anonymity makes political dissension safer" (Saco,2002 119) and advances democracy through secret assemblies (p. 193). She notes that the secret ballot box was to protect voters and that anonymity, rather than visibility, can be a stronger form of resistance.

Anonymous communication, especially as it may occur online, can provide several advantages in the workplace as well because it facilitates desired practices. Marx (1999), for example, suggests anonymity is a key element associated with whistleblowing, informational audits, anonymous gift giving, caller-id blocking, and review of applications without pictures and gender known. Anonymous (1998) discusses the level of anonymity in organizational flyers, upward appraisals, some forms of electronic mail, and some types of online workplace meetings. Scott and Rains (2002) specifically explore anonymous organizational communication, where they review existing work related to the function of anonymity in whistleblowing, feedback/appraisal, and use of electronic meeting tools. Without this anonymity, which often occurs through online tools, people will not blow the whistle as readily, give less honest feedback, feel more scared to report crime, have their input's merit considered less, and perhaps not be evaluated or considered fairly in hiring and promotion decisions. Scott and Rains also report several findings regarding anonymity use and appropriateness. Specific to online anonymity, they note that anonymity is viewed as generally appropriate for organizational surveys/assessment and formal evaluation (either of which may be done electronically), but anonymous communication is only moderately appropriate for informal evaluations and use of certain technologies for anonymous messages. In other ways, because so many legal protections do not extend to most workplaces, anonymity may provide a critical means for the expression of dissent, both internally through tools such as electronic suggestion boxes and externally through the variety of "suck" sites on the web (e.g., www.starbucked.com and www.gapsucks.org). As organizations are increasingly surveilled, monitored, and controlled (Botan 1996), the need for and benefits of anonymity are likely to increase.

As a more specific example, consider the workplace for many reading this essay. Institutions of higher learning are often considered both intellectually enlightened organizations and professional bureaucracies; yet, we use anonymity (online and offline) because we believe a variety of benefits accrue from such practices. In the classroom, anonymity may allow for freer expression about certain topics (especially when done online), focus teams on content rather than people, and promote generally more truthful communication in the students' anonymous evaluations of instructors. In our research, we may guarantee research participants anonymity as a condition of participation, provide organizations and individuals with pseudonyms to protect their identity, and willingly submit our written work to what we often consider to be an anonymous review process. In academia we tend to value anonymity because of the objectivity, fairness, and legitimacy we attribute to it and the opportunities it provides for truthful communication about scholarship. There are other ways of doing reviews, for example, that are not blind or double blind—but there has been little interest in the communication field to adopt other procedures that remove the anonymity. In most of these cases, the anonymity in the process is accomplished largely through the use of online interactions.

Balance

The challenge then is how to provide for the benefits of online anonymity (which center largely on rights to free speech) without its drawbacks (which tend to focus heavily on issues of accountability). For some, the issue is perhaps better phrased as one of how to eliminate the dangers of online anonymity without completely removing those instances where anonymity serves a vital purpose. Balancing these competing interests, especially in an online environment, has fallen largely to the courts.

Online Anonymity on Trial

Given the array of arguments for and against the use of anonymity, especially in online contexts, it is perhaps not surprising that "courts across the country are grappling with the degree of protection to be accorded anonymous Internet speech" (Steinmeyer 2001 B8). Even though courts in the U.S. have historically recognized the importance and legality of anonymous speech as part of our basic first amendment rights to free speech (see Bowman 2001; Lipinski, 2002), some legal scholars now contend anonymous speech faces unprecedented challenges and attention (Wieland 2001).

The basis for law guiding anonymity online comes from legal opinions regarding offline anonymous speech. Although there is early evidence of court opinions (Lewis Publishing Co. v. Moran) upholding disclosure requirements in the early 1900s (Wieland 2001), almost any review of legal opinions in this area will reveal a clear shift in opinion for much of the 20th century. Most notably, a set of key cases (e.g., *Talley v. California*, *McIntyre v. Ohio Election Commission*, *Buckley v. American Constitutional Law Foundation*) heard by the Supreme Court reiterated the right to speak anonymously, primarily in terms of the right to distribute material anonymously. A very recent 2002 case (Watchtower Bible v. Village of Stratton) extended this right to door-to-door canvassers.

These and other rights were extended to the Internet in a series of cases, beginning with Reno v. ACLU. The court noted "the principles of free speech apply to the Internet and extend to protect those who use the Internet as a 'soapbox,' an updated version of the eighteenth or nineteenth century 'pamphleteer''' (see Lipinski 2002 77). However, the major free speech debate today concerning anonymity online centers on alleged cases of defamation and libel. These are better known as ''cybersmearing'' or ''John Doe'' cases. In almost every instance, a critic has anonymously sent a message (e.g., through a remailer, to a discussion board forum, in a chat room) that others have reacted to by bringing forth legal action that involves the desire to know the identity of the message source. Although courts have addressed defamation claims in a variety of contexts over many years, ''the rise of the Internet has forced judges to grapple with novel legal arguments and design innovative remedies suited to this new medium'' (O'Brien 2002 2745). Thus, the direction of court rulings in this area remains unclear, which continues to concern free speech advocates.

A number of individual cases seem to have recently resulted in victories for anonymous free speech online. As part of a larger securities fraud case against 2TheMart.com, that organization subpoenaed bulletin board operator InfoSpace Inc. requesting the identity of 23 anonymous Internet users who posted messages to their bulletin board—messages that 2TheMart.com claimed lowered their stock prices. InfoSpace emailed the users about the request, and one user known pseudonymously as ''NoGuano'' moved to quash the subpoena on grounds that this would ''violate his First Amendment right to speak anonymously over the Internet'' (Steinmeyer 2001,B8). For a variety of reasons (see Steinmeyer for detailed review), the court concluded that the disclosure of the anonymous speakers' identities was unwarranted. Another case (In Re Subpoena Duces Tecum to America Online) involved a publicly traded company wanting to remain anonymous who subpoenaed AOL to reveal the names of several subscribers who had anonymously posted unflattering messages about the company—with the intent of then suing those individuals for libel and other claims. Eventually, the subscribers' names were protected in an appeal under first amendment rights, but the courts did acknowledge that this right was not absolute and identity could be revealed if a plaintiff could show that the identity of the posters was central to the claim. Even as recently as September, 2004, New York District Judge Victor Marrero ruled against the FBI and in favor of an anonymous Internet service provider (Doe v. Ashcroft), stating ''Every court that has addressed the issue has held that individual Internet subscribers have a right to engage in anonymous Internet speech, though anonymity may be trumped in a given case by other concerns'' (cited in Hamblett 2004 1).

However, the most central case protecting the right to anonymous online communication was a 2001 case involving Dendrite International, Inc. v. Doe, No. 3. Under the screen name ''xxpirr,'' nine comments were posted to a Yahoo! bulletin board concerning alleged changes in accounting practices and efforts by the CEO to sell the company (see O'Brien 2002 for detailed analysis). Dendrite subpoenaed Yahoo! as the Internet service provider to reveal the identity of the poster. The courts denied the request, at least in part on the grounds that the plaintiff had not established a case of defamation based on the messages made and their impact. Furthermore, part of the ruling was a guideline that Internet service providers notify the anonymous posters about the subpoena and thus provide them with an opportunity to present opposition to the legal efforts underway. In his decision Judge Robert Fall wrote that the court must ''balance the defendant's First Amendment right of anonymous free speech against the strength of the prima facia case presented and the necessity for the disclosure of the anonymous defendant's identity to allow the plaintiff to properly proceed'' (cited in Bischof 2001a 18).

Despite these victories for anonymous online communication, legal scholars and free speech advocates remain cautious. As Ekstrand (2003) recently notes, these precedents are new and a handful of state court decisions ''hardly guarantee the trend will continue, particularly with more cases pending'' (425). Others have noted that the result of the 2TheMart.com case was driven more by legal miscues than principles of law (Steinmeyer 2001). In the AOL case cited above, the initial trial court determined a compelling state interest in protecting companies "... from the potentially severe consequences that could easily flow from actionable communications on the information superhighway significantly outweigh [sic] the limited intrusion on the First Amendment rights of any innocent subscribers" (cited in Steinmeyer 2001 B8).

Additionally, Bischof (2001b) cites numerous instances where courts have forced Internet service providers, who may often prefer to cooperate rather than engage in a long legal battle with deep-pocketed corporate interests (see France & Carney 2000; O'Brien 2002), to reveal identities of posters before the underlying merit of the defamation case has been established. This has resulted in individuals having their identity released before they even knew legal actions were being taken against them. Apparently, this is still happening even after the guidelines in Dendrite. In a rather disturbing 2003 case (Freedman v. AOL and others) just ruled on in February 2004 (Dorsey 2004), AOL provided complete subscriber information to police detectives (made all the more curious since this was done on the basis of a faxed warrant that did not even contain a judge's signature). The once-anonymous poster had broken no laws but had engaged in political speech against the police commissioner, prompting efforts to uncover his identity. Most relevant to this essay, the claims against AOL were actually dismissed because of a forum selection clause in the plaintiff's AOL subscription information that essentially allowed them to release this data (however, the judge did rule against the police detectives). In another case, a message poster using the pseudonym "Aquacool_2000" sued Yahoo! for revealing his name to a company about whom Aquacool_2000 had made derogatory remarks. The complaint alleged that the company's claim was meritless and that Yahoo! had failed to notify him before releasing this information. This case was settled out of court—ironically with a confidentiality agreement that protected terms.

Indeed, the John Does Foundation, a nonprofit organization supporting anonymous online users who are sued, notes that of the hundreds of suits filed to unmask John Does, very few have gone to court (Ekstrand 2003). While that may seem beneficial to free speech advocates, it also makes it difficult to establish any sort of uniform standard when the merits of anonymous speech have not been fully litigated. When these cases do reach trial, there is a sense that the courts are treading very lightly because of the constitutional implications involved (Bischof 2001b). As to why some of these cases never reach trial, Law Professor Lyrissa Lidsky notes in some instances the plaintiff in these cases may not really be seeking damages—they simply want to know the identity of the message posters "solely for the purpose of intimidating their critics into silence and that's what makes them so dangerous" (cited in Bischof 2001b 35). Others have noted that the true identity of the individual is sought in order for persons or organizations to enact their own extra-judicial punishments. According to Ekstrand (2003), only about half the U.S. states have laws prohibiting these sorts of lawsuits, known as SLAPP (strategic lawsuits against public participation) suits.

The events of September 11, 2001, may well have contributed to a shift away from online anonymity protections as well. Wieland (2001) contends that Internet service providers are now readily working with government in the interest of national security and several anonymous remailer sites have been shut down since that time. Furthermore, the courts have broadened what they may accept as compelling state reasons in cases seeking to identify anonymous communicators, which further limits protections for anonymous online communication. Even considering the recent Doe v. Ashcroft case mentioned previously, an examination of existing cases seems to confirm what legal experts and free speech proponents have concluded: it is difficult to determine the direction of the courts when it comes to the protection of anonymous online speech. It does not appear that a landmark decision in this area is yet in place, and when this topic has actually been litigated in courtrooms across this country, the results have been rather mixed. As communication scholars, we can offer some critiques of this situation and guidelines that reach beyond legal views in an effort to address this complicated topic.

Critiques and Communicative Recommendations

Rather than wait and hope for better laws and clearer legal standards that provide adequate protection for online anonymous communication, several critiques and recommendations are offered for work in this area. No one, including myself, is proposing anything that would allow for slander or defamation via anonymous online communication; free speech rights do not extend to such abuses and not having substantial checks on online libel might render online speech meaningless in many ways. But, the solution cannot be to ban online speech because of the potential harms or in the interest of national security. The balance that is sought is one that clearly protects free speech, including anonymous speech online as a first amendment right, unless compelling and substantiated evidence clearly suggests the need to reveal one's identity.

A very useful starting point emerges from the Dendrite guidelines. Relying on earlier guidelines from a case on anonymous cybersquatting, the court suggested the following four-part test to be employed in cases involving subpoenas requesting the identity of anonymous communicators (see O'Brien 2002 for details): (a) the plaintiff should make efforts to notify the anonymous posters that they are subject to subpoena, and withhold action until the defendants have reasonable opportunity to respond; (b) the plaintiff should identify the exact statements made by the anonymous poster that constitute actionable speech; (c) the plaintiff must present a prima facie case; and (d) the court must balance the necessity of disclosing the defendant's identity with regard to his/her first amendment rights relative to allowing the plaintiff to proceed with the case. Existing analyses from legal scholars and free speech proponents generally support such guidelines (see Chiger 2002; O'Brien 2002). In extending these guidelines, both Chiger and O'Brien note that the online context in which these comments take place must be considered—because the informal and uninhibited nature of the chat room or message board area really should be considered separately from the newspaper editorial page or a television broadcast on a major news network.

The discussion of differences between channel/technology also demands that efforts to consider anonymous online communication consider the array of tools that may permit such interaction. The focus of current attention has been heavily geared toward online discussion/message boards, with some additional attention to online websites, chatrooms, and remailers. Though an obvious starting point, it does not even begin to address the range of technologies that could be used for anonymous online speech. Simply forwarding emails and stripping off identifying information from previous senders begins to make for anonymous speech. Even in synchronous chat rooms, instant messaging sessions, or during text-messaging, individuals have (and will increasingly have) the ability to copy, cut, paste, and forward messages to environments that reach more and more people. Voice files or Internet telephony raise a whole additional set of issues—and may still constitute anonymous communication when the identity of the sender is unknown (and the voice unrecognized or disguised). It is unclear if existing laws and guidelines cover other forms of mediated communication when it comes to free speech rights, especially when other forms do not share some of the same characteristics of the text-based asynchronous message boards. In possibly parallel legal work related to online privacy, fundamentally different laws are generally applied to recorded (asynchronous) vs. live (synchronous) interactions (see Martucci & Place 1998). And, even though technology is increasingly available to gather Internet traffic data and implement sophisticated data retention programs (which may themselves violate first amendment rights (see Crump 2003), individuals have technological solutions as well to preserve their anonymity—including the use of public computers, identity-masking programs, and anonymizing services (though these can vary vastly in the degree of anonymity they ultimately provide). In short, the Internet is not a singular environment—and the types of anonymity made possible and the degree of protections provided may well vary depending on the specific application/tool used.

Existing models/frameworks for anonymity may also be instructive. Marx (1999), for example, suggests that there are seven different types of identity knowledge that vary in degree of identifiability. These range from legal name, through various forms of pseudonyms, to broader social categories. Legal efforts seem focused entirely on legal name, though issues related to locatability and reachability (his second category) are often part of the identity-uncovering and identity-protecting efforts as well. Since much of the anonymous communication on the Internet is actually pseudonymous, there is a great deal of identifiability in place already. Is it possible that a pseudonym (as an extension of an offline self) can be sued or criminally charged in ways that meet others' needs but still protect the identity of the communicator? Little serious attention has been given to such issues to date. Anonymous's (1998) model of communicator anonymity may also be relevant in several ways. First, a determination of the motivations/reasons one has to communication online anonymously may be informative when courts are evaluating the importance of free speech relative to someone else's rights. If lowered status or concerns about credibility and retribution are the motivation, that may carry more weight than motivations done simply because it was easy to do so or fun. Relatedly, the motivations of the party trying to overcome the anonymity of the message sender should be considered, as certain motivations may again carry more weight than others. Finally, the model suggests the importance of anonymity or identification efforts over time. If one's identity is revealed even once, we should understand that action may deter future uses of anonymous communication—effectively chilling speech well beyond any intended frame.

Another critique and focus for future work centers on reading/hearing anonymous communication. Although first amendment rights generally include rights to receive and read communication also, rarely has this been considered in terms of its extension to freely reading/hearing anonymous online speech. Froomkin (1999) notes that even though logic would suggest such an extension, there is "no directly relevant decision of the Supreme Court to support this assertion" (122). Yet, as Crump (2003) notes, since so much online activity centers on reading web pages (and people generally spend more time reading online versus sending anyway), this is a vital issue to consider. Furthermore, the advantages of anonymous speech depend almost entirely on others' ability to view such material—and doing so anonymously may be essential at times. In an age of increased Internet monitoring, the same tools that identify anonymous message senders can also tell us who has received (anonymously or otherwise) such messages. In the dialogue and exchange of ideas that depends heavily on sending/speaking, reading/hearing and responding, legislation and legal interpretations that cover the entire anonymous communication process are needed.

An extremely important set of players in this anonymity-accountability debate are the intermediaries involved. For the most part, this has meant the Internet service provider organizations that maintain information on their otherwise pseudonymous posters; however, intermediaries could include organizations providing other tools (e.g., anonymizer.com), neutral third-party organizations, or even private individuals operating certain anonymizing services. Even though laws have reduced the extent to which these intermediaries are liable for users' messages, most Internet service providers still do little to protect user anonymity. Ironically perhaps, the growth of suits requesting user identity information from these providers has moved them toward "a critical new role as potential defenders of anonymous speech" (Ekstrand 2003 426). Ekstrand argues that the time may be appropriate for these service providers to step forward in defense of those subscribers who wish to criticize anonymously. Yet, as the recent case involving Freedman vs. AOL (and others) illustrates, even these service providers moving toward such roles are clearly still not there on a consistent basis. This suggests that other types of intermediaries—as long as they are not government based—may be a more viable means of protecting user identities until compelling reasons are provided otherwise. Whoever the intermediaries are, they must make very clear and communicate regularly their institutional policies on disclosure of identifying information.

A discussion of institutional policy brings us to consideration of the organizations in which most of us work as another site for anonymous organizational communication. My own formal and informal efforts to examine anonymity in this area suggest that most organizations do not think much about anonymity—and if they do, it typically goes against desired cultural norms favoring openness and directness. Yet, Lipinski (2002) suggests that institutional policies that reflect legal precedents "can help preserve a spirit of free speech, yet allow for the continued functioning of the organization" (p. 108). Thus, policies should be established and communicated in the workplace. Tools that provide for anonymous input should be made available for those situations where people may need them to speak openly. If organizations adopt an attitude of valuing members' rights to anonymous communication and viewing anonymous input as an important form of feedback—often times more honest feedback—there are almost certainly more rewards than potential problems to be gained. Such considerations are especially important to the extent that so many individual protections from the government do not extend to the nongovernmental workplace. One final area relevant to organizations concerns the external message boards or "suck sites" that exist. As opposed to constant legal efforts to shut down such sites, many organizations would be well advised to monitor them to gain feedback about how they might improve operations. Another option is to use these and other interactive media to post an organization's perspective or to provide an alternative viewpoint on the subject.

Perhaps the most important observation and need from all this concerns education of users. Even with the rapid growth of technology, the legal process takes time and it is already clear that there are rather mixed views and competing forces at work here that will likely prohibit an immediate solution to the issues surrounding anonymous online communication. In the meantime, users should be educated in two broad areas. First, "people have a false sense of security about technology and place more trust in it than is warranted. In this way, they are blind to the fact that there exists no such thing as guaranteed anonymity or guaranteed security. Almost anything one does to conceal one's identity can be defeated" (*Teich et al* 1999 75). Education in our classrooms, in our workplaces, in various online communities, and by some of the nonprofit groups that deal with this and related issues (e.g., Electronic Privacy Information Center, John Does Foundation) are key first steps. People need to understand how they are only partially anonymous, and that decisions to communicate this way must be informed of that fact. But at the same time, people should be informed about the technological tools that do provide even this partial anonymity so that those in need are aware that such options exist. Relatedly, these same sources of information can help better educate users about current laws, about when others might be forced to reveal their identities, and when their identities will be protected. Second, we need to be educated as consumers of anonymous information. Again, understanding the motivations as to why something may have been communicated anonymously or pseudonymously may help us to evaluate the credibility of such messages even in the absence of a known source. Relatedly, users in anonymous environments can sometimes manipulate the message so as to make it seem widely supported among a community of users (e.g., having multiple pseudonyms belonging to a single person support an idea) or to play with people's minds by posting frivolous ideas. Although similar behaviors occur offline, they may be even harder to detect in anonymous online communication. Teaching people to be skeptical without rejecting all anonymous messages provides a starting point.

Of course, numerous other challenges and directions emerge here as well. In one sense, the U.S. can pass all sorts of laws on this issue—but the international access to the Internet and the variety of legal standards and norms that exist globally may make such laws increasingly less forceful over time. Additionally, in one of the more ironic cases involving anonymous speech (Wasson v. Agrella; see Hereford 2000), a dismissed employee accused of sending anonymous letters to a college president was not granted first amendment protections because she denied ever sending the messages—meaning that this government employee had to own up to the anonymous speech before such speech could be protected (under the idea that you can't be protected for something you did not say; for related discussion about rights of attribution (see Lemley 1999). These two examples, and many others, point to the numerous challenges still ahead for anonymous online communication.

In closing, even as communication and speech scholars, some of us are hesitant about the use of anonymity. Somehow, it seems secretive and indirect, and a substitute for how communication should really take place. And, ideally perhaps, there would be no need for anonymous communication because we would live in a world where people really could freely express their ideas without any fear of attack or ridicule (or worse). But, at the turn of the 21st century, we are perhaps no more living in that ideal world than was Publius over 200 years ago. In many ways, the growth of various new communication technologies facilitating both the appropriate and inappropriate use of anonymous speech makes today's world even more complicated in this regard. As a result, it is important that we not bemoan the anonymous speaker's rapidly approaching death, but instead celebrate the potential for its resurrection in the online chatrooms, bulletin boards, and other virtual environments we use for communication today.

Endnotes

1. Anonymous remailers, which may be unfamiliar to many, remove all the information in the address header to make the message sender anonymous to message receivers. By sending messages through numerous remailers (across various networks and servers), the messages can become largely untraceable (see Barnes 1999). Anonymous web surfing allows one to go online without websites, governments, or others being able to track one's activities while in cyberspace. The most sophisticated systems are based on onion routing, where messages are relayed via a distributed network of random servers; furthermore, messages in this network are unwrapped by an encryption key at each server that peels off one layer to obtain further instructions (Harrison 2004).

Works Cited

Anonymous (1998). ''To reveal or not to reveal: A theoretical model of anonymous communication.'' *Communication Theory, 8,* 381-407.

Barnes, S. B. (1999). ''Ethical issues for a virtual self.'' In S. J. Drucker & G. Gumpert (Eds.), *Real law @ virtual space.* Cresskill, NJ: Hampton. 371-398

Barnes, S. B. (2003). *Computer-mediated communication: Human-to-human communication across the Internet.* Boston: Allyn & Bacon.

Bischof, D. (2001a). ''Apeals court affirms right to anonymity online.'' *News Media & The Law, 25(3),* 18.

Bischof, D. (2001b). ''Through accusations of defamation, companies are starting to unmask anonymous online critics.'' *News Media & The Law, 25(1),* 35-35.

Botan, C. (1996). ''Communication work and electronic surveillance: A model for predicting panoptic effects.'' *Communication Monographs, 63,* 293-313.

Bowman, L. M. (2001, August 13). ''*Online anonymity wins again.*'' Retrieved August 16, 2001, from http:// news.cnet.com.

Chiger, S. J. (2002). ''Cybersmear: Telecommunication's 200-year-old riddle.'' *Communications and the Law, 24(2),* 49-67.

Crump, C. (2003). ''Data retention: Privacy, anonymity, and accountability online.'' *Stanford Law Review, 56,* 191-229.

Dorsey, P. C. (2004, February 7). ''*Ruling on plaintiff's motion for partial summary judgment.*'' Retrieved February 15, 2004, from http://www.ctd.uscourts.gov/Opinions/020403.PCD.Freedman_partialSJ.pdf.

Ekstrand, V. S. (2003). ''Unmasking Jane and John Doe: Online anonymity and the first amendment.'' *Communication Law & Policy, 8,* 405-427.

Erickson, K. V., & Fleuriet, C. A. (1991). ''Presidential anonymity: Rhetorical identity management and the mystification of political reality.'' *Communication Quarterly, 39,* 272-289.

France, M., & Carney, D. (2000, February 28). ''Free speech on the net? Not quite.'' *Business Week,* 93-94.

Froomkin, A. M. (1999). ''Legal issues in anonymity and pseudonymity.'' *Information, Computers, & Technology, 14,* 79-88.

Godin, S. (2001, October). ''In my humble opinion.'' *Fast Company, 51*, 86-88.

Habermas, J. (1989). *The structural transformation of the public sphere: An inquiry into a category of bourgeois society* (Trans. T. Burger). Cambridge, MA: MIT Press.

Hamblett, M. (2004, September 30). ''Judge disallows secret FBI demand for customer data.'' *New York Law Journal,* p. 1.

Harrison, A. (2004, August 5). ''Onion routing averts prying eyes.'' Retrieved February 5, 2005, from http://www.wired.com/news/privacy/0,1848,64464,00.html.

Hereford, L. (2000). ''California court rejects professor's 'anonymous' free speech.'' *Community College Week, 12(17),* 8-9.

Johnson, D. G. (1997). Ethics online. *Communications of the ACM, 40(1),* 60-65.

Kling, R., Lee Y., Teich, A., & Frankel, M. S. (1999). ''Assessing anonymous communication on the Internet: Policy deliberations.'' *Information Society, 15,* 79-90.

Lemley, M. A. (1999). ''Rights of attribution and integrity in online communication.'' In S. J. Drucker & G. Gumpert (Eds.), *Real law @ virtual space* (pp. 251-266). Cresskill, NJ: Hampton.

Lipinski, T. A. (2002). ''To speak or not to speak: Developing legal standards for anonymous speech on the Internet.'' *Informing Science, 5,* 95-111.

Martucci, W. C., & Place, J. M. (1998). ''Privacy rights and employee communication in the workplace.'' *Employment Relations Today, 25,* 109-120.

Marx, G. T. (1999). ''What's in a name? Some reflections on the sociology of anonymity.'' *Information Society, 15,* 99-112.

Marx, G. T. (2001). ''Identity and anonymity: Some conceptual distinctions and issues for research.'' In J. Caplan & J. Torpey (Eds.), *Documenting individual identity: The development of state practices in the modern world.* Princeton, NJ: Princeton University. 311-327

Nissenbaum, H. (2003). ''Securing trust online: Wisdom or oxymoron?'' In B. E. Kolko (Ed.), *Virtual publics: Policy and community in an electronic age* (pp. 134-171). New York: Columbia University.

O'Brien, J. (2002). ''Putting a face to a (screen)name: The first amendment implications of compelling ISPs to reveal the identities of anonymous Internet speakers in online defamation cases.'' *Fordham Law Review, 70,* 2745-2776.

O'Sullivan, P. B., & Flanagin, A. J. (2003). ''Reconceptualizing 'flaming' and other problematic messages.'' *New Media & Society, 5,* 69-94.

Saco, D. (2002). ''*Cybering democracy: Public space and the Internet.*'' Minneapolis, MN: University of Minnesota. Samoriski, J. (2002). *Issues in cyberspace: Communication, technology, law, and society on the Internet frontier.* Boston: Allyn & Bacon.

Scott, C. R. (1999). ''The impact of physical and discursive anonymity on group members' multiple identifications during computer-supported decision making.'' *Western Journal of Communication, 63,* 456-487.

Scott, C. R., & Easton, A. (1996). ''Examining equality of influence in group decision support system interaction.'' *Small Group Research, 27,* 360-382.

Scott, C. R., & Rains, S. A. (2002, November). *Anonymous communication in organizations: Assessing appropriateness, use, and adequacy.* Paper presented to the annual convention of the National Communication Association, New Orleans, LA.

Shedletsky, L. J., & Aitken, J. E. (2004). ''*Human communication on the Internet.* Boston: Pearson. Spears, R., & Lea, M. (1994). Panacea or panopticon? The hidden power in computer-mediated communication.'' *Communication Research, 21,* 427-459.

Stein, E. (2003). ''eers anonymous: Lesbians, gay men, free speech, and cyberspace.'' *Harvard Civil Rights-Civil Liberties Law Review, 38,* 159-203.

Steinmeyer, P. A. (2001). ''Anonymous speech.'' *The National Law Journal, 23,* B8.

Teich, A., Frankel, M. S., Kling, R., & Lee Y. (1999). ''Anonymous communication policies for the Internet: Results and recommendations of the AAAS conference.'' *Information Society, 15,* 71-77.

Turkle, S. (1995). *Life on the screen: Identity in the age of the Internet.* New York: Simon & Schuster.
Wieland, J. B. (2001). ''Death of Publius: Toward a world without anonymous speech.'' *Journal of Law & Politics, 17,* 589-629.
Williams, R. (1988). ''Reflections on anonymity.'' *Perceptual and Motor Skills, 67,* 763-766.

The Supreme Court and Freedom of Speech, 2003-2004

Paul Siegel
University of Hartford

The 2003-2004 Term was not a very busy one from the perspective of *Yearbook* readers. To be sure, campaign finance reform was a major feature of the year, and the federal legislation before the Court had more direct implications for the act of communication than the issue usually enjoys. No need for parroting such slogans as ''money equals speech'' this time around, in that the statute set forth explicit instructions to candidates which have resulted in advertisements carrying the oft-parodied assertion that ''my name is __________, and I approved of this ad.''

Then too, the Court also issued the latest in a series of rulings on sexual communication on the Internet, again finding that Congress had overstepped its bounds in its laudable zeal to protect children from indecent speech. The Term also featured a more minor decision concerning the logistics for handling licensing schemes for ''adult'' businesses.

The third and last communication-relevant issue addressed by the Court in its 2003-2004 Term was access to information. In one of two such cases, at issue was the application of privacy interests under Exemption 7C of the Freedom of Information Act to surviving family members; the second dealt with far more arcane matters governing separation of powers, executive privilege, and the standards to be used in determining when to issue a writ of mandamus. The case is discussed here because at its core was whether public interest groups would ever get to learn the extent to which unidentified energy industry executives helped create the Bush Administration's policies as formulated by a task force chaired by the Vice President back in 2001.

Before beginning our extended discussions of this handful of decisions, passing mention should be made of one non-decision that received much press attention during the 2003-2004 Term. *Elk Grove United School District v. Newdow* (2004) appeared as if it would settle definitively whether insertion of the words ''under God'' into the Pledge of Allegiance was constitutional as applied to public school children. But alas, the Court managed to skirt the issue by finding that Mr. Newdow, as a *non*-custodial parent, did not have standing to bring the suit on behalf of his minor daughter.

CAMPAIGN FINANCE REFORM

McConnell v. FEC, 540 U.S. 93 (2003).

Key provisions of the Bipartisan Campaign Finance Reform Act of 2002 governing political contributions and expenditures, and explicitly regulating content of broadcast campaign advertisements, are generally not violative of the First Amendment.

The Bipartisan Campaign Finance Reform Act of 2002 (popularly known as ''McCain-Feingold,'' after its main sponsors) constituted a multi-pronged Congressional attempt to reduce corruption and the appearance of corruption in the electioneering process. Chief among the statute's provisions ultimately upheld by the Supreme Court were ones that:

- Prohibit national political parties from accepting or spending "soft money" (unlimited contributions by corporations, unions and individuals);
- Limit state and local party committees to accepting no more than $10,000 from individuals, to be used only for "get-out-the-vote" and voter-registration activities in federal elections;
- Prohibit even such activities to refer to any specific candidate for federal office;
- Raise the amount of regulated "hard money" that individuals can give to candidates and parties ($2,000 to each candidate and $25,000 to any political party, with an overall total of $95,000 in each 2-year election cycle);
- Require that any broadcast advertisements aired within 30 days of a primary or 60 days of a general election that mention the name of a candidate for federal office, the Court's opinion refers to these as "electioneering communications," must be paid with regulated "hard money." Thus, individuals or organizations spending independently of candidates may not even take to the airwaves during these time frames (unless they avoid mentioning candidates by name).
- Limit[1] a long-standing requirement that broadcasters sell time to candidates at bargain rates only to candidates who either promise not to mention their opponents by name, or who include in their ads their own image together with a sentence to the effect that "my name is ________, and I approved this message."[2]

A coalition of 80 plaintiffs including both the Democratic and Republican parties of California challenged the law's constitutionality. An unusually lengthy 2-day hearing was held in front of a special 3-judge panel in December, 2002. An even more unusually lengthy decision over 1,600 pages worth emerged in May, 2003 (*McConnell v, Fec* 2003). The court struck down and/or limited some provisions eventually upheld by the Supreme Court. But since the lower court stayed its own decision, pending the Supreme Court outcome, fund raising and advertising activities in the 2004 election cycle were governed by the provisions of McCain-Feingold.

The Supreme Court heard arguments in the case—four hours worth instead of the usual one a few weeks earlier than its usual first Monday in October term commencement, and issued its rulings in December 2003. Not surprisingly, the Court's eventual opinions in the *McConnell* case were extraordinarily lengthy, over 250 pages in the *United States Reports*. Moreover, the LEXIS database broke the case up into 3 separate online documents all sharing the same citation. Another unusual feature of the case was that Justices Stevens and O'Connor wrote one portion of the majority opinion together. (Other portions of the majority opinion, as the votes shifted on different features of this terribly complex statute, were written by Chief Justice Rehnquist and by Justice Breyer). So complicated was the array of opinions that the usual breakdown of majority, concurring and dissenting opinions provided at the end of this discussion will need to be broken down, title by title of the act.

The Stevens-O'Connor majority opinion upheld what were seen as the law's chief provisions from Title I and Title II of the act (the prohibition on political parties raising "soft money;" the limitation on "electioneering communications"[3]). Chief Justice Rehnquist's section of the majority opinion (dealing with Titles III and IV of the act) was the one that has resulted in all those candidate appearances in their own commercials, telling us that they "approved this message." The Rehnquist opinion also struck down a provision of the law that had forbade minors from making contributions to candidates or parties. As to the portion of the majority opinion written by Justice Breyer, it upheld more minor provisions of the statute, ones requiring broadcast licensees to maintain careful records of three kinds of politically-oriented "requests:"

- ***"Candidate requests"*** (made by or on behalf of any legally qualified candidate for public office);

- ***"Election message requests"*** (requests made by anyone to broadcast messages that refer either to a legally qualified candidate for federal office, or to a pending federal election);
- ***"Issue requests"*** (requests made by anyone to broadcast messages related to a national legislative issue of public importance or otherwise relating to a political matter of national importance).

None of these provisions are especially onerous, Breyer held. Indeed, "broadcaster record-keeping requirements simply run with the territory" (*McConnell v. FEC* 520 U.S. 235).

Title I:

MAJORITY: Stevens and O'Connor; Souter, Ginsburg, Breyer
CONCURRING: Kennedy (in part); Rehnquist (in part)
DISSENTING: Scalia; Thomas; Kennedy (in part)

Title II:

MAJORITY: Stevens and O'Connor; Souter, Ginsburg, Breyer
CONCURRING: Scalia (in part); Thomas (in part)
DISSENTING: Scalia (in part); Thomas (in part); Kennedy, Rehnquist

Title III:

MAJORITY: Rehnquist, O'Connor, Scalia, Kennedy, Souter, with (in part) Stevens, Ginsburg, Breyer, and Thomas
CONCURRING: Thomas (in part)
DISSENTING: Thomas (in part)

Title IV:

MAJORITY: Rehnquist, O'Connor, Scalia, Kennedy, Souter; Thomas (in part)
CONCURRING: Scalia; Thomas (in part)
DISSENTING: Stevens, Ginsburg, Breyer

Title V:

MAJORITY: 'Breyer, Stevens, O'Connor, Souter, Ginsburg
DISSENTING: Scalia; Thomas; Rehnquist, Kennedy

SEXUAL COMMUNICATIONS

Ashcroft v. ACLU, 124 S. Ct. 2783 (2004).

The Child Online Protection Act was properly enjoined from enforcement, in that less restrictive means of protecting children from sexually charged Internet content, such as filtering and blocking software, are readily available.

We first reported on the Child Online Protection Act in the *Yearbook's* review of the Court's 2001-2002 Term. The law was scheduled to take effect in 1998, but was blocked by a federal district ruling later upheld by the Third Circuit Court of Appeals.

In 2002 the Supreme Court, while keeping in force Judge Reed's order enjoining the law from taking effect, vacated the federal appellate court's ruling that Congress violated the First Amendment by using "contemporary community standards" as a criterion to define "material harmful to minors (*Ashcroft v. ACLU (I)* 2002). (The appellate court had been concerned that the contemporary community standards doctrine, applied to the Internet, would put content providers at the mercy of the nation's ''most puritan communities.'').

There was no clear majority telling us exactly why the Supreme Court vacated this aspect of the lower court's ruling. Some sections of Justice Thomas's opinion commanded 4 votes, some 3; only those sections relating the history of the adjudication and the Court's actual decision were signed by a majority of the Court.

Upon remand the appellate court again upheld Judge Reed's injunction (*ACLU v. Ashcroft* 2003), this time managing to avoid reliance on the ''community standards'' issue and the Supreme Court again granted review. At the end of its 2003-2004 term, a 5-4 majority of the Court continued to enjoin enforcement of the law (*Ashcroft v. ACLU (II)* 2004). While stopping short of actually invalidating the statute outright, Justice Kennedy's majority opinion suggests that parental use of any of the filtering software on the market might be a more suitable means of protecting children from sexual messages than the statute's mechanism of having commercial Internet speakers require customers to provide credit card information. Many minors, after all, have their own credit cards, and could thus flout Congress's intent. Then too, the federal statute can only criminalize conduct conducted within America's shores, but a high per cent of sexually explicit web sites originate overseas. Indeed, were the statute to be enforced aggressively, domestic Internet pornographers would likely view the acquisition of offshore-based servers as just one more cost of doing business.

Kennedy suggested also that sending the case back to the lower court for further factual development was especially appropriate in this case, which has dragged on so long that the Internet itself may be a very different entity from what it had been when the law was first passed. Some of those differences might have constitutional import. Moreover, the efficacy of filtering and blocking software has certainly changed in the ensuing years, and here too the lower court would benefit from an updating of the factual record.

Justice Stevens (with Ginsburg joining) wrote a separate concurring opinion in which he suggested that the majority had based too much of its decision on practicality and not enough on First Amendment principle. Stevens agreed with the district court's initial assessment that traditional notions of ''community'' standards have no place on the Internet, a medium designed to transcend geographic communities and to build new visions of community. While allowing that protecting children is itself a laudable enterprise, he expressed concern that criminal law should not be used as a substitute for parental oversight.

Justice Breyer wrote a dissenting opinion, joined by Justice O'Connor and Chief Justice Rehnquist. In it he argued that the majority manifests a bit too much deference to the interests of speakers whose online messages are covered by the statute's scope. For Breyer that scope is virtually isomorphic with long-established definitions of obscenity, which is wholly beyond the First Amendment's protection. Yes, the statute makes reference to communications designed to appeal to *minors'* prurient interests, and that lack serious value *for minors*, but such language does not create a much broader set of covered works than ordinary definitions of obscenity.

Even for those few, yet unidentified, artifacts that might be otherwise protected by the First Amendment (i.e., which are not obscene for adults), the statute does not prohibit dissemination, Breyer added; it merely requires purveyors to take specified actions to reduce the chances that minors will be exposed to the works.

Breyer also accused the majority of misapplying the ''less restrictive means'' test. Filtering software, he points out, is not an alternative legislative proposal; it is rather part of the extra-legal landscape, the status quo. Parents always have the opportunity (if they can afford it) to purchase Internet filters. The Court should have asked whether Congress' requirement of a credit card or similar identity verification is likely to protect more minors from being exposed to obscene commercial sites. For Breyer, it is obvious that Congress has acted reasonably, in that filtering technology is imprecise (filtering out too many non-obscene images, while allowing too many truly obscene images in).

Justice Scalia wrote a short dissenting opinion, in which he claimed that the pornographers whose interests are protected by the Court majority are guilty of sexual pandering at least, even if not peddling obscenity. As such, the Court never should have employed the high degree of First Amendment scrutiny reserved for other kinds of speech. For Scalia, then, not only should the Court have upheld the statute in *toto*; it should have been an easy case.

MAJORITY: Kennedy, Stevens, Souter, Thomas, Ginsburg
CONCURRING: Stevens, Ginsburg
DISSENTING: Scalia; Breyer, Rehnquist, O'Connor

City of Littleton, Colorado v. Z.J. Gifts, 122 S.Ct. 2219 (2004).

A town ordinance governing ''adult'' businesses is not constitutionally infirm for lack of an explicit right to expedited review of license applications, in that state law already provided for such review.

The named municipality had a local ordinance governing the licensing of ''adult businesses.'' Rather than avail itself of the licensing application procedure, Z.J. Gifts opened a covered business in an area of town not zoned for such enterprises, and then brought suit to challenge the constitutionality of the local law.

The city offered two arguments. First, it claimed that its only obligation to owners of adult businesses was to offer prompt judicial *review* of any adverse decision, citing the Court's 1990 decision in *FW/PBS, Inc.* v. *Dallas*.[4] The plaintiffs, relying in large part on language from the much earlier *Freedman v. Maryland* (1965), claimed that the city must be prepared to offer a prompt judicial *decision*). Concerning the variation in language, Justice Breyer's majority opinion accuses the city of ''making too much of too little'' (*City of Littleton, Colorado v. Z.J. Gifts* 2224). The Court's *FW/PBS* decision did not loosen the *Freedman* requirements; indeed, in that same 1990 decision the Court tells us that ''the license for a First Amendment-protected business must be issued within a reasonable period of time'' (2224 citing 493 U.S. 228). Granting a license sounds much more like making a decision than it does merely performing a review of arguments.

The city's second argument was that its licensing scheme did meet the constitutional promptness requirement, however construed by the Court. Here the Court agreed. First, Justice Breyer pointed out, we have no reason to presume that Colorado will fail to offer prompt judicial review of any denied license for an adult-oriented business. As is commonplace in the states, Colorado's own judicial rules provide for expedited review of claims that encompass fundamental constitutional rights. Since the plaintiff in this case never availed itself of the licensing process, choosing instead to mount a facial challenge to the governing statute, it is at best premature to find fault with the city.

Breyer also went out of his way to emphasize what he saw as important factual distinctions between the licensing scheme at issue here and the law struck down by the Court in *Freedman v. Maryland.* The earlier case involved a Board of Censors to which films must be submitted and which had the power to completely prevent the showing of any artifacts it found ''pornographic'' (a far broader category under the statute than *obscene* films).

By contrast, Littleton intended only to employ content-neutral criteria[5] to determine if a license for an adult-oriented business should be granted. Such criteria, applied fairly, might result in some applicants failing to obtain a license to run an adult-oriented business. But others would get such licenses, and so it would be very unlikely that any specific book or film or similar artifact would be wholly unavailable within the city limits. As Breyer put it, "a supplier of that material should be able to find outlets; a potential buyer should be able to find a seller."[6]

Justice Scalia wrote a short concurring opinion in which he suggested that the majority was a bit too solicitous of the license applicant's claims. This ordinance is aimed at "sex-pandering businesses," he chided Breyer; the First Amendment is applicable only peripherally, if at all.

Justice Stevens wrote a separate, partial concurrence, in which he expressed concern with what he saw as the majority's conflating of two distinct promises from the *Freedman* and *FW/PBS* cases. After today's decision, he feared, "assurance of a 'prompt judicial decision' means little more than assurance of the *possibility* of a prompt decision" (2227).

Critiquing the majority from an opposite direction, Justice Souter, joined by Justice Kennedy, also wrote a separate partial concurrence. They allow that the licensing scheme here does not amount to "full-blown censorship," but they caution that it is also not "as innocuous as common zoning." The mechanism is more of a hybrid, using content-neutral criteria that are nonetheless "triggered by the content of expressive materials" (2227).

ACCESS TO GOVERNMENT INFORMATION

National Archives and Records Administration v. Favish, 124 S.Ct. 1570 (2004).

FOIA's Exemption 7 C may properly be construed to apply to the privacy rights not only of the target of a law enforcement investigation, but to surviving family members as well.

Exemption 7 of the federal Freedom of Information Act (the law enforcement exemption) is really six exemptions in one. Section 7C provides for the non-disclosure of law enforcement records the revelation of which "could reasonably be expected to constitute an unwarranted invasion of personal privacy." In its 2003-2004 Term, the Court had to consider a novel issue, must the person objecting to disclosure be the subject of the files, or can that person's survivors also inject themselves into the litigation?

In dispute were photographs of the Vincent Foster death scene in a park outside of Washington, DC. Foster, it will be recalled, was President Clinton's deputy counsel, whose apparent suicide shocked the Washington establishment and provided fodder for conspiracy theorists of many persuasions, despite the unanimous conclusions of the U. S. Park Police, the Senate, the House, the FBI, and independent counsels Robert Fiske and Kenneth Starr that this was, in fact, a suicide.

Allan Favish of the group Accuracy in Media was unconvinced, and sought disclosure of the official police photos under the FOIA. When the case, actually a handful of consolidated, related cases, reached the Supreme Court, Justice Kennedy concluded for a unanimous Court that the privacy interests of Foster's surviving family members were strong enough to outweigh Favish's interest in disclosure. It would be different if the family members were merely arguing as a proxy for Foster's own privacy interests, Kennedy admitted, but they had their own independent claims:

> They seek to be shielded by the exemption to secure their own refuge from a sensation-seeking culture for their own peace of mind and tranquility, not for the sake of the deceased. . .Foster's sister, Sheila Foster Anthony, stated that the family had been harassed by, and deluged with requests from, "political and commercial opportunists" who sought to profit from Foster's suicide. In particular, she was "horrified and devastated by [a] photograph [already] leaked to the press." "Every time I see it" [she] wrote, "I have nightmares and heart-pounding insomnia as I visualize how he must have spent his last few minutes and seconds of his life." She opposed the disclosure of the disputed pictures because "I fear that the release of [additional] photographs certainly would set off another round of intense scrutiny

by the media. Undoubtedly, the photographs would be placed on the Internet for world consumption. Once again my family would be the focus of conceivably unsavory and distasteful media coverage.''[7]

Kennedy also emphasized that Congress never intended for Exemption 7 C to be so narrowly construed as to reach only the privacy interests of the subject of a requested file. The ''could reasonably be expected to. . .'' language is far broader, he pointed out, than the corresponding language associated with Exemption 6 of the Act which makes reference to disclosures of personnel, medical, and ''similar'' files that ''*would* constitute'' an invasion of privacy. The difference may seem small, but the legislative record indicates it was intentional. And this makes sense, Kennedy suggested in that ''law enforcement documents often have information about persons whose link to the official inquiry may be the result of mere happenstance.''

Interestingly, Kennedy phrased the Court's main holding in the *Favish* case so narrowly as to suggest case-by-case jurisprudence. The Court tells us only the ''FOIA recognizes surviving family members' right to personal privacy with respect to their close relative's death-scene images'' (1579).

Secondarily, the Court also speaks of FOIA requesters' burden of proof in cases involving Exemption 7C. Specifically, Kennedy tells us that ''where there is a privacy interest protected by Exemption 7C and the public interest being asserted is to show that responsible officials acted negligently or otherwise improperly in the performance of their duties, the requester must establish more than a bare suspicion in order to obtain disclosure. Rather, the requester must produce evidence that would warrant a belief by a reasonable person that the alleged Government impropriety might have occurred'' (1581).

MAJORITY: (Unanimous)

Cheney v. United States District Court 124 S.Ct. 2576 (2004).

Lower courts should pay great deference to the executive branch's need for secrecy, even in the absence of a formal invoking of executive privilege.

Were analogies still part of the Scholastic Aptitude Exam, the stem of a practice item for political junkies might read ''Bill Clinton is to Health Care as George W. Bush is to ________,'' with the correct answer being energy policy. Soon after taking office in 1993, Clinton appointed Hillary to head a task force charged with creating new health care policy, and that task force was the subject of litigation seeking to reveal some of its secret proceedings. A key issue in contention was whether the Clinton committee was the kind of advisory committee Congress had in mind in the Federal Advisory Committee Act, or whether it was exempted from disclosure in that its entire membership (it was initially asserted) were full-time government employees. (Whether the First Lady counts as a government official was a corollary issue) (*Association of American Physicians and Surgeons v. Clinton* 1993).

Similarly, shortly after taking office in 2001, Bush appointed Vice President Cheney to head an energy task force, which was also subject to litigation seeking information about the kinds of witnesses appearing before it. At issue was the same Federal Advisory Committee Act that was involved in the Clinton case. No one disputed this time that the entire official membership of the committee were government officials. But it was equally clear that several energy industry representatives attended meetings and participated actively in meetings, likely even voting. Did such practices render the guests ''quasi-members,'' thus triggering the FACA's disclosure requirements? In that the energy task force's report resulted in sweeping changes, perhaps this is where the Clinton analogy breaks down. Public interest groups from the Sierra Club to Judicial Watch sued to open the group's books. A federal trial court ruled in favor of plaintiffs, at least to the extent of compelling disclosure of the industry representatives' identities (information which, presumably, would have helped determine whether the suit should be able to go further). Upon appeal, the D. C. Circuit Court of Appeal refused to issue a requested writ of mandamus to undo the trial court's ruling, hinting that it might rule differently had Cheney explicitly invoked executive privilege. But, as many commentators have suggested, the Vice President was loath to do so in the context of the looming re-election campaign (Savage and Milligan 2004).

The Supreme Court, in a 7-2 ruling, found that the appellate court had been too timid, that it did not need to wait for the formal invoking of executive privilege. Writing for the majority, Justice Kennedy suggested that the appellate court had followed too closely the spirit of earlier cases involving the Nixon Watergate tapes[8] and the Clinton compelled testimony in front of the Paula Jones grand jury (*Clinton v. Jones* 1997). In both instances courts decided in favor of disclosure, but those cases are distinguishable, Kennedy found. With respect to the Nixon controversy, allegations of criminal wrongdoing were at issue: "The need for information for use in civil cases, while far from negligible, does not share the urgency or significance of the criminal subpoena requests in *Nixon*" (*Cheney v. United States District Court* 2589). In the more recent Clinton debacle, the focus had been on the president's private rather than official conduct.[9]

Justice Stevens' brief concurrence indicates he would have preferred that the appellate court had simply vacated the federal district court's discovery order. Justice Ginsburg, joined by Justice Souter, dissented, indicating they would have preferred that the federal district court be permitted to determine for itself how much pre-trial discovery to permit the plaintiffs. Finally, Justice Thomas (with Scalia joining),[10] wrote a separate partial concurrence, in which he concluded that the appellate court should have been ordered to issue the requested mandamus writ against the district court (thus effectively denying any discovery for plaintiffs).

MAJORITY: Kennedy, Rehnquist, Stevens, O'Connor, Breyer
CONCURRING: Scalia, Thomas (in part)
DISSENTING: Ginsburg, Souter

Endnotes

1. Technically, this section was not *upheld* by the Court. Rather, plaintiff Senator McConnell was deemed not to have standing to challenge the provision, in that he would not be personally affected by it until his next re-election campaign in 2008. Thus, the Court simply refused at this juncture to entertain arguments for overturning the provision.
2. Pundits wondered what effects the new regulations on the actual content of political ads would have. Would politicians eschew negative ads altogether—presumably the only reason to mention an opponent's name is to say something bad about him—in order to receive the lowest unit price on their advertising buys? Or if they used the "my name is. . ." option instead, would having their voice and image appear in the ad lead them to at least tone down the negative attacks? An episode of the *West Wing* aired in early 2005 pretty accurately depicted the statutory provision's real effects which were, in a word, minimal. Candidates tend to insert the "I approve" clip at the very beginning of their ads, and save the most negative assertions about their opponents until the end. Thirty seconds may not seem like a long time, but in fact by the end of that time many viewers do indeed forget the face and voice of the candidate who sponsored the ad.
3. This category of speech was a significant change from the narrower category of regulated communications that began with *Buckley v. Valeo,* 424 U.S. 1 (1976). Messages were regulated only to the extent that they used the "magic words" that explicitly called for a candidate's election or defeat. It had long been felt that advertisers got around this restriction by focusing instead on specific reasons why viewers should be impressed with or disappointed by a candidate's stance on a given issue, but stopping short of calling for the voters to act on their feelings.
4. 493 U.S. 215 (1990).
5. Among the offenses for which an applicant would be denied a license were having had a license revoked in the prior year, or failing to pay taxes or to obtain a sales tax license. None of the criteria made reference to the subject matter of materials to be sold (except for the threshold definition of "adult" business in the first place).

6. 122 S. Ct. at 2225.
7. 124 S. Ct. at 1577-8.
8. *U.S. v. Nixon*, 418 U.S. 683 (1974).
9. Admittedly, special prosecutor Kenneth Starr would not agree with this assessment.
10. Scalia's participation in the case at all had generated more press attention than the Supreme Court's ultimate decision. The justice, it will be recalled, had refused a request to recuse himself after it had been discovered that he had socialized with Vice-President Cheney in the infamous duck hunting episode while the case was pending.

Works Cited

Elk Grove United School District v. Newdow 124 S.Ct 2301 (2004).
ACLU v. Ashcroft 322 F. 3d 240 (3rd Cir. 2003).
Ashcroft v. ACLU (II) 124 S. Ct. 2783 (2004).
Ashcroft v. ACLU (I) 535 U.S. 564 (2002).
Association of American Physicians and Surgeons v. Clinton 997 F. 2d 898 (D.C. Cir. 1993).
Cheney v. United States District Court 124 S.Ct. 2576 (2004).
City of Littleton, Colorado v. Z.J. Gifts, 122 S.Ct. 2219 (2004).
Clinton v. Jones 520 U.S. 681 (1997).
Freedman v. Maryland 380 U.S. 51 (1965).
McConnell v. FEC, 540 U.S. 93 (2003).
McConnell v. FEC, 251 F. Supp. 2d 176 (D.D. C. 2003).
National Archives and Records Administration v. Favish, 124 S.Ct. 1570 (2004).
Savage, C. & Milligan, S. (2004, June 25). "High Court Won't Rule on Cheney Records Case." *Boston Globe*. A1.

Media and Modernity in the United Arab Emirates: Searching for the Beat of a Different Drummer

Timothy Walters and Jack A. Barwind
Zayed University, United Arab Emirates

As H.H. Sheikh Mohammed Rashid Bin Al Maktoum manned a booth at Comdex 2000 in Las Vegas designed to attract techies and their businesses to Dubai Internet City, one glib observer noted that the royal was trying to ''pull a Bugsy Siegel in the middle of the Dubai desert'' building a technological city instead of casinos (Gartner 2000). The stakes might be higher for the United Arab Emirates than they were for Bugsy. Roughly the size of Maine, the UAE has undergone a profound transformation from an impoverished region of small desert principalities to a modern state with a high standard of living in a little more than 30 years. But only about 15% of the reported 4.3 million population in 2005 were nationals; the other 85% were the expatriates who actually drive the economy, serving in capacities ranging from service and construction workers to managers to silent partners for ex-pat entrepreneurs. Less than 11% of the native local population is actually involved in this economy.

Today, the UAE has an estimated 2003 GDP per capita of approximately $23,000 (in purchasing power parity) and Human Development Indicators ranking it in the top portion of the Human Development Index (CIA 2005; *United Arab Emirates Yearbook, 2004*; Human Development Indicators 2004). Despite such gaudy numbers, a hidden secret is that the actual standard of living has been in decline for about the last decade. Such factors as hidden taxation, high birth rates, and large paternalistic subsidizes are responsible, and government leaders who can read between the lines are concerned. In addition, today's current generation lacks the hard, competitive edge that their grandparents had. Born to a high standard of living, these children are either unwilling or unable to compete in an economy with a level playing field. Whatever else, they certainly would not work at low-paying, face threatening entry-level jobs. Therein lies the challenge for the nation's political leaders.

Seven absolute monarchs exercise political power over a federation established in 1971. None of the emirates has any democratically elected institutions and their rule has been both tradition-bound and patriarchal (U.S. Department of State 2001). Because political parties and elections are prohibited, the citizens of the UAE cannot change their government democratically. Citizens may express concerns directly to their rulers by traditional means including the open majlis (International Press Review, 2000; see also U.S. Department of State 2001). However, the role of the majlis as a mechanism connecting rulers with people has diminished in recent years for several reasons. One is because increased societal complexity (a derivative of modernity) has led to a burgeoning bureaucracy; another is life is more hectic, fast paced, and chaotic than before.

One ruler from each Emirate serves as a member of the Federal Supreme Council, the highest legislative and executive body. The council selects a president and a vice president from its membership and the president appoints the prime minister and cabinet. The Cabinet manages the Federation on a day-to-day basis. A consultative body, the Federal National Council, comprising advisors appointed by the emirate rulers, has no legislative authority, but questions government ministers in open sessions and makes policy recommendations to the Cabinet (U.S. Department of State 2001).

Each emirate retains control over its own oil and mineral wealth, some parts of internal security, and some regulation of internal and external commerce. The federal government has primacy in matters of defense and foreign policy, some aspects of internal security, and, increasingly, in the supply of government services (U.S. Department of State 2001).

The judiciary generally is nominally independent, but political leadership can (and does) review its decisions. The legal system of the UAE is based on a constitution approved by the Federal National Council in 1996, replacing the provisional documents that had been renewed every five years since the country's creation in 1971 (IPR 2001). Springing from tradition, the constitution, and legislation, the UAE legal system has been influenced by Islamic, Roman, and French law (Emory nd.; University of Ottawa nd). Common law principles have become important in commercial contracts, and intellectual property law has been modernized recently (Al Tamimi & Company (nd); Dubaiinc nd; IPR 2001; Abu-Ghazaleh nd; Rouse and Company, nd.). Nonetheless, actual enforcement depends upon Wasta (connectedness) and tribal last names.

Today's Emiratis live life large. At all levels, their paternalistic governments support them with no-cost public education, low-cost medicine, high-paying jobs, short working hours, marriage grants, enormous pension contributions, and inexpensive housing. Inspired by the benevolent leadership of the late Sheikh Zayed, the country has blossomed in the desert. In doing so, it has moved from petrodollar dependence to a diversified economy with destination tourism a major force, more than a dozen free trade zones, and a state-of-the-art telecommunications infrastructure. Dubai's speculative building boom with free-hold ownership for foreigners has created a get-rich quick mentality and has lined the pockets of a connected few with billions of Dirhams. The country also has become a transportation hub with modern airports and efficient container ports and increasingly serves as a communications gathering place for Arabic-language media who wish to return from their self-imposed Diaspora. To attract media enterprises, the country has adopted public policy to minimize restrictions and has a Constitution offering protection for free expression in most of its forms (Reuters 7 November 2000; see also, Trabelsi 2001). The singular goal of these several initiatives is to eliminate the drag on progress that the lack of raw materials has made for other area countries (Selber & Ghanem 2004).

Realizing that oil and gas reserves are finite, the federal government has invested heavily in tourism, aviation, re-export commerce, and recently telecommunications. In doing so, leadership has recognized that the country must make more of its human resources. Devoid of most natural resources except for petrocarbons and people, the UAE has invested billions of dollars in high tech. The great dream is that human capital, with its various skills and abilities, can create income-yielding activities and serve as pillar of the future (Walters 2001 82).

While tech and its spin-offs is a great hope for the future, that same technology provides significant challenges. For as information science and knowledge come to propel the economy, that same science and knowledge not only will provide jobs but gateways to empowering individuals. This empowerment will challenge not only traditional notions of society, but how that society functions in the UAE. Even today, a visitor to major cities in the Emirates such as Al Ain, Abu Dhabi, Dubai, or Sharjah is immediately confronted with the paradox of a highly technological and modern city operating within a highly traditional, conservative Islamic culture. Seeing an Emirati woman covered with Abaya, Shaila, and often Burka shopping for designer jeans in the local Gucci or Yves St. Lauren retail outlet punctuates this in a very dramatic way.

Because of changes in the media, government policy, and a modernizing economy, the Emirati culture has been evolving. The mind's eye might flash back to vivid pictures of the welcoming campfire of the traditional Majlis and the harsh, close-to-nature life style romantically described in Thesinger's *Arabian Sands* or Burton's *Personal Narrative of a Pilgrimage to Al Madinah and Mecca* (*Volume 1*). This traditional culture was founded on the Bedouin values of honor, prudence, goodwill, nobility, wisdom, gentleness, justice, control, good sense, and dignity. Loyalty and an emphasis on honor, both drawn from a simpler past, were other valued traits (Patai1983). Citizens admired leaders who displayed patience, hospitality, responsibility, honor, honesty, and bravery (Swan & Walters 2004). And, Islam has served as *the* normative force defining personal conduct and acceptable community behavior for hundreds of years (Patai 1983; Lewis 1990).

For sometime though, Emirati society has been moving from this mythic Bedouin-inspired lifestyle to that of an increasingly sedentary highly urbanized society. This new society is faster paced, more secular, less religious, and more urbanized than ever before. Much of this change has been the product of a marketplace economy drive by modern media. The rising knowledge-driven economy uses and depends upon modern media and interacts with that media. As this has happened, Emirati culture has been affected because examples for life have become intertwined with electronic habits of a new "life literacy." Some view this as the 8th day of creation in the Middle East

Metaphors for living have shifted as the range of work has evolved from agrarian to knowledge based and work sites have shifted from small villages or nomadic living to urbanized centers. Cities such as Abu Dhabi and Dubai have populations of about a million and a million plus respectively whose citizens live fast-paced increasingly impersonal, though not quite anonymous, lifestyles. Outlying Emirates such as Ras Al Khaimah, Sharjah, and Umm Al Quain now are threatened with slow depopulation as their younger citizens collect in these larger urban areas for economic opportunity. Forced to look inward, each of these Emirates is grasping for a sensible development model.

As the society begins the search for tomorrow, traditional culture and the Internet-inspired world both will compete in the marketplace of ideas. As this occurs, society will examine regulatory issues (who owns the Internet, who controls the Internet, and how will the Internet be regulated); the why, how, and what to control of content; and how cyberspace can be used to drive economic activity and make the most of human capital (Aizu 1997; see also Price and Krug 2000).

Civic Society

Law does not determine by itself how free, pluralistic, or independent media (including Internet media) will be. That is because the interaction between legal and social/cultural institutions defines this freedom (Price and Krug 2000 8-10). Laws, of course, help, but even authoritarian societies have mastered the vocabulary of free expression (and access to that expression) and have written it into their constitutions. A few examples from recognized authoritarian governments are highly illustrative. Article 14 of Singapore's constitution calls for freedom of speech, assembly, and association subject to such "such restrictions as it considers necessary or expedient in the interest of the security of Singapore or any part thereof, friendly relations with other countries, public order or morality and restrictions designed to protect the privileges of Parliament or to provide against contempt of court, defamation or incitement to any offence. . . ." Article 40 of Saudi Arabia's constitution safeguards all means of communication, guaranteeing that they shall not be confiscated, delayed, read or listened to except in cases defined by statutes. And Article 35 of the Constitution of the People's Republic of China says that Citizens of the People's Republic of China enjoy freedom of speech and of the press. (See International Constitutional Law nd.)

The will of the people and the development of civic society have great impact on the reality of what actually happens (O'Donnell and Schmitter 1986; Geremek 1992; Diamond 1994;

Bryant 1995). Civic society exists above the individual level but below that of the state and is institutionalized and generalized through law, custom, and practice. In civic society complex networks of economic, social, and cultural practices based on friendship, family, the market, and voluntary association influence daily life (Wapner 1995). Sometimes, but not always, civic society is a precursor to a democratic state (O'Donnell and Schmitter 1986; Geremek 1992; Diamond 1994; Bryant 1995). Such civic forces are in play in varying degrees in the UAE and sister GCC countries, where kinship and marriage count, and extended family networks wield enormous power in all aspects of life. Thus, any articulation of Freedom of Expression becomes intertwined with family, tradition, and heritage. (See for example, Essoulami 2001.)

Geography, history, culture, language, and the seven Emirate-based monarchies remain keystones of a millennium-old routine of life. The building blocks of this life require that individuals serve families, families serve society, and the individual serves both (Patai 1983; Nawar 2000). For most, the family and tribal structure are the fundamental metaphors. Traditionally, the freedoms that matter have been those that the ruler offered his tribal "family" or those that the head of the household offered his wife(s) and children.

Besides Islam, other strands of a long, proud history are woven into the cloth of society. The Arabic language is one strand. It is picturesque carrying with it emotions, feelings, and thoughts, creating an artistic expression of sound and rhythm that Naguib Mahfouz describes as "searching for tunes in the air" (Mahfouz 1986, p. 33). As other have noted, the "emphasis is on form over function, affect over accuracy, and image over meaning" in Arabic language and communication. (Zaharna 1995 241).

Regardless of all else, the most critical element in those things that matter is Islam, which permeates all of society as it serves as *the* normative force (Patai 1983; Lewis 1990). Until most recent economic developments, Muslims have felt little particular need for secularism. Even today, the mere recognition that secular transparency is valuable in mundane corners such as the economy remains grudging. That is because conservative Muslims envision the West imposing an entire system of political and social values from such small beginnings (Ringle 2001). They use the prognostication of small, step-by-step change as a way to inject fear into even the most moderate of their numbers.

The advent of political Islam has made Freedom of Expression issues inherent in the development of cyberspace a three-sided problem. Government has the power to suppress; religious fundamentalists want to eliminate those who oppose; but a brave few advocate enhanced free expression (Nawar 2000).

Legal Norms

As do many other countries, the United Arab Emirates guarantees Freedom of Expression in its written constitution. Article 30 of the Constitution protects "freedom of opinion and expressing it verbally, in writing or by other means of expression shall be guaranteed within the limits of the law" (Human Rights Watch, June 1999 at www.hrw.org/advocacy /internet/mena/uae.htm). Article 31 guarantees "freedom of communication by post, telegraph, or other means of communication and (that) the secrecy thereof shall be guaranteed in accordance with the law" (Human Rights Watch June 1999, http://www.hrw.org/advocacy/internet/mena/uae.htm).

Nevertheless, it is Article 7 of the Constitution that gives an idea of how "accordance with the law" is defined. This article declares Islam the official state religion and that Islamic shari'a shall be a principal source of legislation (Legal Profiles, Islamic Family Law http://www.law.emory.edu/?IF L/legal/UAE.htm). Shari'a is derived from principles of the Quran, explicated by Ijma, or rules that develop through debate and the resultant consensus of religious leaders

(Kabbani, nd). On a practical level, this means that creating secularism in any corner of the society is difficult.

Federal Law 15 of 1988 requires that all publications be licensed with the ministry of education and delineates acceptable subjects of reporting. Journalists censor themselves on sensitive subjects such as the ruling family, Islam, and national security, government policy, religion, and relations with neighboring states. The information minister, a son of Sheikh Zayed, has been quoted as telling the media to "criticize freely," though there is no evidence that journalists have complied, particularly with respect to Emirati rulers and their extended families (Al Bakry 2001; Human Rights Watch, June 1999; Owais and Matthew 2000). Local Arabic and English newspapers convey the impression the country is an idyllic place to live with few of the problems facing other countries like revolutions, crime, or corruption.

Reporters have established Warren Breed-type boundaries themselves, practicing self censorship akin to prior restraint. "Freedom without responsibility may invite chaos," Ayesha Ibrahim Sultan, head of the UAE journalist's union has said. "Freedom and responsibility have to go hand in hand. If we separate them and allow total freedom, it will lead to chaos. . ." (Rahman 2001). Freedom, then, is not absolute; it is limited because certain social aspects including the morals and values guiding a society must be considered (Rahman 2001). Some scholars of journalism would consider this a form of "development journalism" and appropriate to the stabilization of society. They should recall that the Emirates, as a political reality, are little more than 30 years old.

In establishing boundaries to expression, the UAE is no different than other societies. Remember that, while the First Amendment of the US Constitution states in part "Congress shall make no law . . . abridging the freedom of speech, or of the press; or the right of the people peaceably to assemble," common law values some expressions more than others and also permits exceptions for limiting expressions such as obscenity and national security. That common law is greatly influenced by the ebb and flow of history, the tenor of the times, and, of course, culture.

Even Article 19 of the United Nation's Universal Declaration of Human Rights does not advocate unlimited free expression. Article 19 says that "Everyone has the right to freedom of opinion and expression; this right includes freedom to hold opinions without interference and to seek, receive and impart information and ideas through any media and regardless of frontiers." Even so, under international law, governments can restrict information to protect certain interests such as national security, public order or health or morals in what amounts to prior restraint (Human Rights Watch 1999).

The differences about what constitutes a threat to national security, public order or health or morals rests, as late Associate Justice of the United States Supreme Court Potter Stewart might have said, in the eyes of the beholder. Up and down the GCC, stakeholders are considering what the limits should be. In a 1998 editorial, Abu Dhabi-based *Al Ittihad* urged people to adopt a modern cultural concept of freedom while practicing responsible decisions in real life. The paper also called for the formulation of an Arab concept of freedom (UAE Editorials 1998.)

Just what that formulation might be remains the subject of vigorous debate. Some social forces have voiced hostility to the Internet or to its availability to the public at large. Legislators in Kuwait and elsewhere have denounced the Internet as a threat to local culture, morals, or religious sensibilities (Human Rights Watch 1999). Other GCC governments and their supporters have sounded these same themes to justify a go-slow, paternalistic approach to allowing public access to the Internet.

That viewpoint includes the Saudis. Saleh Abdulrahman al-'Adhel, the head of the King Abdul-Aziz City for Science and Technology, reportedly stated that the Internet presents "an important service in relaying and distributing information but also has a negative side that conflicts with our faith and our Arab Muslim traditions" (Associated Press 12 May 1997).

Worries about material considered offensive delayed Internet access in Saudi Arabia, where foreign publications are strictly controlled and censored. State telecommunication monopolies capable of blocking Net access to politically, socially, or culturally sensitive material help to keep a lid on the problem (Reuters 1998; see also, Lee 2001; Associated Press, 12 May 1997; Trabelsi, 1998).

The UAE, sensing an economic opportunity, has been more liberal than GCC sister states Saudi Arabia or Kuwait (Wheeler 2000; see also Dubai Press Club 2000). On 10 May 2001, General Sheikh Mohammed, Crown Prince of Dubai and UAE Minister of Defense speaking in rather de Tocquevillean terms at the launch of Media City (a campus of media enterprises such as Reuters, CNN, Emirates Media, among others) said that:

> We who live in today's cyber age increasingly understand the importance of information and the media that carries this information. The TV set, the newspaper, the radio and the mobile phone are the tools that allow us to utilize this information. But pause and think. If knowledge is power, then the media that brings it to us is the source of that power.
>
> As we look at the dynamic and fast changing media world around us we are continually reminded of the power of media. Improvements in technology are breathing new life into familiar media like TV, radio and print. New and advanced technologies such as the mobile phone and the computer have expanded the horizons and transfer of knowledge and information, making the world like a small village where people can communicate with each other.
>
> I guarantee Freedom of Expression to all of you. . . . Let us do so responsibly, objectively and with accountability and in the spirit of the social and cultural context in which we live.
>
> This freedom will allow and encourage the Arab media to return home, to broadcast and publish once again from Arab land, and contribute to this new regional media industry.
>
> Always remember, the human mind, once stretched by a new idea, never returns to its original size. It only grows larger. Media has the power to effect change and evolve (*Gulf News*, 11 May 2001; for more information also see, Wheeler, 21 January 2001).

The Federal National Council has echoed this sentiment, has offered its support for freedom of the expression, and has stressed the need to support efforts to guard freedom of opinion and expression as provided by the constitution, but within the boundaries of the law (Dawood 11 January 2001).

Exactly what those boundaries are remains unclear because no bright line exists in the sometimes-shifting sands. Despite the seductive notion of a sweeping era of globalization, uniform regulation of cyberspace is improbable because different societies with different cultures have differing viewpoints and frameworks for exercising control. A key contradiction stands out. One pole is that community standards must be vigilantly protected. The other is that free speech is paramount, even if standards are sometimes violated (Whittle 16 May 1996; Ang 1997; Sussmann 2000). These viewpoints are drawn from the wellsprings of culture, one of whose functions is to serve as an ecological boundary between groups.

Regulatory Schemes

Despite the advent of globalization, a uniform regulatory standard may be impossible with respect to cyberspace because each country has specific cultural and legal imperatives driving the regulatory process (Ang 1997). Different societies with different cultures have differing viewpoints for exercising control. "Every culture has the right to express itself," said Milagros De Corral, UNESCO's deputy assistant director speaking in Abu Dhabi on 23 April 2001 before the second International Summit on Internet and Multimedia (Wired 2001). "But when it comes to cultural content, the problem is that the moment you change a character . . . you can erode something" (*Wired* 2001).

The debate over eroding values has, like Janus, two faces in the United Arab Emirates. Decentralization of information is one. Deployment of information and communications technology facilitates decentralization of power, creating distributed information available to all, including the women who sometimes live a cloistered existence. Those cloisters a prison do not make, if women have the freedom to soar over them via the Internet. Evidence suggests that women in the United Arab Emirates do so (Walters, Quinn, & Jendli 2005). The second of the twins, globalization, raises the specter of homogenized, largely Westernized, values. Because of these twin concerns, the United Arab Emirates has carefully considered the spread of the technology (Dahan nd).

Several general potential regulatory schemes exist, ranging from individual self sanctioning to a state-imposed rule set (Ang 1997; see also CCPJ 2000). Advocates of unfettered speech tend to support the person as the regulator. Advocates of state control look toward the government as the ultimate regulator. Between these two extremes, resides a third way. (See Figure 1 below.)

Figure 1
Regulatory schemes

Regulator	**Rules**	**Sanctions**	**Mechanism for sanctions**
The person	Personal ethics	Self-sanction	Self
Second party	Contract	Various-self help	PICS[1], filter software
Non hierarchically organized social forces	Social norms	Social sanctions	Code of Conduct
Hierarchically organized nongovernmental organizations	Organization rules	Organization sanctions	Industry self-regulation
Government	Law	State enforcement with coercive sanctions	Legal system

Adapted from Ang, 1997

Many regulators argue that curbs on Freedom of Expression on the Internet are needed to protect children from harmful content, preserve religious values, safeguard local cultures, protect national security, thwart terrorists, and silence racists (Balmer 2002). The United Arab Emirates agrees. Many nationals believe that community standards inherent in Islam and the society into which Islam is inexorably woven must be protected. Thus some advocate a paternalistic system, passionately arguing against unfettered access to certain classes of information. They do so fearing a lack of media literacy among the population at large, using the logic of the 3rd person effect to advocate what they consider a benign, benevolent censorship.

Certainly authorities do so with non-cyberspace information. The College of Family Sciences at Zayed University, an all-women's university with campuses in Abu Dhabi and Dubai, regularly censors reproductive science texts, covering pictures, redacting text, and ripping out whole sections to eliminate offensive material including inappropriate contact and subjects such as alcohol and drug use. They also eliminate case studies that might offend. Art books containing nudity are placed in a secured room and only students obtaining written parental permission can access these books.

Few Emirati officials will admit that blocking unwelcome political information is among their objectives in imposing controls on the Internet. As Burkhart and Goodman have noted that pornography is ''almost always first mentioned'' when it comes to what the Internet ''may do to national, cultural and religious values.'' Other forbidden topics are ''proselytizing by other religions and the availability of un-Islamic information (such as how to commit suicide), the potential effects on women's roles in society, (and) dilution of local cultural norms'' (Burkhart and Goodman1998 taken from Kettman 24 April 2001 Za'Za' 16 March 2005).

Print copy publications such as *Cosmopolitan* and *Elle* with international circulation eliminate many of the problems with cultural norms because they have versions adapted to the marketplace. ''Versioning'' reduces the potential for cultural conflict by creating different editions of the same magazine that are audience appropriate. Yet, versioning is probably impracticable with respect to e-sites because of economies of scale, international and national law, and the difficulty created in developing (and maintaining) multiple sites.

Although Saudi Arabia has gone furthest in defining the scope of Internet data it wishes to keep from its people, others have adopted similar logic to block data (Burkhart and Goodman 1998). The Qatar ambassador to the United Nations once wrote (in what can only be described as *1984*-esque language) ''the high-level moralities in preventing the indecent and corrupt material will undoubtedly nourish morality at the human level. Prohibition, in this respect, therefore, is not deprivation but enrichment; not suppression but discipline, and not limitation but expansion'' (Quoted in Sussmann 2000).

The United Arab Emirates is among those countries who so ''protect'' her citizenry. The UAE filters and blocks based on content and retains the capacity for electronic eavesdropping (Human Rights Watch, June 1999; see also, Bell, 2001). One recently blocked was a German-based website offering ''escort service'' in Dubai. Carrying pictures, profiles, and prices, EIM blocked it because it did not comply with the region's ''Islamic values'' (Staff Reporter 9 May 2004).

UAE dial-up users who employ the local telephone service do not access the Internet directly. They dial in to a proxy server of Etisalat, the government telephone monopoly and single ISP in the country. The proxy denies access to web sites if the URL requested is on a list of banned sites, or if a content check of the site by the proxy server turns up objectionable material (See Human Rights WatchJune 1999; see also 2000 World Press Freedom Review). Terms and conditions of usage permit Etisalat to terminate services if a consumer uses the service for a ''criminal activity or unlawful purpose such as but not limited to vice, gambling or obscenity or for carrying out any activity which is contrary to the social, cultural, political, economical or religious values of the UAE'' (Etisalat 2005).

If you venture somewhere Etisalat finds objectionable, the following message pops up.

Emirates Internet denies access to this site.
For more information on Emirates Internet services click here

When you click **here**, the message takes you to the Emirates Internet & Multimedia homepage; it *does not* explain *why* the site was blocked.

What is it that would make this site objectionable? Why would it be blocked? UAE Government officials say the sole purpose of its blocking policy is to eliminate pornographic sites. A senior official in the Ministry of Information and Culture told Human Rights Watch in a telephone interview on June 10, 1998:

> ''There is no restriction on the political, social, economic side. Politically, in the U.A.E., we do not hold value for censorship, especially political or censorship of ideas: we don't believe in that. You can access on the Internet any material, from Israel or anywhere. The whole idea [of the proxy system] was to block X-rated materials. You can see the first pages [of sexually explicit sites], but not whatever is after that'' (Human Rights Watch 1999).

The Etisalat staff reviews web sites, sometimes responding to complaints or tips from users, using broad guidelines focusing on the ''sexually explicit'' to root out objectionable sites. Apparently the system was set up to respond to concerns and fears of teenage abuse. Yet it is just these teenagers who have the technical expertise to circumvent the system. A committee at Etisalat examines the site, verifies the pornographic content, and then blocks it (Human Rights Watch June 1999).

The official cited above added that, although Etisalat attempts to block sites, the proxy filtering system was not foolproof. ''You can get to porno,'' he said, ''because you can always just dial a foreign server. We try our best to limit X-rated material, but you can never really build a wall'' (Human Rights Watch June 1999).

This official was correct. For those with the technical means and money, blocking is ineffective. The Web-savvy can circumvent it; the petro rich can dial around it, reaching an ISP outside the country (Campagna 2000). For those who can afford the best, there is always satellite Internet service. (For example, see http://www.startv.com/eng/.)

Emirati authorities maintain that they do not track individual users' online activities. Nonetheless, they retain the technical capability to do so if they choose, an ability facilitated because all dial-in users are channeled through a proxy server operated by this public utility (Human Rights Watch June 1999). When a *Gulf News* staffer complained to Etisalat that some of his e-mail was not getting through the proxy system, he was told that yes, indeed, the message had left at a specific time en route to a specific individual. Lloyd's bank Dubai has long refused to create on-line banking for its customers because of Etisalat-related security issues.

If pornography is an Internet-related direct threat that it is believed might diminish Islamic society, another more insidious threat is the ascendancy of English on that media. Viewed through the lens of Islam, this dominance could be interpreted as a sign of Western imperialism (Patai1983). This fear is not without some validity. Noting the potential for damage, UNESCO issued a warning in 2000 regarding the possible disappearance of half of 6,000 existing world languages (Human Rights Watch 1999). Arabic speakers do not intend that the language of the Prophet will be one of them. At the January 19, 2002 meeting of the Session of the Islamic Commission for Economic, Cultural and Social Affairs in Jeddah, The Secretary General of the Organization of the Islamic Conference (OIC) Dr. Abdelouahed Belkeziz called for rectifying the cultural warfare being practiced against Islam. (See http://www.oic-oci.org/.) The implications of using the metaphor of war suggest polarization, antagonism, and intent.

Because total censorship is virtually impossible once citizens have the means, skill, and opportunity to go on line, the Internet will be a catalyst for change for those so empowered. That is because the Internet evaporates distance while combining text, speech, and pictures in a compelling convergence of communication that potentiates real-time, far flung, unfiltered information gathering (Pool 1990 8). Such a threat will necessarily compel introspection on how the Arab world can resist the perceived ''evils'' of globalization on the one hand while modernizing on the other (Kettmann 2001). Yet, the logistics and legalities of a modern economy suggest that transparency, not opacity, must constitute the standard operating logic.

In a region where nearly every government censors or punishes speech critical of the authorities, fear that democratizing Internet access can undermine the state chokehold on information has been a significant factor in slowing Internet growth (Dahan nd; see also Committee To Protect Journalists www.cpj.org/countrystatus; Reporters sans Frontières, www.rsf.fr; Human

Rights Watch www.hrw.org; and the U.S. State Department's *Country Reports on Human Rights Practices* www.state.gov///www/global/human_rights/hrp_reports_mainhp.html). Yet, despite purposive foot dragging, the Internet has begun spreading as pro-Internet forces in government and in the business, academic, and research communities, wishing to keep current and globally competitive, have pushed for easier access to online data and communications (Human Rights Watch 1999; Human Rights Watch June 1999; Dahan 2001; United Nations 2001). A government trying to free itself from a petrocarbon dependent economy in a land with few other natural resources must embrace globalization, modernity, and technology if it is to continue or improve its current standard of living.

Content control is difficult once the ''jinn'' are out of the bottle. Those jinn are now out of that bottle and would be hard to put back in. A Reuters report on 20 September 2000 quoted Mohammed Al-Abbar, director general of Dubai's Economic Department, as saying that the increase of satellite access and Internet usage makes censorship more difficult to achieve in the country.

''In today's world censorship doesn't exist,'' he said. ''We can pick up hundreds of channels here plus the internet. The world is changing. We are already a global city, traveling the world, and we know exactly what is happening around the world and we cannot hope to stop, nor would we want to stop, whatever is happening. So censorship is no longer an issue. We want the same freedom to operate as if a channel was in London, Atlanta or wherever'' (Reuters 20 November 2000). A media savvy 20ish generation has begun practicing what Al-Abbar has preached (Walters, Quinn, & Jendli 2005).

The United Arab Emirates wants it all, but policy makers seem confused about how to get from today to tomorrow. At a recent media conference in Abu Dhabi, Sheikh Mohammad, Crown Prince of Dubai, issued a clarion call for the media to present a Gulf message. The Crown Prince called for a ''message of enlightenment to encourage development, to build men up and to call for modernization . . .'' (Stent,2005a). Sheikh Abdullah bin Zayed Al Nayhan, Minister of Information and Culture, chipped in at that same meeting, calling on the media to be risk takers, encouraging ''innovative thinking and dialogue'' about delicate subjects (Stent 2005b.) Yet, at another venue at that same meeting Dr. Ali Al Shauibi, a senior Dubai police official, accused the media of ''promoting ideas which are damaging to the UAE's future.'' Calling some television channels ''scandalous,'' he called on the press to regulate itself. On the one hand the Crown prince of Dubai has advocated a freewheeling open debate of all issues; on the other the Dubai police chief says he will take television channels off the air that violate his view of what is the cultural norm. (See, for example, Stent 2005a and 2005b.)

Chiming in on that same subject, the director of the Al Arabiya channel, Adbul Rahman Al Rashid called for rules and discipline to ''control our freedoms'' (Sands 2005). A few months earlier the Ministry of Education had gagged reporters by denying access to information and from quoting any of its officers (Hoath 24 March 2004).

Such schizophrenia about information, its control, and its value to the marketplace, epitomizes the difficulty of reconciling the old with the new. Leaders are still searching for a practical way to incorporate local standards and practices into a meaningful Arabic version of modernity. The United Arab Emirates hopes to leapfrog to the future without pain but that may be impossible because creating a cycle of virtuous change offers stark choices. Thus, it seems that if progress is to occur, a transitional generation of the United Arab Emirates faces the conundrum of adapting the best that modernity offers while retaining the best of traditional society. Some argue that the steady advent of technology makes the evolution towards markets and modernity inevitable (Amin 2004). How (or whether) this society can dance to the beat of a different drummer and succeed remains unclear.

Works Cited

Abu-Ghazaleh. (nd). Abu-Ghazaleh Intellectual Property. http://www.agip.com/Default.aspx?&lang=en. For example, see http://www.agip.com/news.aspx?id=379&lang=en

Aizu, I. (1997). Social, legal, and policy issues around Internet in Asia. Asia Network Research. For PAN Meeting, 1997.6.10. See http://www.panasia.org.sg/.

Al Bakay, A. (24 October 2001). Media Told to Exercise Freedom. *Gulf News*, Section 1, p. 3.

Al Tamimi & Company. (nd). Intellectual Property in the UAE. http://www.ip-emirates.com/copyright.htm.

Amin, H. Y. (Spring, 2004). Social Engineering: Transnational Broadcasting and its Impact on Peace in the Middle East. *Global Media Journal*, 2(4).

Ang, P.H. (1997). How Countries are regulating Internet Content. http://cad.ntu-kpi.kiev.ua/events/inet97/B1/B1_3.HTM.

Associated Press, 12 May 1997. Taken from Susan Gavi , *Online Journalism Review*, Crossing Censorship Boundaries, 24 November 1999, located at http://ojr.usc.edu/content/story.cfm?request=283#1.

Balmer, C. (22 January 2002). Pope Says Internet ''Wonderful'' but Needs Regulating. Reuters. http://www.reuters.com/news_article.jhtml?type=internetnews &StoryID=534471.

Bell, T.W. (2001). *Internet Privacy and Self Regulation: Lessons from the Porn Wars*. Cato Institute Briefing Papers, No. 65.

Bryant, C. (1995). Civic Nation, Civil Society, Civil Religion in J. Hall, *Civil Society: Theory, History, Comparison*, Cambridge: Massachusetts: Polity Press, pp. 136-157.

Burkhart, G., and Goodman, S. (March,1998). The Internet Gains Acceptance in the Persian Gulf, Communications of the ACM, 41(3):19-25 Doanloadable at http://doi.acm.org/10.1145/272287.272290. The ACM is the Association for Computing Machinery.

Burton, R. (1964). Personal Narrative of a Pilgrimage to Al Madinah and Mecca (Volume 1). Mineola, New York: Dover Publications.

Campagna, J. (2001). Middle East and North Africa 2000: Regional Overview. CPJ, www.cpj.org/attacks00/mideast00/mideast.html.

CCPJ. (2002). Internet Censorship Report. www.cfje.org/publicaztions/internet.

CIA. (2001). *The World Factbook 2005*. http://www.cia.gov/cia/publications/factbook/geos/ae.html#Econ

Dahan, M. (nd). Internet Usage in the Middle East: Some Political and Social Implications. Middle East Virtual Community. http://www.mevic.org.

Dawood, A. (11 January 2001). FNC declares support for freedom of the media. *Gulf News*.

Diamond, L. (1994). Rethinking Civil Society: Toward Democratic Consolidation. *Journal of Democracy*, *5*(3):4-17.

Donnell, G., and Schmitter, P. (1986). *Transitions from Authoritarian Rule: Tentative Conclusions about Uncertain Democracies*, Baltimore, Maryland: Johns Hopkins University Press.

Dubai Press Club. (5 November 2002). Dubai Launches its Media City. www.dpc.org.ae.

Dudaiinc. (nd). Facts and Figures. http://www.dubaiinc.com/.

Emory. (nd). United Arab Emirates. www.law.emory.edu/IFL/legal/UAE.htm.

Essoulami, S. (2001). The Press in the Arab World: 100 years of suppressed freedom. www.cmfena.org/magazine/features/100_years.htm.

Etisalat. (2005). Terms and Conditions. http://www.etisalat.co.ae/html/ custom_info/customer_care/customer_care_-terms.htm.

Gartner, J. (14 November 2000). It's Sheik to Be Techie. *Wired*, http://www.wired.com/news/print/0,1294,40167,00.html.

Geremek, B. (1992). Civic Society Then and Now. *Journal of Democracy, 3*(2):3-12.

Gulf News. (11 May 2001). Power of ideas and media.

Gulf News. (22 January 2002). Al Tayer praises Etisalat's great role. *Gulf News* online. www.Gulfnews.com/Articles/News.asp/ArticleID=38545.

Hoath, N. (24 March 2004). FNC offers mediation to resolve ministry-press row. *Gulf News*, p. 5.

Human Development Indicators. (2004). New York, New York: United Nations Development Program or go to http://hdr.undp.org/reports/global/2004/pdf/hdr04_complete.pdf.

Human Rights Watch. (June 1999). *The Internet in the Middle East and North Africa: Free Expression and Censorship*. http://www.hrw.org/advocacy/internet/mena/.

Human Rights Watch. (1999). Freedom of Expression on the Internet. www.hrw.org/wr2k/Issues-04.htm.

International Constitutional Law. (nd). http://anduin.eldar.org/~ben/scout/html/430.html or http://kclibrary.nhmccd.edu/constitutions-subject.html

International Press Review. (2000). *2000 World Press Review: UAE*. www.freemedia.at/wpfr/uae.htm.

IPR. (2001). United Arab Emirates. www.infoprod.co.il/country/uae2a.htm.

Kabbani, Shaykh Hisham Muhammad. (nd). Questions on IJMA' (Consensus), *Taqlid* (Following Qualified Opinion), and *Ikhtilaf Al-Fuqaha'* (Differences of the Jurists). As-Sunna Foundation of America. http://www.sunnah.org/fiqh/ijma.htm.

Kettmann, S. (10 June 2001). Oil Realm Embraces a Wired Economy. *New York Times*, Late edition, Section 3, page 7.

Kettmann, S. (21 April 2001). Abu Dhabi does the net. *Wired*. http://www.wired. com/news/culture/0,1284,42633,00.html.

Lee, J. (19 November 2001). Companies Compete to Provide Internet Veil for the Saudis. *New York Times*, Late Edition—Final, Section C, Page 1, Column 2.

Lewis, R. (September 2000). The Roots of Muslim Rage. *The Atlantic Monthly online*. www.theatlantic.com/issues/90sep/rage.htm. Originally from *The Atlantic Monthly, 266*(3):47-60.

Mahfouz, M. (1986). *The Beggar*. Translated by Kristin Walker Henry and Nariman Khales Haili al-Warraki. Cairo, Egypt: The American University in Cairo Press.

Nawar, I. (2000). *Freedom of Expression in the Arab World.* Aspen Institute Conference on Freedom of Expression, Wye River, May 30–June 1, 2000.

O'Donnell, G. and Schmitter. P. (1986). *Transitions from Authoritarian Rule: Tentative Conclusions about Uncertain Democracies*. Baltimore, Maryland: Johns Hopkins.

Organization of the Islamic Conference. (nd). http://www.oic-oci.org/.

Owais, R., and Matthew, A.P. (5 November 2000). Media City launched as beacon of creativity. *Gulf News* online. http://www.gulfnews.com/Articlesv /News.asp?ArticleID = 1898.

Patai, R. (1983). *The Arab Mind.* New York, New York: Charles Scribner's Sons, pps. 307-313.

Pool, Ithiel da Sola. (1990). *Technologies without Boundaries*, Cambridge, Massachusetts: Harvard University Press.

Price, M. and Krug, P. (2000). *The Enabling Environment for Free and Independent Media*. Programme in Comparative Media Law & Policy. Oxford, England: Oxford University.

Rahman, S. (1 May 2001). Media Freedom without responsibility 'may invite chaos.' *Gulf News.*

Reuters. (6 May 1998). Leery Saudis Get Wired. Taken from *Wired*, http://www.wired. com/news/politics/0,1283,12131,00.html.

Reuters. (20 September 2000). Taken from 2000 World Press Review, http://www.freemedia.at/wpfr/uae.htm.

Reuters. (7 November 2000). Taken from 2000 World Press Review, http://www.freemedia.at/wpfr/uae.htm.

Ringle, K. (23 October 21). The Crusaders' Giant Footprints: After a Millennium, Their Mark Remains. *Washington Post*, Page C01.

Rouse and Co. International. (nd.) MEISCA ip express. http://www.iprights.com/publications/meiscaipexpress/index.asp.

Selber, G.M. & Ghanem, S.I. (2004). Modernization and Media in the Arab World. *Global Media Journal*, 2(4): http://lass.calumet.purdue.edu/cca/gmj/SubmittedDocuments/Fall2004/contentsfa04.htm.

Star-duo. (2002). Satellite Internet service provider in the Middle East. http://www.startv.com/eng/.

Staff Reporter. (9 May 2004). Website offering escort services in the UAE blocked. *Gulf News*, p. 1.

Stent, M. (10 January 2005a). Be bold in tackling issues, Mohammed tells media. *Gulf News*, p. 1.

Stent, M. (10 January 2005b). Confines of law must be eliminated. *Gulf News,* p. 1.

Sussman, L. R. (2000). *The Internet and Press Freedom 2000.* Freedom House: Press Survey 2000. www.freedom-house.org/ pfs2000/sussman.html.

Swan, S., & Walters, T. (2004). A People in Transition? Unpublished manuscript. Zayed University, Dubai.

Thesinger, W. (1991). *Arabian Sands.* New York, New York: Penguin Press.

Trabelsi, H. (17 November 2001). Technology: Arab ministers alarmed by digital gap with West. *Nando Times*, from Agence France-Pressee, http://www.nando.net/technology/story/172634p-1, 669862c.html.

Trabelsi, H. (15 July 1998). Saudis Near End of Seven-Year Wait To Surf the Net. Agence France-Presse, taken from Human Rights Watch, The Internet In the Middle East and North Africa: A Cautious Start, 2001, http://www.hrw.org/advocacy/internet/mena/int-mena.htm.

UAE Editorials: Zayed's talk to FNC stresses Freedom of Expression. www.uaeinteract.com/uaeint_main/newsreport/19980106.htm.

UAE Yearbook. (2005). Dubai, United Arab Emirates. Trident Press or go tohttp://82.195.132.90/uaeint_main/yearbook/yr_his_trad/yrbk_side.asp

United Nations. (2001). *Human Development Report.* New York, New York: United Nations. Downloadable as a pdf file at http://www.undp.org/hdr2001/.

University of Ottawa. (nd) http://www.droitcivil.uottawa.ca/world-legal-systems/eng-monde.html.

U.S. Department of State. (February 2001). Country Report on Human Rights Practices 2000—United Arab Emirates. http://www.unher.com/. Also at www.humanrights-usa.net/repo45w/unitedarabemirates.html.

Walters, Gregory J. (2001). *Human Rights in an Information Age*. Toronto, Canada: University of Toronto Press.

Walters, T., Quinn, S., & Jendli, A. (2005). A New Roadmap to Life: Media, Culture, and Modernity in the United Arab Emirates. 2005 International and Intercultural Communication Association (IAICS), *Taipei, Taiwan, on July 6-8.*

Wapner, P. (1995). Politics Beyond the State: Environmental Activism and World Civic Politics, *World Politics, 47*:311-340.

Wheeler, J. (25 November 2000). Dubai sheikh pioneers online chat. BBC News Online: World: Middle East. www.bbc.co/uk./low/english/world/middle_east/newsid_1040000/1040672.stm.

Wheeler, J. (21 January 2001). Dubai launches Media City. BBC News Online: World: Middle East.

Whittle, R. (21 May 1966). Internet censorship and PICS in 900 Words. *The Australian.*

Wired. (23 April 2001). Preserving Culture on the Net. *Wired*, http://www.wired. com/news/culture/ 0,1284,43217,00.html.

World Press Freedom Review. (2001). *2000 World Press Freedom Review*. http://www.freemedia.at/wpfr/uae.htm.

Zaharna, R.S. (1995). Understanding Culture Preferences of Arab Communication Patterns. *Public Relations Review, 21*(3): 241-255.

Za'Za',. B. (16 March 2005). Two Americans released after being detained for promoting Christianity. *Gulf News*, p. 5.

Book Reviews

Edited by
Thomas R. Flynn
Slippery Rock University

Religious Expression and the American Constitution
East Lansing: Michigan University Press, 2003

Franklyn S. Haiman

In *Religious Expression and the American Constitution*, Franklyn S. Haiman examines the evolving legal interpretations of the role of religion in a republic whose Constitution guarantees a separation between expression and authority. Despite his being a "self-confessed First Amendment junkie," Haiman provides a balanced, even disinterested, survey of the evolution of our understanding of the meaning of the stand on church and state as expressed in the First Amendment, enhanced by the Fourteenth Amendment, and interpreted by the various levels of American courts.

The First Amendment to the Constitution not only forbids the establishment of a particular church or religion, but also any Congressional interference with the free exercise of religion. Haiman's study examines the legal implications in both prohibitions and traces the Supreme Court decisions in several key cases regarding the role of religion in a pluralistic society. Haiman grounds his discussion in the struggle between church and state for autonomy and control. He surveys these tensions in Europe and later, its American colonies, as religions struggled to maintain power in a secularizing world. The gradual move toward disestablishment and tolerance that accompanied the Enlightenment led to a new relationship between church and state in American society. By the time the Constitution was being drafted, religion in America had become a contractual affair between the citizen and his God, and governance had become a contractual relationship between the citizen and his state. Haiman notes, for example, the use of God "the Creator" in the Declaration of Independence and the distinct absence of any such reference in the Constitution, drafted only seven years later. He argues from this that there is no genuine basis for the concept of a true "Christian America."

Haiman then examines the First Amendment and the challenges that have fueled its interpretation over time, raising a number of significant questions regarding the foundations of the amendment and its application to modern America. For example, can or should the United States of the twenty-first century be legally bound by the intentions of the eighteenth century framers? What constituted "an establishment of religion" in the eyes of the framers? Although the Amendment treats each of its freedoms as separate and distinct elements, the matrix of all five is expression, rather than worship. What does that imply for judicial interpretation of the separation of church and state? Is evenhanded support of all claimants, religious and non-religious, constitutional, or did the framers envision an absolute wall between church and state?

Did the framers intend the Amendment to apply also to the states? Or, were the states independent entities in a joint enterprise, like the various members of the United Nations or the European Economic Union?

Haiman's analysis of various court decisions finds that they fall into two major schools of thought: "original intent," which holds that the Amendment must be interpreted on its own terms, and "living document," which holds that the framers saw the document as a set of guidelines to be amended as time and situations demanded. Within this discussion, he raises the question of how far the concept of the constitution as a "living document" can move from that of the original words and intentions of the framers without destroying the basis of the nation and its government. Both methods contain internal weaknesses, which Haiman examines in detail, using both low- and high court decisions to reveal the evolution of First Amendment understanding. He also notes that decisions regarding interpretation of the church/state dichotomy fall into two categories: non-preferential or evenhanded, and absolute or disinterested. Another issue Haiman raises is that of the gradual extension of the First Amendment provisions to the separate states as the issue of states rights itself has evolved over time.

Throughout the volume, Haiman grapples with the basic question: can a document that is almost 250 years old continue to have much to say to a post-industrial, post-modern society comprised of a multicultural population? The increasing complexity of America's religious systems demands that these questions be addressed, as more people from non-Judeo-Christian traditions and cultures are assimilated into the American mainstream.

Bringing his essay up to the religious fervor that followed the terrorist attacks of September 11, 2001, he expresses concern with the possible misuse of that event as a spur to a shallow "and exclusive" religiosity, and with the possible use of religion as a diversionary tactic for political activity that might not have been passed on its own merits.

The volume is both informative and well written. For the general reader who is less familiar with First Amendment legal history than Haiman, however, greater clarity in presenting the various layers and sequences of decisions, appeals, reversals, and remandings that shape that history would be helpful. Although certain cases he cites may well be "famous" within the field of constitutional law, they are not necessarily recognized as such by the nonprofessional. Overall, however, the volume is so informative that these minor inconveniences should not deter the reader.

The book is a useful tool for several disciplines, Constitutional Law, as well as Cultural History, Religion, and Rhetoric. One of the major assets of this volume is the inclusion of significant portions of the pertinent original documents that Haiman cites throughout the text. Together, the narrative and the appendices provide a solid analysis of the First Amendment issues that must be addressed if the nation is to continue to develop as a multicultural society in which the views of every minority are respected and protected.

Barbara M. Kelly
Hofstra University

Christianity and the Mass Media in America: Toward a Democratic Accommodation

Quentin J. Schultze

East Lansing, Michigan: Michigan State University Press, 2003

The mass media in America are always under scrutiny. Daily, the media in all its forms presents the public with information to be digested, evaluated and used. Public decisions are made based on what we as the recipients of mediated information conclude from what we read, hear and see. The power of the media is vast. Likewise, for many Americans, another force influences the decisions we make and the way in which we interpret what we read, hear and see: Christianity. Quentin Schultze's work explores the complexities of the relationship between the media and Christianity in America. He concludes "[a] healthy tension between the media and Christianity is ultimately a good thing for democracy in America" (6). Along the way Schultze provides complex arguments, thoughtful rhetorical analysis, interesting historical information and a strong critique of what he calls "mainstream journalism as informational fundamentalism" (276). His intertwining of rhetorical analysis, mass media and popular culture criticism and history creates a fascinating and thought provoking work. Additionally, he includes an analysis of how all these topics reflect upon and rely upon both freedom of speech and freedom of religion as guaranteed by the First Amendment. Schultze reminds us that freedom of religion is such an important part of the Constitution because our founding fathers believed it to be a necessity for freedom of speech, since the colonists left their homes because there they were generally denied any right to speak or participate in political affairs because of their religion. To Schultze, it is important that we remember the essential nature of religion to the formation of the American Constitution. He is concerned that the importance of religion in American culture is being overlooked, and his concern is certainly justified when the Supreme Court must decide if the words "under God" in the Pledge of Allegiance violate the separation of Church and State.

Schultze is meticulous both in his research and in his organization. He begins by setting out the five rhetorical topoi "that serve as doors to the public arenas in which Americans imaginatively discussed the media and faith": conversion, discernment, communion, exile and praise (9). An important move Schultze has used is to provide his reason for using the conversations of people occurring in the media rather than to use official church documents. He also stipulates that he will reconstruct some of these conversations occurring in the mass media and will use "the theory of communication developed by the Chicago School of Social Thought to illuminate the dynamic interplay of religion and the media in American life" (9). Clearly defining the five topoi, Schultze goes on to illustrate and analyze their use throughout the history of the media and Christianity in America.

What is important is that Schultze is emphasizing the importance of religion in America and its importance to mass media. He has constructed a careful argument that shows the positives and negatives of Christianity in mass media over the history of the United States beginning with Alexis de Touqueville's work from 1830. Using Toqueville as a primary source, he begins his retelling of the history of media from Toqueville's observations. Moving more or less chronologically, he points out how religious media and religious publications were involved in the public conversation about important issues of each time period. Using case studies he constructs a careful argument for why religious viewpoints are essential to America's democracy. He even looks at Revolutionary and pre-Revolutionary journalism and concludes that the events of the day and the decisions made by government officials were seen as part of the plan of Divine Providence. Additionally, Schultze connects the rise of religious programs to the way evangelical radio preachers learned to market themselves in the crowded airwaves of radio. These preachers paved the way for televangelists such as Jimmy Swaggert and Pat Robertson. His discussions that recount and evaluate the history of early radio and the conflict over regulation and his discussion of "mainstream journalism as informational fundamentalism" make strong points about how media has influenced the public and the growth of the media (276). He concludes with a summary of his argument for strong faith communities in America to enliven and sustain democracy in America based on the best practices of religion and democracy in American history. He supports this call with the results of a 2000 poll that shows that Americans believe that "the religious life should help guard public as well as private morality and should even influence mass media practices"(329-330).

Schultze ends his work with a strong argument for the importance of a close interrelationship of mass media and Christianity. Throughout the work he has shown how each informs the other. Since he is particularly concerned that the negative values and influences of mass media and unreflective use of technology will supplant the positive values of democracy and Christianity, his work's structure has carefully prepared the reader for this conclusion. Although he is careful to include diversity and include the non-Christian world religions whose adherents are continuously becoming American citizens and whose freedom of religion is guaranteed, he is so strongly steeped in the Christian tradition that he stresses the history of the Christian religions which have used the media, especially print and broadcast media within the twentieth century.

Revealing of Schultze's methodology and rhetorical critiques are the ways he addresses freedom of speech. In his discussion of the religious periodicals, *Commonweal, America, Catholic World, Christian Century and Christianity Today,* during the years 1920 to 1970, he illustrates his contention that these were the most significant and important sources of tribal discussion of broadly cultural or mainstream concerns free of any ecclesiastical controls. His contention is well supported and argued, but of equal interest to freedom of speech scholars is his discussion of how these five journals responded to the movement for regulation of radio broadcasting during the 1930's and 1940's.

Radio was the first of the broadcast media used to spread religious programs. As the number of radio stations increased and as more and more individual churches and preachers established stations, the limited airwaves became crowded and stations overlapped each other. Federal regulation was definitely needed to provide clear broadcasts. While this history is generally known to those interested in broadcasting, Schultze's analysis goes several steps further by presenting and critiquing the stances of each of these journals on the issue of regulation. Not only does he set out each journal's position, but he also includes a rhetorical analysis of the impact of that position on the resolution of the issue, on the faith community that published the journal, and the effect on the general public. Schulze's summary clearly lays out the praise he brings to *Commonweal* as well as the values that he believes are what should inform the media in America.

Commonweal served from 1924 to 1970 partly as a public space for lay Catholics to discuss seriously the impact of broadcasting on American culture. The journal sought to balance the freedom of the press and broadcasting with the common values that Americans held—or should have held—as a democracy and a national community. Moreover, *Commonweal* defined those shared values not as purely Catholic but instead as public ones. By upholding the rights of other religious traditions to use radio and television to express their tribal beliefs publicly, *Commonweal* maintained a strong belief in the overarching communal values of freedom of speech for the entire nation. In summary, *Commonweal's* conversation about broadcast regulation highlighted a remarkably subtle but rhetorically powerful integration of individual freedom . . . and public values. . . . *Commonweal* combined a rhetoric of Catholic communion, a strong rhetoric of public discernment, and a rhetoric of praise for freedom of speech in America (107). Similarly, Schultze evaluated the contributions of the other four journals to this and similar conversations. For example, he concludes that *Christian Century*, a Protestant journal, ''hoped to leverage its ecumenical rhetoric of discernment into a new plea for a cross-tribal rhetoric of communion'' (125). While *Commonweal* called for self-regulation, *Christian Century* supported a ''wide range of regulatory and broadcasting efforts'' (125). This is but a partial example of the intricate arguments Schultze presents for each journal he evaluates. Ultimately he concludes that this period between 1920 and 1970 has not been repeated in religious journalism and that this strong religious voice is sorely missed from the public arena.

Of great interest and importance is Schultze's critique of journalism in the late twentieth century and early twenty-first centuries. He calls it ''mainstream journalism as informational fundamentalism'' (276). Schultze ''argues that professional journalism has contributed to the privatization and secularization of religion in the United States. This development has worked to the advantage of professional journalists, who increasingly have taken over some of the social functions and cultural authority formerly held by religious institutions. Like religion, modern news is an epistemology, a way of knowing about the world, and a means of locating ourselves in the world'' (264). The following critique stresses the way in which the media almost tell the people what they imagine we wish to hear. ''Contemporary journalism is a ritual of imaginative storytelling designed to convince both journalists and their audiences that the world is more or less like the way that they have imagined it''(266). At a recent Harvard Institute on the Media and American Democracy I attended, the journalists who spoke repeatedly stressed that they ask the questions we the people want answered. They also claim that interviewees from President Bush to local politicians evade or do not answer these pressing questions. Schultze faults journalists, not for asking the questions and getting the facts, but for their interpretation of the facts and their reliance solely on those facts, conflict and human actions in presenting news. . . ''News reporters ignore stories that point to the meaning of and coherence in life because these topics suggest stability and longevity rather than conflict and change'' (279). His critique goes further when he declares that ''[r]eporters' own professional fundamentalism limits their worldview to narrow-minded immanence'' (283). What Schultze firmly believes is missing in contemporary journalism is the point of view that connects and evaluates news in terms of the ''essential value, transcendent virtue or even inherent good'' of human thought and conduct (266). Using examples from religion news he pursues the idea that motives are only looked at from a simplistic self-interest rather than from the true complexity of human nature. He decides, ''Reporters' own professional fundamentalism limits their worldview to narrow-minded immanence''(283). Finally, he argues that ''[j]ournalists' secular-rational 'faith' establishes a bias against religion within the profession''(287). He suggests that ''[t]he best reporters simply reject such a telegraphic approach to reporting; they use history, philosophy, theology—indeed all fields of study—to help them make imaginative sense of the world. They implicitly break from informational fundamentalism into the wider epistemological horizons of the humanities"(288). In defense of this strong position, Schultze points out that ''[a]part from some forms of religious fundamentalism, Christianity in America largely challenges dogmatic ideologies and promotes democratic and republican ideals. . . . Journalists are obligated as public fiduciaries to take religion seriously as part of the discourse that makes democracy possible, not to promote one or another religion any more than the government does'' (303). This emphasis finishes his critique of informational journalism and stresses what Schultz believes religious journalism and a religious perspective as part of a journalist's world view bring to media in a democracy.

In conclusion, Schultz's work brings a necessary view to the discussion of the methods used by the media to influence the public's understanding of public affairs and issues of importance to America and Americans. Freedom of speech and freedom of religion are basic guarantees of our Constitution. Schultze proves that ''[a] healthy tension between the media and Christianity is ultimately a good thing for democracy in America'' (6).

Jean Ann Streiff
Oakland Catholic High School

The Four Freedoms of the First Amendment—A Textbook

Craig R. Smith and David M. Hunsaker
Long Grove, Illinois: Waveland Press, Inc. 2004

This is a book I intend to use the next time I teach my course, "Perspectives on Freedom of Expression." The book is presented without graphics, whether important or cosmetic, and it offers a well written narrative providing both a historical perspective and a contemporary view of freedom in America as guaranteed by the constitutional interpretations and judgments of our federal court system, especially the United States Supreme Court. While my reading of this book finds freedom of expression most apparent, a clear and symbiotic relationship between freedom of the press, freedom of speech, freedom of religion and freedom to peaceful assembly is made clear early in the text. From the influence of European tradition to commercial speech in our time, the authors select incidents, arguments, cases, and decisions that can be meaningful to any college or university student interested in what the First Amendment means and what freedoms it provides through our Constitution as a living document.

My concern with a number of books on communication law or free speech currently available for teaching about the First Amendment is that the student finds more detail to review than what she or he is likely to remember and retain beyond the course examinations. However, the authors make the genesis of the First Amendment from the period of colonial American to meaning for our 21st Century in an intelligent and uncomplicated fashion. Additionally teaching ancillaries are offered within the text to help the students to organize their thinking and engage in important ideas the authors work to establish. The chronology of the important months in the ratification of the First Amendment provides an opportunity to review the journey our national document took from inception to completion. The study questions at the end of each chapter are good ones that will compel the user to genuinely think about what the chapters are aimed at accomplishing. The simulation exercises can add substance interpretation and evaluation of First Amendment issues and decisions if they are used in the class activity to be included in our courses.

The text is organized somewhat differently than others covering the same period these authors examine. For example, after offering an important historical background culminating in the ratification of the Constitution and Bill of Rights, the book moves importantly through information on the religious clauses of the First Amendment, the regulation of political speech, and the regulation of broadcast speech. Chapters on libel, hate speech, obscenity, indecency, and commercial speech follow. In the final chapter the reader is treated to what the authors have to say about the future of free expression. I am pleased their observations are thoughtful, challenging, underscoring the importance of citizens knowing about their rights and what speech is protected by the First Amendment.

We can easily agree that the First Amendment of the U.S. Constitution provides a foundation for all of our liberties. In our culture there is always some degree of tension if not clash between an impulse to censor, if not constrain, basic freedoms for what are argued as necessary constraints. Nonetheless, our courts have provided a great deal of freedom under the Constitution that we all are privileged to be able to enjoy. The preservation and protection of our basic freedoms produces some limitations under our laws, especially when freedom and basic rights appear to be in conflict with each other. Smith and Hunsaker inform their readers about the American condition as a young democracy so that the readers can understand and appreciate that without these freedoms, especially freedom of expression, our nation will neither thrive nor survive.

John J. Makay
Bowling Green State University

Writing Dissent: Taking Radical Ideas from the Margins to the Mainstream

Robert Jensen
New York: Peter Lang, 2004

Students and Scholars of free speech are aware of two historical trends: First, we know historically that the ideas that bring social change often originate on the political margins of society. Second, we are also aware that media monopolies increasingly control much of the ideas that enter into our national conversation. How can individuals seeking to help bring about social change exert influence in our present media environment? *Writing Dissent: Taking Radical Ideas from the Margins to the Mainstream* by Robert Jensen is a useful and usable guide to writing and publishing op/ed pieces in newspapers. It is more than that, however; it is a clear, brief introduction to radical political perspectives, to the values and practices of the contemporary craft of journalism, and to why radical commentary needs to be written for publication in newspapers.

Jensen has written a concise book (150 pages including the bibliography) that can be read in a single sitting, but I predict that many readers will find occasion to refer to it over and over again. As author of this book, Jensen takes the role of a mentor for writers (and potential writers) with radical ideas they'd like to see published in a newspaper. As the title indicates, Jensen focuses principally on publishing in the mainstream press; however, publishing in the alternative press is also briefly addressed.

In his Introduction, Jensen states that he wants to give readers confidence that they can write and be published, as well as tools to address the question: ''Is writing for the mainstream media worth the time and effort?'' (2). In the chapters that follow, he provides succinct but helpful introductions to (or reviews of) fundamentals of radical politics and journalism as well as reprints of a number of his own published op/ed pieces, with comment, that pursue both of his stated goals. Between this introduction and the conclusion, the book is divided into two parts, Part I: Getting Ready to Write, and Part II: Writing Strategies and Examples.

Chapter 1 is titled: What Makes Radical Analysis Radical? Jensen's answer reminds readers that the Latin origin of the word ''radical'' means root and that radical analysis ''often . . . means realizing that what is taken as an aberration or deviation from a system is actually the predictable and/or intended result of a system'' (7). He illustrates, using examples. He observes that mainstream politicians typically argue for or against a particular policy (an example he uses is raising or lowering capital gains tax), but that questions that go to the root of the matter go unasked. To illustrate, Jensen mentions this one: ''Why should we accept a system in which some individuals are allowed to accumulate large fortunes while others work much harder but have no material security?'' His writing is clear on basic issues such as these and he illustrates his generalizations—and makes some of them more problematic—by reference to his own experiences and his own positioning within radical politics. For example, he notes controversy related to ''the role of identity-based movements'' (e.g., rights for gays and lesbians) in ''the broad struggle for justice'' (9). He observes, however, that ''identity-based movements'' share a core resistance to power inequities and the naturalizing of social dominance; and, thus, he finds room for each such movement in a radical politics that works to substitute ecology for current power-based hierarchies.

The remainder of Part I is a tightly written and helpful introduction (or review) of principles of the craft of journalism and the art of working with journalists. Jensen notes, with admiration, "the ideal of holding the powerful accountable" but he also argues that the craft, as he has practiced it and has seen others practice it, rarely lives up to the ideal. In these chapters concise instruction and recommendations are given on topics ranging from the inverted pyramid, to journalistic values such as balance and neutrality, to working with editors—illustrated with examples from Jensen's own published writing and sprinkled with solid recommendations for further reading.

Part II explains and provides models of strategies and tactics for writing and publishing radical political commentary. As a teacher and writer concerned both with the rhetoric of social movements and with the practice of journalism, I found the advice offered here to make good, practical sense and the models included generally to be strong, engaging illustrations. In Chapter 4, for example, Jensen uses a piece published in the *Houston Chronicle* on November 30, 1999, to illustrate strategies for advanced planning that can lead to publication while a predictably newsworthy event is still hard news. In addition to providing guidance on how to deal with tight deadlines in commenting upon current news, Jensen provides a variety of other suggestions. Some of these suggestions are useful but hardly surprising—such as timing commentary to coincide with anniversaries and "piggybacking" on news-created openings to publish basic critiques of oppressive institutions and practices. Others, however, such as those in Chapter 10, Personal Connections and Dumb Luck, provide fresh, useful examples of how to use one's privilege to help others without privilege (an idea Jensen later attributed to Salvadorian Archbishop Oscar Romero. See 147). And, the final chapter in the section makes an argument for publishing in the alternative as well as the mainstream press—putting a communitarian spin on the common observation that such publications are "preaching to the choir." Specifically, Jensen observes that political dissent can bring about social isolation and so "having a place where one feels like part of a choir, even if it is a small choir, is important" (131).

Beginning on page 145, the conclusion to Jensen's book is only a little over three pages long. And, as happens when I encounter a particularly moving piece of photojournalism, I was unprepared for the impact of Jensen's acutely self-reflective concluding essay. It is about being a feeling person and striving for creative self-realization though writing dissent. Please read it.

Susan Mallon Ross
University of Southern Mississippi

Censorship, Inc.
The Corporate Threat to Free Speech in the United States

Lawrence Soley

New York, New York: Monthly Review Press, 2002

Lawrence (Larry) Soley's book *Censorship, Inc.* provides a challenging new frame of reference or brand new lenses through which to view constraints on mass-media-produced information. Those of us who have taught First Amendment law courses have no doubt often pointed to the government as the source of censorship, but Soley cautions us to remember that big business and "big media" are more likely to place constraints on information than is the government. Soley explains: "When government capitulates to private groups and commits speech-stifling acts, the acts are described as 'censorship.' When private entities commit the same acts, they are described as exercises in 'property rights,' 'editorial control,' or simply 'business policies'" (ix). Of course, conglomerates cannot threaten prior restraint as the government can, so the conglomerates rely on the economic threat of withdrawing advertising money whenever a news report might displease them.

Soley begins with a close look at how easy it has been for big tobacco companies such as R. J. Reynolds to intimidate magazine editors into avoiding articles about the health hazards of smoking. After all, as *Cosmopolitan* explained, it would not want to jeopardize $5-to-$10 million worth of advertising from the tobacco companies (3). Soley also considers the problem of large corporations withholding information about their products. For example, the tobacco companies never told anyone that they were "spiking" [adding nicotine to] cigarettes (6). American Home Products "withheld information that fen-phen, a diet drug combination, caused dangerous heart valve problems" (13). Lead pigment manufacturers knew that lead paint could cause brain damage but they did not bother to tell the public (14).

For those who need a refresher course in American history (or those who never learned it when they should have), Soley's second chapter on company towns, labor unions, and the mine owners' ability to control information is a chilling reminder of the brutality with which coal miners were treated. Soley comments: "So severe was the control [of available reading materials] that not even Stalinist Russia could match it" (37). Lest we complacently assume that these are problems of the past, Soley cites a 1997 case in which an employer of migrant farm workers called in the county sheriff to keep television and newspaper reporters from examining conditions in a farm workers' camp on his property (50).

Soley devotes separate chapters to blacklisting, SLAPP (Strategic Lawsuits Against Public Participation) suits, and the loss of freedom of speech not only at privately owned shopping malls, but also in "planned unit developments" (PUDs) and "common interest developments" (CIDs). Readers who have never lived in PUDs or CIDs may be astonished to learn how much control a homeowners' association can have over one's individual speech. Soley cites the case of Jerry Warsing, who lived in Brandermill, Virginia and posted a sign reading: "This is a shrink-well soil damaged home." Soley explains that the sign "was meant to protest the use of shrink-well soil, which Warsing believed caused $28,000 to $32,000 worth of damage to his home'' (172). The homeowners' association fined Warsing $820 and ordered him to remove the sign. Soley explains: ''If the Brandermill housing association were a municipality rather than a private corporation, it could not legally silence Warsing'' (172).

One of Soley's most fascinating chapters focuses on the perishable product disparagement (''veggie libel'') laws (complete with a discussion of the Texas cattlemen's libel suit against Oprah Winfrey for her comments about the practice of feeding dead cattle to living cattle and spreading mad cow disease). Although Winfrey prevailed, a less visible effect of the cattlemen's suit was to cause a wave of self-censorship among broadcast and cable networks. For example, actor Alec Baldwin could not persuade the History Channel, the Discovery Channel or even PBS to air a documentary on the economic and political determinants of food consumption called *The History of Food* (128). In contrast, a few brave journalists with hidden cameras have exposed appalling practices in supermarkets such as ABC's exposé of Food Lion employees bleaching and repackaging dated meat (108-110). And thanks to NBC's *Dateline,* consumers could learn that a company called AgriGeneral took eggs with expired dates, mixed them in with new eggs, and then shipped them back to supermarkets (126).

This chapter on journalists' relationship to the food industry also raises thorny questions, however. In a second edition of *Censorship, Inc.* Soley might place more emphasis on the fact that, in a world in which the best sound-byte wins, the average consumer without a degree in biochemistry is ill-equipped to analyze scientific research. For example, was daminozide (marketed as Alar) really a carcinogen (111)? Did the apple growers in Washington State lose $75 million as a result of false and unnecessary scare tactics by the Natural Resources Defense Council? Unless high school science teachers can bring *everyone* up to speed so that all of us can read the original research and interpret raw data ourselves, we will be forever dependent on journalists who may be merely parroting what others have told them without any real understanding of it themselves. Soley might also provide more detail to accompany some of his illustrations in a second edition. For example, he mentions one of the battles by the People for the Ethical Treatment of Animals (PETA) to prevent mistreatment of pregnant mares that are kept immobile in order to collect their urine, but there is no explanation given for why farmers engage in this strange practice.

Turning from the farm back to cities and suburbs, for those of us who teach large introductory courses on the mass media, Soley's chapters on advertisers and the ''corporate media Goliaths'' will be especially helpful. Soley recounts Gloria Steinem's experience as publisher of *Ms.* Magazine when it still accepted advertisements before 1990. Steinem reported that Procter & Gamble prohibits its products from being advertised ''in any issue that included any material on gun control, abortion . . . or the disparagement of religion'' (198). In addition to advertisers, Soley observes that retailers such as Wal-Mart can ban any magazine or CD that displeases it from its entire chain. For example, singer Sheryl Crow wrote the song ''Love Is a Good Thing,'' which included the lyrics ''Watch our children while they kill each other with a gun they bought at Wal-Mart discount stores.'' Wal-Mart demanded that Sheryl Crow delete the lyrics, but when she declined, Wal-Mart refused to carry her CD in any of its stores, costing Sheryl Crow an estimated $500,000 in sales (212-213).

Soley's chapter on the ''corporate media Goliaths'' provides a sobering look at the shrinking ''marketplace of ideas'' as media mergers result in ever larger conglomerates where making a profit as opposed to informing the public is the bottom line. It is common knowledge that General Electric (GE) owns NBC, for example, but is it common knowledge that a number of Ohio utilities sued GE in 1987 for fraud and cost overruns at the Zimmer Nuclear Power Plant? Is it common knowledge that GE has a long list of criminal convictions? (230-231). NBC waited two months to cover this story, and then mentioned it just once (230).

Soley also recounts the clash-of-the-titans incident in which Time Warner disagreed with the amount of compensation Disney wanted for re-transmitting its ABC television stations and various Disney channels on Time Warner's cable system. In July 2000 Time Warner blacked out Disney's ABC network programs from its cable systems for a few days until the FCC ordered Time Warner to reinstate ABC and the Disney channels (238). Of course, when cable subscribers cannot watch the ABC television network, this gets their attention. But very few members of the general public might have known that the FCC created a new class of low-power FM radio stations in the late 1990s. The public was no doubt unaware that the National Association of Broadcasters quietly lobbied the House of Representatives to pass the Radio Broadcasting Preservation Act of 1999 (H.R. 3439), effectively banning the low-power FM stations before they even went on the air (246-247). Needless to say, the broadcast news media never discussed H.R. 3439 (247).

In his final chapter Soley argues that a ''significant way to curb the power of corporations, and their control over speech, is to declare that corporations are not individuals [persons] and therefore should not be accorded the same rights as individuals'' (256). Soley acknowledges that to recognize that corporations are *not* individuals ''requires the reversing of a century of court decisions beginning with *Santa Clara County v. Southern Pacific Railroad* (1886) that have extended constitutional rights to corporations, falsely equating corporations and their massive power . . . with that of individuals. Courts and legislatures need to recognize that [the U.S. Constitution is] designed to protect individuals, not 'artificial entities''' (257). Soley is fully aware that this change will be a long time coming, and suggests that we need to begin with campaign finance reform. ''Laws that ban [political action committee] PAC contributions outright are a good start'' (257).

In the preface to his book, Soley acknowledges his indebtedness to the late Herb Schiller (xi). Indeed, Soley's book is a tour de force; it is a welcome addition to classic works in this area such as Herb Schiller's *Mass Communications and American Empire* (1992) and Ben H. Bagdikian's *The New Media Monopoly* (2004). Soley documents his points with meticulous thoroughness. If we allow Soley's arguments to sink in throughout *Censorship, Inc.* we realize that he is truly challenging us to re-think our entire paradigm regarding freedom of speech and the free flow of information in the United States. After all, conglomerates are *not* democracies; they are run more like small dictatorships. Although the CEOs of large corporations might enjoy a return to the 1800s in which the press functioned generally as a lapdog to the ''robber barons,'' one hopes that the general public can see that we must find a way to maintain genuine diversity of sources of information. Here, Soley's arguments that corporations do *not* need the same legal status as persons are well taken.

Juliet Dee
University of Delaware

Regulating Cyberspace: The Policies and Technologies of Control

Richard A. Spinello
Westport, Connecticut: Quorum Books, 2002

McLuhan argued that ''the medium is the message.'' In a similar vein, Spinello argues that ''code is the regulation.'' Or does he? This is the thesis of *Regulating Cyberspace*. Beginning with the theoretical framework of the Internet and the early U.S. policy precedents, Spinello discusses the evolution of cyberspace and the challenges posed by its open and dynamic architecture. While the text does not immediately assume a basic regulatory philosophy regarding the Internet and computer-mediated communication (CMC) in general, the author's cautiousness towards innovation is buttressed by his belief in the need for intelligent (read: censoring) code and heavy-handed government intervention.

Spinello initially seems to advocate a free market libertarian approach to Internet regulation, but fails to sustain this argument. Early in the text, Spinello seems obsessed with regulating access to pornography, particularly on code-based solutions (e.g. content filters) even in light of their apparent technical and policy-based infeasibility. As Spinello comments,

> The United States might have ironclad anti-porn laws, but what's to stop the purveyors of pornography from setting up their Web servers . . . where the United States has no jurisdiction? Given the burdens imposed by laws on free speech of regulatory arbitrage, a more decentralized approach may be feasible. But before we consider the roots of any opposition, let us review the code that can make content control possible (116).

While the author's opposition to mass-mediated obscenity ostensibly stems from a desire to protect minors from accessing explicit media, Spinello's solutions significantly impact consenting adults and the free market. In brief, adult users are not to be trusted in an increasingly complex world. Indeed, if the ''code is the regulation,'' who is to regulate the progressively independent-minded programmers? What of our timeless Constitution and the rule of law? Such questions remain unanswered, as the author seems all too willing to leave technocrats to their own devices.

Paradoxically, Spinello stresses the need to shape technological innovation vis-à-vis emphasizing the interplay between public (i.e. community) good and private interests (e.g. corporations, IP holders etc.). Again, the author seems to suggest a compromise between these ostensibly disparate arenas. As stated earlier, Spinello seemingly praises the virtues of the self-regulation (i.e. individual choice) and the free market. However, much of *Regulating Cyberspace* stresses moderation in policy-making in lieu of innovation and the liberty-producing aspects of the Internet (e.g. free speech, freedom of association etc.). Despite such erroneous conclusions, Spinello generally does a solid job in marshalling some of the salient arguments inherent to sound decision making indigenous to the private and public sectors. Perhaps, what is most troubling about Regulating Cyberspace is its tendency to control as default and its abstinence from more hands off approaches to self-regulation, while refraining from the necessary logical proofs endemic to the collective morality it seems to claim so audaciously.

That being said, Spinello does illuminate some basic universal truths: 1) Pornographic material is generally deleterious to minors; 2) Law does not keep pace with technology; and 3) The Internet poses serious challenges to privacy. Furthermore, the author's analysis serves to fruitfully engage readers in the sort of necessary dialogue so needed in an increasingly complex and fragmented world.

To this end, Spinello's augmentation of previously discussed, but overlooked discourse regarding technological effects is to be commended. Far from accepting the technological status quo, Spinello examines the technical foundations (e.g. APANET) as well as the tributaries of cyberspace in an interdisciplinary, knowledge-synthesizing manner. While this process is admittedly incomplete and necessarily brief, *Regulating Cyberspace* is complete in terms of its sequence and logical progression. Despite its contradictory dynamics between state control and individual liberty, the needs and introspection expressed by the author seem sincere and thorough. For instance, on pornography, Spinello asserts that government regulation must be done in a way that mindfully assesses the needs of the community (e.g. protecting minors) as well as protecting the free speech rights of consenting adults. Along this vein, Spinello argues for self-regulation among those in the community (e.g. teachers, parents etc.), but foresees difficulty in this approach.

However, as with so many areas, the author urges for the strategic use of code, in this case, content controls. As mentioned earlier, Spinello cites the difficulties in controlling CMC vis-à-vis legislation, the courts, or even individual common sense. Still, the author is quick to point out software-based remedies are an imperfect solution at best. Specifically, Spinello names two hurdles to effective list-based filtering:

The first is a reflection of the inherent volatility of the Web. Lists are doomed to be incomplete: Pornographic Web sites come and go, so it is difficult for even the most scrupulous software vendor to identify all objectionable sites. Also, most vendors do not release information about which sites they block and some are not even forthcoming about which criteria or categories they use. How do they define what constitutes "objectionable material"? (117).

The second hurdle is the biases inherent to code-programmers and software companies. The text cites X-Stop, a popular filtering software, which, according to Spinello, blocked access to non-pornographic material such as websites on "Safer Sex" and the "Books for Gay and Lesbian Teens/Youth" (118). At the center of this issue was the American Library Association's use of the above-mentioned technology and their position to allow "unfettered" Internet access (even to minors) which is based on the Library Bill of Rights, which states, "'a person's right to use a library should not be denied or abridged because of origin, age, background, or views'" (118). Unfortunately, Congress did not follow Spinello's general minimum necessary involvement argument and in late 2000 "passed a bill requiring schools and libraries to install filtering technology as a condition for receiving federal funds . . . the Children's Internet Protection Act (CHIPA)" (120).

Encouragingly, the author takes a laissez-faire approach to Internet hate speech in the United States, but also cites the complexities surrounding the issue such as the jurisdiction of nations and the threats posed by differing global standards regarding which sorts of speech are protected (i.e. what is protected in U.S. may not be protected in France). Perhaps, more crucial is Spinello's assessment of spam, or unsolicited bulk e-mail. According to the author "The war against spam has been relentless but futile" (129). Certainly, the realities of the marketplace support the general veracity of this claim. To be sure, some spammers assert that unsolicited bulk e-mail represents their sovereign property and any attempt to destroy or filter it constitutes a violation of their ownership rights. Therefore, given the general seriousness of this matter, Spinello wisely dedicates sufficient analysis of the issues therein. As such, the text accurately describes unsolicited bulk e-mail as a negative externality, "since it clogs the pipes through which all

Internet communications must flow and slows down the entire system'' (129). This distinction is key. In doing so, Spinello contrasts spam with free speech-unsolicited bulk e-mail as low on the free expression hierarchy. Fortunately, the text does not attempt to revert to a black and white analysis of this issue, but instead chooses to concentrate on the nuances inherent to each argument (i.e. for and against commercial CMC speech). Does all spam constitute worthless discourse, not worthy of First Amendment protection or is some positioned to transform the Internet into the '''democratizing force''' envisioned by its innovators and early mass communication theorists? (130).

In brief, Spinello suggests several solutions to solving the burgeoning spam problem. These include the following: 1) A public policy solution banning spam or mandating a labeling requirement; 2) Code-based solutions (i.e. filtering programs); and 3) Internet ''black hole'' lists. Unfortunately, all of the above-mentioned solutions are problematic. In general, public policy initiatives proved ineffective as law generally has had a difficult time anticipating the technical choices enacted by spammers (e.g. alternate mail servers, erroneous return addresses etc.). Second, similar to webpage filters, spam filtering is not an exact science and filtering the right ''types'' of e-mail (i.e. spam) proved elusive. Third, Internet ''black hole'' lists are controversial. As Spinello explains, ''Those ISPs and network providers that are blacklisted will have all of their e-mail bounced, not just the e-mail of the spammer. Thus if ISP X [a suspected spam-friendly network] is blacklisted, other ISPs that subscribe to the RBL list will boycott all of the e-mail from X's service'' (132). The Wall Street Journal and similar publications ask whether organizations such as the Mail Abuse Prevention System (MAPS) should hold the power to determine whether millions of e-mail messages arrive at their final destinations in the interest of a public good (i.e. stopping or deterring spam)? As the text concludes, the courts will render critical decisions in this arena.

In terms of intellectual property (IP), Spinello raises looming questions regarding the nature and scope of IP protection in the digital age. During the summer of 2000, the two most prominent cases in this area were the DeCSS and the Napster trial (Spinello 142). In essence, DeCSS dealt with whether the dissemination of code designed to crack DVD reproduction encryption constituted a form of protected speech. Likewise, the courts were left to determine the culpability (if any) of Napster in providing a peer-to-peer forum for the unauthorized file swapping of copyrighted (primarily music) material. Barow (1994) poses the fundamental problem indigenous to the above-mentioned cases as well as symptomatic of the broader challenges posed by digitized forms of expression, '''if our property can be infinitely reproduced without cost, without our knowledge, how can we protect it? How are we going to get paid for the work we do with our minds''' (as cited in Spinello 143-144). In application, DeCSS and Napster are significant as the decisions rendered were the first attempt to answer these questions. As Spinello summarizes:

In February 2001 a three-judge panel of the U.S. Court of Appeals for the Ninth Circuit issued a ruling that supported Judge Patel's original order. The appeals court ruled that Napster's music-sharing site facilitated copyright infringement on a massive scale. The substance of the injunction remained unaltered: It was Napster's responsibility to prevent the exchange of any copyrighted music (158).

Similarly, the DeCSS trial ruled in favor of the plaintiffs. In January 2000, several Hollywood studios (e.g. Paramount Pictures, Universal, and MGM) filed suit against three New York men operating a website distributing DeCSS (Spinello 161). According to the text, ''In February 2000 Judge Lewis Kaplan issued a preliminary injunction prohibiting the defendants from posting DeCSS on their respective Web sites pending the trial. Following this court order two of the defendants settled with the movie studios. But the third . . . Eric Corley, refused . . . and the case continued'' (161). That being said, Corley's defense was two-fold. First, his lawyers challenged the ''absolute right'' of the movie industry to determine how DVDs are played (Spinello 161). The reasoning was that DeCSS represented a form of ''fair use'' in digital media as it permits DVDs to work on PCs not using Windows or Mac operating systems (Spinello 161-162). Second, the defense argued that linking to DeCSS code was an ''important form of First Amendment expression'' (Spinello 162). However, on August 17, 2000 Judge Kaplan shot down both arguments, siding with the movie industry. In sum, Judge Kaplan stated unequivocally that DeCSS violated the 1998 Digital Millennium Copyright Act (DMCA).

Clearly, the breadth of Spinello's knowledge regarding IP and the larger CMC constructs is impressive if not outstanding. The author succinctly summarizes as well as supplements contemporary legal arguments made in recent times. In doing so, Spinello's analysis serves to synthesize knowledge areas as well as draw conceptual parallels within the multi-discipline mass communication sphere. Clearly, such adeptness is to be commended. However, Spinello's desire to regulate and control the Internet's core is troubling, if not all together philosophically disconcerting. Even in light of key economic and technological externalities, Spinello approaches regulation as a default, rather than a last resort. Indeed, the Internet proliferates and associates freely-it resists regulation. As readers are reminded, ''information wants to be free.'' The truth of the matter is we may not have a choice.

David M. Mercer
George Mason University

From Megaphones to Microphones: Speeches of American Women, 1920-1960

Sandra Sarkela, Susan Mallon Ross, & Margaret Lowe
Westport, CN: Praeger, 2003

''From Megaphones to Microphones: Speeches of American Women, 1920-1960'' is an interesting read and an important contribution. This work ''scratches the surface'' of the history of women's public speeches, documenting the women from all walks of life who commonly gave public speeches on a regular basis to a variety of audiences. Thoughtfully organized, this anthology offers a collection of women's public speeches ranging from 1920 to 1960. The speeches document women's voices during the ''quiet'' decades beginning after the passage of the Nineteenth Amendment to the U.S. Constitution in 1920, through the birth of the second wave of the women's movement. This collection of speeches answers the question: ''What happens to activist voices once a political movement ends?''

This collection of speeches offers a glimpse into the lives, history, and speech-giving record of a diverse group of activist women during the middle decades of the twentieth century. The authors surveyed unpublished records in public and private archives, as well as published material in books, newspapers, magazines, and journals of the period to create this collection of women's public speeches. They chose women from all walks of life, regions, ethnicities, and social classes who spoke in public and maintained records of their speeches in the form of notes, manuscripts, publications, and recordings.

The text holds many speeches previously unpublished. The authors selected speeches that raised national issues and were given before national organizations or audiences. Specifically, the speeches chosen were given by working, middle-class, and elite women; African American, Native American, and Latina women. The speakers are notable and less well-known women. Well-known speakers include: Jane Addams, Nannie Helen Burroughs, Frances Perkins, Eleanor Roosevelt, Margaret Sanger, Mary McLeod Bethune, Clare Boothe Luce, Mary Anderson, Helen Gahagan Douglas, Mary Church Terrell, Margaret Chase Smith, and Pauli Murray.

Readers will learn that women of the period did not speak in one unified voice. The women public speakers of the period learned how best to articulate their goals and shepherd their agenda forward. These speakers debated issues of economic policy, social justice, New Deal programs, labor movements, war and peace, corporate power, and international diplomacy. They debated the issue of equal rights and encouraged women to immerse themselves in the political life of the nation. The authors suggest that the place of women in public life is revealed through these speeches, as well as the dreams and demands for the nation. As the authors note, ''American women acquired and honed their ability to maneuver their way through the democratic political process. They mastered the intricacies of local election laws, parliamentary procedure, national party platforms, union tactics, environmental codes and diplomatic decorum'' (xviii).

The book is divided into four parts covering specific thematic periods. The first section is titled Part I: ''What Next? 1920-1931'' and covers the period immediately following passage of the Nineteenth Amendment to the Constitution. The authors address such questions as: Would all women have the right to vote, or would literacy tests, poll taxes, and anti-immigration laws bar minority and working-class women from the voting booth? What issues might women champion? Would the vote improve women's political or economical position in American life? Would politicians and unions court female workers?

The authors assert that in the 1920's, women redefined what it meant to be political and feminist and to speak in public (2). The collected speeches reflect the state of women's place in public life. Women addressed issues of war and peace, consumerism, conservation, and education. Readers will learn that radio opened the door for women's voices because women spoke in a conversational tone and the microphone compensated for weak vocal projection. Radio provided an intimate link between female political activists and women listening at home. Audiences could not see the speaker and didn't have to leave home to hear the words of the female political activist. The use of radio made it possible for women's recorded speeches to be disseminated to a national audience.

The first speech featured in Part I is Jane Addams' ''Address at 'Portrait Monument' Dedication'' delivered on February 15, 1921 at the United States Capitol. The authors offer an accurate and thorough description of the lead up to Addams' speech. Using contextual details, the authors explain such things as why and where the speech was given, as well as historic events that precipitated the speech. Mary Church Terrell's life spanned from the ''Emancipation Proclamation to the groundbreaking *Brown v. Board of Education* Supreme Court decision in 1954'' (11). Two of Ms. Terrell's speeches were selected to provide a survey of her range in politics as well as devotion to racial and sexual progress: ''The Black Mammy Monument'' (1923) and ''Talk to Young Men of Howard University'' (1925). In the first speech, Terrell rejects a proposal to erect a Black Mammy Monument while the second speech ''demands that African American men improve their conduct, for the sake of women and their race'' (13). The authors also include Nannie Helen Burroughs describing her as ''a renowned orator, tall with a strong voice . . .'' (43). In her address to the National Republican Party Convention, Burroughs called on the ''Negro'' to keep fighting for racial equality in the speech titled ''What the Negro Wants Politically'' (1928). Other speakers included in section one: Florence Ellinwood Allen, Ruth Muskrat Bronson, Gertrude Simmons Bonnin, Elizabeth Manroe Sippel, Florence Jaffray Harriman, as well as a collection of convention speeches from the General Federation of Women's Clubs.

Part II, titled ''Whose New Deal? 1932-1940,'' moves into the tumultuous years of the Great Depression. Women public speakers confronted ''how they might best respond to the worst economic catastrophe the nation ever witnessed'' (75). Authors explain ''New Deal programs were primarily designed to restore white, male workers to their socially ascribed breadwinner status'' (75-76). Further, the authors assert that women speakers of the 1930s drew upon their prior activist experience and the rhetorical traditions of preceding generations. They describe two trends that emerged during this period: (1) More women gave speeches as representatives of state due to numerous government appointments, and (2) Women's workplace experience. The authors note that women continued to debate the merits of the Equal Rights Amendment created by the National Woman's Party founder Alice Paul. In this section, the authors chose to include Ruth Morgan's speech ''Campaign Issues Challenging Political Parties, Challenge of the Woman Voter'' (1932). Morgan was affiliated with the National League of Women Voters and encouraged her audience to make sure that members continued to play an active role in shaping the national agenda.

Mary McLeod Bethune's speech ''Clarifying Our Vision with the Facts'' was presented in 1937 before the Association for the Study of Negro Life and History. The authors suggest ''Bethune implores her audience to instill racial pride in themselves and others by learning and teaching the history of achievement . . .'' (127). Several other important speeches of the period include: Frances Perkins' "Social Insurance for U.S." (1935); Anna Kelton Wiley's "Philadelphia Branch of the National Woman's Party" (1935); Eleanor Roosevelt's "What Libraries Mean to the Nation" (1936); and Margaret Sanger's "Woman and the Future" (1937). Other women speakers included: Ella Reeve Bloor, Blanche Ames Ames, Aimee Kennedy Semple McPherson, Mrs. Helen Robbins Bitterman; Mrs. Laura Hughes Lunde; and Luisa Moreno.

Part III, "Speaking of War! 1940-1945," highlights women's statements regarding U.S. war policy as well as the specific duties each speaker believed women should fulfill during the war, both on the home front and abroad. The speeches included in this section indicate that "women expressed a wide range of opinions" during this period (163). This section opens with Eleanor Roosevelt speaking to the 1940 Democratic National Convention in Chicago. According to the authors, the First Lady's appeal to support FDR brought "order out of chaos . . ." (167). Journalist Dorothy Thompson's speech "The Great Democracy of the Free," presented at a *New York Herald Tribune* forum in 1940, made the war a voting issue. Clare Booth Luce presented "The Role of American Women in Wartime" to the Bridgeport, Connecticut, Women's Committee on American Institute of Banking in 1942, reminding her audience that "their lives remained relatively comfortable, despite the war. . . ." and soon they would be called upon to sacrifice in pursuit of victory (197). Other speakers in this section include: Hattie Caraway, Dorothy Day, Mary Anderson, Mary Beard, Ella Reeve Bloor, and Florence Jaffray Harriman.

Part IV, "Is That All There Is? 1945-1960," reflects women's response to a wide range of political and social issues in the aftermath of war, the growing fear of nuclear weapons, the cold war, and environmental devastation, as well as women's expanding role in the nation's economy as activists, workers, entrepreneurs, and professionals. These voices reveal the growing anxiety and discontent among many politically active women. This section begins with a speech from Democrat Helen Gahagan Douglas titled "My Democratic Credo" which was given on the floor of the House to "set the record straight on her commitment to democracy" (229). Republican Margaret Chase Smith's "Address to Business and Professional Women's Clubs," delivered in1949, mapped out themes such as world peace through the United Nations, Equal Rights Amendment, health care, minimum wage, education, and working conditions. The authors include a third speech from Mary Church Terrell in the form of her testimony before the House Judiciary Committee on the Equal Rights Amendment, held in 1948. Pauli Murray's speech "Being Good Neighbors—The Challenge of the Mid-Twentieth Century," delivered in 1959, focused on civil rights and her determination to fight for justice with an emphasis on love and compassion rather than hate and anger. In this speech, Murray quoted Adlai Stevenson, "Freedom demands infinitely more care and devotion than any other political system. . . ." Other speakers included in this section: Emily Greene Blanche, Maida Springer-Kemp, Dorothy Kenyon, Margaret M. Henderson, Justine Wise Polier, Katie Louchheim, Dorothy Shaver, Fannia Cohn, Rachel Louise Carson, and Martha May Eliot.

Each section begins with a brief overview that sketches the historical and social context for the era, emphasizes key trends in women's public activism, and points to shifts in speechmaking styles. Each section ends with an excellent list of suggested readings to better understand the time period. Each speaker is represented by a carefully chosen photograph to give the reader an image of the woman. The Appendix holds Speeches by American Women Published in Vital Speeches of the Day, October 8, 1934-December 12, 1959.

In conclusion, this book is solidly researched and well written. Sarkela, Ross, and Lowe have created an excellent resource that is thoroughly researched with insightful analysis, which greatly adds to our understanding of the period. Readers will learn that the "quiet" period between 1920 and 1960 was not so quiet after all. "From Megaphones to Microphones" is a welcome addition to the study of women's discourse. For scholars in communication, rhetoric, women's studies, black studies, history, and sociology, this book provides proof that women's voices were expressed during the "quiet" period.

Paula McKenzie

Morality and the Mail in Nineteenth-Century America

Wayne E. Fuller

Urbana, Illinois: University of Illinois Press, 2003

''You've got mail,'' had a very different meaning for my great-grandmother than it does for my daughter. In this fascinating and exhaustive work, Wayne E. Fuller explores the causes and consequences of U.S. mail policy during the nineteenth-century. Those interested in the place of communication technology in the development of a country's identity, or interested in a people's incipient sensitivity to the balance between freedom of speech and other interests, will find this book particularly intriguing. Fuller, an emeritus professor of history from the University of Texas at El Paso, had previously published *The American Mail: Enlarger of the Common Life*. His expertise prepares him well to address the very complex history of the U.S. mail and nineteenth-century American morality. *Morality and Mail* contains ten chapters, each considering a different aspect of the mail.

I cannot remember a time when the post office was open on Sundays, and truthfully, I'd never thought much about why until I read Fuller's opening chapter, ''Mail on the Sabbath.'' Fuller describes how in 1810, very quietly, Congress decided that post offices would be open on Sundays. This action became the country's first clash between church and state and a total puzzle. According to Fuller's account, there had been no public demand or business need which would require mail on the Sabbath. Rather, the decision to open post offices on Sundays reflected the entrenched animosity between the Jeffersonian Republicans and the Hamiltonian Federalists, between the well settled North which could support post roads and the sparsely settled South which could not. Fuller provides a fascinating and detailed account of why Jefferson was so determined to erect the wall of separation between church and state. And why evangelical Protestants were adamant in their opposition.

In chapter two, Fuller further develops the religious dimensions of postal service. By 1828, more than just post offices were open on Sundays. With the expansion of postal roads came the expansion of service and the transportation of the public in the stage coaches carrying the mail. Fuller recognizes that an unexpected outcome of better mail service was the expansion of a reading public. Fuller demonstrates that the presidential campaign between John Quincy Adams and Andrew Jackson was conducted largely through the mail. After Jackson's election, Fuller shows how the Sabbatarians began to concentrate on the constitutional issues raised by Sabbath mail, including the violation of the First Amendment rights of postmasters required to work on Sundays and the Tenth Amendment issues of state's rights. He also demonstrates nicely that the postal system began to make large sums of money for some individuals and lost large sums of money for the government. The congressional investigation that eventually occurred confirmed the high level of graft and corruption in the awarding of postal contracts. The 1830s also marked the period when those opposed to slavery began to use the mail to try to introduce their position into the South, in violation of state law. Fuller does an excellent job of developing the various historical strands that animated these issues.

The third chapter explores the change of strategy employed by the Sabbatarians to end Sunday mail service. They changed their focus from the religious mandate of the Sabbath to conceiving

Sunday as a day of rest. By 1841, the volume of Sunday mail had markedly declined. Not for long, however. In response to pressure by private carriers, Congress reduced the postage on religious newspapers, causing the postal system to be flooded with religious newspapers. One of the most notable was Lewis Tappan's *National Era* which contained a serial of *Uncle Tom's Cabin.*

The evangelical's long standing fears of bringing God's wrath onto the nation by violating the Sabbath seemed to come to pass through the Civil War. Their sense of God's hand on the country was demonstrated by the timing of Lee's surrender and Lincoln's assassination. Fuller's inclusion of details like these enriches this historical account. He then explores how the Christian character of the country seemed to be further threatened by the dramatic expansion of the rail system. Not only did the rails carry more mail, but they shifted the nation from a rural to urban center. The Sabbatarians were now supported by the National Reform Association, the Woman's Christian Temperance Union, and the American Sabbath Union. Freethinkers, fully accepting Jefferson's "wall of separation," continued to work in earnest against what they perceived to be unconstitutional intrusions of religion into state activities. Sunday mail continued to be a focus of concern. Just when the reader believes the issue will be resolved in the Sabbatarians' favor, Fuller highlights that those supporting the "day of rest" drive could not overcome the desires of publishers to send Sunday newspapers through the Sunday mail.

Fuller examines the history of Sunday newspapers in chapter four. He outlines the two goals Congress had in developing postal rates for newspapers: (1) the dissemination of information to the public, and (2) maintaining a diversity of news sources because of their fear of large urban newspapers. The focus of much congressional concern was on the price of mailing newspapers and periodicals, and the classes of mail. Fuller does an excellent job of developing the historical effects of both religious and secular presses on the changing nature of American culture.

In chapter five, Fuller shifts his attention to an issue perhaps closer to the interests of those in free speech, pornography. Fuller's history of this issue is fascinating. The Civil War becomes the impetus for the mailing of a great deal of obscene material and the response by evangelicals in the mailing of religious tracts. In an attempt to stem the tide of obscenity to troops, Abraham Lincoln, just before his second inaugural, signed the first law prohibiting obscene materials from being mailed. Since the law contained no means of enforcing the statute, obscene material continued to be mailed.

The creation and dissemination of obscene material centered in New York City where a huge number of young men had moved following the war. The Young Men's Christian Association (YMCA) attempted to stop the "dissipation" of these men by controlling the distribution of obscene materials. In this historical context, Fuller turns his attention to Anthony Comstock and his rise to power and influence as this very young man begins his battle against all things corrupting. With the passage of the Comstock law in 1873 and his subsequent appointment as a special agent for the Post Office Department, Comstock worked to rid the city of those selling obscenity with new vengeance. Such was the ferocity of his attack that the YMCA ended its association with him. Subsequent revisions of the Comstock law further strengthened Comstock's position. Fuller's account of the clash between Comstock and the National Liberal League is particularly animated. Fuller describes the National Liberal League as being "composed of free thinkers of nearly every persuasion—'freelovers,' atheists, and free religionists" (111). Members of the League saw themselves as defenders of freedom of speech and press.

A previously banned work, *Cupid's Yokes*, became the focus of debate and legal proceedings. The judge presiding at the trial of publisher Dr. DeRobigne Mortimer Bennett determined that the jury need not consider the work as a whole and that it only need find that certain passages could degrade or damage those individuals who were susceptible and who could acquire the work. As such, Fuller demonstrates how an English common law case, *Regina v. Hincklin*, becomes the nation's standard for determining obscenity until 1957. Fuller concludes this chapter by describing the effects of adding "filthy and disgusting" when describing materials that could not be mailed (119). Evangelicals, still determined to rid the mails of offensive materials, now turned their attention to paperback books that were considered to be impure.

In chapter six, Fuller explores the history of the attack on what was perceived to "impure literature." He addresses both the financial issues—the loss to the government in the mailing of these books at the 2nd class rate approached $25 million dollars in 1896, and the human costs—those that asserted that reading "trashy" novels lead to the destruction of young men in particular.

Chapter seven explores the developing conflict between the Post Office, the postage rate, and the mailing of paperback books. Fuller's knowledge of the intricacy of postal rates is truly extraordinary. In addition to abuses of the second-class privilege were those of the sample-copy privilege which allowed publishers, once granted, to mail as many sample copies of a publication as they wished. Abuses by mail order companies became the most egregious. Adding to the Post Office's problems was Congress's decision to allow colleges and universities to send materials through the second-class mail at the going rate of a penny a pound. Suggestions were even made that the mail should be privatized. But the focus of attention remained paperback books. Fuller provides a vivid account of the attempts by Eugene Loud to revise postal law. Eventually the Loud Bill failed, leaving the Post Office to continue mailing paperbacks at a penny a pound.

In chapter eight, Fuller considers attempts to ban "immoral things" from the mail. The Women's Christian Temperance Union (WCTU) sought to expand the Comstock law to include information and devices regarding contraception and abortion. With the development of large scale newspaper advertising, medicines to prevent conception and produce abortion began to find their way through the mail. In response to the increased advertisement of these materials, an antiabortion crusade developed in the mid-century. Fuller's history of these issues provides a nice juxtaposition between changes in postal practices, including the development of parcel post, Anthony Comstock's activities, Congressional inclusion of contraceptives and abortafacients as obscene materials, and the outcome of these controversies.

In the midst of these very serious issues were some lighter moments that Fuller captures nicely. Particularly noteworthy would be the defense offered by those charged with mailing advertisements for these products, who argued that they could not be found guilty since their products were useless. Some judges accepted this argument, others did not. Fuller shows that while evangelicals failed to cleanse the mail of advertisements or the materials of contraception or abortion, the evangelical attempt to link these ideas to pornography stigmatized the practice of all forms of reproductive control.

Fuller turns his attention to lotteries, providing a lively account of the very complex issue of lotteries and their relationship to the mail. Routine early in the nineteenth-century, by the 1830's their destructive nature was recognized by evangelicals. Attempts to control them again raised issues of states' rights especially since many lotteries operated in southern states. In 1878, the Supreme Court entered the fray in *Ex Parte Jackson,* giving Congress the constitutional right to determine what could be mailed, but prohibited the postmaster general from opening letters. Fuller's account of the complex twists in the effort to end the Louisiana lottery is particularly compelling. In the end, Congress overcame the issue of states' rights, and its early reluctance to legislate morality, and took into it's own hands far-reaching powers to control of the content of the mail.

In his final full chapter, Fuller returns to the issue of obscenity, this time in the form of obscene letters. As Fuller describes, complicating attempts to control this type of mail was the fact that special agents, mail inspectors, were essentially political appointments who operated on behest of the political party in power. Not until 1888, when President Grover Cleveland made special agents civil servants, was this problem corrected. Soon after the Division of Mail inspection developed a very efficient method of responding to complaints about mail handling, including obscene mail. Anthony Comstock and R.W. McAffee were again involved in trying to control the mailing of obscene advertisements, pictures, and stories. They included in their campaign freethinkers who merely advocated the position of free love, marriage, and contraception. Postal inspectors were also faced with the growing problem of obscene mail which was used to sexually harass or blackmail the recipient. Fuller's account of the process of finding the senders of such letters makes for charming reading.

Wayne E. Fuller's account of the mail in nineteenth-century America is a wonderful story well told. There are only minor weaknesses in the work. Most significantly, Fuller neglects to provide a definition for ''obscene'' (98) when the word is initially used. The legal definition is developed later in chapter 3, but given the slippery nature of the word, a definition from the historical context would have been helpful. Fuller's book demonstrates that a form of communication technology, in this case the mail, can be used as a lens to understand the transforming moral culture of a country. Fuller highlights the growing role of the Supreme Court in determining the limits of Congressional power, the conflict between states' rights and a strong federal government, the tension between church and state, the clash between evangelicals and free thinkers, the fears surrounding the erosion of family life, the role of technology and media in homogenizing America, the shift from rural to urban centers, and the hostility between political parties. While the form of communication technology may well have changed, the issues faced by my great-grandmother and my daughter in dealing with that technology may not be that different at all.

Mary Elizabeth Bezanson
University of Minnesota, Morris

The Free Speech Movement: Reflections on Berkeley in the 1960s

Robert Cohen and Reginald E. Zelnik, Eds.
University of California Press, 2002

''There is a time when the operation of the machine becomes so odious, makes you so sick at heart, that you can't take part, you can't even tacitly (passively)[1] take part, and you've got to put your bodies upon the wheels, upon the levers, upon all the apparatus and you've got to make it stop. And you've got to indicate to the people who run it, the people who own it, that unless you're free, the machine will be prevented from working at all! Now, no more talking. We're going to march in singing 'We shall Overcome.' ''

On December 2, 1964, University of California, Berkeley, philosophy student Mario Savio spoke these words to an audience of ten-thousand at a rally in front of Sproul Hall, exhorting students to participate in a sit-in to protest recent disciplinary actions against four leaders of the Free Speech Movement (FSM). An estimated 1,500 people had entered the building and nearly eight hundred stayed to be arrested in ''the largest mass arrest of students in American history'' (Cohen & Zelnik, 1).

What was the free speech movement, what were the perspectives of faculty and student participants, and what were its consequences? The essays contained in *The Free Speech Movement: Reflections on Berkeley in the 1960s*, edited by Robert Cohen and Reginald E. Zelnik, offer viewpoints on these questions. The editors contend that the history of the FSM has largely been told from the perspective of participants who were at the center of the movement. It is their intent to ''open the door to a wide variety of historical interpretations'' (p. 9). To this end, editors include thirty-three contributions from students who led the FSM, students whose participation was more peripheral, faculty who supported the movement and facilitated resolution of the conflict, the UC Berkeley president during the FSM, historians, and also friends, spouses, and colleagues who remained close to Mario Savio after the FSM.

The essays in this volume provide a variety of interesting perspectives on the Free Speech Movement. This reviewer will highlight five insights that stood out to him. Readers who are interested in topics such as freedom of speech on college campuses, the sixties, and student activism, will undoubtedly discover many insights of their own in Cohen and Zelnik's compilation.

First, the essays indicate that the Free Speech Movement was truly a struggle for free speech. The precipitating event came at the beginning of the fall semester in 1964, when the Chancellor terminated the Sather Gate Tradition, under which student organizations had been allowed to engage in political advocacy on a strip of land near an entrance to campus. Student organizations responded by setting up tables for advocacy in defiance of the rules. Police were summoned on October 1. Jack Weinberg (author of the slogan ''never trust anyone over thirty'') was arrested while sitting at the CORE table and placed in a police car (128). A crowd of students surrounded the police car, producing a thirty-two hour standoff. A compromise ended this situation and committees were formed to resolve disciplinary issues and revisit campus advocacy rules. These efforts may have been making progress toward a consensus, but then students returned from Thanksgiving break and learned that the Chancellor had sent out letters of discipline to four leaders of the movement. This act led to the Sproul Hall sit-in, the arrest of the protesters, and a subsequent strike supported by many teaching assistants and students (384). On December 8, the Academic Senate overwhelmingly passed a resolution, 824 to 115, opposing university control over the content of speech, calling for an Academic Senate Committee to resolve disciplinary issues, and calling for political activity on campus to be governed only by time, place, and manner rules. One week later, the University of California Board of Regents voted that political activity on campus ''would only be regulated by the First and Fourteenth Amendments'' (124).

The Free Speech Movement had a relationship to other emerging social movements. One component of political activity on the Berkeley campus was recruiting students to participate in civil rights protests off-campus. Members of the FSM had been active in civil rights protests in the Bay Area and even Mississippi, and borrowed nonviolent civil disobedience strategies from the civil rights movement. The strategies of the FSM would later be used by opponents of the Vietnam War. Despite these connections to other movements, the FSM began because speech rights were denied to advocates of all persuasions (107-08) and the result of the movement was the Regents' acknowledgment that student speech on campus was protected by the First Amendment.

A second insight gleaned from the essays is a more detailed understanding of Mario Savio. This movement leader is discussed in many of the essays which highlight his importance to the FSM and the high esteem in which he was held. Several authors suggest that he was motivated by the social justice emphasis of his Catholic upbringing (resist evil) and by his participation in the Mississippi Freedom Summer Project, not by the teachings of Marx or Mao, as media reports at the time suggested. An FBI probe of Savio found no evidence of Communist beliefs or affiliations (250). Savio was an emergent leader of the FSM and he preferred open, democratic decision-making (37). His style was analytical and reflective and he carefully considered the facts and issues before acting (148, 164). He often interacted with others in a manner that communication scholars would recognize as invitational. The ''Operation of the Machine'' speech was effective, not because of its fiery rhetoric, but instead because Savio's commitment to ''bring intellect to the issues'' for two months had given him credibility (184).

A third insight can be gained by reading the accounts by students, both leaders and the rank-and-file, who participated in the movement. There were students who had long been active in the causes of the left, but also a self-identified ''Valley Girl from Encino'' whose neighbors included John Wayne (185), and a student who identified his involvement as marginal, but became intensely interested in his graduate seminar readings and how they related to the FSM (182). A freshman who came to Berkeley from New York City to remake herself recalls that she was too timid to deliver a speech during the police car incident, although she thought of several as she listened (115). The pledge mother for Delta Phi Epsilon, who went on to achieve prominence as a Democrat in the California Assembly, reserved her highest praise for one of the Republican leaders who worked with her in the FSM (108).

A chilling aspect of the FSM was the fact that almost 800 people were arrested, tried, and convicted for participating in the Sproul Hall sit-in. Alameda County detention facilities were not the Abu Ghraib prison, nevertheless, the arrestees described rough treatment at the hands of the police (187) and crowded facilities with no toilet paper (121-22). Another referred to the incident as a ''nightmare of finger printing, mug shots, newspaper headlines, charges of 'Communist''' (234).

Upon their conviction, the judge asked the protesters to submit statements explaining why they participated in the sit-in. A summary of these responses along with details from about sixty defendants' statements (229-49) is a fascinating section of this book. Less than 10% of the 515 statements offered a radical critique of capitalism or the University. Less than 10% offered moderate statements that expressed doubts about participating in civil disobedience. Few were apologetic, even though a contrite statement would have improved their chances for lenient sentencing. A strong majority was proud to have engaged in civil disobedience because the administration had trampled cherished constitutional rights.

A fourth insight, particularly interesting to professors who read this book, can be gained by reading the essays of faculty members. Some of the key participants were junior faculty members who did not have tenure (296-97, 342, 427). There were divisions within the faculty, evidenced by the fact that on December 3, the day after the Sproul Hall sit-in, over two hundred faculty (including four Nobel prize winners) telegraphed the governor with a message of support for the administration (309). About the same time, another faculty group which came to be known as the Committee of 200 (with supporters from a variety of disciplines including math and the life sciences, along with law, political science, and sociology) drafted a set of principles supporting free speech. These views carried the day and the subsequent Academic Senate 824-115 vote in support of free speech was essential to the FSM's victory (265).

Despite this landslide vote, the interests of the students were rarely "isomorphic" with the interests of the faculty, even its liberal members (322). A large number of the "yes" voters were primarily motivated by a desire to bring peace to the university (313). Faculty who strongly supported the movement still had to devote much of their time to writing "tenure articles" (427), setting up labs, and obtaining grant funding (346). These competing priorities limited their opportunities to participate in free speech efforts. Notwithstanding their sympathy for the students, most faculty members did not support the sit-in and other acts of civil disobedience (314). Although some faculty participated in campus FSM protests, none were among those who remained in Sproul Hall to be arrested (322).

A final insight consists of critical observations about the FSM. Although Mario Savio prided himself on consensus decision-making, women who were active in the movement were more critical of his leadership (109-110). Men dominated the meetings while women did most of the clerical work and provided food (130). Another problem was the political backlash provoked by the FSM. The movement was detested by politicians, the media, and much of the public. Ronald Reagan was elected governor on a platform that included cleaning up the mess in Berkeley. Several authors contended that Reagan's stance against Berkeley was an important causal factor in his election (24, 377, 511). Finally, there is debate about whether civil disobedience was necessary for the FSM to achieve its goals. The administration had made some concessions to the FSM, including a change to allow on-campus political advocacy of legal actions. Perhaps it would have been possible to secure the movement's objectives through legal means (379, 383).

Cohen and Zelnik's *The Free Speech Movement: Reflections on Berkeley in the 1960s* should be interesting to students and scholars of freedom of speech. This book review has identified some of the highlights, but with thirty-three chapters and 618 pages, there are more insights to be discovered. The inclusion of a variety of FSM participants, including student leaders, less-active students, and faculty members provides a diversity of first-hand accounts of the movement. Free speech scholarship and teaching often focuses on landmark Supreme Court decisions. This work is unique because it details a campaign by students to secure their own free speech rights without resort to the courts. The book may well be too long to assign as required text in a Freedom of Expression course, but it would be worth considering as a reserve reading. Students would be likely to find chapters written by other students who were active in the FSM very interesting. Sections of the book that relate to allegations of Communist influence in the FSM would go well with a unit on the McCarthy era. The question of whether the Free Speech Movement's disobedience was morally justified would provide the topic for an interesting classroom debate.

Douglas Fraleigh
California State University, Fresno

Silencing the Opposition: Antinuclear Movements & the Media in the Cold War

Andrew Rojecki
Chicago: University of Chicago Press, 1999

Perhaps the most important justification given for bestowing substantial First Amendment protections to the media is that the press acts in the best interests of the public it serves by providing a platform for criticism of the government. The myth of a vigilant press is propagated by cases like the Pentagon Papers in which the media's role as political watchdog was reified. Our meta-narrative about the importance of a free press in a democracy does not include cases where the media were complicit with the government's positions and served to limit argument about important public issues. *Silencing the Opposition* serves as a reminder that the press may not always be on the side of American citizens.

Rojecki meticulously examines how the media covered the oppositional rhetoric of the anti-nuclear movements during the Eisenhower, Kennedy and Reagan administrations. In particular, his work examines the relationship between press coverage, administration policies and the rhetoric of anti-nuclear movements. Rojecki's primary question is whether the news media provided nuclear protest groups with a "secure forum for their ideas" (1). He found, not only did the press limit coverage of these organizations, they also systematically de-legitimated the movements by using rhetorical strategies that restricted the movements' abilities to be perceived as legitimate voices in public debate. Although the anti-nuclear movement was granted some credibility and coverage, Rojecki finds that the movements were only accorded credibility when the administration's goals were consistent with the movement's goals.

Chapter One is an introduction to the politics of social movements. It is in this section that Rojecki discusses the importance of the press in the proliferation of the marketplace of ideas. After a short introduction of Milton's and Mill's theories, Rojecki establishes the failure of the market to promote a robust debate, in part because of the consequences of the economic paradigm on citizens' access to information. The author's analysis of the limitations of the market provides a nuanced analysis of the problems of the press. Rojecki finds that a poor flow of information and an un-involved public contribute to the lack of an informed citizenry (6).

Two primary case studies drive Rojecki's project: the first is an examination of the movements that sought the United States to stop nuclear testing in the late 1950s and early 1960s; the second is an analysis of the movements that were protesting the nuclear policies of the Reagan administration. For each of these cases, the book includes a detailed explanation of the administrations' policies, a description of the media coverage of the movement including both quantitative and qualitative data, and an analysis of the strategies and timing of the media coverage.

Rojecki analyzed the coverage of the test ban movements in the *New York Times* and *Time* magazine for his first case study. Although the movements gained some credibility when Eisenhower's administration debated internally about its policy on the test ban, overall he found that these movements were damaged by press coverage. The *New York Times* questioned the legitimacy of the movement by undermining the quality of its leadership. Linus Pauling, a renowned chemist from the California Institute of Technology, was the primary spokesperson for the movement and his treatment by the *New York Times* is typical of the strategies the media used to silence the campaign. Pauling was repeatedly described as ''left''; the attribution called into question his credibility. Thus, the movement was marginalized as being attached to communists and other radical political groups.

Time magazine, whose editorial policy was virulently anti-Soviet, derided the movement as futile and uneducated about political issues. *Time*, however, did provide some legitimacy to the movement's leadership because it divided its coverage of the issue into the political and scientific spheres. In the scientific sphere, Pauling was accorded credibility due to his status as a scientist, but in the political sphere, *Time's* coverage diminished Pauling's status in much the same fashion as the *New York Times*.

Perhaps the most chilling example of the media's disregard for the test ban movement is Rojecki's discovery that the *New York Times* suppressed its knowledge about Project Argus. The Project was a series of high altitude nuclear tests over the South Atlantic. The paper had learned about the tests, but did not publish the story in a timely manner, despite Eisenhower's pledge to join the Soviet Union's moratorium on testing. The *New York Times* decided against timely publication so that the tests would not draw the ire of the protestors and risk being cancelled. This incident vividly displays the power of the media to shape the public debate; by holding back the story, the paper furthered the government's agenda and frustrated the movements' abilities to use these tests as a rallying point.

Rojecki's second case study of the 1980s anti-nuclear protest movement analyzes coverage in *The New York Times* and *CBS Evening News*. He once again locates moments when the movements were granted credibility by the media, when White House staff was uncertain as to its own policy, but finds that overall the movement was trivialized by the press. He found that the coverage of the movement focused on its membership and on its inability to effect meaningful change. In the 1980s the debate over the legitimacy of nuclear programs shifted from the public to the technical spheres of communication and, in doing so, made ordinary citizens unimportant in policy decisions.

Of particular interest in the analysis of the television coverage is the way that children became the predominant visual symbol of the movement. Rojecki argues that their prominence in the coverage made the issues seem infantile, further diminishing the power of the movement to effect change. ''The increasing prominence of children . . . as movement spokespersons suggested a linkage with naïveté and symbolic politics'' (143). Visually, this strategy enforced the Reagan administration's assertion that the people could not participate in the nuclear debate.

Silencing the Opposition is an important case study of how public argument is subverted by government power in conjunction with media complicity. Free speech scholars, however, may find the work lacking a solid foundation in first amendment theory and cases. Outside of the limited discussion of the marketplace of ideas in the first chapter, Rojecki devotes little attention to the implications of skewed news coverage to the freedom of the press. Although Rojecki's primary objective is not to examine first amendment protections of media, his argument would most definitely be served by much of the first amendment scholarship on the role of the free press in creating a robust debate.

Despite Rojecki's lack of direct analysis of first amendment issues, free speech scholars will find this a useful work. *Silencing the Opposition* serves as a case study of how the media frame argumentation about important issues. The questions of nuclear war and development of nuclear technologies were of critical importance to the American public; that the media skewed American's understanding of these issues raises important questions about the legitimacy of the media in promoting democratic governance. Readers are left wondering how many other crucial issues have been skewed in favor of administrative policy.

Rojecki's book also serves as a warning about the monopolization of the channels of discourse; as media ownership is centralized in a few large corporations, it is more likely that even more cases of silencing oppositions will surface. Despite the recent ruling in the 3rd Circuit Court, which threw out FCC rules that allowed increased ownership of broadcast stations in the same market (Sutel), FCC rulings on media ownership issues insure that even fewer voices will be allowed to surface in public debate.

Works Cited

New York Times v. United States, 403 U.S. 713, U.S. Supreme Ct., 1971.

Sutel, Seth. "3rd Circuit Decision Rejects FCC's Rules of Media Ownership." *The Legal Intelligencer* June 25, 2004, p. 4. *Academic Universe*. Lexis-Nexis. Montana State University, Billings Library. 14 July, 2004. (http://proxybl.lib.montana.edu:2084/universe)

Susan Balter-Reitz
Montana State University